STEPHEN OPPENHEIMER is a world-recognized expert in the synthesis of DNA studies with archaeological and other evidence to track ancient migrations. He is a Research Associate at the Institute of Human Sciences, Oxford University.

Praise for *The Real Eve*

'Wonderfully readable and excitingly controversial . . . Readers who liked Jared Diamond's *Guns, Germs and Steel* will love this.'

John Terrell, Director of Anthropology,
The Field Museum, Chicago

'To discover the real daughters of Eve, read on.'

Martin Richards,
Researcher in Human Evolutionary Genetics

'Readable but authoritative.'

Andrew Sherratt, Professor of Archaeology,
University of Oxford

By the same author

Eden in the East:
The Drowned Continent of Southeast Asia

THE REAL EVE

Modern Man's Journey Out of Africa

STEPHEN OPPENHEIMER

CARROLL & GRAF PUBLISHERS
New York

Carroll & Graf Publishers
An imprint of Avalon Publishing Group, Inc.
245 W. 17th Street
New York
NY 10011
www.carrollandgraf.com

AVALON
publishing group incorporated

First published in the UK by Constable,
an imprint of Constable & Robinson Ltd 2003

This revised paperback edition published by Carroll & Graf 2004

ISBN 0–7867–1334–8

Printed and bound in the EU

Library of Congress Cataloging-in-Publication Data is available on file.

To my daughter Maylin and son David,
to my wife Freda, and to my father and mother.

To know where we are going, we have to know where we are;
to know that we have to know where we came from
Filipino version of an Oceanic proverb

CONTENTS

ILLUSTRATIONS

ACKNOWLEDGEMENTS

SINCE PUBLICATION of the landmark Cann, Stoneking and Wilson out-of-Africa paper sixteen years ago, many in countries from all round the world have contributed to the understanding of our past through the growing gene trees of modern humans. These include the participants in the studies, lab staff, PhD students and post-docs right up to the heads of particular laboratories. As far as possible I have tried to give appropriate credit by citing relevant papers; but while refereed publications are scientists' main visible research product, they depend not just on thorough, careful, hard work, but to some extent on that more fluid and transferable currency, original ideas. Ideas, like good tunes move from lip to lip sometimes hiding their origins. They are rarely explicitly credited and, in multi-author papers, the originator is sometimes difficult to deduce.

Work on mitochondrial DNA was pioneered in the US, during the late 1970s, by Wesley Brown and Douglas Wallace. The late Allan Wilson, the senior author on the 1987 Cann paper, is acknowledged by all to have been an inspiration to those who followed him. In this book I cite mainly papers from after that time. With the increasing pace of research during the 1990s and after the turn of the twenty-first Century, new people entered the scene. Without underplaying the work of many other groups and associates, I would like to identify what I regard as an inner circle of scientists who have pioneered the 'phylogeographic approach' to tracing prehistoric human movements. Based in scattered parts of Europe, in some ways they are self-identified, since several other geneticists disagree with their methods. Among this inner circle are geneticists Martin Richards, Antonio Torroni, Silvana Santachiara-Benerecetti, Peter Forster and Toomas Kivisild working with Richard Villems. Their work was revolutionized by the mathematics required for the new tree-building. Again I would like to identify Hans-Jürgen Bandelt poly-math and mathematician and Vincent Macaulay physicist, statistician and mathematician, who did much to pioneer such methods and have both helped many teams including several, recently, from Russia and China. In a tensely competitive research field members of this group are surprising in the degree to which they all share their insights with each other.

The Y chromosome picture was pioneered initially by English geneticists from Leicester (Mark Jobling and Matt Hurles) and Oxford (Chris Tyler-Smith), but has subsequently been dominated by well-financed American laboratories with Peter Underhill's (under Luca Cavalli Sforza) and Mike Hammer's teams being the best examples. With large panels of gene markers, they have made extraordinary strides in bringing the Y-chromosome tree up to the same fine detail as that of mtDNA. Since mtDNA is relatively short there is a limit to what she can reveal and the Y chromosome will inevitably overtake her although dating will continue to be a problem. Lluis Quintana-Murci (now in Paris) made significant contributions to both the mitochondrial and Y chromosome stories.

When not expressing my own ideas and opinions, I have cited relevant papers that signaled a particular advance. Giving credit, where due, can be as important a function of the bibliography as that of showing the text-argument really is evidence-based. Popular genetics books without bibliographies run the risk of giving the reader the impression that the author worked it all out on his own. But citing publications is only one aspect of acknowledging my debts in compiling this book. While writing *Out of Eden* I have received an enormous amount of help directly from various people in terms of their time spent patiently explaining things to me, constructively criticizing my ideas, and offering their own insights. First and foremost is Martin Richards who, by good luck, I contacted when his own boss was unavailable a few years ago. Martin has given of his time unstintingly, including a critical reading of the book. He is, in my view, one of the main illuminati in this field. Next, in terms of hours on the phone and otherwise, is Vincent Macaulay followed by Hans Bandelt, Peter Forster, Toomas Kivisild and Chris Tyler-Smith. For the Malaysian Orang Asli genetic study, in addition to UK co-authors Catherine Hill, Martin Richards, William Meehan, James Blackburn, Mike Ward and Douglas Clarke, I would also like to thank our overseas collaborators, in particular Adi Taha without whose extraordinary efforts the study would have failed, Patima Ismail my Malaysian genetics collaborator, David Bulbeck who encouraged me to follow the route of his study, Muhamad Mahfuz Bin Nordin, and Norrulhuda Mohamad Halim, Norazila Kassim Shaari, Joseph Maripa Raja, Antonio Torroni, Chiara Rengo, Orang Asli participants, the JHEOA and, of course, Discovery Channel for financial support.

There are other geneticists who have given me their time and insights. Over several years and while writing this book, I attended a magnificent series of guest seminars organized by the late Ryk Ward covering many aspects of bioanthropology. Tim Crow explained his view of human speciation on the Y-chromosome to me. Chris Tyler-Smith, Peter Underhill, Mark Jobling, Matt Hurles, Mark Stoneking and Lluis Quintana-Murci have all given good counsel. Roger Dawkins and Joe Williamson kindly read my proofs in record time and offered very useful advice.

I have also had much educational help from archaeologists, including particularly Derek Roe, who taught me hands-on about blades, Andrew Sherratt, who corrected some of my misconceptions on the importance of size reduction and hafting in the Palaeolithic, again hands-on, read the whole book and gave constructive criticism on the Prologue and Chapters 2–3, David Bulbeck, who read Chapters 4–7 wearing both his archaeological and anthropological caps. Zuraina Majid took me through the cultural sequence of Lenggong Valley pebble tools. Susan Keates gave much assistance in references and read Chapters 5 and 6 for me. Seife Berhe organized the Eritrean field visit and kindly took me over the ancient reefs he had found. Ipoi Datan facilitated my visit to Niah caves. Graeme Barker, Ian Lilley, Chris Stringer, Mike Morwood, Tim Reynolds, Beatrice Clayre, Sandra Bowdler, Rob Foley, Marta Lahr, William Davies, Paul Pettitt all gave me their time and insights.

I cannot praise and recommend my agents Julian Friedmann and Carole Blake highly enough to anyone who is lucky enough to get on their list. They went over and above the call of duty.

Constable & Robinson, my publishers, have put much patient and good-natured effort into transforming something written with half an eye to academics into something with more sparkle and accessibility. I think they did a good job. At the top of the list are the editorial team: Pete Duncan (my editor), John Woodruff, Anna Williamson, Sara Peacock and Jane Anson. Bill Smuts, the illustrator, translated my numerous sketches into great maps. But there are others, including Gary Chapman, Sallie Robins and Jennifer Duthie.

There are a number of others not in the above groups who have helped me. Georgina Harvey who researched on the Toba literature and put me in touch with Eelco Rohling oceanographer, who illuminated the pre-history of Red Sea salinity for me. An old friend, George Wells, brought me up to scratch on the 200-year history of the two language origin paradigms. Roger and Geeta Kingdon introduced me to Jonathan Kingdon's work, John Robinson was a great source of references and support. Finally of course, Freda my wife, who has always taken better photos than me, has supported me throughout.

Acknowledgement of the above does not necessarily indicate their agreement with the views expressed in this book.

PREFACE

IMAGINE AN AIRLINE CHECK-IN QUEUE in Chicago or London. Seven people stand there, looking in different directions. One is a solicitor of Afro-Caribbean origin, another a blonde-haired girl whose family come from northern Europe, another a computer expert who was born in India. The fourth is a Chinese teenager listening to music on a Walkman. The fifth, sixth, and seventh are all attending a conference on rock art and come respectively from Australia, New Guinea, and South America. All seven are quiet, and avoid eye contact because they neither know one another nor feel related in any way. Yet it can be proved they are all related and ultimately all have an African female and male ancestor in common.

In all our cells we have genes. Genes are made up of DNA, the string-like code of life that determines what we are, from our fingernails to our innate potential for playing the piano. If we analyse the genes of any one of these seven people, we can trace the geographic route taken by their ancestors back to an ultimate birthplace in Africa, at the dawn of our species. Further, if we take any pair of them and compare their genes, we will find that they share a more recent ancestor – living, in all probability, outside Africa (see Figure 0.3). What is more, I believe that we can now prove where those ancestors lived and when they left their homelands. This remarkable proof has become fully possible only within the last decade, as a result of pioneering work by a number of people.

Many of us have wondered what we would find if we could perhaps board a time machine and travel back through the generations of our ancestors. Where would it take us? Would we find ourselves to be distantly related to some famous or notorious person? How many generations would we pass through before we arrived at the first humans? Does our line continue back to monkeys, and beyond to worms and single-celled creatures, as Darwin maintained? We know from dry biology lessons at school that this ought to be so, but as with the uncertainty of what happens to us after we die, it is hard to grasp.

We are now so used to the pace of technical advances that the sense of wonder fades with each new one. Yet, until very recently, geneticists could only dream of using our genes to trace the detailed history of how we conquered the world. The reason for their pessimism was that the majority of the genes they examined shuffled themselves around at each generation and were common to most populations anyway. Their task was like trying to reconstruct a previously played card game from the pack of cards *after* it has been shuffled. So it was nearly impossible to draw an accurate genetic family tree going back even a few hundred years, let alone back to the beginning of our species. Most human populations look very similar beneath the skin, so where could one start?

The use of gender-specific gene lines, the so-called Adam-and-Eve genes, has in the last ten years changed all that. In contrast to all other genes, mitochondrial DNA (a collection of genes outside the cell nucleus) is inherited only through our mothers, and the Y chromosome is inherited only by men. These two sets of gender-linked genes are passed on unchanged from generation to generation, with no shuffling, and can therefore be traced right back to our ancestors, to the first mammals, and even beyond to worms and worse. We can thus construct two family gene trees, one for our fathers and one for our mothers. As a result, in any population, of whatever size, we can trace any two individuals through one of these two gene trees back to a most recent shared ancestor on the tree. Such an ancestor may have lived 200, 5,000, or 150,000 years ago, but all ancestors can be assigned a place on the newly constructed Adam-and-Eve genetic trees. These are real family trees of modern human gene lines, with real branches. Each branch on each tree can be dated, although the accuracy of such dating still leaves much to be desired.

Many regional human gene trees have now been fitted together, like a large jigsaw that is started by assembling the edges using certain clear landmarks. In this way, a picture of the Adam-and-Eve gene lines spreading from Africa to every corner of the world has been pieced together over the last decade. It has got to that satisfying point, as with jigsaws, when the whole structure suddenly links up and takes shape; the remaining pieces, though many, are now being placed on the tree and on the map with increasing ease and speed. The pace is now so rapid that people working at the cutting edge on one geographic region may still be unaware of breakthroughs in another region. The whole branching tree can now be laid flat on a world map to show where our ancestors and their gene lines travelled in their conquest of the world.

The new knowledge has resolved some of the apparent paradoxes thrown up by the contrast between the cultural and biological stories of the last 150,000 years. We can now even start to hang the regional human fossil relics of that period in their correct places on the genetic tree of life.

Many questions have been answered. It turns out that, far from the world being a common genetic melting pot with massive to-and-fro prehistoric movements and mixings, the majority of the members of the modern human diaspora have conservatively stayed put in the colonies their ancestors first established. They have dwelt in those localities since well before the last ice age. We can also trace the dates of specific migrations over the last 80,000 years. Thus, from a picture of great diversity and lack of definition, we have the opportunity to move to a highly specific and regional focus on the branching networks of human exploration.

Several other obvious examples of long-standing archaeological questions have been resolved by the new gene trees. One is the 'Out-of-Africa' *v.* 'Multiregional' controversy. The Out-of-Africa view is that all modern humans outside Africa descend from a recent movement from Africa less than 100,000 years ago. This exodus wiped out all earlier human types around the world. The multi-regionalists, in contrast, argue that the archaic human populations, *Homo neanderthalenis* (Neanderthals) in Europe and *Homo erectus* in the Far East, evolved into the local races we now see around the world.

The Out-of-Africa view now wins the contest because the new genetic trees lead straight back to Africa within the past 100,000 years.[1] No traces of Adam-and-Eve gene lines from older human species remain on our genetic tree, except of course at the root, from which we can measure our genetic distance from Neanderthals. Neanderthals have now been genetically typed using ancient mitochondrial DNA, and it seems that they are our cousins rather than our ancestors. We share with them another common ancestor, *Homo helmei*.

Current Out-of-Africa proponents have usually hedged their bets, claiming that Australians, Asians, and Europeans came as separate migrations of *Homo sapiens* from Africa. Not so: the male and female genetic trees show only one line each coming out of Africa. This is my central argument in this book. There was only one main exodus of modern humans from Africa – each gender line had only one common genetic ancestor that respectively fathered and mothered the whole non-African world.

Other prejudices have also foundered. Some European archaeologists and anthropologists have long held that Europeans were the first to learn to paint, carve, develop complex culture, and even to speak – almost as if Europeans represented a major biological advance. The structure of the genetic tree denies this view. Australian aboriginals are related to Europeans, and share a common ancestor just after the exodus from Africa to the Yemen over 70,000 years ago. Thereafter they moved progressively round the coastline of the Indian Ocean, eventually island-hopping across Indonesia to Australia where, in complete isolation, they developed their own unique and complex artistic cultures. The first Australian rock art has been dated at least as early as the first European one. This must mean that humans came out of Africa already painting.

Another old archaeological controversy concerns the spread of the Neolithic culture across Europe from Turkey 8,000 years ago. Did the farmers from the Near East wipe out and replace the European hunters, or did the new ideas spread more peacefully, converting the pre-existing Palaeolithic hunter-gatherer communities? The genetic answer is clear: 80 per cent of modern Europeans descend from the old hunter-gatherer gene types, and only 20 per cent from Near Eastern farmers. The old ones were not such a pushover.[2]

Finally, moving to the other side of the world, there has always been colourful speculation over the origins of the Polynesians. Thor Heyerdahl was not the first. In fact, Captain Cook was nearer the mark in arguing for a Polynesian link to the Malay archipelago. For the past fifteen years archaeologists have thought that Polynesians came from Taiwan. The genetic tree discounts this now: the ancestors of the sailors of the great canoes started out further along the trail, in Eastern Indonesia.[3]

Coming back to our airline queue, we should also remember that we are participants in this genetic story, since 99 per cent of the work of reconstruction of our ancient gene trees was carried out using modern DNA given voluntarily by people living in different parts of the world today. This is a story of relevance to each and every one of us.

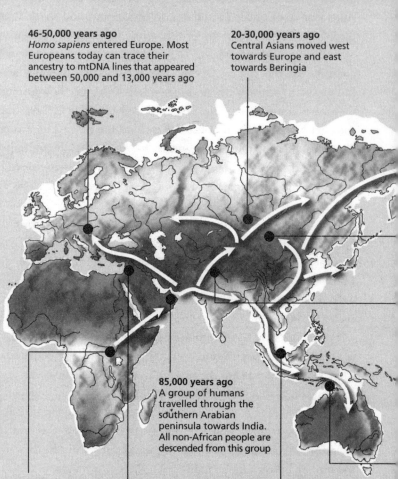

46-50,000 years ago
Homo sapiens entered Europe. Most Europeans today can trace their ancestry to mtDNA lines that appeared between 50,000 and 13,000 years ago

20-30,000 years ago
Central Asians moved west towards Europe and east towards Beringia

85,000 years ago
A group of humans travelled through the southern Arabian peninsula towards India. All non-African people are descended from this group

African origins
Over 150,000 years ago modern humans - our mtDNA ancestors - lived in Africa

120,000 years ago
A group of humans travelled northward through Egypt and Israel but died out 90,000 years ago

75,000 years ago
Modern humans moved east from India into Southeast Asia and China

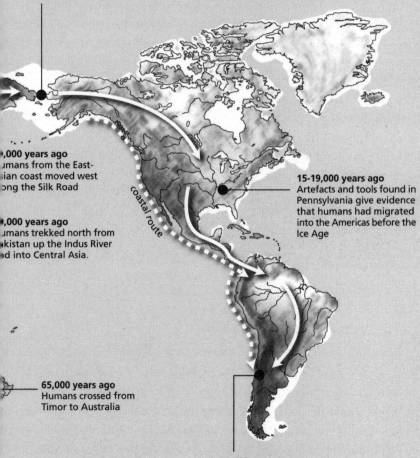

22-25,000 years ago
Humans crossed the Bering land bridge that connected Siberia and Alaska

,000 years ago
...umans from the East-...ian coast moved west ...ong the Silk Road

,000 years ago
...umans trekked north from ...kistan up the Indus River ...d into Central Asia.

coastal route

15-19,000 years ago
Artefacts and tools found in Pennsylvania give evidence that humans had migrated into the Americas before the Ice Age

65,000 years ago
Humans crossed from Timor to Australia

12,500 years ago
Evidence of human habitation and artefacts found, Monte Verde, Chile

PROLOGUE

MANY ANTHROPOLOGISTS NOW SAY that we came out of Africa, but how do they know? If we all have a single recent origin there, why do there appear to be different races of humans? How closely are these races related? Is 'race' a valid concept? Are we all part of one family, or do Africans, aboriginal Australians, Europeans, and East Asians all have different parallel evolutionary origins? And why us? What key forces in our evolutionary history took descendants of apes that had just left the trees to walk the African savannah and catapulted them onto the Moon within a couple of million years?

Jacob Bronowski's *The Ascent of Man* and Richard Leakey's *The Making of Mankind* were landmark documentaries that stimulated public interest in human evolution. Yet, as with any consensus view, they left many questions unresolved. Lack of relevant evidence at the time meant that they also inevitably left what are now recognized as gaps in knowledge and understanding. Subsequent archaeological and biological findings have allowed us to pose new questions and plug some of those gaps. We are also now in a position to correct the distorted perspective we have of what really separates us from our ancestors and from our living cousins, the great apes, and to challenge the myths that have hindered past progress.

DNA analysis has led to extraordinary advances in our under-standing of the regional biological history of modern humans. As we shall see, the so-called Adam-and-Eve genes really do allow us to track back in time and space to follow the human family in its wanderings round the globe. But not all the advances have been in molecular biology. Palaeoanthropology, the study of our ancestors, has leapt forward in several important fields since Leakey's presenta-tion, over twenty years ago. First, a number of newly found early human skulls, both within and outside Africa, have resolved the timescale and geographical extent of the repeated out-of-Africa movements of the past 2 million years. Other skull finds have pushed the branch between our ancestors and those of chimps back even earlier. Second, the comparative analysis of skull shape has, with the advent of fast computers, been put on a more scientific basis, with the result that key skulls of prehistoric peoples from around the world can now be placed near branches on the human genetic tree, and today's descendants on the twigs.

This approach to defining the branches of the modern human biological tree by comparing skulls fell under the cloud of poor science linked to racism as a result of the activities of Nazi anthro-pologists in the middle of the last century. Since the 1960s, different motives, more objectivity, and better maths have allowed palae-ontologists to resolve more detail in the hominid tree and even that of modern humans. The intense public interest in this field, and the persisting fear of it being hijacked to serve nationalist and racist agenda, have unfortunately led to a minefield of 'politically correct' euphemisms laid by Western anthropologists to protect us from our prejudices. Although such language has the expressed aim of defin-ing differences between peoples more clearly, the result has been to obscure and proscribe discussion. 'Race', for instance, is now a politically incorrect term, and in some circles so is 'ethnicity'. Such hypersensitivities should be regarded as a challenge rather than an obstacle. Discussion of human differences is racist when the agenda are competitive, exclusive, and derogatory. It can equally be a positive celebration of our diversity.

In this book I am concerned mainly with questions about our recent story, over the past 200,000 years, which can be answered by tracing our way back through our genes. But to do that properly, and understand what it was that made us explore every corner of the Earth and then some, we do need to ask, 'Why us?' in the first place. The forces that drove our adaptive survival against overwhelming odds in the African savannah are the key to our nature and to our extraordinary story. We were not 'put' here fully formed, thinking, talking, and unique among animals. We were specially selected and moulded by a fierce, blind, unthinking environment. Like all evolving species, we had ancestors and cousins who shared some of our abilities but perished in adversity. Our physical and behavioural adaptations were focused on surviving the struggle with our greatest enemy and stern teacher, the climate.

One of Rudyard Kipling's immortal *Just So Stories* tells of the Elephant's Child, who in those early days had no trunk and plagued his uncles and aunts with irritating questions. He made the mistake of going to the Crocodile to ask him what he normally ate for dinner. The Crocodile told him to bend down close to hear the answer. As soon as he did, the Crocodile clamped his jaws hard on the end of the elephant's nose and tugged him towards the river. After a prolonged tug-of-nose, the Elephant's Child managed to release himself – only to find that his nose had stretched into a fine, new trunk. This Kipling fable, like others in the anthology, cocks a crude snook at Jean-Baptiste Lamarck's notion of evolution by the inheritance of acquired characteristics, but there is a hint of Darwinian reality in the result. Through non-benign means, the Elephant's Child gained a uniquely useful modified nose, although he took a bit of time to realize it. Similarly, modifications to our brain, our free hands, our feet, and our family and social life have been selected by the recurrent cruel weather of the past few million years, and we have put them to unique new uses.

One of the more surprising insights has come from a growing understanding of the effects of repeated glacial cycles during the past 2.5 million years on human evolution and expansions out of Africa. Whereas severe climatic change generally causes widespread megafaunal extinctions, the appearance of new and more successful human species seems to have coincided with severe glaciations and expansions of the African savannah. But climate may have been a major force behind hominid evolution for much longer than that. Primates have, in general, more dextrous hands, relatively larger brains, more varied diets, and more complex social lives than most other contemporary mammals. Ten million years ago, Africa was a lush paradise with vast open forests and home to several species of ape. Even then, various primate species, not just apes, were experimenting with life on the ground and in the grassland around islands and tongues of forest. Africa's grassland has expanded progressively since then, as the world's climate has cooled and dried, but this has happened in cyclical fits and starts of increasing frequency and severity.

Walking apes

As we know from the effects of our recent ice age, the worst phase of the climate cycle, although brief, can cause widespread extinctions. Only the survivors of such climatic episodes can pass on their own genetic type, holding special features that may have been selected for by the environment. Around 7–8 million years ago, a dramatic reduction in the number of ape species coincided with several million years of global cooling and grassland expansion. Some have suggested that this short ice epoch already marks the time of the split between our ancestors and the ancestors of modern chimpanzees. The most important initial physical change in our ancestors, bipedalism (walking on two legs) may have its roots in that time. At present, however, the first clear evidence for bipedalism is seen only in skeletons of *Australopithecus anamensis*, a walking ape dating from 4 million years ago and found on the shores of Lake Turkana, in northern Kenya, in 1995.[1]

Many think that there was a cause-and-effect relation between the spread of the grasslands and the change from quadrupedal forest-living to easy walking around the savannah. This may well be true but, judging by the toothed predators with which they shared their environment, the early bipedal apes probably did not stray too far into the plain and away from the protection of the wooded islands. In any case, other primates, such as the ancestors of baboons, managed to get along surprisingly well in the savannah on four legs (as do modern baboons).

Others have suggested alternative theories of why it was advantageous to adopt a two-legged posture, such as literally keeping a cool head[2] or, like the African meerkats, keeping an eye out for predators on the plain. However, our ancestors' brains, although larger than those of most other land mammals, were no bigger than that of our cousin the chimpanzee, so there was less danger of them over-heating. Nor is standing upright – which many mammals do, including monkeys, chimpanzees, bears, and meerkats – the same thing as habitually walking on two legs for long periods. The idea of leaving hands free to do other mischief such as wielding heavy sticks for hunting (or more likely for defence against predators, since our ancestors were mainly vegetarian) is attractive as an evolutionary force. Unfortunately we have no direct proof, since wood is perishable and stone tools are not found from that time.

Those early walking apes, for whom there is still only fragmentary evidence, were followed by the famous 'Lucy' family, *Australopithecus afarensis*. Lucy's partial female skeleton was discovered by Donald Johanson in 1974 at Hadar, in Ethiopia. Living between 3 and 4 million years ago, her kind were 1–1.5 metres (40–60 inches) tall, more clearly upright and bipedal, with a pelvis

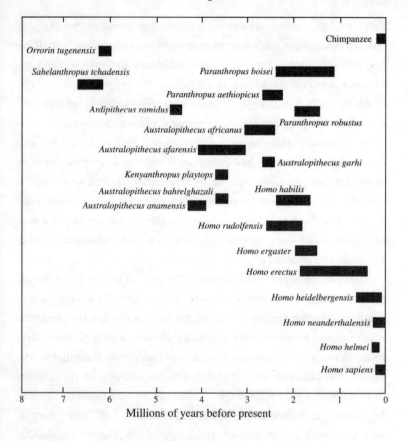

Figure 0.1 The 'untidy tree'. Over the past 8 million years of hominid evolution (including here only our nearest living relatives, chimps), several species usually co-existed at any one time, so drawing a tree of direct descent on the basis of chance fossil finds may be misleading – hence the lack of branches on this tree.

more similar to ours. Above the neck the similarity ceased, for their skulls and brains were like chimpanzees' (375–500 cm^3 in volume), although they had smaller canine teeth (see Plate 1). As with gorillas, their females were much smaller, suggesting a harem society. A different two-legged version (*Australopithecus africanus*) lived between 2 and 3 million years ago and, although the same size, had a slightly larger average brain size than chimps at between 420 and 500 cm^3. Their teeth were also smaller and more like ours. It should be said that these two particular bipeds are not necessarily steps on a direct evolutionary sequence towards ourselves: our ancestor at this time could easily have been a sister species as yet undiscovered. For instance, our nearest ancestor could have been a recently discovered species from about 3.6 million years ago called *Kenyanthropus platyops* – quite literally, 'flat-face' (Figure 0.1). The flat face, a feature of humans, might represent a bridge between the walking apes and us. What is certain, though, is that over the few million years in which the australopithecines ('southern apes') and their immediate ancestors walked Africa's grasslands, we see only a moderate, not a dramatic, increase in brain size.

Growing brains in the big dry

Things were about to change, because 2.5 million years ago the world started getting colder. Within a million years, the wet and warm Pliocene geological period gave way to the Pleistocene ice epoch. This was a grinding cycle of repeated dry ice ages, with alternating advances and retreats of African grassland lasting right up until the most recent glaciation, which climaxed 18,000 years ago. Soon after the start of this unstable, icy, and dry period, the first humans (the *Homo* genus) with their stone tools and larger brains made their entrance on the African savannah stage. As had happened a few million years before with the split into four-legged and two-legged locomotion, this was a parting of the ways for the descendants of the walking apes. One branch, known as *Paranthropus*, developed larger jaws to cope with grinding up tough vegetable matter. The other branch, *Homo*, made stone tools, developed substantially larger brains, and set off down the road towards becoming better hunter-gatherers and then, finally, us.

Naturally, we are inclined to think of humans as being special and set apart from the other apes. Many think that it is our especially large brain that makes us what we are. Some even think that an increase in brain size led to tool-making, but this argument seems unlikely. Fashioning *stone* tools, unlike walking on two legs or manual dexterity, may be unique to humans (and possibly to *Paranthropus*[3]), but even chimpanzees make crude but effective tools out of wood, and they have smaller brains and branched off much earlier than the walking apes. Although we do not have the evidence in wood from the last 7 million years, chimps still have roughly the same sized brain as our common ancestors who lived at the beginning of that time. This does not seem to constitute a strong link between simple tool-making and achieving a critical brain size. Nor does it rule out the possibility that the common ancestors of chimps and humans were making tools so long ago.

One of the earliest human tool-makers, *Homo habilis*, had an average brain volume of 650 cm^3, but among the known habilis skulls is one 1.9 million years old with a chimp-like brain volume of only 500 cm^3, which is at the top end of the range for the earlier australopithecines.[4] The small body and brain size and the other ape-like features of *Homo habilis* have led some anthropologists to call for their expulsion from the *Homo* genus or 'human club', but in spite of the well-argued case, this seems more like size prejudice than scientific reasoning. *Homo habilis* were unlikely to have been our direct ancestors, but that can be said for most hominids; and they made stone tools.

The idea that we somehow grew a big brain first, then decided what it was for, is a negation of Darwinian principles. Any new kind of behaviour always precedes the physical adaptation that evolves to exploit that behaviour. Well before the start of the Pleistocene ice epoch there must already have been some aspect of our behaviour – something to do with the way we faced the climatic challenge, perhaps – that gave large, energy-expensive brains survival value. The problem of finding food in an increasingly dry environment must have taxed our ancestors' resourcefulness. Larger brains clearly helped them in some way. That behaviour must still be with us today, because over subsequent major glaciations during the past 2.5 million years, new human species with larger brains and more skills appeared in Africa. As the climate briefly warmed after each glacial maximum, the Sahara would become green for a few thousand years and the new human species would venture out to try their luck in Eurasia. By 1 million years ago, brain volumes of various human species living both within and outside Africa had increased from 400 to 1,000 cm^3, and even into the modern size range. In other words, human brains had grown to three-quarters of their modern size long before we came on the scene.[5]

Why did we grow big brains?

There have been various suggestions as to what the key behaviour selecting for big brains might have been. The ice ages forced Africa into extreme aridity and would have inspired the dwindling numbers of savannah humans to greater resourcefulness and cooperation. We can see the value of larger brains in such circumstances, but why should *our* brains have grown, and not those of the other mammals living at the edge of the savannah? One behavioural characteristic that is still very much with us today is our fondness for meat with our vegetables. Indeed, London-based anthropologist Leslie Aiello and her colleague Peter Wheeler (the originator of the cool heads theory) suggested that we needed to eat meat in order to facilitate our brain growth.[6] Brains need lots of calories to fuel them, and require high-grade nutrients in order to grow. Yet, as Aiello and Wheeler acknowledged, meat-eating is more a means than a motive for brain enlargement. They also argue that the parallel reduction in size of human intestines, as shown by an alteration of the shape of the ribcage in *Homo ergaster*, is evidence for a change to eating more meat than vegetables. In other words, the oldest true humans had lost the vegetarian pot-belly so characteristic of australopithecines. But this change in the ribcage happened before the dramatic brain growth.

Early humans such as *Homo habilis*, *Homo rudolphensis*, and *Homo ergaster* may have been more scavengers than hunters. Perhaps they learnt that by arming themselves with sticks and stones they could drive larger predators away from kills, and as their tool-making and cooperative hunting abilities improved they became more confident. But without evidence, all such arguments for the role of climate and meat-eating in the enhanced brain growth of early humans remain largely armchair speculation. We know that, at least in Africa, stone tools were used by *Homo erectus* to butcher meat,[7] but to establish a link between meat-eating, worsening weather, and brain growth we would need a comparison with purely vegetarian primates in the same environment over the same period.

Recently, Sarah Elton,[8] an anthropologist based at the University of Kent at Canterbury, has provided just that – but her results rather shake our sense of the uniqueness of the human line. She measured brain size in a number of fossil skulls from primate species over the period roughly from 2.5 million years (the start of the cooling) to 1.5 million years ago. She studied the two main branches of hominids that diverged during that period, *Homo* and *Paranthropus*, covering a total of six species. As a comparison primate group she chose several prehistoric species of large, grass-eating, baboon-like *Theropithecus* monkeys that lived in the same environment over the same period. The results were startling. The large vegetarian monkey species showed no trend of increasing brain size over that time period, but hominids from both the *Homo* (*ergaster* and *habilis*) and *Paranthropus* (*boisei*) branches did. So, not only were several new *Homo* and *Paranthropus* species appearing with successively larger brains, but brain size was increasing specifically *within* each species of each genus. The latter observation is even stronger evidence for a shared new behaviour selecting for larger brains held by the common ancestor of the *Homo* and *Paranthropus* branches, but not shared with other contemporary primates. The relative increase in size in both hominid branches is also surprising since the *Paranthropus* branch, with their huge jaws, were supposed to be specialist vegetarian grinders. Over the million-year period that Elton studied, the average hominid brain size for all species increased from 400 cm^3 to 900 cm^3.

If we compare this early era of phenomenal brain growth with more recent times in the human line, there is a clear discontinuity between ancient and modern. Between the earliest *Homo habilis* just under 2 million years ago and the first so-called *Homo rhodesiensis* fossils of 1.07–1.3 million years ago,[9] a period of roughly 700,000 years, brain volume increased by two and a half times. In the subsequent 1.2 million years, although there were modest trends in brain size increase in individual human types outside Africa, such as Asian *Homo erectus* and European Neanderthals, a net increase of only 6 per cent was required to reach the brain size of today's humans. (In fact there has been an overall *decline* in brain volume in modern humans over the past 150,000 years – see Figure 0.2). So, from a physical point of view, the earliest period of the human tree was the most dramatic.

These results suggest that the earliest period of increased climatic adversity at the end of the Pliocene, and over the Pliocene–Pleistocene climatic changeover, selectively favoured brain growth in the various new hominid species, but not in other primates sharing the same environment. What does this mean? First, it supports the view that all these hominids belonging to the *Paranthropus* and *Homo* branches, and by implication their common ancestor, possessed some new behaviour selectively favouring brain growth, which they had shared from at least the beginning of the cool period. In other words, the behavioural seeds of our extraordinarily rapid brain development may already have been in place in walking apes 2.5 million years ago. Second, it puts the meat theory under some strain, although in her defence of that theory Elton argues that

Paranthropus were neither strict vegetarians, nor were they incapable of making tools to assist in extracting food from a variety of sources.[10] Third, the selection for brain size seemed to have its greatest acceleration at the beginning of our genus, over 2 million years ago.

There is a further problem with the 'meat makes brainy hunters' theory. Higher primates were not the only cooperative hunters on the African savannah. Yet we do not see lions, hyenas, or the African hunting dog wandering the veldt with huge craniums. To be sure, these committed carnivores do have relatively larger brains and appear more calculating than their prey, but they do not compare to humans, or even chimps. They are true, blinkered specialists in tooth, claw, and muscle. Hominids, by contrast, have always retained their physical and mental flexibility in exploiting food resources. We still eat vegetables – lots of them, including fruits, roots, leaves, seeds, nuts, and berries. Our hands and teeth have become more generalist and flexible rather than specialist. The only physical feature that has developed in relation to our hands, apart from the opposable thumb, is the part of the brain devoted to their manipulation.

A remarkable number of the behavioural differences and dietary strategies that set us apart from the carnivores are in fact characteristics that we *share* with our nearest living primate relative, the chimpanzee. We even share the social significance of cooperative hunting with them. Astonishing film sequences of chimps hunting colobus monkeys in Africa reveal the differences between primate hunters and specialist carnivores. We are told that those smart primate hunters have much higher success rates than lions. Their quarry meat, although highly prized, is not an essential part of their diet. Not all chimp troops hunt, nor do all chimps in a hunting troop get to eat the meat. Those that do partake may be trusted lieutenants or females with whom the dominant hunting male may wish to copulate. So, hunting among chimps could be more a prestige than a survival strategy, as it is among some humans. Sexual favours would ensure that hunting males passed on their genes more successfully. We all know where runaway sexual selection leads: to peacock tails – or, just maybe, to big brains.

Sexual speculation aside, the point I wish to make is that we should be looking much more closely at the behaviour of our closest living relatives for the seeds of our success. The history of primates over the past 10 million years has not been of specialist ruminants who decided to stop eating vegetables and start eating vegetarians instead, and who in the process became much smarter. It is the history of an already intelligent, large-brained order of forest-based generalists who made a virtue of their flexibility, even when they changed habitat. They all preserved the dexterity of their five-fingered hand and in most cases their teeth got smaller rather than larger.

One group, the ape-like ancestor of chimps and ourselves, became larger. As masters of their environment they exploited a wide range of forest vegetable food. In their trend towards omnivory they experimented with a diet of animals smaller than themselves. In their intense competition for mates, hunting may have stuck as a self-perpetuating prestige cultural practice. Being smart and cooperative, they became good at it; but neither chimps nor our ancestors ever gave up the flexibility and survival value of a diverse diet, nor the flexible social cooperation that they used to exploit their environment so well.

The single most important physical specialization that our ancestors the australopithecines evolved was the ability, unique among mammals, to habitually walk on two legs. Whether this adaptation was in response to the encroaching savannah, the need keep a cool head, or – more likely – to free up their hands, it happened millions of years before the sudden acceleration of our brain growth. When the weather became seriously worse 2.5 million years ago, their behaviour and physical form were appropriate for the next step. Their hands were free, their head was smart and cool, and their intelligent, cooperative exploitation of a wide range of foods, including meat, was still the rule. The dry climate merely turned up the selective pressure on the savannah primates to make the best of diminishing vegetable resources. Instead of aping the big cats and growing their canines into sabres and their claws even longer, and becoming true carnivores, they did what they had always done in the past: they used their brains and hands. It was against this long-established background of flexibility and social cooperation that some unique new behaviour associated with rapid brain growth kicked in 2.5 million years ago with the start of the Pleistocene ice epoch. This new behavioural trait offered the potential to cope with climatic adversity. That it was present 2.5 million years ago, before the first humans, is evidenced by the rapid brain growth shared by humans' sister genus *Paranthropus*.

Ever newer models

Although other intelligent apes, including several *Paranthropus* species, continued to walk the African savannah from 2.5 million years ago, it is humans – genus *Homo* – with whom we are concerned. Humans represented a new evolutionary concept in a number of ways, not only with their enlarged brains, mixed diet, and smaller teeth, but in their adaptive behaviours, including the making of the first shaped stone tools by the very earliest human species.

If we take *Homo habilis* as the prototype, then *Homo erectus* was the line-defining human – the Model T Ford of the new genus. Even more successful than the Model T, they dominated the planet for a million and a half years. With a sad, wary face, a flat nose, and, initially, a rapidly growing brain, *Homo erectus* was just like us from the neck down (see Plate 2). They had stone tools – simple retouched pebbles at first, but later more sophisticated hand-axes. Their African progenitor *Homo ergaster* was the first human to leave Africa, 1.95 million years ago, to become the Asian *Homo erectus*. The latter were slightly smaller than ourselves, and rapidly spread to the Middle East, Russia, India, the Far East, and Southeast Asia, carrying with them their so-called 'pebble-tool' technology.[11] There are controversial claims that the smaller predecessor on the tree *Homo habilis* also made this leap at the same time. There is better evidence, however, that all subsequent human species made it out of Africa at the first available interglacial warm-up between ice ages.

Homo erectus types then dominated the world for nearly a million years until another terrible series of ice ages dried up much of Africa over a million years ago and brought about the emergence of a new, more specialized family. The first African representative of this new model was *Homo rhodesiensis*. The same size as us and with a brain volume of as much as $1,250 \text{ cm}^3$, they used a more sophisticated stone tool kit known as Acheulian, named after a village in France near where the style was first found. Acheulian tools included largish flat stones shaped on both sides to form teardrop-shaped pointed hand-axes. This new arrival first made it out of Africa to Europe, and possibly to China, during a brief warm-up about half a million years ago, and carried the Acheulian technology with them.[12]

Then, 350,000 years ago, another severe ice age struck, perhaps forcing yet another large-brained human onto the African stage around 300,000 years ago. They are known to some as archaic *Homo sapiens*, and to others as *Homo helmei*. To avoid confusion I shall use the latter name. Beetle-browed, the same size as us, and with an average brain volume slightly larger than ours at $1,400 \text{ cm}^3$, they represented the plateau as far as dramatic brain growth was concerned. As we shall see in Chapter 2, they were also associated with the start of one of the most important revolutions in human technology, known as the Middle Palaeolithic. Some have gone so far as to suggest that if brought up in a modern family, these heavy-browed creatures might fit into our society.[13]

A larger and longer out-of-Africa movement, during a warm period, saw *Homo helmei* spreading throughout Eurasia 250,000 years ago. *Homo helmei* may have given rise to *Homo neanderthalensis* in Europe and Asia (see Plate 4) and had several possible relatives in India and China from the same period. The source human family containing our own ancestors remained in Africa, for the time being, physically separate from their Neanderthal cousins in Europe.[14]

Our own species, *Homo sapiens*, was born over 170,000 years ago, out of what was nearly a human extinction in which the total population fell to an estimated 10,000 in a mother of all ice ages.[15] Although *Homo sapiens* duly made it out of Africa to the Levant at the next interglacial, 120,000 years ago, the genetic and archaeological evidence indicates that their descendants died out there without issue in the ice age after that. (The Levant – an old-fashioned label, but useful in this context – comprises modern Syria, Lebanon, Israel, Palestine, and Jordan: the Mediterranean Near East minus Egypt.) When modern humans finally spread out of Africa to the rest of the world around 70,000–80,000 years ago, Eurasia was still inhabited by several other human species. The European Neanderthals, and possibly the Southeast Asian *Homo erectus*, persisted until less than 30,000 years ago, but no genetic traces of them remain in living humans.

Significantly, both Neanderthals and those modern humans living before the last ice age 20,000–30,000 years ago had rather bigger brains than do people living today.[16] It seems that the magic brain-enlarging effect of ice ages had played itself out before the time of our birth as a subspecies of *Homo helmei* (Figure 0.2). Maybe the obstetric risks of large heads were limiting. Either that, or brain size was no longer the most important determinant of success, and

Figure 0.2   Brain size and cultural evolution. A graph of brain growth reveals three phases over the last 2.5 million years, as separated by vertical dashed lines. The curve below shows how rapid cultural acceleration occurs during brain size reduction. (Recognized cultural milestones given equal weighting. Log-log Regression lines 1–6 relate to closely related contemporary regional human types as shown by symbols.)

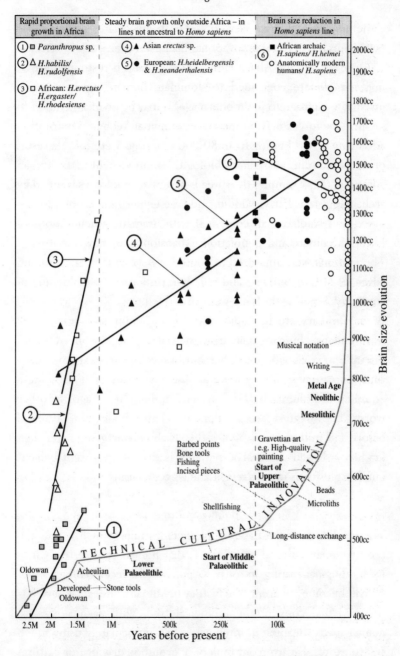

Brain size evolution

Years before present

something new that we were doing with our brains – some other behavioural or cultural innovation – had taken over.

Once we had left Africa, although our brains had stopped growing, the climate continued to dominate human expansions and inventions right up to the modern age. It may be no exaggeration to say that the forces driving the waves of human technical innovation advancing across Eurasia from 80,000 years ago were more a result of stress and relief than of any biological improvement in the human computer. For example, the spreads of new technologies labelled by archaeologists as Early, Middle, and Late Upper Palaeolithic, Mesolithic, and Neolithic all coincided with dramatic ameliorations of Europe's climate and population expansions into new territories. These events were mirrored in Southeast Asia with expansions and advances of boat-building and sailing in response to the flooding of continental shelf as the sea level rose and fell.

In summary, then, rapidly increasing brain size was a key feature that set humans apart from the walking apes that lived before 2.5 million years ago. Since then our brains have trebled in volume. This increase was not gradual and steady: most of it came as a doubling of volume in *Homo erectus* 2 million years ago. In other words, the greatest acceleration in relative brain size occurred before 1.5 million years ago, rather early in our genus, and then gradually slowed down. The paradox is that our apparent behavioural explosion is mostly recent and is accelerating.

Baldwin's idea

The resolution of the paradox of ancient brain growth versus the recent human cultural explosion is that human culture feeds into itself, thus generating its own, exponentially accelerating tempo. As will become apparent, the history of human cultural evolution is not a virtual copy of the biological tree, with each successive human species leaping in intelligence and immediately using much smarter tools. Far from our biological evolution driving our cultural innovations, it was always the other way round, and although our brains stopped growing a long time ago our culture continues to evolve. The coevolution of culture and genes underlies recent human revolution. Although a deceptively simple concept, it runs counter to all our ethnic and species prejudices.

The mechanisms by which behavioural innovations or 'new culture' drive evolution were first elaborated by American psychologist Mark Baldwin a century ago.[17] Baldwin gave a behavioural interpretation of Darwin's view of evolutionary phenomena even as simple as the giraffe growing a long neck to eat the leaves at the tops of bushes and trees. He suggested that behavioural flexibility and learning could amplify and bias the course of natural selection. Once new, invented, or learnt habits had changed the context or habitat of a particular group of animals, natural selection could favour genetically determined behavioural and physical characteristics that best exploited that new environment. Known as 'coevolution' or 'genetic assimilation', this simple argument avoided the pitfall of Lamarck's discredited theory of inheritance of acquired characteristics, while retaining one of the forgotten but more prescient of his ideas.

Coevolution is not relevant only to our own species' history. Far back on the tree of life, new, invented, or perhaps randomly adopted but adaptive behavioural skills drove the genetic changes that determined the subsequent development of special physical traits to exploit those habits. All Darwin's finches were descended from a single ordinary Central American finch species that had to try different solutions in order to survive in the challenging new environment of the Galapagos Islands. Later, multiple new species of finches evolved physically, the better to exploit those different skills.

Just as far back on the vertebrate tree, at the start of each generation, the young of many species imitated and re-learnt the 'innate' skills of their parents. We know of many instances among higher vertebrates where the parents actively participate in teaching their young. So at first these new 'invented' behaviours were transmitted not primarily by genes, but by parents and others teaching – and by the young learning. Subsequently, genes favourable to the new behaviour would begin to be selected by biological evolution, thus equipping new species to better exploit the new behaviours. In other words, genes and culture coevolved.

The development of culture need not necessarily be so tightly bound to genetic inheritance. Throughout most of mammalian evolution, such teaching of culture was strictly confined to members of the immediate family or group; as a result, behaviour was bound to genes. Among social mammals, however, survival skills are transmitted among members of a social group that are not always related. Thus, at some time over the last few million years of primate biological evolution, the evolution of culture gained a degree of independence from the genes coding for the animals that carried it. By analogy, the evolution of the violin family could equally have been achieved by a guild of viol-makers as by a family that passed the skill from father to son.

What is the evidence for this? Some purely learnt rather than innate cultural traits are geographically localized in a way which may be independent of genetic relationships. We know of Japanese macaques that wash sweet potatoes in the sea – a local cultural trait, with a recorded historical and geographical origin, which was subsequently passed on from generation to generation. It is extremely unlikely that this new behaviour depended on any new genetic trait; but, to follow this trivial example through, if there was a special survival advantage to washing sweet potatoes *and* they became the main dietary support for this local race of macaques over many generations, natural selection of random genetic alterations in those future generations could enhance the practice of sweet potato washing in some way. That would be coevolution.[18]

The geographical localization of invented culture in higher non-human primates is seen particularly clearly among chimps. In chimp tribes, specific tool-making techniques are possessed by members of a particular group and by other nearby but unrelated groups. These techniques are culturally acquired and not genetically determined and are therefore not necessarily found farther afield. At some point, perhaps even before the appearance of hominids, culture jumped the species barrier and was shared between different apes. Long before this time, cultural evolution can be said to have entered its teens and to possess its own prehistory in parallel with genetic evolution.

From this Baldwinian perspective, we can make one prediction and one observation. The prediction is that if complex deliberate communication requires a developed brain, then simple deliberate communication of some sort must have preceded the evolution of big brains. The observation is that the extraordinary invention and sophisticated flowering of writing happened some 5,000 years ago, and the invention of musical notation much more recently. These two coded non-oral systems of communication unleashed, arguably, the highest peaks of human achievement, yet we do not invoke a new species of human with special genes and a new brain to account for each of them.

How did our brain grow, and why does size matter?

Much of the perceived difference between modern humans and other animals has been related to a large brain. Several things, however, need to be pointed out. Size is very important but it is not everything. Bigger may not necessarily be smarter. For instance, pigs, being big, have much larger brains than small, expert, hunters such as wild cats. Humans who for medical reasons have had half their brain removed in childhood can enjoy near-normal human intellect and skills with the remaining 700 cm^3. Clearly, connections do count for something, and we definitely have more interconnections inside our brains than do other mammals; but how did this come about?

In general, larger bodies require larger brains. To put it crudely, this is because the larger organs and muscles of larger bodies need more brain to control them, or at least a minimum share of the attention the brain pays to the larger bulk of the body. This relationship between body and brain size, although predictable in most mammals, is not a simple ratio – if it were, then mice, for example, would have much smaller brains than they actually possess. The relationship becomes even less straightforward in the higher mammals since the body/brain size ratio has been distorted in several profound ways. Primates, for instance, have proportionately larger adult brains than do other mammals, because they have bodies that, from early life, grow more slowly for the same absolute rate of brain growth.

Humans also have a slower clock for brain maturation than do other apes. In all mammals, brain growth switches off before body growth in a way that matches the functional needs of the adult body size. Humans, however, differ from other primates in that their internal clock keeps their brains growing for longer than would be expected for their final body size as primates. The result of the prolongation of foetal and infant development stages is a brain size more appropriate for a 1,000 kg ape such as the extinct *Gigantopithecus.*[19]

Another simple gene-controlled difference in humans is that the parts of the brain originally sited on the back of the early developing embryo grow relatively larger than in other primates.[20] In the adult human, this means that the cerebellum and the cerebral cortex end up disproportionately large. These two parts of the brain are essential for coordination and higher thought. The genetic changes that brought about these dramatic effects were probably simple and involved rather few developmental genes. The resulting relative changes in the sizes of different parts of the brain have profound effects.

All these distorting size effects are genetically programmed to start in the embryo at a very early stage, before most brain cells develop their connections. The ballooning of the cerebral cortex endows it with far more neural tissue than is required for the mundane tasks of keeping the rest of the body running. In other words, in humans (and to a lesser extent in modern apes) there is a huge volume of apparently redundant cortex without a civil service role.

If the overexpansion of the cortex happens in the embryo long before the different parts of the brain start connecting up with one another, how might this affect the quality of the final connections? The answer is that when nerve cells in distant parts of the brain do start connecting up with one another, later on in the embryo's development, size plays a strong role in determining the strength and number of connections that the cortex makes internally with itself and externally with the rest of the brain and spinal cord. The resulting overgrowth in cortical connections may be described as a powerful 'ministry without portfolio' that is truly well-connected and has its fingers in every executive pie. The increased internal cortical connections may, in particular, make us humans hard-wired for mischief, creativity, and associative symbolic thought. The increased external connective power of the cortex has also given us direct control of motor nuclei in the brain stem which govern speech production. Those nuclei were previously under a sub-cortical autopilot control. All this, merely as a result of the crude resetting of perhaps half a dozen controller genes.[21]

Most of this 'upsizing' happened long before we came along. Simple comparison of brain and body size in earlier humans shows that the these changes moved into overdrive with the evolution of *Homo erectus*. So, with the knowledge that just a few genetic altera-tions brought about a huge growth of functional potential in the human brain, we come back again to the question of what new behaviour drove that rapid growth 2.5 million years ago.

Food for thought or just talking about food?

Evolutionary psychologist Robin Dunbar, from the University of Liverpool, has argued that animals with relatively large brains can remember, and interact closely with, a larger social network. In theory, he argues, those with the greatest 'social capacity' are humans. From comparison with other animals we could extrapolate a group size of over 300 for both modern humans and Neanderthals. From a personal point of view I have to say that, although I could probably recognize over a thousand individuals when I was at school, this does not fit with the number of people I am personally familiar with on a regular basis today. In a more relevant context, there is also a limit to the density of population a given area of dry savannah can support. Studies of the !Kung hunter-gatherers of southern Africa show average extended family group sizes in the teens and a maximum, dry-season, extended family camp of forty. Clearly, in the larger groups social interaction may be more super-ficial than in the smaller ones. Palaeolithic expert at the University of Southampton, Clive Gamble, has argued that our ancestors (and, more recently, our own societies) shared different sized networks with different functions. The immediate *intimate* group or network size, mainly consisting of the nuclear family, may have been only around five; a larger, effective network might have been around twenty, and an extended network, with less frequent face-to-face contacts, could have been 100–400. The opportunities for sharing or exchanging material goods would arise only in the first two of these networks, while exchange would have more of an element of calculated self-interest in the third. It does not add up to a strong case for sociability, in itself, driving brain growth.[22]

While the ability to recognize large numbers of colleagues may be associated with a large brain, it is difficult to see such a network-ing effect fuelling each jump in human brain size over the past 2.5 million years – especially if the network interaction was little more than grooming for lice and fleas and being nice to one another. Time left over for the serious business of finding food could well be diminished by too many such contacts.

Robin Dunbar and Leslie Aiello have suggested that language might originally have been an energetically cheap means of social grooming in this context,[23] although it also serves as a means of exchanging information. Most of us spend much of our time in social talking. I find it difficult, however, to conceive that complex spoken language – our own unique skill – evolved more as a form of reciprocal grooming and gossip than as a means to extend our cooperation productively and to teach our offspring by transmitting practical information. The human family moved from lowly scavenger-gatherers to one of the top predators on the African plain in the period before our fully modern ancestors left Africa. Surely this was not by dint of gossip and social point-scoring. Chimps that have been taught to communicate by sign language certainly concentrate much more on food issues in their communications than on social chit-chat.

In fact, I would turn it the other way round. I argue that language was that unique behaviour shared between the sister genera *Homo* and *Paranthropus* 2.5 million years ago which enabled them, co-operatively and flexibly, to survive the barren cycles of the Pleistocene ice epoch and thus drove their brain growth. According to Baldwin's 'new behaviour before adaptive physical change' co-evolution theory, they must have had some form of language to start with. It would be hard to argue that the symbolic coded lexicon and syntax of complex language and the productive cooperation it unlocks should not benefit in a graded way from an increase in computing power. Put simply, it is much more likely that we were already communicating usefully and deliberately 2.5 million years ago, and that this drove our brain growth, than that our brain grew until some threshold size was reached and, like Kipling's Elephant's Child with its new trunk, we suddenly discovered we could talk.

Symbolic thought and language: purely human abilities?

Deliberate communication of one form or another undoubtedly started a long time ago in animals. Vocal speech is merely the most sophisticated form of animal communication, and has selected for a number of specialized physical changes in humans. Vocal speech has special advantages over simple gesture language apart from its ability to convey complex ideas. We can communicate in the dark, through trees, and without looking at the person we are speaking to. It is much easier to con, deceive, and tell lies, and to hide our communication from strangers speaking other tongues. Children learn to lie at around the age of four. Some have suggested that males' prowess at telling jokes, and making females laugh, might have been an element in sexual selection. Like all other aspects of culture, however, language was invented and has to be internally reinvented in every child learning to speak.

We modern humans justifiably differentiate ourselves from our other living primate relatives by our power of speech. Unfortunately we do not leave the qualitative comparisons there. In the same way that we exaggerate religious and ethnic variations among our own kind, we try to take perceived differences from other apes much further in order to establish an us/them framework. A recent and extreme manifestation of this habit of exclusion between modern human groups was seen in the term *untermensch* (literally 'under-people' or 'less-than-human') used by the Nazis to describe the people they persecuted, robbed and murdered.

We have also credited ourselves with having multiple unique intellectual and manipulative skills that fence us off from the rest of the animal kingdom. Trying to look through that fence is condemned as 'anthropomorphism'. In spite of this, since the beginning of the twentieth century our nearest living relative, the chimp, has surprised careful observers by charmingly picking the wicker from these hurdles one by one. Old myths of unique human skills have died hard. First, people maintained that humans were the only animals to use tools. When that idea lost credibility, the prejudice was refined to state that humans were the only animals to *modify* tools. When this was disproved, we had to content ourselves with the assertion that only humans were capable of inventing and making tools. Again, chimps proved us wrong.

Much of this simple information was available from Wolfgang Köhler's studies in the early 1920s of a chimp colony on the island of Tenerife. Köhler, a Gestalt psychologist, went much further than showing that chimps could solve problems. He elegantly demonstrated that they were capable of both abstract and rational thought.[24] Unfortunately, few humans were able to look at his experimental results rationally at the time. It took Jane Goodall and others with their patient observation and brilliant camera-work in the field to convert the scientists and the public to the implications of Köhler's results, much later in the century.

The big surprise in the second half of the twentieth century was to find that chimps, a non-speaking ape species separated from us by at least 5 million years on the evolutionary tree, have a nascent language ability. Chimps have been taught to communicate with humans. More impressively, they are able to take their new skill and use it to communicate with one another using symbolic and coded signs. The greatest star of this story is Kanzi, a bonobo (bonobos are close relatives of chimpanzees, with several behavioural traits reminiscent of ourselves). Kanzi learnt to communicate using a complex coded symbol language on a computer. He also spontaneously learnt to comprehend spoken English, correctly interpreting syntax. The scale of his achievement could have something to do with the fact that he was a bonobo (it appears that bonobos may be slightly closer genetically to humans than other chimps) but it seems more likely the result of his having picked up the skills spontaneously as an infant at his chimp foster mother's side, when his childlike learning ability window was open and at its best. She was actually the intended target of the language teaching and, as an adult, was struggling to learn these new symbols. Chimps have also been shown to demonstrate abstract, symbolic, and rational thought, as well as what is termed 'symbolic inference' and 'symbolic manipulation', although they are clearly not as good at these skills as we are. Most likely, this is simply a matter of degree. As far as language is concerned, chimps are obviously hampered by lack of vocal control and are either not disposed to or unable to see the value of extended non-verbal communication.[25]

Surprisingly, the full implications of these experiments are still largely ignored by linguists. To understand this obstinacy we have to appreciate the dichotomy in current theories of the origins of language and thought. Two lines of argument have run in parallel since the nineteenth century. The first of these, in which language is seen essentially as an invention, was initiated by the eighteenth-century Enlightenment *philosophe* Étienne Bonnot de Condillac. He argued that spoken language had developed out of gesture language (*langage d'action*) and that both were inventions arising initially from simple association. The Condillac view anticipated the concept of cultural evolution and, with some development, can be traced through Darwinism and a mid-twentieth-century thinker, Ronald Englefield, right down to the present day with the work of New Zealand psychologist Michael Corballis and others. The full theory sees gesture language as arising originally among apes, and then becoming conventional or coded as the new skill drove its own evolution. Subsequently, verbal signals, some already present in the 'innate' primate repertory, were co-opted and developed into deliberate coded communication. Evolutionary pressures then promoted the development of the vocal apparatus and also of part of the brain immediately next to that responsible for gestures. This speech centre is often called Broca's area.[26]

Touched with the gift of speech?

The other, at present dominant view of the origin of language is almost creationist in its denial of the process of evolution. Language, in this case specifically the spoken word, is seen as having arisen suddenly among modern humans between 35,000 and 50,000 years ago as some kind of 'big bang' speciation event. According to Noam Chomsky, the ability to speak words and also to use syntax was recently genetically hard-wired into our brains in some kind of language organ. This view of language is associated with the old idea that logical or rational thought is somehow dependent on words. This concept originated with Plato and was much in vogue in the nineteenth century with writers such as Jakob Grimm – 'Animals do not speak because they do not think' – and Max Müller – 'Language is our Rubicon, and no brute will dare to cross it' and 'without speech, no reason, without reason, no speech'.[27]

The creationist notion of a great leap forward in the quality of human thinking is further reflected in a common interpretation of Upper Palaeolithic art in Europe. European cave paintings and carved figurines which have been dated to over 30,000 years ago are seen, according to this perspective, as the first stirrings of symbolic and abstract thought and also of language. However, the mature sophistication of the earliest paintings found in Chauvet Cave in the south of France seems to deny this view.[28] In any case, such a Eurocentric interpretation ignores the knowledge that Australians were already painting on rocks on the other side of the world at the same time as the early Europeans. It is absurd to suggest that they and the rest of the world had to learn their own speech and painting from Europeans. There is every reason and much evidence, as will be discussed in this book, to suppose that their common African ancestor had already mastered the skills of speech, art, and symbolic representation long before leaving Africa 80,000 years ago.

Another problem with the creationist or 'big bang' view of modern humans' unique abilities is that there is evidence that Neanderthals had the same specialized vocal anatomy that we have. The possession of a similar hyoid bone, an enlarged thoracic spinal cord, and an enlarged orifice to carry the hypoglossal nerve to the tongue, are consistent with Neanderthals speaking. On Baldwin's hypothesis, these attributes also indicate that Neanderthals' (and our own) common ancestor *Homo heidelbergensis* was already speaking over half a million years ago. Since *Homo heidelbergensis* also had an equally enlarged nerve orifice and some other key anatomical features of speech, the argument could possibly be stretched back further to *Homo erectus*, who shows evidence of a lopsided brain. The latter is thought to be an important associated phenomenon of language. *Homo habilis* is thought by some to show an impression, inside the skull, of Broca's area, consistent with the view that the process of specialized enlargement to adapt to speech had already begun 2 million years ago.[29]

This anatomical speculation brings us back to the first humans and the dramatic sprint in brain enlargement in *Homo* and *Paranthropus*. If there ever was a big bang in the speciation of smart hominids, this was it. Tim Crow, a professor of psychiatry in Oxford, has argued that two important speciation events can be inferred from two closely related mutations on the Y chromosome, sometime after the split between chimps and ourselves. There is some reason for supposing that one or both of these mutations might be associated with cerebral asymmetry, and possibly with language. If so, then we might speculate that the first mutation occurred in the common ancestor of *Homo* and *Paranthropus* and the second in *Homo erectus*, since the latter shows the first evidence of cerebral asymmetry.[30]

Modern neurophysiological research, using a variety of techniques including active imaging, has further undermined the biologically deterministic view of thought and language evolution and acquisition. We now know that the syntax of different types of language is handled in different parts of the brain. Syntax is not hard-wired: it is *inferred* by young children, who, compared to adults learning a new language, have a greater and more flexible ability to decode symbolic associations and guess the correct syntactic inference. Humans are not unique in having a critical period in development when language skills are acquired. The same phenomenon is seen in the 'singing' non-primates, such as birds and whales. The complex, often unique songs sung in later life by these animals are learnt, modified, and imprinted at an early stage. Moreover, research shows that speech is not necessarily limited to a particular part or parts of the brain.[31]

These neurophysiological studies have suggested an alternative to the Chomskian theory of language evolution, one which incorporates the ideas of Condillac, Englefield, and Corballis. This is the view that spoken language was ultimately a primate invention, like toolmaking, which drove the biological evolution of the brain and vocal apparatus. As a cultural invention, it has also evolved separately outside our bodies within specific cultural communities. The unique combination of lexical and syntactic features of a language such as French are the cultural possessions of the French community, and clearly do not result from a unique biological aspect of being French. Each language and its syntax evolves from one generation to the next, constantly adapting itself to cope with the learning biases of each new set of young immature minds.

In summary, of all the mental and practical skills that philosophers have put forward as qualitative differences between modern humans and chimps, the only one that remains is human speech. Clearly, there is a great quantitative difference in intellectual ability, but human intellect did not suddenly flower 35,000 years ago in the European Upper Palaeolithic – it had been evolving over the previous 4 million years. For the past 2 million years humans have been improving on the walking-ape model by using their brains, but they may have been aided in this by speech-driven coevolution in brain size. Just like the flexible new trunk of the Elephant's Child in Kipling's fable, the enhanced abilities of our new brain to manipulate symbolic concepts and sets has been turned to a variety of complex tasks other than speech. The fact that we can speculate about the geometry of the universe and its origins, and even start to explore it, suggests that our intellect has few limits of flexibility and fresh application.

We have seen that the cycles of African desiccation accompanying ice ages encouraged the growth of human brains over 2 million years ago. This also happened in our sister genus *Paranthropus*, but not in large savannah-dwelling monkeys, suggesting that some special behaviour which depended on brain size was already being shared exclusively by those hominids. There is a tendency to see runaway brain growth as a recent event among humans, but if we look at the evidence we find that the opposite seems to be true. The most rapid proportional brain growth happened between 1 and 2 million years ago. By the time modern humans came along, brain growth had largely slowed down. The paradox is that our apparent behavioural explosion is mostly recent and is accelerating geometrically.

Rather than accept the obvious – that human culture feeds into itself, thus generating its own accelerating tempo – many anthropologists, archaeologists, and linguists believe that something 'genetic' happened to the way our brains worked within the last 100,000 years, producing a different kind of human brain with new wiring. Some go even further, suggesting that language is the most obvious candidate for that new and unique behaviour.[32] Frankly, I think this is perverse logic and un-Darwinian. Deliberate coded communication, or 'language', is certainly a useful, new, and unique behaviour. How much simpler, though, if this was what had differentiated our early ancestors from other large savannah primates and had driven evolution of their brain size 2.5 million years earlier so that they could communicate better and cope with their worsening environment in a more inventive way.

*   *   *

So far I have made little reference to genetics, which is going to figure prominently in this book. Much of the human history of the past 2.5 million years has been reconstructed by a combination of studies of fossil bones and past climates. All but one human species became extinct, some of them long ago, so we do not have their living genes to study. This is not to say that genetics has nothing to tell us about the dark ages of our evolution, before modern humans appeared on the stage. In the 1970s, some geneticists began to use crude immunological tools to measure protein similarities between species, and suggested that humans and chimps were even more closely related than had been thought. Their suggestion was met with derision at the time, but as techniques of comparison turned from immunology to demonstrating a basic genetic similarity and then eventually to measuring precise genetic differences, they were vindicated. The realization has grown that we are much closer to chimps than to the other great apes, the gorillas and orang-utans, our common lineage having split not much more than 5 million years ago.[33]

To say that there are no genes left over from past human species is also not quite true. Most of our nuclear genes are inherited nearly intact from ancestral humans and apes. Some human genes can be found in several forms that split from one another long before we appeared on Earth. Scientists have also extracted short fragmentary stretches of mitochondrial DNA from a number of Neanderthal bones, and are now in a position to answer basic questions about how closely we are related to them and whether there are any of their genes left in modern human populations.

However, the real revolution in understanding human genetic prehistory covers the last 200,000 years, which is what concerns us here. For this period, the new genetics has shone a bright light onto a contentious field previously dominated by collections of European and African stone tools and a few poorly dated skeletal remains. Before turning to details of genetic tracking, it may help to look at some of the ideas behind genetic inheritance and how they have evolved. The concepts are mainly simple, being related to our own everyday understanding of and pre-occupation with inheritance, but are often misrepresented, either for reasons of hype or because they are veiled in jargon.

The secrets of the peas

Humans have been aware of some idea of genetic inheritance ever since the first animals and plants were domesticated. Farmers made deliberate attempts to breed out unwanted features such as large size or aggression. Cereal grain was bred for increased size and ease of cropping. However, much of the detail of 'farmer's lore' was fundamentally wrong, though crudely functional. Speculation about the exact mechanisms and rules underlying inheritance increased in the mid-nineteenth century with the publication of Charles Darwin's *Origin of Species*, but Darwin's understanding of the principles of heredity was not much more sophisticated than that of his predecessors. Instead it was his contemporary, the nineteenth-century Austrian cleric Gregor Mendel, who first laid down a logical framework for understanding how parental characteristics were transmitted, based on his obsessive mathematical calculations on the inheritance of the colour and shape of pea plants.

Basically, Mendel showed that, for any particular physical feature, or *character*, such as flower colour, each pea plant possessed two genes (although he used another term) that determined the *expression* or outcome of the character. Variation in relative dominance between these two genes determined their expression in the plant. During the process of sexual procreation, only one of these genes would be donated by each parent to each offspring plant. Thus, each offspring inherited a mixture of characters from each parent, with

the combined effect of two genes determining each physical character at each generation. Since either parent could have different
functioning gene types, for instance different petal colours, for each
(and any) pair of genes, and only one of the two was chosen at
random, the proportions of different varieties of offspring formed a
pattern that could be predicted from a knowledge of the characters
possessed by each parent. In this way, Mendel showed that inheritance of characters took place by the transfer of discrete packets of
information. The variation in the offspring was down to the precise
but random mix of these packets, or genes, in each individual,
whether it be a pea seed or a human.

Mendel was careful to choose simple, common, easily distinguished characters and to study them individually. In reality, the
expression of some physical characters is determined by more than
one gene, and we all have around 30,000 pairs of functioning genes
because we are rather complex organisms. Thus the visible random
variation between siblings in the same family is not the result of any
vagueness in the process of heredity, but arises because there are
large numbers of gene pairs being randomly chosen during sexual
procreation. With so many gene pairs in different combinations,
there is huge potential for variety. By way of contrast, the extreme
similarity of identical twins gives us a glimpse of how precise the
conversion of heredity into physical form really is. The extraordinary achievement of Watson, Crick, and Rosalind Franklin was to
translate Mendel's discoveries into biochemistry – or molecular
biology, as this aspect of biochemistry came to be known.

Cardboard keys to life

'We are the products of our genes.' The secret keys to this Edward-
ian truism were traced and cut out on bits of cardboard by two
adventurer-scientists, Jim Watson and Francis Crick, in 1953.[34]
Their 'keys' were scale diagrams of four chemicals (nucleotide

bases), whose unique interlocking relationship, set in the double-stranded zip-locking deoxyribonucleic acid (DNA), holds the code for life on Earth. Those bits of cardboard unlocked the mechanism linking Mendel's work to the theory of evolution by natural selection as set out by Darwin in the *Origin of Species*. Watson and Crick explained exactly how thousands of unique characteristics, varying from one individual to another, are passed on intact from generation to generation. In short, it was the greatest advance in biological understanding in the twentieth century.

Within each of the cells of our bodies we all have incredibly long strings of DNA. It is the stuff of the genes. It stores, replicates, and passes on all our unique characteristics – our genetic inheritance. These DNA strings hold the template codes for proteins, the building blocks of our bodies. The codes are 'written' in combinations of just four different chemicals known as nucleotide bases (represented by the letters A, G, C, and T), which provide all the instructions for making our bodies. We inherit DNA from each of our parents, and because we receive a unique mixture from both, each of us has slightly different DNA strings from everyone else. Our own DNA is like a molecular fingerprint.

During human reproduction, the parents' DNA is copied and transmitted in equal proportions. It is important to know that although most of the DNA from each parent is segregated during reproduction, small bits of their respective contributions are shuffled and mixed at each generation. The mixing here is not that of mass random allocation of genes inferred by Mendel, but tiny crossovers, duplications, and swaps between maternal and paternal DNA contributions. This is known technically as *recombination*. Luckily, for the purposes of genetic researchers, there are two small portions of our DNA that do not recombine. Non-recombining DNA is easier to trace back since the information is uncorrupted during transmission from one generation to the next. The two portions are known as mitochondrial DNA (mtDNA) and the non-recombining part of the Y chromosome (NRY).

Mitochondrial DNA: the Eve gene

To say that we get exactly half of our DNA from our father and half from our mother is not quite true. One tiny piece of our DNA is inherited only down the female line. It is called mitochondrial DNA because it is held as a unique circular strand in small tubular packets known as mitochondria that function rather like batteries within the cell cytoplasm. Some molecular biologists say that, aeons ago, the mitochondrion was a free-living organism with its own DNA, and possessed the secret of generating lots of energy. It invaded single-celled nucleated organisms and has stayed on ever since, dividing, like yeast, by binary fission. Males, although they receive and use their mother's mitochondrial DNA, cannot pass it on to their children. The sperm has its own mitochondria to power the long journey from the vagina to the ovum but, on entry into the ovum, the male mitochondria wither and die. It is as if the man had to leave his guns at the door.

So each of us inherits our mtDNA from our own mother, who inherited her mtDNA intact from her mother, and so on back through the generations – hence mtDNA's popular name, 'the Eve gene'. Ultimately, every person alive today has inherited their mitochondrial DNA from one single great-great-great-. . .-grandmother, nearly 200,000 years ago. This mtDNA provides us with a rare point of stability among the shifting sands of DNA inheritance. However, if all the Eve chromosomes in the world today were an exact copy of that original Eve mtDNA, then clearly they would all be identical. This would be miraculous, but it would mean that mtDNA is incapable of telling us much about our prehistory. Just knowing that all women can be traced back to one common ancestral Eve is exciting, but does not get us very far in

tracing the different geographic lives of her daughters. We need
something with a bit of variety.

This is where DNA point mutations come in. When mtDNA is
inherited from our mother, occasionally there is a change or mutation in one or more of the 'letters' of the mtDNA code – about one
mutation every thousand generations.[35] The new letter, called a
point mutation, will then be transmitted through all subsequent
daughters. Although a new mutation is a rare event within a single
family line, the overall probability of mutations is clearly increased
by the number of mothers having daughters. So, within one generation, a million mothers could have more than a thousand daughters
with a new mutation, each different from the rest. This is why,
unless we share a recent maternal ancestor within the past 10,000
years or so, we each have a slightly different code from everyone
else around us.

Using mutations to build a tree

Over a period of nearly 200,000 years, a number of tiny random
mutations have thus steadily accumulated on different human
mtDNA molecules being passed down to daughters of Eve all
around the world. For each of us this represents between seven and
fifteen mutational changes on our own personal Eve record. Mutations are thus a cumulative dossier of our own maternal prehistory.
The main task of DNA is to copy itself to each new generation. We
can use these mutations to reconstruct a genetic tree of mtDNA,
because each new mtDNA mutation in a prospective mother's ovum
will be transferred in perpetuity to all her descendants down the
female line. Each new female line is thus defined by the old mutations as well as the new ones. As a result, by knowing all the
different combinations of mutations in living females around the
world, we can logically reconstruct a family tree right back to our
first mother.

Although it is simple to draw on the back of an envelope a recent mtDNA tree with only a couple of mutations to play with, the problem becomes much more complex when dealing with the whole human race, with thousands of combinations of mutations. So computers are used for the reconstruction. By looking at the DNA code in a sample of people alive today, and piecing together the changes in the code that have arisen down the generations, biologists can trace the line of descent back in time to a distant shared ancestor. Because we inherit mtDNA only from our mother, this line of descent is a picture of the female genealogy of the human species.

Not only can we retrace the tree, but by taking into account where the sampled people came from, we can see *where* certain mutations occurred – for example, whether in Europe, or Asia, or Africa. What's more, because the changes happen at a statistically consistent (though random) rate, we can approximate the *time* when they happened. This has made it possible, during the late 1990s and in the new century, for us to do something that anthropologists of the past could only have dreamt of: we can now trace the migrations of modern humans around our planet. It turns out that the oldest changes in our mtDNA took place in Africa 150,000–190,000 years ago. Then new mutations start to appear in Asia, about 60,000–80,000 years ago (Figure 0.3). This tells us that modern humans evolved in Africa, and that some of us migrated out of Africa into Asia after 80,000 years ago.

It is important to realize that because of the random nature of individual mutations, the dating is only approximate. There are various mathematical ways of dating population migrations, which were tried with varying degrees of success during the 1990s, but one method established in 1996, which dates each branch of the gene tree by averaging the number of new mutations in daughter types of that branch,[36] has stood the test of time and is the main one I use in this book.

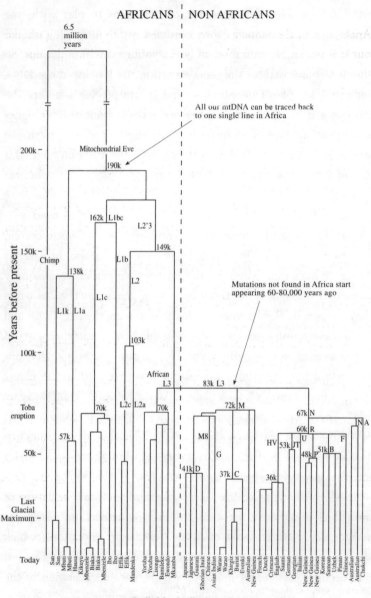

AFRICANS | NON AFRICANS

6.5 million years

All our mtDNA can be traced back to one single line in Africa

Mitochondrial Eve

Mutations not found in Africa start appearing 60–80,000 years ago

Years before present

Individual tribe/country

Y chromosome: the Adam gene

Analogous to the maternally transmitted mtDNA residing outside our cell nuclei, there is a set of genes packaged within the nucleus that is only passed down the male line. This is the Y chromosome, the defining chromosome for maleness. With the exception of a small segment, the unpaired Y chromosome plays no part in the promiscuous exchange of DNA indulged in by other chromosomes. This means that, like mtDNA, the non-recombining part of the Y chromosome remains uncorrupted with each generation, and can be traced back in an unbroken line to our original male ancestor.

Y chromosomes have been used for reconstructing trees for less time than mtDNA has, and there are more problems in estimating time depth. When these are solved, the NRY method may have a much greater power of time and geographical resolution than mtDNA, for both the recent and the distant past. This is simply because the NRY is much larger than mtDNA and consequently has potential for more variation.

Yet Y chromosomes have already helped to chart a genetic trail parallel to the mtDNA trail. At the major geographical branch points they support the story told by mtDNA: they point to a shared ancestor in Africa for all modern humans, and a more recent ancestor in Asia for all non-Africans. In addition, because men's behaviour differs in certain key ways from women's, the story told by the Adam genes adds interesting detail. One difference is that men have more variation in the number of their offspring than women: a few men father considerably more children than the rest. Women, in contrast, tend to be more even and 'equal' in the number of children they have. The main effect of this is that most

Figure 0.3 Real maternal gene tree of 52 randomly selected individual people from around the world. Note the age of Mitochondrial Eve. Branch dating by author based on complete sequence data; the chimp–human coalescent date arises from analysis, i.e. not assumed from fossil evidence – see note [22] in Chapter 1.

male lines become extinct more rapidly than female lines, leaving a few numerically dominant male genetic lines.

Another difference is in movement. It has often been argued that because women have usually travelled to their husband's village, their genes are inevitably more mobile. Paradoxically, while this may be true within one cultural region, it results in rapid mixing and dispersal of mtDNA only within that cultural region. For travel *between* regions, or long-distance intercontinental migrations, by sea for example, the burden of caring for children would have limited female mobility. Predatory raiding groups would also have been more commonly male-dominated, resulting in increased long-distance mobility in the Y chromosome.

A final point on the methods of genetic tracking of migrations: it is important to distinguish this new approach to tracing the history of molecules on a DNA tree, known as phylogeography (literally 'tree-geography'), from the mathematical study of the history of whole human populations, which has been used for decades and is known as classical population genetics. The two disciplines are based on the same Mendelian biological principles, but have quite different aims and assumptions, and the difference is the source of much misunderstanding and controversy. The simplest way of explaining it is that phylogeography studies the prehistory of individual DNA molecules, while population genetics studies the prehistory of populations. Put another way, each human population contains multiple versions of any particular part of our genome, each with its own history and different origin. Although these two approaches to human prehistory cannot represent exactly the same thing, their shared aim is to trace human migrations. Tracing the individual molecules we carry is just much easier than trying to follow whole groups.

Naming gene lines

In this book I refer interchangeably to maternal or paternal clans, gene lines, lineages, genetic groups/branches, and even haplogroups. All these terms mean much the same thing: members of a large group of genetic types sharing a common ancestor (usually through their mtDNA or Y chromosome). The size of the group is to a certain extent arbitrary and depends on how far back the base of the branch is on the genetic tree. One thing that quickly becomes apparent from study of genetic trees is the lack of uniformity in the nomenclature of these branches. For the Y chromosome in particular, each new scientific paper proposes a new system of scientific nomenclature based on different 'in-house' genetic markers used by different research laboratories. This can make comparison between different studies tedious and repeatedly tests the limits of the reader's memory. The underlying tree, however, is more or less the same from lab to lab. Recently, a consensus Y nomenclature was published, with letters from A to R describing the main genetic branches in the tree.[37] I use this nomenclature as far as possible in my referencing and figures. The trouble is that even these eighteen letters and their location on the tree are difficult to hold in the mind – at least in mine. The fact that they are just letters makes it worse.

Luckily, our memory is often aided by context and association. For this reason, and this reason alone, I have introduced names for the major branches and for other branches I refer to frequently. Some of the names are regional, such as Ho for one Chinese/ Southeast Asian Y-branch (after the Southeast Asian explorer Admiral Cheng Ho and also for Ho Chi Minh, the revered Vietnamese nationalist hero). Others are biblical, like the out-of-Africa Y-line founder Adam and his three descendent lines, Cain, Abel, and Seth (see Appendices 1 and 2). There is no intention with these names to infer any deeper meaning – they are simply aides-mémoires.

The mtDNA picture is slightly easier. Many of the different labs agreed at an early stage to try to use a single nomenclature. (Perhaps there was less testosterone involved in the process!) For instance, there are two agreed non-African daughter lines, 'N' and 'M' from the single out-of-Africa line L3. I have called them Nasreen, in keeping with a southern Arabian origin, and Manju, to be consistent with an Indian subcontinental origin.

1

OUT OF AFRICA

ONE OF THE MOST ENDURING media images of popular genetics in the 1980s was a cover of *Newsweek* showing sophisticated and attractive nude portraits of a black Adam and Eve sharing the apple, with the snake looking on approvingly between (see Plate 5). This cover sold record numbers of the magazine. But in spite of the media hype, *Newsweek* was reporting a major advance. There were two stunning insights portrayed in the picture and described in the lead article. The first was some new genetic evidence published in 1987, using genes that could be passed down only through our mothers. This work, by American geneticist Rebecca Cann and colleagues, resolved an old argument about the birthplace of modern humans. The new evidence said that we, 'the modern human family', had originated as a single genetic line in Africa within the last 200,000 years, and not as multiple separate evolutionary events in different parts of the world. This single line, which leads back eventually to the ancestor we share with the Neanderthals, gave rise to the half-dozen major maternal clans (or branches) that are, even today, clearly of African origin.[1]

The second reason for using a biblical allegory on the *Newsweek* cover was that this new genetic approach used only maternally transmitted mitochondrial DNA. Ten years later, a small group of geneticists would use this newly discovered method to identify a single twig from those dozen or more ancestral African maternal genetic branches as forming the sole founding line for the rest of the world.[2] In other words, there was a single common ancestor or 'Mitochondrial Eve' for all African female lines and then, much later, came a subsidiary 'Out-of-Africa Eve' line whose genetic daughters peopled the rest of the world. It proved to be an extraordinary discovery.

The label 'Eve' or 'First Lady', so celebrated by the media at the time, was not the exact truth as geneticists saw it. Using mitochondrial DNA, they had identified a root female genetic line for only a tiny part of our genetic heritage. Mitochondrial Eve was not a sole individual 'First Mother' as often implied by the media. Tracing a maternal genetic marker back to a shared ancestral type does not mean that *all* our genes literally derive from one woman. In each of our cell nuclei we have tens of thousands of genes, each with their own history, that can be mapped. Any one of these genes could be used as a marker system to trace back to a common ancestor.[3] Because much of our DNA mixes around at each generation, the gene trees would not necessarily all go back to the same ancestor. In fact, the genetic heritage of modern humans may be derived from a core of 2,000–10,000 Africans who lived around 190,000 years ago.

Although the reality of parallel 'gene trees' rather than 'people trees' may seem to take the romance out of the Eve tale, it does not diminish the exceptional power of such genetic tracing to tell the grand story of human wanderings over the past 200,000 years. The ability to tell the same story using a number of different genes confirms and enriches the tale. Male gene lines, for instance, tend to show a rather more adventurous intercontinental spread than do female ones. In South Africa, for example, a self-proclaimed 'lost tribe of Israel' was recently identified by geneticists as having Jewish ancestors, but only through the male line.[4]

Objections from multiregionalists and geneticists

The bold and clear trail of spreading humankind drawn by the mitochondrial markers was bound to raise objections. The multiregionalists certainly dissented. These were mainly palaeoanthropologists who still believed that the different world 'races' each broke out of pre-modern ancestral forms – from various parts of the world such as 'Java Man', 'Peking Man', and the Neanderthals. A major problem here is that, in many ways, the regionally defined modern human peoples resemble one another more than they do their supposed ancestors. To cope with this observation, some multiregionalists now argue that different regional 'human species' subsequently mixed and exchanged genetic material with one another to form the complex modern races we have today (Figure 1.1).

Yet the genetic evidence fails to show such fine inter-regional mixing. The geographical distributions of the branches and twigs of the modern out-of-Africa mitochondrial DNA and Y-chromosome trees are regionally very specific. In a last stand by the multiregionalists, the 'inter-regional mixing compromise' has been extended further to encompass the out-of-Africa hypothesis by suggesting that regional archaic human populations, such as Neanderthals, occasionally interbred with incoming anatomically modern – that is, 'like us' – Cro-Magnons. ('Anatomically Modern Humans' are members of the species *Homo sapiens* (*sensu stricto*), possessing a combination of skeletal features that collectively distinguish ourselves and our immediate ancestors in Africa within the past 200,000 years from extinct archaic versions of *Homo sapiens* (*sensu lato*), including our relation *Homo helmei*. The main 'anatomically modern' characteristics are a high round cranium, a pronounced chin, small face and jaws, and brow ridges.) Inter-regional mixing of old-timers and newcomers is in effect a soft compromise of the out-of-Africa hypothesis, which would allow some leftover genes from archaic peoples to be present in the modern gene pool. A child's

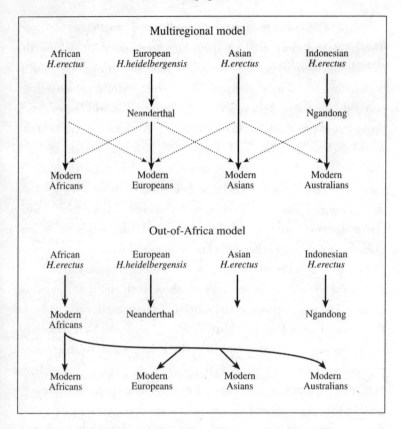

Figure 1.1   Comparison of multiregional and out-of-Africa models. In the out-of-Africa model 'Anatomically Modern' Africans recently completely replaced all other humans worldwide; in the multiregional hypothesis a variable degree of genetic and physical inheritance remains today from older regional species of humans.

skeleton in Portugal, showing short robust limbs and dated to 24,500 years ago – after Neanderthals died out – has been cited as evidence of such hybridization. Yet, again there is no evidence among the tens of thousands of non-Africans who have had their mtDNA and Y chromosomes studied for even a minimal degree of this kind of mixing.[5]

To be fair, that is not the end of the story. While there is no evidence in the 'Adam' and 'Eve' lines of any such modern/archaic admixture, these lines hold but a tiny fraction of our huge genomic library of DNA. Because only one version each of mtDNA and the Y chromosome (NRY) are transmitted at each generation, rather than two, Neanderthal-specific mtDNA lines may on a very few occasions have admixed into Cro-Magnon populations and then become extinct. But there could still be evidence of miscegenation lurking among the rest of the vast nuclear genome. Because such nuclear DNA shuffles and splices at each generation, it is harder to build a tree for each of the numerous gene lines and be sure what was brought in by modern humans and what derives from regional archaic peoples.[6] So it could just be that, as some people claim, the beetle-browed appearance of some rugby internationals and soccer hooligans eventually turns out to be a Neanderthal throwback, rather than the more likely event (in my view) of normal variation in modern humans.

Another kind of dissent was shown by traditional population geneticists. They were surprised and perhaps even upset that mitochondrial DNA gave such a clear picture when their own genetic methods, using hundreds of traditional nuclear gene markers (transmitted by both males and females), had for years indicated a more blurred division between Africa and the rest of the world. Several factors contributed to this blurring. Most important was the traditionalists' classical, population-based approach to constructing mass-migration trees rather than building trees of gene lines. In effect, they persisted in following a broad, albeit mathematically based concept of 'racial migration' rather than tracing the migrations of individual gene lines found in those populations. Another important factor was the mixing and shuffling of nuclear gene lines at each generation – something that does not happen to mtDNA or NRY. Also, most of the gene markers they used had simple trees with a small number of very ancient branches, and the twigs were common to many populations.

For all these reasons, the traditional way of comparing populations of different regions by measuring multiple nuclear gene frequencies was a fundamentally flawed approach to looking at ancient
migrations. As if to demonstrate this, a study by Oxford-based
James Wainscoat and colleagues using nuclear genetic evidence from
just a single nuclear locus (i.e. not Adam or Eve genes), and arguing
for an out-of-Africa model, had already been published in *Nature* in
1986. This was a year before Rebecca Cann's findings, popularized
in the *Newsweek* article, and it used samples from human participants
from all around the world, including samples I had collected in New
Guinea in 1984. Instead of comparing frequencies of many genes,
Wainscoat created a simple family tree of populations from just one
genetic locus. The result was broadly the same as Cann's findings in
suggesting an out-of-Africa origin. Other geneticists also raised a
series of highly technical objections to the analysis of the 'Eve'
genes. The technical objections have since all been overcome one by
one.[7]

With the recent analysis of the other non-mixing system, the
Y chromosome, and studies of many other genetic markers,[8] the
original out-of-Africa picture suggested by the mitochondrial
markers has emerged triumphant, and the multiregionalists have
become an isolated, albeit vociferous minority.

Two routes out of Africa?

Humans had to come out of Africa in the end, as all their primate
relatives had – but the timing and the route, as always, were determined by climate swings. There were two potential routes out of
Africa, a northern and a southern, and the weather determined
which was open at any particular time. The one that was open, in
turn, directed the explorers where to go next – north, or east.
Modern humans first left Africa over 120,000 years ago through an
open northern gate. As we shall see, that first foray ended in disaster.
Their second, successful venture set them on a path through Asia to

the south and east, already well worn by their predecessors. Europe was bypassed and ignored until 50,000 years ago.

Africa was the birthplace of all the various human species to walk this planet. This vast and isolated natural laboratory moulded humans over endless cycles of alternating desert and greening. The unique patchwork of savannah and forest that is sub-Saharan Africa is effectively separated from the rest of the world by two sets of environmental gates and corridors. For the last couple of million years these corridors have acted like a huge livestock corral, with several gateways alternately open and closed. When one set of gates was open the other was usually closed. One gate led north, over the Sahara to the Levant and Europe, while the other led east, across the mouth of the Red Sea to Yemen, Oman, and India. Which gate was open depended on the glacial cycle and determined whether mammals, including humans, migrating from Africa went north to Europe or east to Asia.[9]

Today, Africa is physically linked to the Eurasian continent by only one of these corridors, via the Sinai Peninsula in the north. Normally an unforgiving dry desert, the potential route through the Sahara and the Sinai to the rest of the world opens, like some science-fiction stargate, only when variations in the Earth's orbit and the tilt of its polar axis produce a brief episode of warming. This fleeting event in geological time happens only once every 100,000 years or so, when the Sun's heat causes a polar meltdown and a warm and humid global climate ensues. The Sahara, Sinai, and the deserts of Australia grow lakes, become green, and flower in the short geological spring (Figure 1.2). But because this warm interlude is so brief, the North African weather-gate can act as a deadly trap to migrants.

For most of the last 2 million years, humans have shivered in the grip of the Pleistocene ice epoch, so the brief but marked warming of our planet's surface, which opens up the gates of Eden, is known to geologists as an interglacial optimum. These short lush spells contrast with the normally cold and dry glacial conditions of the Pleistocene. We modern humans have had only two such glimpses of paradise during our time on Earth. The most recent interglacial optimum was only about 8,000 years ago, and we are lucky to be still basking in the after-effects of its autumnal glow. For perhaps a couple of thousand years the Sahara was grassland, and all kinds of game from the south spread throughout North Africa and across into the Levant. Ironically, today's pollution-driven global warming is actually helping to stave off the inevitable relapse into the cooler, drier, more unstable conditions that have characterized most of our time on Earth.

Usually, evidence for such climatic dramas in prehistory has to be teased out by scientists digging the ground and drilling into ice caps and the seabed. In this case, however, we do not need the abundant scientific record of archaeology and climatic change to demonstrate the truth to us. We can see for ourselves by looking at the wonderful paintings on cliffs in the central Sahara region. Thousands of naturalistic images of extinct buffaloes, of elephants, rhinos, hippos, giraffes (see Plate 6) ostriches, and large antelope, were painted there 8,000 years ago. This colourful historical record has continued intermittently up to recent times. Later paintings tell us that the Saharan game disappeared over 5,000 years ago, to be replaced by camels.

This period when African game briefly flowed into Morocco, Egypt, and the Levant was, on a larger scale, similar to rare downpours in deserts that activate the long-dormant seeds of beautiful flowers. The lush paradise was short-lived; the game retreated, and the desert returned. Big mammals do not have seeds that can hide themselves away in the sand. Even non-mammalian drought wizards like the desert frog and lungfish can only cocoon themselves for a short period while waiting for the next downpour. So also during the previous interglacial, the first in our time on Earth, a brave band of pioneers headed north out of Africa and reached the Levant before the Saharan gate slowly shut behind them.

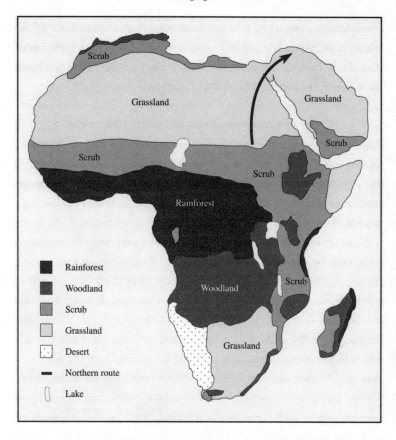

Figure 1.2 The Northern route out of Africa. This map shows vegetation in Africa during an interglacial such as happened 125,000 and 7–8,000 years ago. At these times grassland spread across the Sahara, allowing people from the south to follow the game into North Africa and beyond to the Levant. For simplicity, scrub and savannah are combined, as are semi-desert and extreme desert.

The earlier interglacial, known to scientists as the Eemian or Ipswichian, came 125,000 years ago, soon after the birth of our human family. We know that early modern humans travelled out of sub-Saharan Africa into North Africa and the Levant at a very early stage because their bones have been found in those places. In fact,

the earliest remains of modern humans anywhere outside Africa –
dated to between 90,000 and 120,000 years ago – were found in the
Levant.[10] The big question is whether they made a lasting impression there. It looks as though they failed to do so.

Out of Africa into Europe: the failed first exodus

Until these very early dates were confirmed, the out-of-Africa scientific camp assumed that the early northern exodus of modern
humans to the Levant formed the nucleus from which Europeans
and most Asians evolved. But there were basic flaws to these arguments. The early trail of modern humans sadly petered out in the
Levant around 90,000 years ago. From climatic records we can see
that there was a brief but devastating global freeze-up and desiccation 90,000 years ago that turned the whole of the Levant to
extreme desert. After the freeze, the deserted Levant was soon
reoccupied but this time by other, older residents – our first
cousins, the Neanderthals – who were presumably forced southward to the Mediterranean by glaciers advancing from the north. We
have no further physical evidence of modern humans in the Levant
or in Europe for another 45,000 years, until the Cro-Magnon
people made their appearance (as indicated by the presence of
Aurignacian technology) 45,000–50,000 years ago and successfully
challenged the Neanderthals for their northern birthright.[11]

Thus most authorities now accept that the first modern humans
out of Africa must have died out in the Levant on the return of the
dry glacial conditions that caused North Africa and the Levant to
revert to extreme desert. Trapped in the northern corridor by the
Sahara, there was no way back for them and few places to take
refuge. The gap of 50,000 years between the disappearance of the
first Levantines and the subsequent invasion of Europe obviously
raises serious doubts about the prevailing theory that a northern
African exodus gave rise to Europeans.[12] We shall now see why.

To help us to understand why many European archaeological and anthropological authorities argue that Europeans arose separately from a northern African exodus, we need to acknowledge that there may be a Eurocentric cultural agendum in what a northern exodus tries to explain. Most important is the lingering twentieth-century European conviction that the Cro-Magnons who moved into Europe no more than 50,000 years ago (see Plates 9, 12, 13, 14) defined the beginning of our species as 'modern humans' in the fullest intellectual sense. This human epiphany, with its extraordinary flowering of art, manufacturing skills, and culture, is known to archaeologists rather dryly as 'the European Upper Palaeolithic'. For many of them, it was the creative explosion that heralded our coming of age as a sentient species. The magnificent cave paintings of Chauvet and Lascaux and the voluptuous, finely carved Venus figurines found throughout Europe date back to this culture.

The argument goes like this: if we ultimately came from Africa, and if this ancient artistic revolution that speaks so evocatively of abstract thought came from the Levant, then it is only a short walk from Egypt. Ergo, 'we Westerners' (for the proponents of this view are all European by origin) must have come from North Africa. The northern route is thus, for many experts, the conceptual starting point for out-of-Africa migrations. In the next chapter we shall see how it is logically impossible that Europeans were the *first* 'fully modern humans', and how it was that Africans were fully modern, singing, dancing, painting humans long before they came out of their home continent.

There are real problems, however, in explaining how the sub-Saharan ancestors of Europeans could have got out through North Africa at that time. For a start, with an impassable Sahara Desert in the way for most of the past 100,000 years, any late North African invasion of Europe could only have come from a green refuge left in North Africa, such as the Nile Delta, after the interglacial from over 100,000 years ago. The Europeans could not have come directly, non-stop from sub-Saharan Africa 45,000–50,000 years ago unless they floated all the way down the Nile on logs – which the genetic story denies.

A green refuge in Egypt?

If there was such a North African green refuge during the long dry period after the interglacial, it would thus have been the temporary home for European ancestors for at least 45,000 years. Green North African refuges there were, such as the Nile Delta and the Mediterranean coast of Morocco. The recent find of a child's skeleton buried at Taramsa Hill in Egypt, dated to somewhere between 50,000 and 80,000 years ago, suggests that a relict population could just have survived there. Several leading out-of-Africa proponents are attracted by this possibility since it offers a clear explanation of the 45,000–50,000-year gap. Foremost among them is a champion of the out-of-Africa hypothesis, Chris Stringer, who is based at London's Natural History Museum. He argues that the Egyptian child of Taramsa Hill belonged to a North African refuge colony and that the ancestors of Levantines and Europeans evolved out of such colonies from 50,000 years ago.[13]

Yet there is little other archaeological evidence in North Africa for the ancestors of the Cro-Magnons. Even the single child buried at Taramsa Hill in Egypt was found with Middle Palaeolithic stone tools that could equally have been made by Neanderthals and show no hint of the new technology about to explode into Europe.

The Australian problem

The greatest problem for the Eurocentric cultural agenda underlying the northern route out of Africa, however, is posed by the Australians, who evolved their own singing, dancing, and painting culture far earlier than, and with no help from, the Europeans. Which part of Africa did they come from? What route did they take?

Were they part of the same exodus that gave rise to the Europeans? And, above all, how did they get to Australia so much earlier than the Europeans got to Europe? This conundrum has generated a number of clever rationalizations.

Clearly, none of these questions is easily answered by a single northern exodus to Europe 45,000 years ago, followed by a spreading out into the rest of the world, as suggested by Chicago anthropologist Richard G. Klein in his classic *The Human Career*. The dates are too late for the finds from Australia, and therefore wrong for that theory. The zoologist, Africa expert, artist, and author Jonathan Kingdon has gone even further and argued that the first 'failed' northern exodus to the Levant, which took place 120,000 years ago, had already spread eastward from the Levant to colonize Southeast Asia and then Australia before 90,000 years ago. This solution thus allows only one early exodus from Africa – via the northern route. Chris Stringer has taken the simplest approach by proposing that Australia was colonized independently long before Europe by a separate exodus round the Red Sea.[14]

Like Chris Stringer, the Cambridge team of archaeologist Robert Foley and palaeontologist Marta Lahr also argue that a North African refuge, expanding via the northern route through the Levant, was the crucible for Europeans and Levantines. They have no problem with the number of movements out of Africa, postulating instead that there were multiple breakouts from refuges scattered across Ethiopia and North Africa. This view takes into account the interglacial population expansions in Africa 125,000 years ago. Lahr and Foley see the return of the dry ice-age conditions in effect splitting the African continent into isolated human colonies corresponding to islands of green (see Figure 1.6) that remained separated from one another by intervening desert for the next 50,000 years. Under the Foley–Lahr scheme, the ancestors of the East Asians and Australians could have broken out from Ethiopia and moved east across the Red

Sea at any time. They would thus have had to take the southern route independently of the ancestors of the Europeans. Foley and Lahr have recently taken this north-and-south viewpoint further by teaming up with American Y-chromosome expert Peter Underhill in a recent genetic-prehistoric synthesis. They describe an early exodus to Australia via the southern route, with the main out-of-Africa movement going north later via Suez and the Levant to Europe and the rest of Asia (Figure 1.3) between 30,000 and 45,000 years ago.[15]

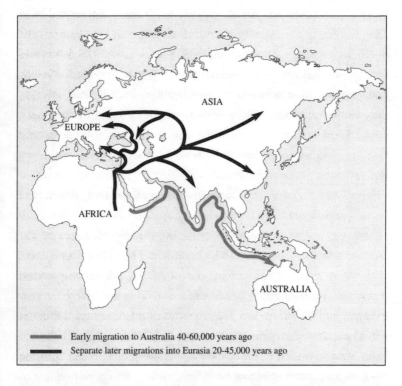

Early migration to Australia 40-60,000 years ago
Separate later migrations into Eurasia 20-45,000 years ago

Figure 1.3　The multiple-exodus hypotheses. Most recent out-of-Africa syntheses argue for at least one northern exit to Europe and further to the rest of Asia within the past 50,000 years, while acknowledging the possibility of an earlier southern route to Australia (Stringer et al. (1996, 2000),[14] Lahr and Foley (1998),[15] Underhill et al. (2001)[15]).

So, the insistence by many experts that Europeans came out via North Africa can be seen to depend on various rationalizations. These include North African refuges and either multiple out-of-Africa migrations or an early onward migration from the Levant towards the Far East. There are problems with all these rationalizations in their attempt to preserve the hallowed northern route for Europeans. Taking the most straightforward first, Jonathan Kingdon has suggested that the world was peopled by a single early northern out-of-Africa movement during the Eemian interglacial 120,000 years ago.[16] Since many of the desert corridors in Africa and West Asia were green at that time, the would-be migrants to Australia could have walked briskly eastward, straight from the Levant to India. They could then have taken a rest in green parts of South Asia before proceeding to Southeast Asia, arriving by 90,000 years ago, and then colonizing Australia. (By 'South Asia', I mean those countries between Aden and Bangladesh that have coasts facing the Indian Ocean. This includes the countries of Yemen, Oman, Pakistan, India, Sri Lanka, and Bangladesh, and the southernmost parts of those that border the Arabian Gulf: Saudi Arabia, Iraq, Beirut, the United Arab Emirates, and Iran.)

As evidence of an ancient skilled human presence east of the Levant, Jonathan Kingdon points to abundant Middle Palaeolithic stone tools found in India starting from 163,000 years ago. The problem with this view is that there is no skeletal evidence for modern human beings anywhere outside Africa of that antiquity. Kingdon acknowledges that these tools could easily have been made by late pre-modern or archaic humans (the Mapas, as he calls them) who were in East Asia at that very time.

Clearly, to get to Australia, Australians must have gone through Asia, but this kind of logic is still no proof that Anatomically Modern Humans migrated across Asia before 90,000 years ago, let alone 120,000–163,000 years ago.

The eastern barriers

There is another problem with Kingdon's 90,000–120,000-year bracket for the colonization of Southeast Asia. If his early migration into Southeast Asia had left the Levant any later than 115,000 years ago, they would most likely have perished in the attempt. Analysis of human and other mammalian movements from Africa to Asia over the past 4 million years suggests that, except during an interglacial, there were a variety of obstacles to movement between the Levant and the rest of Asia. When the world was not basking in the moist warmth of an interglacial, there were major mountain and desert barriers preventing travel north, east, or south from the Levant. To the north and east was the great Zagros–Taurus mountain chain, which combines with the Syrian and Arabian Deserts to separate the Levant from Eastern Europe in the north and the Indian sub-continent in the south.[17] Under normal glacial conditions this was an impassable mountainous desert. There was no easy way round to the north because of the Caspian Sea and the Caucasus.

As in Marco Polo's time, the alternative overland route from the Eastern Mediterranean to Southeast Asia was to get to the Indian Ocean as soon as possible and then follow the coast round. To the south and east of the Levant, however, are the Syrian and Arabian Deserts, and the only option was thus to follow the Tigris Valley round from Turkey and down the western border of the Zagros range to the Arabian Gulf (see Figure 1.8). But this route, through the Fertile Crescent, was also extreme desert outside interglacial periods and was therefore closed.

The practical impossibility of modern humans getting from the Levant or Egypt to Southeast Asia 55,000–90,000 years ago means that a northern exodus from Africa during that period could have given rise only to Europeans and Levantines, not to Southeast Asians or Australians. Now, Europe and the Levant were not colonized until around 45,000–50,000 years ago, and Australia, on the other side of the world, was colonized well before then. This in turn means that, in order to preserve the northern route for Europeans, Chris Stringer, Bob Foley, and Marta Lahr have all had to postulate separate southern routes for Australians and even for Asians. This tangle is resolved by the genetic story.

What the genes say about the northern route

All such speculations have previously rested on an archaeological record consisting of a few inaccurately dated bones separated by huge time gaps. From the turn of the century, published work on the European genetic trail by scientists such as Martin Richards, Vincent Macaulay, and Hans-Jurgen Bandelt has changed all that and allowed us to examine the first leap out of Africa with a much clearer focus on the timing and location.[18] This work does two things. First, it confirms that the Levantine expedition over 100,000 years ago perished without issue, so that the first doomed exodus of modern humans, like the Neanderthals who in turn died out 60,000 years later, left no identifiable genetic trace in the Levant. Second, although sub-Saharan Africans may have much more recently left their genetic mark surviving in one-eighth of modern Berber societies, it reveals no genetic evidence that either Europeans or Levantines came directly from North Africa.

How do I know this? The construction of a precise genetic tree using mitochondrial DNA makes it possible to do more than just identify our common ancestors. Figure 1.4 shows our mitochondrial tree, starting at the base as many clans in Africa, then sending a single branch (L3) out into South Asia (India). L3 became our Asian Out-of-Africa Eve and soon branched many times to populate Arabia and India, then Europe and East Asia. We can date the branches in this tree and, by looking at their geographical distribution, show when and where the founders arose for a particular prehistoric migration. On a grander scale, this method is how the out-of-Africa hypothesis was proved.

Using this approach, we can see that Europe's oldest branch line, designated U (50,000 years old and shown in Figure 1.4), which I have called Europa after Zeus' lover of the same name, arose from somewhere near India out of the R branch, which I have called Rohani after its Indian location. R, in turn, arose out of the N branch, which I call Nasreen, and which arose from the Out of-Africa Eve twig, L3. If Europeans were derived from North African aboriginal groups such as the Berbers 45,000 years ago, we would expect to find the oldest North African genetic lines deriving directly from the origin or base of the L3 branch.[19]

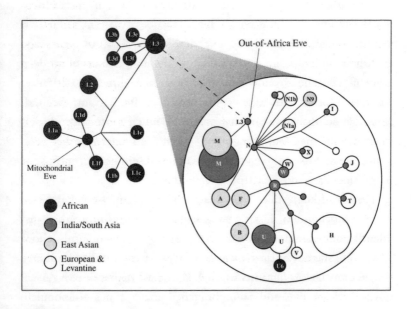

Figure 1.4 A single expansion from Africa. Simplified network of mtDNA groups showing how only one of 13 African clans gives rise to all non-Africans. N (Nasreen) group is expanded to emphasize West Eurasian ramifications, while M (Manju) has no representation there and heavy presence in India. (For detail and dating of tree branches see Appendix 1.)

Instead, when we look at North Africans, in particular the Berbers, who are thought to be aboriginal to that region, we find the very opposite. North African lines are either more recent immigrants or very far removed from the root of L3. First, there is no evidence in North Africa for the earliest out-of-Africa branch nodes, Nasreen and Rohani. Those are found instead in South Asia – as shown in the figure. In fact, we find that North Africa has been populated mainly by recent southward migrations of typical European and Levantine genetic lines. The oldest indigenous North African mtDNA line, sometimes referred to as the Berber motif, is dated to have arrived from the Levant around 30,000 years ago, and is a solitary derived sub-branch (U6 – see the figure) of the West Eurasian Europa clan (West Eurasia being Europe and the Middle East). U6 shows every sign of having come *from* the Levant rather than the other way round. About one-eighth of maternal gene lines in North Africa come from more recent migrations from sub-Saharan Africa, and over half are recent movements south from Europe. Finally, the other daughter clan of Out-of-Africa Eve, the Asian M supergroup which is found in India, is completely absent from Europe, the Levant, and North Africa. This makes it extremely unlikely that North Africa could have been the source of Asians, as put forward in Jonathan Kingdon's scheme.[20]

All this adds up to a view of both Europe and North Africa as recipients of ancient migrations from farther east. In other words, there is no evidence of a first northern exodus from sub-Saharan Africa into North Africa – but rather the opposite. Just where in the East these 'Nasreen', 'Rohani', and 'Europa' branches came from, we shall see shortly.

Just one exodus

The strongest evidence against the north as the primary route for Europeans, or for any other modern humans for that matter, comes again from the structure of the maternal genetic tree for the whole world. As can be seen in Figure 1.4, only one small twig (Out-of-Africa Eve) of one branch, out of the dozen major African maternal clans available, survived after leaving the continent to colonize the rest of the world. From this small group evolved all modern human populations outside Africa. Clearly, if there was only one exodus, they could have taken only one of the two available exit routes from Africa. I cannot overemphasize the importance of the simple and singular fact that only one African line accounts for all non-Africans.

In any exodus from Africa there would have been a mix of different potential founder genetic 'Eve' lines. The same applies for any random group of people. Yet only one of these genetic lines survived. How this came about holds the proof for how many sorties from Africa were successful. Let us say there were fifteen genetically different types or lines of mtDNA that left Africa in a particular group (it could be more or less, as in Figure 1.5). This is a realistic number; even today there are fifteen surviving African maternal lines older than 80,000 years (see Appendix 1). These could be viewed as fifteen different kinds of marbles in a bag. From those fifteen lines only one mitochondrial line would, over many generations, become the Out-of-Africa Eve line or the common ancestral 'mother line' of the rest of the world. In other words, there would be only one kind of marble left. This random selection and extinction process is called *genetic drift* because the original mix of lines has 'drifted' towards one genetic type.

The mechanism behind drift is simple. From time to time, some mothers' lines will die out because they have no daughters surviving to reproduce. These gene line extinctions are shown in Figure 1.5. In a small isolated population, this will eventually leave a single surviving ancestral line. Drift has strong effects in small groups. A common modern example of drift, seen through the male side, is that of small isolated Alpine or Welsh villages ending up after

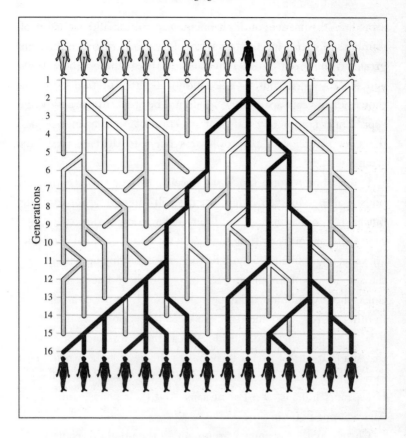

Figure 1.5   Genetic drift. Diagram to show how, over the generations in a small isolated population of constant size (e.g. 100–400), there is a tendency for natural variation in reproductive success to reduce diversity – so from many varieties of mtDNA to a few or just one line (highlighted in black). Tracing back from the 16th generation here shows they all have the same ancestral mother.

generations with just one family surname – Schmidt or Evans, perhaps – on all the shopfronts.

If we now take two identical African exodus groups and isolate them in different regions (two bags of marbles in our analogy), each group will drift down to one gene line. Because drift is due to random extinction, the two groups will not usually both drift to the same line (the chances of this happening are 1 in 15 if there are equal numbers of each type to start with). If we then take two different groups coming out of different parts of Africa (the northern route and the southern route – see below) at different times, tens of thousands of years apart, they would not be at all similar and would represent a completely different selection of African lines. Again, the two groups would be even less likely to drift down to the same line.

It does not require much statistical knowledge to see that the odds against two such independent small migrant groups moving out at different times and in different directions from Africa, and each then randomly drifting to exactly the same maternal gene line, are vanishingly small. It would be the same as ending up with exactly the same kind of marble in each bag. Had there been two migrations, there would inevitably be at least two Eves for non-Africans. In other words, the genes confirm to us that if only one mitochondrial gene line survived outside Africa, there was only one group that made it out of Africa to populate the rest of the world. That same small group eventually gave rise to Australians, Chinese, Europeans, Indians, and Polynesians. And their genes came out of Africa at one point in time.

Clearly, with this unitary argument, if the northern route could not give rise to Australians, then logically nor could it give rise to anyone else outside Africa. But before rejecting the northern route and exploring the feasibility of the single southern route, we should pinch ourselves and ask whether the rest of the genetic evidence really is consistent with this single exodus view. The short answer is yes, when we look at genetic markers other than mitochondrial DNA. If we look at the Y chromosome, we find that all non-Africans belong to only one African male line, designated M168. Using markers passed down through both parents, several studies have again shown evidence for only one expansion out of Africa.[21]

Another issue that is very relevant here is the prediction of dates.

When we look at the founding African genetic line, Out-of-Africa Eve, which gave rise to non-Africans, we find an age of around 83,000 years[22] (see Figure 0.3). This does not fit with the archaeo-logical and genetic evidence of a much later colonization of the Levant and Europe from only 50,000 years ago.

In contrast to the very derived nature of genetic lines in North Africa, there is another African region that holds an extraordinary diversity of genetic lines, close and parallel to the very roots of the out-of-Africa branch. This is Ethiopia, with its green hills standing out among the surrounding desert and dry savannahs of the Horn of Africa. But Ethiopia is to the south-east of the Sahara, literally at the gates of the southern route. Geneticists are now in a race to study Ethiopians, some of whom may be descended from the source population of that single exodus. This leads us now to look at the southern route.

The southern route

To fully understand the alternation of corridors that potential emi-grants from Africa had to contend with, we have to go back to the first human to leave Africa. Millions of years ago, when the super-continent Pangaea was in the process of breaking up, Africa shivered and cracked her flank. This huge fault in the Earth's crust connects to the rift valley system of East Africa. Its most visible effect is a deep cleft between Africa and Arabia – the Red Sea. At the northern end of the Red Sea now lies Suez, and at the southern end is an isthmus, 25 km (15 miles) wide and 137 metres (450 feet) deep, known as the Gate of Grief (Bab al Mandab) from its numerous reefs (see Plate 7). Two million years ago, Africa was still joined to Arabia and the strait was dry. A wide range of Eurasian and African mammals were able to cross between Arabia and Africa at both the northern and southern ends of the Red Sea. At that time, however, Africa was already moving away from Arabia at a rate of 15 mm per year, gradually opening the isthmus and eventually closing the southern gate out of Africa.

Recent evidence shows that one of the last mammals to walk out of Africa, before the Gate of Grief finally flooded and closed, was our second cousin *Homo erectus* (see Plate 2), carrying with them a few basic pebble tools. At this stage, since both the northern and southern gates were open, our cousin spread rapidly eastward through India to East Asia and also up through the Levant, reaching Dmanisi in the Caucasus by 1.8 million years ago.[23]

The flooding of the Gate of Grief was not the only barrier raised to mammalian movement into Asia. Two more hurdles had been erected. The first of these, as referred to above, was a long range of mountains, the Zagros–Taurus chain. These had been pushed up in the previous few million years at the same time as the Himalayas. Stretching from Iran to Turkey, this rocky barrier has effectively prevented access from the Levant to India, Pakistan, and the Far East ever since humans first moved out of Africa. The second land barrier separated the northern and southern gates from each other (Figure 1.6) and is known today as the Arabian Desert, or by such grim terms as 'the empty quarter'. One of the driest deserts in the world, it increased in size to occupy the whole Arabian peninsula as our present ice epoch, the Pleistocene, began to bite 2 million years ago.

Ice ages mean cooler weather and less evaporation from the sea; this, in turn, meant less rain in the desert belt. In a really severe ice age, like the one we have just had 18,000 years ago, huge volumes of water are locked up in ice sheets over a kilometre thick. During a glacial maximum the sea level falls sufficiently for the normal water exchange between the Indian Ocean and the Red Sea to almost stop.[24] There have been two of these events in the past 200,000 years, during our own time on Earth, when the Red Sea effectively became an evaporating salt lake. Most of the plankton died off. Although the Red Sea was more or less sterile, there was still a very narrow water channel of a few kilometres at the mouth, broken up by reefs and islands.

Like the greening of the Sahara, such extreme glaciations have been rare and rather short-lived. When they do happen, roughly every 100,000 years over the past 2 million, humans from Africa could easily make the southern crossing across the mouth of the Red Sea, with the aid perhaps of primitive rafts, island-hopping where necessary. (The raft option was of course not available to other big mammals.) Even when accessible like this, the main part of the Arabian Peninsula is not a very attractive prospect for emigrants, always being bone dry in the depths of an ice age. There are, however, green refuges in the Yemeni highlands above Aden. The south Arabian coast also benefits from the monsoons thus allowing the beachcombing trail towards the Gulf. Humans may have crossed out of Africa by this southern route at least three times in that past 2 million years.[25]

After humans first walked across into Asia 2 million years ago, the desert barriers separating Europe and the Middle East from Asia were closed. Crossing from Africa by the southern route, they could move on and into India only by making their way along the coast, while those taking the northern route could only go into the Levant, the Caucasus, and Europe.

These complex corrals and barriers to migration into Asia set the pattern for the human colonization of the rest of the world. As each new version of the genus *Homo* arose in Africa, some tribes would take the northern route during a warm interglacial, while others would take the southern route during an ice age. The first humans to take the northern route during an interglacial, around 1.8 million years ago, reached Dmanisi in Georgia. To look at, they were perhaps closer to *Homo habilis*, the earliest and most primitive African human, than to their East Asian *erectus* contemporaries. Somewhere between early African *erectus* (*Homo ergaster*) and *Homo habilis* they have been assigned a new species name, *Homo georgicus*. This parallel

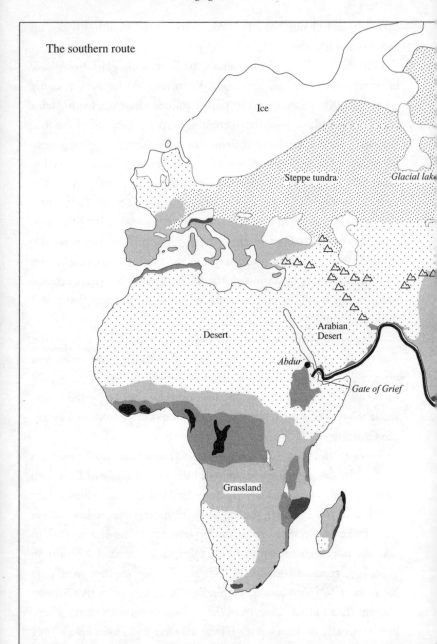

The southern route

Ice

Steppe tundra

Glacial lake

Desert

Arabian
Desert

Abdur

Gate of Grief

Grassland

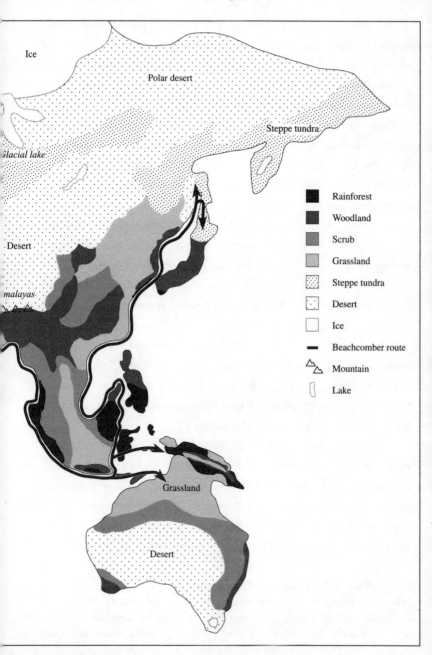

colonization by two different early human species taking different routes supports the view that human exits from Africa before the closing of the southern route had more to do with opportunities of geography available to any African mammal than with some special behaviour of *Homo erectus*, as was previously thought.[26]

Dmanisi humans seem, on the face of it, to have died out long ago in the Caucasus and the Levant, when it got colder. As we have just seen, the same tragedy struck modern humans some 2 million years later, after the Eemian interglacial. When the Levant dried out after a few thousand years, the Dmanisi humans were unable to escape north, south, or east, and so perished. It is perhaps a tribute to the next emigrants, *Homo heidelbergensis*, that their offspring were more successful in repeatedly colonizing Europe, possibly three times over the last 800,000 years. The last of these northern migrations may have taken place during an interglacial as recently as 250,000 years ago. By this time the African source *Homo* species, although still beetle-browed, had evolved larger brains and now made the more advanced Middle Palaeolithic tools. Foley and Lahr call the ancestor of that last African emigrant *Homo helmei*.[27] They postulate that *Homo helmei* evolved in Europe into our first cousin, *Homo neanderthalensis* (see Plate 4 and Chapter 2).

Over nearly the same period (160,000–800,000 years ago) there could have been a similar number of human migrations to the Far East by the southern route. These large-brained Asians were similar, though not identical to, their European cousins. In the same way that the Neanderthals acquired bigger brains, later eastern migrations out of Africa 200,000 years ago may also have given rise to

Figure 1.6 (see previous pages)   Single southern route out of Africa. The full beachcomber route from the Red Sea along the Indo-Pacific coast to Australia and beyond, including likely extensions to China, Japan and New Guinea. Vegetation and sea-level shown as at 65–85,000 years ago. Note how the extent of desert throughout this period prevented access to Northern Eurasia.

larger-brained types such as the Maba and Dali skulls in China,[28] and even possibly 'Madeleine' in Java (see Figure 0.2).

We can even approximately date the last of these southern emigrations from Africa to a time before the appearance of modern humans. The valley of Narmada in central India was home to a large-brained archaic human whose skull has been only poorly dated but who certainly lived over 150,000 years ago. Although it has yielded few pre-modern human fossils, India is much richer in the stone artefacts that they made. The older, so-called Acheulian (Lower Palaeolithic) tools in India date roughly from 160,000 to 670,000 years ago, while the newer Middle Palaeolithic tools from Africa appear in India at the end of that period, around 160,000 years ago.[29] This suggests that the last movement of pre-modern humans out of Africa could have taken place as recently as 160,000 years ago, during the dry glacial age that preceded the dawn of modern humans.

The final change from Middle Palaeolithic to the Upper Palaeolithic tools is also seen in the Central Narmada and Middle Son Basins in northern India, associated with a volcanic ash layer from the great Toba explosion on the island of Sumatra around 74,000 years ago. This suggests a major culture change around that time.[30] Upper Palaeolithic tools were characteristic of the first modern humans to arrive in the Levant and Europe, 25,000–30,000 years later.

Cold feet?

A southern route across the Red Sea which is most accessible when the Earth is glaciated goes some way to explaining the mounting evidence for our own defining exodus from Africa. I think it came not during the warm Eemian interglacial period 125,000 years ago, but 45,000 years later, at the threshold of a prolonged glaciation. As we now look at the evidence for this founding migration and even try to narrow the date down, there are three obvious, related questions: why we crossed the Red Sea, when we did, and why we did not cross before.

The answer to the last of these questions – why we waited so long before taking such a short sea-hop – 11 km (7 miles) during glacial periods, narrower than the mouths of many rivers – is perhaps the most revealing. We humans may be wilful, aggressive, and impatient, but we are also resourceful and smart. We would not think of migrating en masse to another planet, or overseas to the next continent, if we were not happy with conditions as reported by scouts. We would also like to be convinced of the chances of surviving the round trip, should we be forced to return. Reconstruction of the stepwise prehistoric migrations by the Polynesians in the Pacific over the past few thousand years tells us that much.

Judging by how rapidly modern humans subsequently spread around the coast of the Indian Ocean to Australia, the first modern Asians could easily have taken rafts or boats across the narrow mouth of the Red Sea many times during the first 70,000 years that their forebears lived in East Africa. So what was stopping them? The answer, almost certainly, was the presence of other people on the other side of the water – perhaps detected by scouting expeditions. Clearly those other people would not have been modern humans, but more likely the nearest thing: Asian descendants of African *Homo helmei*. The Indian evidence referred to above supports this view, as do the abundant Middle Palaeolithic tools found across the water in the Yemen and southern Arabia.

A recent book on human origins[31] has used the multi-species bar scene in the movie *Star Wars* to emphasize that, in the few hundred thousand years before modern humans arrived, a number of human species had succeeded in cohabiting on this planet for long periods without exterminating one another. This probably had more to do with the fact that each subspecies usually occupied separate continents and islands than with their being good neighbours.

When several human species did try to share a continent, the result was usually a rapid reduction to one species. Fossil evidence in Africa shows that the birth of modern humans 130,000 or more years ago signalled the rapid end of the record for our parents *Homo helmei* there. The last of these were dated to around 130,000 years ago. Whether the near extinction of all African human species during the very dry period 140,000–190,000 years ago simply left modern humans as the only survivor, or whether they 'cleansed' Africa of *Homo helmei*, we can make a good guess. This guess is based on our recent track record of successful and attempted genocides in Tasmania, Germany, Rwanda, and the Balkans. The Tasmanian extinction in the nineteenth century was the only complete racial annihilation achieved in these deliberate attempts at destroying an entire people, and took a relatively short time, presumably because the victims were all confined to and could not escape from what became their island grave. So, according to modern historical records, we are ready, willing, and able to exterminate a neighbour of our own kind. Given a few thousand years there is every reason to suppose we could have achieved the same result on another species at continent level.[32]

The first steps into a new continent are the most difficult. The extraordinarily successful prehistoric expansion from Island Southeast Asia in which the ancestors of the Polynesians occupied the islands of the Indo-Pacific region tells us something about moving into new territory. Although they had supreme sailing technology, envied even by Captain Cook, they always avoided settling islands that already had people living on them. Where the length of their eastern sailing trips left no choice but to make a 'guest' landfall, for instance on the large inhabited island of New Guinea, their colonies have remained literally 'on the beach' to this day, thousands of years later.[33] For a small band of invaders to cross by sea and, with superior military technology, easily take over a populated continent has become possible only in the past 500 years.

As survivors, modern humans may have had the continent of Africa to themselves from 130,000 years ago. If, as is likely, the earliest modern East Africans were aware of archaic beetle-browed neighbours with similar abilities across the water in the Yemen, they may well have decided that their dominance in Africa was good enough for them, and that discretion was the better part of valour for the time being. We will know better what was waiting on the other side of the Red Sea when the Palaeolithic of the Yemen is more thoroughly investigated and dated. The early excavations conducted by Cambridge archaeologist Gertrude Caton-Thompson have, however, clearly established that there was human occupation there during the Palaeolithic.[34]

Time to move

Much has been made recently of a 'beachcombing' lifestyle among the first modern Africans as a motive for spreading out of Africa and around the Indian Ocean (see Figure 1.6). For most of their first 2 million years on Earth, humans were roaming the savannah as hunter-gatherers. Like the Kalahari of southern Africa, they exploited the rich nutritional value of group-hunted game, supplemented by salads of roots, fruit, and leaves. As the major glaciation of 130,000–190,000 years ago began to reduce their savannah range, someone had the idea of foraging and eating shellfish and other marine produce from the beach. It is always possible that beachcombing started even earlier, but since the beaches are now under water, we will never know. Such a diet, being rich in protein and Omega-3 fatty acids, is nutritious, good for the brain, and easier to obtain than game. Beach tucker has the added advantage of remaining available when the savannah dries up during an ice age.

Evidence for such beachcombing is unexpectedly easy to assess, since characteristic piles of split shells (shell middens) are left behind. There is, however, a problem in knowing just how long humans have been doing it. Shell middens are generally found just above the high-tide line, but for most of the past 200,000 years sea levels have been many metres below today's beaches. This means we would expect to miss most ancient middens except those laid down during the high sea levels of an interglacial, such as the one 125,000 years ago.

Neanderthals combed beaches in Spain and Italy 60,000 years ago, so it is possible that they brought the practice with them from Africa. Until recently, however, the earliest evidence for African beachcombing came from Klasies River mouth in South Africa, dated to between 100,000 and 115,000 years ago. In 2000, however, new evidence was discovered for early beachcombing at Abdur (see Plate 8) on the Eritrean west coast of the Red Sea, just to the north of the Gate of Grief. Dated to 125,000 years ago, at the peak of the Eemian interglacial, the same beach site yielded butchered remains of large mammals, indicating a mixed diet. The implements, which included blades made from obsidian, a volcanic glass, are most likely to have been made by modern humans.[35]

The great interest in this site on the Red Sea is twofold: it provides us with the oldest evidence for beachcombing anywhere and it is very close to the southern route out of Africa. Both aspects feed into an attractive model, which may be called the 'beach-buggy to Australia'. We get a compelling story of beachcombers multiplying until their patch of beach could support them no longer, then moving on to the next unexploited beach, and so on. By such rapid progression, once over the Red Sea the vanguard would just have followed the coast of the Indian Ocean, eating their way right down to Indonesia within 10,000 years. The low sea levels of the time would have allowed a dry walk from Aden to the tip of Java, and then easy island hops to Australia, where shell middens are found from the earliest traces of human habitation.

I am pretty sure that this model of the early colonization of Australia is correct, but the dates have to fit, not only for the archaeological evidence but also for the molecular clock on the gene tree for all the other Eurasian dispersals. If, on top of this beach buggy model, we impose only a *single* out-of-Africa exodus to colonize both Australia and the rest of the world, we can start to make strong predictions for the order and dates of colonization en route of India, Southeast Asia, and the parallel movement to New Guinea. These predictions should be the test of the theory.

Why and when did we leave Africa?

One problem with the genetic molecular clock is that we have to allow rather generous margins for error. Thus, although we can be confident that the gene tree is telling us there was only one successful exodus, the approximate genetic dates say that this could have taken place any time between 65,000 and 95,000 years ago.[36] Our ancestors could thus have been collecting shells for some 60,000 years on the western shore of the Red Sea – from at least 125,000 years ago – before deciding to move on.

Before looking at the archaeological evidence for that move, it might help to establish whether there was a precipitating climatic event, as in so much of our prehistory. Could a transient increase in the severity of glaciation have brought the sea level at the Gate of Grief to a point where our ancestors could have walked across from reef to reef? The increasing aridity of the East African coast might have reduced available drinking water, thus making the rather wetter monsoon conditions on the southern Yemen coast more attractive to the beachcombers. A ford across to Arabia might have been just the inducement to overcome any remaining fears of the neighbours. The latter, in turn, perhaps lacking beachcombing skills, may have left southern Arabia altogether because of the drought.

In spite of the attractive biblical allusion of this scenario, the problem with a dry exodus across the mouth of the Red Sea 60,000–90,000 years ago is that oceanographic evidence denies that the Gate of Grief was ever completely dry during our time on Earth.

Such an event nearly happened three times during major glaciations of the past half million years: 440,000 years ago, 140,000 years ago, and at the last glacial maximum 18,000 years ago.[37]

The strait was very much narrower during glacial periods, allowing easy island-hopping across the shallows and the reef islands of the Hanish al Kubra, at the northern end of the isthmus. As we have seen, this must have been where Asian *Homo erectus* crossed, so it should not have been much of a problem for our pioneers to complete the journey to Australia within a few thousand years. Although the Red Sea did not part, there was a major cold event around the time of our first exodus from Africa (Figure 1.7). Measurements made on the Greenland ice cap show that the second-coldest time of the last 100,000 years was between 60,000 and 80,000 years ago.[38] At its coldest, 65,000 years ago, this glaciation took the world's sea levels 104 metres (340 feet) below today's levels. The way in which this sea lowstand (as it is called) was measured in the Red Sea holds an unexpected clue for what might have been the stimulus to move.

Oceanographers have been able to measure interglacial sea-level highstands by looking at coral reefs. Sea-level lowstands which occurred during glacial maxima are more difficult to confirm. Eelco Rohling, an oceanographer at Southampton University, has found a way to use the Red Sea to overcome this problem. He measured prehistoric levels of Red Sea plankton. During a glacial maximum, the Gate of Grief approaches closure and the Red Sea becomes effectively isolated from exchange with the Indian Ocean. Evaporation causes the Red Sea's salinity to increase so much that plankton, the base of the marine food chain, disappears. During an interglacial period, like now, the high sea level allows the Red Sea to flush out its salt, and sea life can start again. Sea-level lowstands like the one 65,000 years ago did not completely block the mouth of the Red Sea, so the plankton, although severely affected, did not completely disappear. The low level of plankton allowed Rohling and colleagues to improve the previous estimates for the sea-level depression at this time.[39]

Depression of plankton is worsened by low oxygen levels and high water temperatures in the shallows, as happens near beaches at Abdur in Eritrea and at the mouth of the Red Sea. Low levels of plankton in the Red Sea are, in turn, likely to have affected the success of the beachcombers. By contrast, the beaches of the Gulf of Aden just across the water in the Yemen were outside the Gate of Grief and had nutrient-rich, oxygenated upwelling water from the Indian Ocean. In other words, over on the southern Arabian coast the beachcombing conditions were probably excellent.[40]

So perhaps dwindling food resources on the western shores of the Red Sea, attractive beaches on the Gulf of Aden, and cool wet Yemeni uplands for refuge were what spurred our ancestors to take their momentous step. The question still remains of when: did they wait until the sea levels were lowest and the beachcombing was at its worst, 65,000 years ago, or did they move earlier, when things first began to deteriorate? Again, the Red Sea plankton may give a clue. Plankton and sea levels did not decline evenly between 100,000 and 65,000 years ago. Instead there was a short, sharp depression of both at 85,000 years ago, with sea levels falling to 80 metres below present, followed by an equally dramatic and brief improvement 83,000 years ago.[41] Maybe that 85,000 year old dip was the spur that set our ancestors on their beachcombing trail.

Evidence of another great climatic catastrophe during that sea-level trough comes from cores drilled in the Arabian seabed.[42] This was the volcanic eruption of Toba in Sumatra, 74,000 years ago.

Figure 1.7 Timeline of climatic events and human expansions. The interglacial 125,000 years ago allowed the first northern exit. A climatic downturn at 85,000 years affected Red Sea salinity and may have prompted the southern exit. Toba's explosion caused genetic bottlenecks both in and outside Africa. An ice age at 65,000 years then allowed access to Australia, while two clusters of interstadials from 50,000 years allowed colonization of Europe.

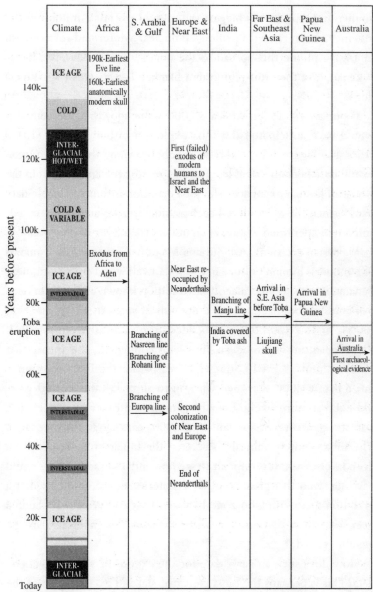

	Climate	Africa	S. Arabia & Gulf	Europe & Near East	India	Far East & Southeast Asia	Papua New Guinea	Australia
140k –	ICE AGE	190k-Earliest Eve line 160k-Earliest anatomically modern skull						
	COLD							
120k –	INTER-GLACIAL HOT/WET			First (failed) exodus of modern humans to Israel and the Near East				
100k –	COLD & VARIABLE							
	ICE AGE	Exodus from Africa to Aden		Near East re-occupied by Neanderthals		Arrival in S.E. Asia before Toba	Arrival in Papua New Guinea	
80k –	INTERSTADIAL				Branching of Manju line			
Toba eruption								
	ICE AGE		Branching of Nasreen line Branching of Rohani line		India covered by Toba ash	Liujiang skull		Arrival in Australia
60k –								First archaeol-ogical evidence
	ICE AGE		Branching of Europa line	Second colonization of Near East and Europe				
	INTERSTADIAL							
40k –								
	INTERSTADIAL			End of Neanderthals				
20k –	ICE AGE							
	INTER-GLACIAL							
Today								

Years before present

Major events in peopling of world

Known to be by far the biggest eruption of the last 2 million years, this mega-bang caused a prolonged nuclear winter and released ash in a huge plume that spread to the north-west and covered India, Pakistan, and the Gulf region in a blanket 1–3 metres (3–10 feet) deep.

If our ancestors left Africa 85,000 years ago, their descendants would have anticipated the Toba explosion in Sumatra by 11,000 years (see Figure 1.7), and beachcombers around the Indian Ocean would have been in direct line for the greatest volcanic ash fall in the whole of human existence. The Toba eruption is thus a valuable date mark, since the ash covered such a wide area, is accurately dated, and can be identified wherever an undisturbed layer of it is found.

Malaysian archaeologist Zuraina Majid has explored the remains of a modern human culture in a wooded valley in Perak State, near Penang. A continuous Palaeolithic tradition known as the Kota Tampan culture goes back tens of thousands of years there. At one site, tools from this tradition lie embedded in volcanic ash from Toba.[43] If the association with modern humans is confirmed, this means that modern humans got to Southeast Asia before the Toba eruption – more than 74,000 years ago. This, in turn, makes the 85,000-year-old exodus more likely. Equally, genetic and other evidence for a human occupation of Australia by 65,000 years ago fits this scenario. The Toba event specifically blanketed the Indian subcontinent in a deep layer of ash. It is difficult to see how India's first colonists could have survived this greatest of all disasters. So, we could predict a broad human extinction zone between East and West Asia. Such a deep east-west division, or 'furrow', is still seen clearly in the genetic record.

How does such an early date for the exodus fit with the genetic data? This is perhaps the most controversial and exciting part of the story. The short answer is that the genetic dates and tree fit the early exodus well (see Chapters 3 and 4). This also resolves the question I left hanging earlier about the origins of the Europeans: why it was that Europe was colonized only after 50,000 years ago, yet arose from the same maternal ancestor as the Australians and Asians.

The first Asian Adam and Eve clans

As we saw above, a small number of founding Eve clans from Africa landed in the Yemen and became isolated from Africa. After many generations these lines eventually drifted down to just one mitochondrial Out-of-Africa Eve, otherwise known by the rather dull technical label L3. L3 soon gave rise to just two daughter female clans: Nasreen (N), and a sister clan, Manju (M) (see Figure 1.4).

Manju's most ancient and diverse family is found in India, and Nasreen, for her part, was the only mother for Europeans – there being virtually no daughters of Manju in West Eurasia. Both Nasreen and Manju's descendants are now, however, found in every other part of the world except West Eurasia (see Appendix 1 and Figure 0.3). This fact on its own confirms that every non-African in Australia, America, Siberia, Iceland, Europe, China, and India can trace their genetic inheritance back to just one line coming out of Africa: it confirms that there was only one exodus. After the exodus, it seems, L3's own unique African identity went the way of genetic drift and was lost except for a few local remnants, leaving just Nasreen and Manju and their daughters. We can thus trace every modern non-African descendant waiting at a shop counter in, say, Outer Mongolia, Alice Springs, or Chicago, back to that first out-of-Africa group.

There are a couple of exceptions that prove the rule. One of these is U6 (already mentioned), who moved back from the Levant into North Africa. The other is M1, who moved back across the Red Sea into Ethiopia about the time of the last ice age. How do we know that? Some exciting recent work by Estonian geneticists Toomas Kivisild and Richard Villems has showed that M1 does not go back as far in Africa as does the Manju clan in Asia.[44] In other words, M1 was a more recent recolonization of East Africa back from Asia.

Eve's daughter line Manju is found only in Asians, not in Europeans. When we look at the oldest Manju branches in Asia we find a date of 74,000 years for the Manju clan in Central Asia, 75,000 years in New Guinea, and 68,000 years in Australia. India, as I have said, has the greatest variety of Manju sub-branches and may even have been the birthplace of Manju from L3; one Indian subclan alone (M2) has a local age of 73,000 years.[45]

When we look at the genetic trail of our fathers, written in the Y chromosome, we see a similar picture. Of all the African male lines present before the exodus, only one gave rise to all non-African male lines or clans. This 'Out-of-Africa Adam' line gave rise to three male primary branches outside Africa, in contrast to the two female ones (Nasreen and Manju). Known to geneticists as C, D/E (or YAP), and F, I have chosen for simplicity to call these three clans Cain, Abel, and Seth after Adam's three sons (see Appendix 2). As with Out-of-Africa Eve's line, there are also modern day sub-Saharan African representatives. In Adam's case this is Abel's line, which has both an Asian and an African/West-Eurasian branch. The latter has a high representation, particularly in Bantu peoples, who recently and dramatically expanded from the north to the south of Africa. To keep things simple at this stage, however, I will leave more detailed discussion of Adam's three sons to Chapters 3–7.

The origins of Europeans

The genetic tree tells us something clear and quite extraordinary about Europeans and Levantines: they came, not directly from Africa, but from somewhere near India in the south. Their matriarch, Nasreen, was probably the more westerly of Eve's two Asian daughters to be born along the coastal trail. She is different from Manju in that her daughters are found among non-Africans throughout the world, in Eurasia, Australia, and the Americas. This difference from the Manju clan, which is absent from Europe and the Levant, means that the separation of Nasreen into Easterners and

Westerners could have happened near where the beachcombers reached India. By genetic dating, Nasreen's Asian and Australian descendants are at least as old as Manju.[46] The most likely point on the route for the birth of Nasreen is the Arabian Gulf. At that dry time it was not a gulf at all, but an oasis of shallow freshwater lakes fed by underground aquifers and the Tigris and Euphrates rivers. There in the south, Nasreen had a daughter, Rohani, 60,000 or more years ago. This beautiful desert refuge must have survived throughout the following tens of thousands of years, for, although these western clans clearly originate in the south, we find no genetic or archaeological evidence of Nasreen's and Rohani's daughters having arrived in Europe or the Levant until 45,000–50,000 years ago.

As always, there is a climatic reason for the late colonization of Europe by Nasreen's daughters from the Gulf region, and we can find it in cores drilled from the seabed off the Indian coast, in the submarine delta of the Indus. As explained above, access between Syria and the Indian Ocean was always blocked by desert during glaciations. Almost exactly 50,000 years ago, however, there was a brief but intense warming and greening of South Asia, with monsoon conditions better than today. This climatic improvement can be detected as a carbon-rich layer in the undersea delta of the Indus.[47] Since the warm spell lasted perhaps only a few thousand years, geologists call it an 'interstadial' rather than 'interglacial', but the effect on the dormant Fertile Crescent of Iraq was the same.

For a short while that narrow green corridor opened (Figure 1.8), allowing migration from the Arabian Gulf to Syria, and the great-granddaughters of Asian Eve went north-west up the Fertile Crescent to the Levant (see Chapter 3). The original South Asian source for these European migrants is revealed by the genetic trail: as can be seen from the genetic tree (see Figure 1.4), for each Nasreen branch that went north-west to Europe, another Nasreen branch went east to India.

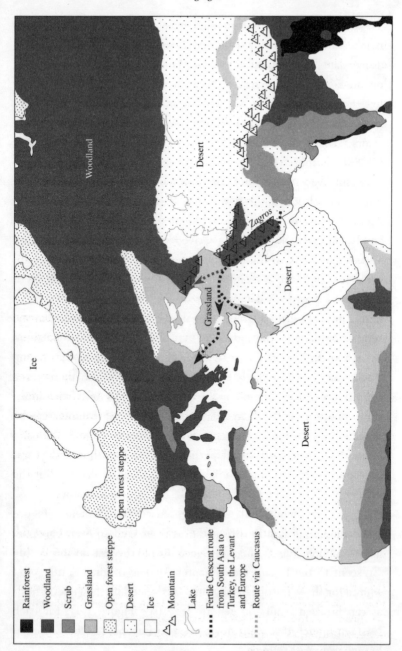

Rainforest
Woodland
Scrub
Grassland
Open forest steppe
Desert
Ice
△△ Mountain
Lake
Fertile Crescent route from South Asia to Turkey, the Levant and Europe
Route via Caucasus

Woodland

Desert

Zagros

Grassland

Desert

Ice

Open forest steppe

Desert

Such a picture of Europeans' genetic roots in South Asia over-turns the northern out-of-Africa theory. It also fundamentally changes the Eurocentric view of Europeans as the first fully modern human culture outside Africa. So, to be safe, we must ask whether there is any archaeological evidence to contradict the idea of the first Europeans coming from South Asia. There does not appear to be any – rather, it seems to be the other way round.

The earliest archaeological evidence in West Eurasia for technology of the Upper Palaeolithic is no more than 47,000 years old. The Belgian archaeologist Marcel Otte challenges the conventional view of Europeans' ancestors having come out of North Africa, developing their Upper Palaeolithic technology en route, and points instead to the Zagros Mountain range in the present-day ethnic region of Kurdistan, just north of the Gulf, which he argues was the core region for Upper Palaeolithic technology.[48]

Sri Lanka, then a peninsula to the south of India, is extraordinary in that it turns the east–west cultural tables. Reliable evidence gives a date of 28,000 years ago for manufacture of microliths on Sri Lanka. These tiny, specialist stone blades did not appear in Europe and the Levant until 10,000 years ago. Indeed, in a tantalizing find, one level below those microliths, another more basic microlith layer has been dated to between 64,000 and 74,000 years ago. If the date of this find is confirmed, then it could be the smoking gun of the trail out of Africa around 70,000 years ago.[49]

Summary

Archaeological and anthropological controversies over our ultimate origins as the latest human species could be resolved by the

Figure 1.8 The Fertile Crescent corridor to Europe. Around 50,000 years ago, weather warmed and moistened sufficiently to open a green corridor (dotted lines) across the desert between South Asia and Turkey. For the first time since the interglacial 75,000 years before, modern humans were able to move into the Levant and then to Europe.

unbroken genetic trail of our Eve line back to the first modern Africans. The genetic evidence has allowed us to focus this perspective down to the precise movements of our immediate ancestors. As a result, we can see only one group of people coming out of Africa over 70,000 years ago. This fundamental departure from the conventional view of multiple movements out of Africa fixes all subsequent migration routes for the rest of human history, starting from that single southern trail. The first out-of-Africa pioneers moved along the Arabian coast to the Arabian Gulf, where they founded the first colony of Westerners, who would colonize Europe much later. The journey from India onwards to the East has another history.

2

WHEN DID WE BECOME MODERN?

THE PAROCHIAL OBSESSION OF EUROPEANS with their past and with their apparent supremacy in Palaeolithic material culture led, in the last century, to a number of presumptions. Roughly speaking, these were that we (for I am European) were the first to think symbolically and in the abstract, and the first to speak, paint, carve, dress, weave, and exchange goods.

In Chapter 1, I suggested that the false assumption that these skills were unavailable to our African forebears paralleled the conviction that Levantines and Europeans arose from a northern move out of Africa separate from those that gave rise to Australians and Asians. This view is undermined if we accept the evidence that European and other Western genetic lines arose as early offshoots of a single South Asian family group that spawned the whole non-African world. In this chapter I argue that the desire to make a centrepiece of the 'coming of age' of modern humans in Europe and the Levant obscured other, valid views of the prehistory of both the East and the West.

The genetic evidence that modern humans emerged from Africa, leaving behind them 'homeland' representatives whose descendants still live in Africa and are self-evidently 'fully modern' in every way, has disturbing implications for continuing Western perceptions of modern Africans. Although the danger of these views is obvious, the mindset of some European archaeologists has remained unchanged.

Out-of-Africa versus the multiregionalists

Archaeologists have continued to argue that a number of innate and fundamental human behaviours sharply distinguished the first modern Europeans from their close European cousins, the Neanderthals, and also, following a similar line of argument, from their immediate ancestors in Africa. One reason for emphasizing this contrast may have been to counter the multiregional hypothesis of human origins and prove that we were not descended from Neanderthals. Implicit in these arguments, however, is the assumption not only that early modern Europeans (the Cro-Magnons) were the first to develop and transmit these new skills to succeeding generations, but that the Neanderthals were somehow biologically not up to it. Extending that type of argument would suggest that the Cro-Magnons' anatomically modern ancestors in Africa were not sharp enough to create Upper Palaeolithic technology either. In other words, the Europeans were the first to speak, paint, and carve, and then, we have to assume, they somehow later taught the Africans and Australian aboriginals (not to mention Asians) how to do it. Now, I may have misunderstood what I have read, but this is the message I get even from some recent publications. Before examining the external evidence against this Eurocentric view, I will look at what could have given rise to such a distorted picture.

The problem began in 1856 with the first discovery of a Neanderthal skull. Right from the start, Neanderthals were given a bad press, being ridiculed as beetle-browed idiots. This image was defined in 1921 in a short story, 'The Grisly Folk', offered by popular science writer H.G. Wells, who presented them, in contrast to the modern and articulate Cro-Magnons, as grunting, hunched monsters. Attempts to rehabilitate Neanderthals as our potential equals and cousins never quite succeeded, because even their apologists consistently damned them with faint praise, and film documentaries continued to stress their physical appearance and overlook their large brains.

The truth is that we still all regard the Neanderthals as lesser folk, and experts continue to emphasize perceived cultural differences. When we place their material culture alongside that of their contemporaries, the first modern Europeans, our prejudice seems to be confirmed. The moderns painted cave walls, and even themselves – no indication that Neanderthals did that. The moderns worked non-stone objects such as bone, shell, and antler, and carved figurines – something it was previously thought no Neanderthal could be caught doing. Such artefacts moved hundreds of kilometres across Europe, indicating some kind of trade or exchange – initially, no evidence for that among Neanderthals. How could there be? Neanderthals were not even using these materials. Such long-distance cooperation appeared to complement other evidence which has been used to argue that moderns had larger and more complex social networks than Neanderthals. They, in contrast, have been portrayed as living inflexibly in small groups, lacking the intellectual wherewithal to adapt to changing circumstances – although Clive Gamble points out that exotic high-grade raw stone for knapping had, in fact, been moved up to 300 km (200 miles) around Europe before the Upper Palaeolithic.[1] The moderns made hearths and buried their dead – not a typical feature of Neanderthal culture. Finally, when we look at that most abundant and durable message from the past, stone tools, we find a clear and convenient difference between Neanderthals and moderns. The latter were making *blades* – slivers struck from a stone core that were more than twice as long as they were broad.

Cro-Magnons, the first European moderns, appeared on all these counts to be the 'all-singing, all-dancing' people when compared with the dull, brutish, inflexible Neanderthals – so why? The standard answer has always been that we must have been biologically superior, at least as far as our brains were concerned. The Neander-thals' acknowledged superiority in physical strength, and their thick bones, contrasting with our own thin skeletons, completed the picture of brawn versus brain. The degree of contrast in these cultural differences between the two groups of humans has been used to further enhance the case for a biological coming of age of modern Europeans as sentient beings, but there is little logic in this argument.

What else about our cousins could we speculate on? Among the perceived differences that elevated man from beast are abstract and symbolic thought – and yes, speech. Could we establish that Neanderthals were 'without speech' – in other words, 'dumb'? The fact that they had a very similar 'bone of speech' (the hyoid) in their voice box which is very similar to the hyoid in moderns has not stopped such speculation. There is even a common opinion that all the new skills demonstrated by modern Europeans, including the development of speech, resulted from a special gene or genes that kicked in 40,000–50,000 years ago (see the Prologue).

The first and indeed *most* of the spectacular discoveries of early modern human creativity (Upper Palaeolithic art and technology from roughly 18,000–35,000 years ago) were made in Europe. That is, after all, where archaeology started and where, for the past 150 years, most archaeologists have come from. We are all familiar with the extraordinary grace, realism, and perception revealed in the cave paintings of Lascaux and Chauvet in southern France (see Plate 9). It seems an almost unconscious extension of wondering about the artistic explosion of the European later stone age (also known as the European Upper Palaeolithic) to see this as marking modern humans' coming of age. Some put this thought into plain words and argue that, before this time, 'Anatomically Modern Humans', whose remains date back in Africa to at least

160,000 years ago, may have looked modern but had not quite 'got there' yet.[2]

If modern Europeans were emerging from the chrysalis with such a spectacular unfolding of genius, the extreme argument continues, then surely there must have been some biological (i.e. genetically determined) element which before then had been wanting in our make-up. However, this line of argument seems, dangerously, to conclude that the ancestors of modern Africans and modern Australians would have been biologically less advanced than those of Europeans.

But stop! What are we saying? Isn't this a bit like a city slicker going to a small country village and announcing, 'You country bumpkins are out-of-date biological primitives', or a historian claiming that the invention of writing, the industrial and agricultural revolutions, and musical notation were each the result of new genes? Future historians comparing the sophistication of life and dominance of developed Western countries with that of stone-age cultures in Papua New Guinea would be unwise to attribute the contrast to anything biological.

Many of us, perhaps most, nurture unspoken feelings that other groups are self-evidently inferior to ours. So much so that the American biologist Jared Diamond felt compelled to set the record straight. He wrote his best-selling *Guns, Germs, and Steel*[3] to explain that inequalities of development and global power are more likely to be the result of historical accidents of opportunity rather than of any innate intellectual differences between different populations. He wanted to explain how it was, for instance, that small bands of conquistadors could destroy the populous pre-Columbian civilizations of the Americas.

Yali's question

At the beginning of his book, Diamond poses his main question as it was put to him by a remarkable man and popular local leader, Yali, from one of the world's last surviving Neolithic cultures, on the north coast of New Guinea (see Plate 10). Yali asked, 'Why is it that you white people developed so much cargo and brought it to New Guinea, but we black people had little cargo of our own?' ('cargo', in the context Yali used the word, literally means 'imported goods' such as sacks of Australian rice, and refrigerators and other luxury goods). Yali was no average villager. He was no average human, having spent much of his life actively grappling with the implications of this question from the magico-religious perspective of his own culture. Diamond came under his spell and clearly regarded him as an unusually perceptive, enquiring, and intelligent person.

Yali was also at one time leader of the most successful cargo cult ever launched in New Guinea (cargo cults were centred around the belief that cargo can be created by ritual), and his magnetism extended beyond his fellow New Guineans and one curious bio-logist. His qualities of charisma and leadership found him pride of place in another book, *Road Belong Cargo*.[4] Written by Australian anthropologist Peter Lawrence, this is the best known description of cargo cults, and three chapters are devoted to Yali and his own continuously evolving cults.

I once received a personal account of Yali from someone who had known him better than most. In the early 1980s, I was working as a doctor in Yali's home province of Madang, New Guinea. I had spent a short time as a patient myself, sharing a small cubicle in the provincial hospital with an ancient, craggy, and decrepit Australian planter. Mo Johnson was a diabetic who lived permanently in the ward, having discovered that, thanks to his veteran's status, all his medical expenses and food were paid for. A charming but mis-chievous old man, he had no possession apart from his short-wave radio, with which he infuriated the Samoan ward sister. Mo told me his life story. Red-necked and foul-mouthed, he was incapable of referring to New Guineans except by using racist epithets. It seemed so at odds with the company he kept: there was a steady stream of friendly visitors to his bedside, all of them New Guinean.

Mo was one of the few surviving members of the legendary band of 'coast-watchers' – human moles who had dug themselves into jungle hillsides all along the coasts of South Pacific islands during the Second World War. Mostly former planters, they had volunteered to stay behind after the Japanese invasion to report by radio on enemy troop, plane, and ship movements. They were credited with a major role in the Battle of the Coral Sea. Most of the coast-watchers were killed, died of disease, or were captured and perished in prison camps.

Mo, the war hero, owed his life to Yali – which is the point of this short anecdote. Yali was Mo's 'native helper' and kept him alive through the war, at one point springing him from a Japanese prisoner-of-war camp and then guiding him through 300 km (200 miles) of dense jungle and swamp back to Madang. After the war, Yali, now also a hero, was identified by the British colonial administrators as a charismatic leader, and nurtured by them. But the relationship broke down as soon as the administrators realized that they had a Messiah on their hands, not a puppet. As Mo told me, and as Peter Lawrence recounts in his book, they decided to humiliate him and make an example of him. So they put Yali in jail. And then Mo said something characteristic, unconsciously revealing the attitudes and language of his own culture yet showing deep personal sincerity. He said to me, 'Steve, they broke his heart by jailing him. Yali was the best. He was better than them. He was a real white man.' I have been assured since by Australians that this phrase carries no racist tag!

Yali was no white man, nor was he an Australian. It is clear from both Diamond's and Lawrence's accounts that Yali possessed an abundance of intelligent enquiry; yet with little knowledge of an alien culture he was unable to answer the question he put to Jared

Diamond. Refrigerators were not made on New Guinea, so why should he know how they were made? At the root of Yali's question was all the luxury cargo for the white colonists that regularly arrived on ships docking at the Madang wharf. Cargo cultists, Yali foremost among them, were convinced that cargo was produced by secret magic possessed only by whites. In spite of all his personal qualities and clearly superior intellect, Yali's magico-religious Neolithic cultural background and limited knowledge base made it impossible for him to comprehend the agricultural and industrial complex that lay far across the ocean. A phrase sometimes used to explain cargo belief is 'lack of knowledge of the means of production', but this oversimplifies Yali's quandary since, as we all know, knowledge does not automatically overcome a belief in the 'supernatural'.

The people of the Madang coast are supreme horticulturists. Each gardener maintains up to thirty varieties of taro (a root vegetable) in their plot along with other products, an arrangement which incidentally protects plants against blight. Yet despite their skills, the New Guinean gardeners believe that their success is not simply a matter of learning and experience, but depends on the correct application of planting and growing magic. As Peter Lawrence noticed, they thought that if their crops failed it was down to incompetently applied magic rather than poor gardening skills. After all, everyone knows how to grow taro! This was the New Guinean view of all cultural skills: they were in the possession of 'experts' who knew the right magic. Such a view of the prime importance of magic over the means of production inevitably extended to exotic imported cargo, for which the means of production was unknown or only vaguely understood. The cargo *had* to be made by magic. Yali's attempts to extract or duplicate the white man's cargo magic were doomed, and he was unlikely to realize his error since he presumed that the colonists would hang on to their secret. For their part, the white colonists thought (and said) that Yali and his cultists were both fools and knaves. They too were wrong, on both counts.

Do not judge a people by its culture

What has all this to do with human origins and the first modern Europeans? Well, even some prehistorians continue to make the everyday human mistake of judging human potential by tools, products, and 'cultural development'. They make the mistake when comparing the 'modern' Cro-Magnons with the 'ancient' Neanderthals because they focus on the great contrast in material culture between the newcomers and the established residents. Almost unconsciously, they make the mistake again when comparing Cro-Magnons with earlier Anatomically Modern Humans who had lived in Africa for the previous 100,000 years.

As we have seen, modern humans had colonized Asia and Australia long before they got to Europe. Their descendants still live in those regions and have every reason to resent the Eurocentric implication that Europeans, who were the first into the industrial age, were also the first to become 'really human'. The weakness in this idea is obvious: the reason why we have so much evidence for the glory of the Upper Palaeolithic in Europe is that Europe is precisely where people have looked for it. The greater difficulty of finding evidence of earlier art forms in Africa also relates to time, preservation, and specific cave types. All art is ultimately perishable, and art on exposed surfaces might not have survived as well from earlier ages.

So just how 'dumb' were the Neanderthals, and is the technology comparison fair? We can ask first whether, given the same cultural advantages, they could have matched the achievements of modern humans. The usual view is that they were inflexible losers. They had been around in Europe, adapting to local hardships and cold for well over 200,000 years, yet they failed to advance into the coldest places. By contrast, the newly arrived but tropically adapted moderns were supremely successful at establishing themselves in all sorts of cold places, and they did so within a short space of time. However, it could be argued that the moderns were fortunate enough to have developed technical and cultural advantages elsewhere. Have modern humans always made tools differently from or better than Neanderthals? In other words, if we look at modern humans before they entered Europe, and at their colonization of the rest of the world, do we find the same clear-cut advantage between Anatomically Modern Humans and other contemporary pre-modern humans in the same regions? The answer is, mostly, no.

Anatomically Modern Africans and stone technology modes
Anatomically Modern Humans have been around for at least 160,000 years. For perhaps the first 100,000 of those years, most of them made and used the same general class (or 'mode') of tools as did the Neanderthals. The technology of these tools was already a sophisticated multistage process. Generally called Middle Palaeolithic technology, they were probably first invented well over 200,000 years ago by African *Homo helmei*, possibly our common ancestor with Neanderthals (see Chapter 1). Confusingly, Middle Palaeolithic stone tools from different places are known by different terms. Such tools from Europe, North Africa, and the Levant are called Mousterian, after a site in France where specific examples were found associated with *Homo heidelbergensis* and Neanderthal remains. Those tools from sub-Saharan Africa are known as Middle Stone Age.[5]

Perhaps the most characteristic features of the Middle Palaeolithic period were a reduction in tool size, hafting, and use of the prepared stone core from which tools were struck out. During the previous period of over a million years, African *Homo erectus* typically made large hand-axes by shaping a flat core or flake on both sides; what was left of the core or flake became the finished axe. By contrast, the Middle Palaeolithic technologists first carefully prepared a specially shaped core (a technique that had emerged earlier, perhaps 350,000 years ago) and then struck a series of flake tools from it. A final touching-up shaped the final product but preserved the sharp edge of the carefully designed flake.[6] The flake could be hafted to make a more useful implement.

With a couple of exceptions (discussed on pp. 116–18), modern Africans both north and south of the Sahara continued to make and use Middle Stone Age (and earlier) types of tool until around 50,000 years ago. As we saw in Chapter 1, the first modern Africans to leave the continent set up their ill-fated and short-lived colony north of the Sahara, with outposts in the Levant, between 90,000 and 125,000 years ago. As should have been expected of immigrants from North Africa, they were using Middle Palaeolithic tools just like those used by the Neanderthals who had preceded them out of Africa, and of course like the tools used by other Neanderthals who were soon to reoccupy the Levant.

Human migrants using similar technology

I stress that we should expect the first modern humans emigrating from Africa over 100,000 years ago to have been using mainly Middle Palaeolithic technology, since there is no evidence for any dramatically newer tradition around in North and East Africa at the time. The 125,000-year-old tools at the beachcombing site near the mouth of the Red Sea – the latter being, in my view, the definitive site of the modern human exodus – were Middle Palaeolithic, though no human remains were found that could identify their makers.

The same argument can be made for the tools used by their immediate ancestors, who migrated to Asia. Middle Palaeolithic tools first appeared in India about 150,000 years ago, but are most clearly associated there with the last warm interglacial, 125,000 years ago. Such dates could mean either that these tools were brought in by *Homo helmei*, or that modern humans reached India earlier than has been thought. At any rate, the only skeletal evidence for humans in India between 100,000 and 200,000 years ago, the Narmada skull, was definitely not modern and so suggests the former.[7]

The oldest incontrovertible evidence for modern humans in Southeast Asia, at Niah Cave in Borneo, includes a modern skull dated to 42,000 years overlying a Middle Palaeolithic flake industry said to be typical of the Indian 'Soan' Middle Palaeolithic.[8] Since the genetic evidence tells us that a single migration gave rise to all modern non-African humans, this all supports the general principle that the first modern human emigrants from Africa were still making Middle Palaeolithic tools (i.e. similar to those of the Neanderthals) when they crossed the Red Sea. What is curious about Southeast Asia – and serves again to warn against laying too much store by technology – is that apart from that single report of a Middle Palaeolithic flake industry in Niah Cave and several other examples, most of the Southeast Asian Palaeolithic record shows a regression. After that, Southeast Asians generally stopped using prepared cores for a long period. In other words, it could be argued that they reverted to more old-fashioned stone technology.

The European Upper Palaeolithic: why did blades make it so different?
Modern humans such as Cro-Magnons are credited with inventing the next technological stage after the Middle Palaeolithic – the Upper Palaeolithic. As far as stone tools are concerned, what was the main technical advance of the European Upper Palaeolithic? On the whole it was diversity, but a major feature was the development and use of blades. Like many people, I find the esoteric technical terms used by archaeologists to describe chipped stone tools dry and difficult to get my mind around. So I went to see an expert on the Palaeolithic: Professor Derek Roe, director of the Oxford

University Quaternary Research Unit, a few streets away from my home.

Over some excellent coffee, this charming and knowledgeable expert got my hands around some real flakes and blades. In crude terms, blades are knapped or struck off a prepared stone core just as flakes are; but the exact way this is done results in a longer, slimmer flake, leaving behind a prismatic core from which numerous further blades can be knapped (Figure 2.1). The blade, instead of being oval or triangular like a flake, is a long, slender, parallel, slightly curved, double-edged sliver of stone that can be retouched to produce a wide range of secondary tools such as knives, awls, points, and scrapers. The potential advance opened by that slightly different way of chipping the core is huge. First, you get many tools from one prepared core, not just one. This reduces labour enormously, and if the source of good stone is inaccessible or rare it cuts down on fetching and carrying. Second, a huge range of different products can be made from one core. In other words, the inventors of blades began a revolution that had its own inbuilt acceleration.

I then asked Professor Roe which, in his view, was the greater conceptual leap: in the Middle Palaeolithic, the further development and use of prepared cores from which to strike tools; or in the Upper Palaeolithic, the invention of the struck blade. He thought for a moment. His considered answer was the earlier Middle Palaeolithic achievement, because the use of prepared cores was a multi-stage process that required the final product to be fixed in the maker's mind throughout. Any mistake in preparation, and the artisan would have to start again. Striking a blade rather than a flake off the core, although opening tremendous opportunities, was still a single knack at the end point of an existing sequence. In other words, older humans making prepared cores by the time of the Middle Palaeolithic was a more significant conceptual advance than modern humans developing blades in the Upper Palaeolithic, several hundred thousand years later.[9]

Progression of time

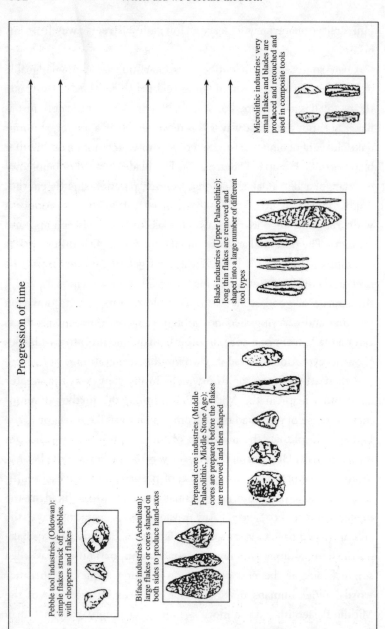

Pebble tool industries (Oldowan): simple flakes struck off pebbles, with choppers and flakes

Biface industries (Acheulean): large flakes or cores shaped on both sides to produce hand-axes

Prepared core industries (Middle Palaeolithic, Middle Stone Age): cores are prepared before the flakes are removed and then shaped

Blade industries (Upper Palaeolithic): long thin flakes are removed and shaped into a large number of different tool types

Microlithic industries: very small flakes and blades are produced and retouched and used in composite tools

Robert Foley takes this 'hallmark' view further, arguing that the prepared core technologies of the Middle Palaeolithic mark the appearance of *Homo helmei* and are also better general markers for the worldwide spread of modern humans than the blades of the Upper Palaeolithic.[10]

To explain the 'conceptual' paradox of the blade revolution to myself, I tried to think of an everyday example of a rather simple technical insight that resulted in an explosion of diverse useful results, and eventually I thought of Velcro patches. With all due respect to the insight (or foresight) of the inventor, the invention had already been made by plants, in the burr seed that hitches a ride on sheep's wool. While the inventive originality of the Velcro patch was humdrum, the diverse applications have been revolutionary in many aspects of everyday life.

Neanderthals were behind the times, but could they catch up?

So, before 50,000 years ago modern humans were at the same stage as Neanderthals in their use of stone tools – that's one side of the argument. What about the period from 28,000 to 40,000 years ago, when Neanderthals came into contact with moderns? We might be able to test the opposing hypotheses of better brains versus same brains by looking at what happened when the two groups interacted. If the Neanderthals, with their large brain volume and close evolutionary relationship to the moderns, had simply missed out on a good idea, then they should easily have picked up the new skills of the invaders. If, on the other hand, they really were dumb and these techniques were beyond them, they should have learnt nothing. In the event they did adapt, and in some places they even developed

Figure 2.1 Prepared cores, flakes and blades. Simplified view of classification of stone tool-making advances (Modes 1–5 from top down), shown in relative, not absolute, chronological order. An advance does not necessarily imply that older modes are discarded – rather, the progress was cumulative.

their own versions of some of the new Upper Palaeolithic technologies. But this adaptation was clearly not fast enough.

The first thing to note, when thinking of possibilities for technology exchange, was that although Neanderthals and moderns
coexisted in Europe for between 5,000 and 12,000 years (at some
time between 28,000 and 40,000 years ago), all the evidence shows
that for most of that time their territories hardly overlapped at
all. As the moderns expanded rapidly from Eastern Europe, the
Neanderthals, who were concentrated in the west, gradually retreated to their last strongholds – in Italy, then southern France, and
finally Spain and Portugal. Careful computer analysis of sites and
dates has recently shown that the areas of coexistence were limited
to after 35,000 years ago, and to just the two last strongholds, in
southern France and in the south-west tip of Spain (Figure 2.2). By
that time it was perhaps too little, too late. The reasons for the
Neanderthals' retreat can still only be guessed at. Was it because of
violent conflict, for instance, or more peaceful competition? The
lack of territorial overlap for 10,000 years suggests a prolonged and
probably unfriendly stalemate. However, more overlap might not
have helped Neanderthals to change their tool-making methods. The
new advances in technology were, after all, something that had
taken moderns tens of thousands of years to develop. In the same
way that Yali's people could never get at the secrets of the Europeans' luxury goods, the Neanderthals could never fully realize the
potential of the newcomers' revolutionary culture if they were not
socially close to them. Maybe Neanderthals rarely got the opportunity to pick up the new technology. In spite of these problems,
they actually picked up quite a few 'modern' habits, mainly during
the periods and in the regions of overlap.[11]

Hearths and burials

Built hearths are claimed to be hallmarks of fully modern Upper
Palaeolithic behaviour, but hearths as old as 50,000 years have been

identified in Russia and Portugal, associated with Mousterian tools, suggesting that the practice was already present in the Middle Palaeolithic and was therefore being used even by Neanderthals. Perhaps one of the most controversial vindications of Neanderthal cultural potential concerns formal burials. Deliberate burial, especially with goods and tools which had been used during life, evocatively suggests at least a concern with what happens after death and perhaps a belief in an afterlife. Such a belief could even be regarded as the first evidence for a particular aspect of religious thought. This kind of philosophical speculation makes it important to identify

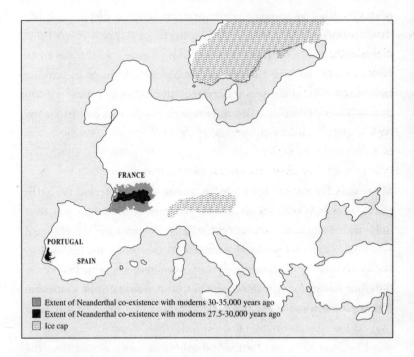

FRANCE

PORTUGAL

SPAIN

▨ Extent of Neanderthal co-existence with moderns 30-35,000 years ago
■ Extent of Neanderthal co-existence with moderns 27.5-30,000 years ago
▨ Ice cap

Figure 2.2 Space-time estimates of Neanderthal–modern coexistence. The Neanderthals' last refuges were in south-west France and Portugal.[11]

whether a particular set of bones was deliberately buried and whether or not grave goods are really present.[12]

Complete skeletons can indicate formal burial, but not always. The presence of complete human skeletons dating to times after 100,000 years ago, and particularly for Neanderthals between 40,000 and 60,000 years ago, could alternatively be the result of change in occupation of caves by hyenas and other carnivores. The degree to which grave goods such as flowers, stone circles, goats' horns, and artefacts were ritually or religiously placed has also been disputed.[13] Perhaps the most important evidence that this was just a locally shared cultural innovation is that early burials happened only among humans in West Eurasia, including the early moderns at Qafzeh in Israel (see Chapter 1). There is no evidence for the practice of burial among their contemporaries in Africa. In other words, burial, like many other aspects of Upper Palaeolithic technology, was a local invention in West Eurasia which spread to Neanderthals, who in turn preceded Modern Africans in burying their dead. This sequence undermines the biological determinism that ascribes particular cultural practices exclusively and progressively to particular human species.

Why talk up Neanderthals at all?

My reason for taking this apologist stance, fair-brokering the skills of Neanderthals with those of early humans, is not to try to prove they had exactly the same 'genetically determined' intellectual potential. There is no way one can claim this on current evidence. Neanderthals, as well as being large-brained, were anatomically different from moderns in other ways, so it would not be a surprise if there were some slight mental differences. No, my purpose is to suggest that the arguments that Neanderthals were culturally backward because they were duller, dumber, or more stupid than the invading moderns are based on a false belief that biological and cultural traits go very closely together. At the very least, as far as

Europe is concerned this argument may have been overstated and may have gone further than is justified by the evidence.

The European Upper Palaeolithic has been glorified as the 'human revolution', with dramatic cognitive advances such as abstract thought and speech. Often explicit in this scenario is the concept of a biological advance: the idea that a genetically determined change – a thought or speech gene – somehow brought about the Upper Palaeolithic revolution in Europe. Many of the most dramatic innovations of the modern newcomers were, however, just that: new inventions that had a clear regional and chronological beginning long after our species' emergence. These late inventions gave the moderns a special local advantage. Neanderthals were outgunned and wrong-footed by the complex culture the newcomers had quite recently developed. By analogy, no anthropologist would dare say that Yali's Neolithic people in New Guinea had less biological potential than Jared Diamond's own metal-age people, but it is clear that, as a result of cultural isolation, they had not benefited from certain Western technical innovations of the past 2,000 years, such as guns and steel.

Why do I defend Neanderthals? The answer is that bad-mouthing Neanderthals, regarding them as people who were like but unlike us, is symptomatic of a deep need among all human societies to exclude and even demonize other groups (see also Chapter 5). I suggest that the unproven dumbing of the Neanderthals is an example of the same cultural preconception that has, by a mistaken geographical logic, cast our own Anatomically Modern African ancestors in the same role, as 'moderns manqués'. The very real problem for this Eurocentric standpoint is that today's modern Africans are the direct descendants of those pre-Upper Palaeolithic peoples, and share with them more of their original genes than do any other people in the world. By denigrating their ancestors, by implication we denigrate them.

The European Upper Palaeolithic: cultural or biological revolution?
Clive Gamble is a world expert on the reconstruction of Palaeolithic
human behaviour. In a very readable book, *Timewalkers*, he summar-
ized conventional views and identified the period from 40,000 to
60,000 years ago as the crucial behavioural threshold between
ancients and moderns. He describes the end of this timespan,
40,000 years ago, as the time after which the great acceleration took
place, with the advent in Europe of art, bone tools, body ornament,
open-site burials, storage pits, quarries, exchange of goods, and
long-term occupation of harsh environments. He takes the threshold argument further, saying, 'There is no doubt that after 35,000 BP
[before the present] Upper Palaeolithic industries sweep the board,
not only in Europe but across much of the Old World, with Australia
forming a notable exception . . .'[14] This Australian 'exception'
clearly does not apply to rock art, since six pages later he mentions
'the rock engravings from Karolta in South Australia, now directly
dated to as much as 32,000 BP'. Such a date makes them almost as
old as the Chauvet Cave art, and in fact does seem to extend his
earlier point, at least partially, to include Australia.

Others, such as Chicago palaeoanthropologist Richard Klein,
take this cultural explosion a stage further and interpret it as a
human biological epiphany. In a standard text, *The Human Career*,
written in 1989, he states:

> it can be argued that the Upper Paleolithic signals the most
> fundamental change in human behavior that the archeological
> record may ever reveal . . . The strong correlation between
> Upper Paleolithic artifacts and modern human remains further
> suggests that it was the modern human physical type that made
> the Upper Paleolithic (and all subsequent cultural developments)
> possible. The question then arises whether there is a detectable
> link between the evolution of modern people and the develop-
> ment of those behavioral traits that mark the Upper Paleolithic.

He then draws attention to the mainly Middle Palaeolithic tools of earlier modern humans, concluding:

> In sum, anatomical and behavioral modernity may have appeared simultaneously in Europe, but in both the Near East and Africa, anatomical modernity antedates behavioral modernity, at least as it is detectable in the archeological record. This observation is difficult to explain. Perhaps . . . the earliest anatomically modern humans of Africa and the Near East were not as modern as their skeletons suggest. Neurologically, they may have lacked the fully modern capacity for culture. This may have appeared only as recently as 40,000 to 50,000 years ago when it allowed [what were by] then fully modern humans to spread rapidly throughout the world.[15]

In these explicit biological statements we have one dominant conventional out-of-Africa model that places the chronological and genetic threshold to our modernity (behavioural and neurological) at no more than 50,000 years ago, in West Eurasia and after the out-of-Africa dispersal. This model was conceived before 1989, at a time when it was believed that Australia was colonized only 40,000 years ago. In other words, Klein could interpret the evidence to allow for Australia – and hence also Asia – to have been colonized by Anatomically Modern Humans only after the start of the European Upper Palaeolithic. This made it possible for him to argue that these new 'neurally enhanced' moderns in Europe could have then moved on to colonize the rest of the non-African world. Klein published a second edition of his book in 1999, by which time he acknowledged, on the last couple of pages, the problem of possible earlier Australian (and Asian) colonization by 60,000 years ago, and the possibility of harpoon fishing in Africa between 90,000 and 155,000 years ago. In his conclusions he still, however, returns to the argument of a neurological evolutionary (i.e. genetically driven) revolution in Europe 40,000–60,000 years ago: 'to me it suggests that the fully modern capacity for culture may have appeared only about this time [50,000 years ago]'.[16]

Even before we consider the evidence, we can see that this argument implies a biologically deterministic approach to cultural evolution. It assumes that each cultural advance is determined or 'allowed' by a genetic change. As I mentioned in the Prologue, human (or other primate) culture is first invented, then learnt and added to from generation to generation. Each advance or skill does not come out of a new gene. Rather, new behaviours come first and the genetic modifications that best exploit those new behaviours come afterwards. In other words, the change of culture precedes the change of body – not the other way round. Furthermore, there are predictable geographical differences of culture. If a particular invention in one region led to other local inventions, the accelerated pace of innovation would give that region a head start. So regional differences in the rate of cultural progression should be expected, even within one human species.

Did a European wisdom gene spread to everyone else?

There are several inescapable logical assumptions in Klein's argument that fully 'neurally modern' humans appeared only after 40,000–50,000 years ago. First there is the explicit implication that early African moderns were biologically less than modern – in other words, they did not have the neurological capacity to develop modern behaviours. This strange conclusion would inevitably apply to those moderns left in Africa, and also to the first moderns migrating into Asia and on to Australia, since it is now generally accepted that these colonizations took place quite some time before 50,000 years ago (the earliest possible time for which the Upper Palaeolithic can be identified in the Eastern Mediterranean). What do these hypothetical conclusions mean? They would mean first that the direct ancestors of today's Africans living between 50,000 and 130,000 years ago were biologically incapable of developing or using Upper

Palaeolithic behaviour and technology. They would not be able to paint, carve, trade, organize, and so forth. Many say that they could not speak – or, if they could, that their speech was 'primitive'. With such disadvantages, presumably they could not, given the opportunity, drive cars or fly planes; compose and play soul, spirituals, reggae, classical music, and jazz; or become doctors, financiers, and geneticists. The mitochondrial DNA and Y-chromosome trees imply that today's Africans are descended mainly from lines present before 50,000 years ago and not from lines outside Africa. So, why can today's African descendants do all these things their ancestors were supposedly genetically incapable of?

There is a further logical problem. If Europeans were the first biologically modern humans and were isolated comparative late-comers, what about the rest of the world? How did they catch up? All living modern humans are fully 'Anatomically Modern', and we can trace back our genetic trail to a small ancestral group that started branching in Africa around 190,000 years ago. At no point after that did the total modern population number less than a thousand,[17] so we have to imagine that one group inevitably led, by expansion and branching, to many groups.

The first nucleus of moderns thus expanded, split, and spread early, some branches never to meet again until recent times. This effect of 'no-return' separation was never so final as when the one and only successful out-of-Africa group crossed the Red Sea and headed for India and Australia. If, as many evolutionists believe, there was some late genetic change in Europe that made us behaviourally modern as opposed to behaviourally 'archaic', this mutation (or mutations) must have occurred at a particular time in individual Europeans after 45,000 years ago – and, obviously, out-side Africa.

A new mutation would have been passed on to all descendant populations that received the mutated gene, but would not have been shared by 'cousins' and their descendants. The only exception to this would be if the mutated gene was subsequently shared as a result of cross-marriage. The chance of such cross-marriage would diminish sharply as groups separated and spread around the world. So if there really was, say, a 'painting mutation' or a 'speech mutation', only those descended from the individual who developed that mutation should inherit the skill. So, if the 'behaviourally fully modern' cluster of mutations initially evolved locally in Europeans 40,000–50,000 years ago, then the rest of the colonized world – the Asians, Africans, and Australians – would not be able to paint, carve, speak, make blades, or place a bet on a horse. Nor would their modern descendants. This is clearly absurd, for they can do all those things.

By this argument, the only way that the original modern colonies of Asians, Africans, and Australians could come up to speed with a European Upper Palaeolithic culture that resulted from a genetic mutation would be if they received infusions of all those new 'culture genes'. The only biological way of infusing genes, or gene flow, is by migration and intermarriage. But it would not be enough just to have a few foreign cousins. To change all the descendants' capabilities, the old hypothetical 'cultural genes' would have to be completely replaced by the 'new'. Curiously, this massive gene flow is just the same argument that the discredited multiregionalists use to explain how modern human populations evolved separately in different parts of the world from local *Homo erectus* variants, yet ended up looking more like one another than the local *erectus* types. The main problem with the gene-flow levelling theory is that the geography of the mtDNA and Y-chromosome trees shows no evidence of such large-scale inter-regional mixing

Let's take a cultural example. For Australians to have been producing rock art 32,000 years ago (which, apparently, they did), at the same time as it first appeared in Europe, would have required an instantaneous and massive gene flow round the globe from Europe to biologically 'enable' them to get to that level. It is a ludicrous idea, which can easily be tested. We can see from the genetic record that although modern Australians share with Europeans the two out-of-Africa M and N ancestors from over 80,000 years ago, they preserve their own M and N types. There is no evidence that they are descended from Europeans. Nor was there any significant gene flow from Europe to Australia during the rest of the Palaeolithic.[18]

Lack of genetic mixing after out-of-Africa is the general rule

The genetic evidence from the male-line and female-line markers, the Y chromosome and mtDNA, in fact shows the opposite of massive gene flow. One of the most important messages of the Y-chromosome and mtDNA stories is that, after the initial modern human dispersals out of Africa, each Old World and Antipodean region became settled, and little if any further inter-regional gene flow happened until the build-up to the last great glaciation 20,000 years ago. Both genetic marker systems show clear regional and intercontinental divisions.

Cultural diffusion (a sort of seepage or spread of culture not requiring much people movement) during the Palaeolithic is a more likely method of long-distance cultural transmission and one which does not necessarily require gene flow. However, could it really have been possible for 32,000-year-old Australian rock art to be derived from that of Europe at the same time? The culture would have to have been passed halfway around the world in an impossibly short space of time.

The simplest answer, which does away with this paradox and similar ones, is that the African ancestors of all non-Africans came out of Africa painting, talking, singing, and dancing – and fully modern! There is thus much biological as well as logical evidence *against* a genetic evolutionary event leading on to fully modern humans 40,000 years ago in the Levant, Europe, or anywhere else outside Africa. This leads us on to examine the direct archaeological evidence and anthropological arguments for the simpler model, namely that the first Anatomically Modern Africans were already fully modern in their intellectual potential.

The cultural evidence

Two well-known teams of anthropologist and archaeologist have recently examined the tools, technology, and lifestyle of our ancestors to measure their potential. Their approaches and discussion frameworks were very different but to my reading, their conclusions were broadly the same. While looking at their work we need continually to put archaeological evidence of variations in technology between different groups back into the perspective of Yali's question. Conventional writing and reading were invented over 4,000 years ago in the West, but no one argues for a writing gene; the same goes for the dramatic developments of the past century – radio, television, computers, computer language, spacecraft, and so on. In other words, we cannot use the sophistication of any particular recent human technical invention as a biological milestone. Also, much evidence of technical and symbolic culture, such as wood-carving and art painted on wood, is perishable, so there may be less evidence of earlier manifestations in a wood-using culture.

This means that, without adequate context, we cannot assume that evidence of technical innovations points to a biological evolution. From our knowledge of how cultural innovations have spread during our own, recorded, history, we would expect a generally slow cultural improvement to be punctuated by apparent local revolutions, which would then diffuse farther afield and eventually result in an overall acceleration. What is perhaps most important when examining the origins of the Upper Palaeolithic revolution is to look for the geographical location of the immediate precursor culture: North Africa, or South Asia?

Using stone trails to follow people round the world

We should of course start with that most abundant and durable record: stone tools. The Cambridge team of Robert Foley, anthropologist, and Marta Lahr, palaeontologist, have carried out an in-depth review of stone and bone evidence from around the world to see if one really can fit stone technology types to different human species, ancient and modern. Their main conclusion was that the worldwide spread of modern humans is most comprehensively defined by the dated appearance of so-called Mode 3 technology (Figures 2.1 and 2.3) – a technical threshold that was passed by our ancestors *Homo helmei* in Africa around 300,000 years ago. Originally defined as the use of a specially prepared stone core from which flake tools could be struck off, Mode 3 is really the Middle Palaeolithic under another name. Another way of looking at Mode 3 is not just as a change in knapping technique, but more in terms of the advance from large, heavy hand-axes to smaller stone tools, including sharp flakes, that could be hafted.[19] Mode 3 thus coincides with the earliest appearance of the large-brained *Homo helmei*, who in Foley and Lahr's view were the common ancestor for both ourselves and Neanderthals. Mode 3 became the main technology used by all members of this latest human family – including moderns – until after 50,000 years ago. The use of prepared cores to generate flakes was conceptually the most complex development, and occurred in the Lower Palaeolithic. If these people were smart enough to make prepared cores, they were probably smart enough to make blades.

Blade production from prepared prismatic cores is the second hallmark technique. However, it is much less useful as a marker of the spread of modern humans, being a late and local event in Europe and around the Mediterranean (and later still in Africa and Asia, though not in Australia). And it is perhaps not reliable as a specific marker for fully modern humans outside Africa, because there is evidence for blade production by others, including contemporary

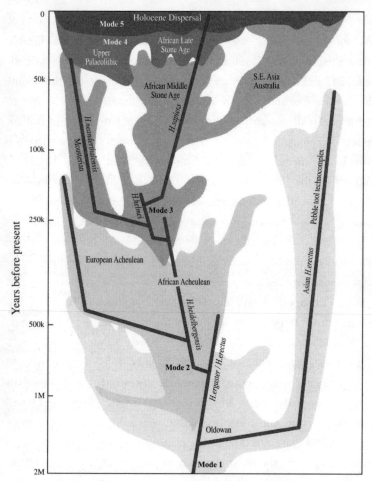

Geographical spread of technology modes and associated humans

Figure 2.3 The worldwide spread in space and time of stone technology. Increasingly dark shading with time indicates successive spreads of Modes 1–5 (moving from Africa to Europe on the left; and to the Far East on the right). The human species associated with the spread of individual modes are superimposed as a branching tree.

non-moderns (such as the Chatelperronian industries, mentioned in note 11) and earlier modern Africans (such as in Howieson's Poort, South Africa, 60,000–90,000 years ago), in what are otherwise Middle Stone Age settings. As a final twist, these short-term African appearances of 'smart' blades were later replaced again by typical Mode 3 industries. Some archaeologists speculate that blades were invented several times before the Upper Palaeolithic and then forgotten.[20] Perhaps the two main practical advances of the Upper Palaeolithic were in blade use: diversity of tools and economy of raw material.

American anthropologist–archaeologist duo Sally McBrearty and Alison Brooks have taken the argument of ancient African Middle Stone Age skills much further. In an in-depth interpretation of the origin of modern human behaviour entitled 'The revolution that wasn't',[21] they challenge the orthodoxy of the 40,000–50,000-year-old 'human revolution'. Instead, in parallel with but using a contrasting approach to Foley and Lahr, who see Mode 3 (Middle Palaeolithic) technologies as defining features of modern human behaviour, McBrearty and Brooks discuss the evolution of modern cultural behaviour in terms of the African Middle Stone Age. The latter ran roughly contemporary with the European Middle Palaeolithic up to the African Late Stone Age, with a prolonged fitful changeover starting sometime after 70,000 years ago. They see the African Middle Stone Age, starting with *Homo helmei* 250,000–300,000 years ago, as a more dynamic and inventive cultural evolutionary sequence than its Middle Palaeolithic neighbour in Europe, anticipating many behaviours more characteristic of the European Upper Palaeolithic. Over several hundred years, they argue, humans in Africa had gradually assembled, by invention, an increasingly sophisticated cultural and material package of skills. Looking at the African record, only a few of these technical and social advances could be linked to biological milestones as *Homo helmei* were replaced by modern humans. Much more could be attributed to purely cultural evolution, which has its own accelerating tempo.

Smart African tools

McBrearty and Brooks show that, in contrast to Europe, where the much-vaunted blade tools were a defining feature of the modern human arrival 40,000–50,000 years ago, blades were used off and on during the African Middle Stone Age for as much as 280,000 years, thus predating modern humans by almost a quarter of a million years.[22] Another type of stone tool that flourished in the Middle and Upper Palaeolithic was the stone point. Points are basically flakes that have been retouched along both faces to make a point suitable for a spear tip. They have a 250,000-year history in Africa – much longer than that in Europe – and, as McBrearty and Brooks point out, show great regional diversity and sophistication there (Figure 2.4).

One specialized and precise type of stone tool that was first made in Africa turned up rather late in European prehistory: the microlith. Less than 25 mm (1 inch) long and blunted like a penknife along one edge, these tiny but accurately fashioned tools were made from small blades or segments of blades. They had a wide range of uses, particularly when set in complex hafted tools and weapons such as spears, knives, and arrows. A damaged individual microlith on such a weapon could easily be repaired or replaced. Regarded as Mode 5 – the ultimate in stone tool sophistication – they are the hallmark of the African Late Stone Age, turning up first in Mumba Rock Shelter, Tanzania, around 70,000 years ago. However, they appeared in Europe much later – mostly from after the last glaciation 8,000 years ago. The earliest consistent non-African record of microlith industries comes not from Europe but, significantly, from Sri Lanka, around 30,000 years ago, suggesting direct fertilization from Africa via the southern route (see Chapter 4).[23]

The use of non-stone materials such as bone and antler to make tools and weapons was another novel skill claimed as a European first from 30,000–40,000 years ago. McBrearty and Brooks, however, point to ample evidence for bone tools in Africa up to 100,000 years ago. Not only that, but some of the first African bone tools were barbed points looking like harpoon tips (see Figure 2.4).

Another fascinating item in the human toolkit that dates back 280,000 years to the time of our grandparents *Homo helmei* is the

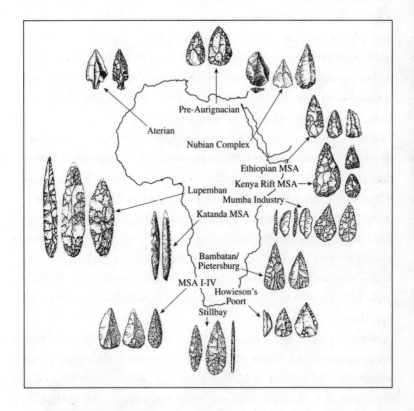

Figure 2.4 Map of the distribution of stone point styles found from the African Middle Stone Age. Note also barbed 'harpoon tips' from Katanda.

grindstone. Grindstones have nearly always had two completely different functions: to grind food, and to grind mineral pigments such as red and yellow ochre from lumps of rock. The latter application is much more relevant to the story of our intellectual evolution.[24]

African artists

Pigment use has been regarded as another hallmark of the European Upper Palaeolithic,[25] so its appearance up to 280,000 years ago, in Africa, shows that the overemphasis on the beautiful Chauvet paintings as a first sign of symbolic behaviour has blinded us to the same stirrings of the mind in our more distant ancestors. Pigment was used so heavily in Africa up to 100,000 years ago that mining for minerals such as haematite was on what might be called an industrial scale. Quarrying began in Europe only 40,000 years ago. At one African mine, at least 1,200 tonnes of pigment ore had been extracted from a cliff face.[26] Some anthropologists and archaeologists get excited about the systematic use of pigment because they believe it to be early evidence, along with burials, for symbolic behaviour. Pigments were used for painting of walls and objects, for body painting, for use in burials, and to cure hides. Neanderthals used pigment, although the dating of finds seems to indicate that they acquired the use by cultural diffusion from early moderns. Sadly, we shall never know how much body hair Neanderthals evolved to combat the cold, but this could have reduced the ease and practicality of body-painting.

Both vegetable and mineral pigments were used by Upper Palaeolithic humans, but much of the clear evidence for vegetable pigments during the African Middle Stone Age will have decayed over time. Actual evidence of representational painting is also limited by time, particularly in Africa, which possesses far fewer limestone caves of the sort in which the Lascaux and Chauvet paintings have

(1) Reconstruction of *Australopithecus afarensis*, from Lucy's family of walking apes, 3-4 million years ago. They had one of the first clearly upright and bipedal bodies, but a skull and brain still the size of a chimpanzee's.

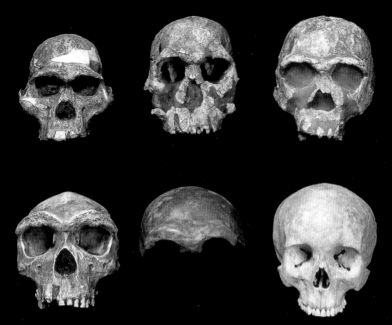

(3) Skulls of (from top, left to right) *Australopithecus*, *Homo rudolfensis*, *Homo erectus*, *Homo rhodesiensis*, Neanderthal and modern man.

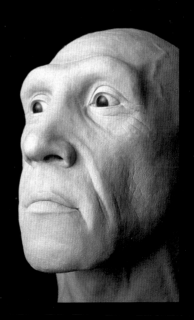

Facing page: (2) Reconstruction of *Homo erectus* head. With a wary face and growing brain, they left Africa at the earliest opportunity, successfully dominating the planet for nearly two million years.

Right: (4) Reconstruction of Neanderthal head. The heavy features, brow-ridges and large nose were partly adaptations to the northern climate.

(5) *Newsweek*'s iconic cover of 11 January 1988 carried the full story of 'Mitochondrial Eve' to the world.

Below: (6) Eight-thousand-year-old Saharan rock images of elephants, hippos and giraffes, like this at Fezzan in Libya, record a time when the region was lush grassland.

(7) The Red Sea, with the Gate of Grief at the bottom, where the crossing out of Africa took place 85,000 years ago. (Colours computer-generated.)

(8) The world's 'first oyster bar' was discovered at Abdur in Eritrea, a 125,000-year-old reef with oyster meal remains and obsidian tools clearly visible together.

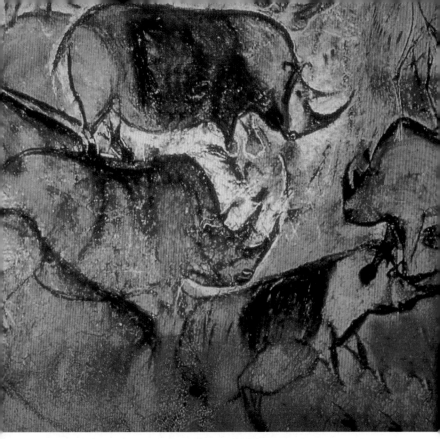

(9) The magnificent cave paintings of Chauvet, like these rhinoceros, are perhaps mistakenly thought to mark a human epiphany or coming of age in Europe.

(10) New Guinean leader Yali at a cargo cult ceremony on the north coast (1956).

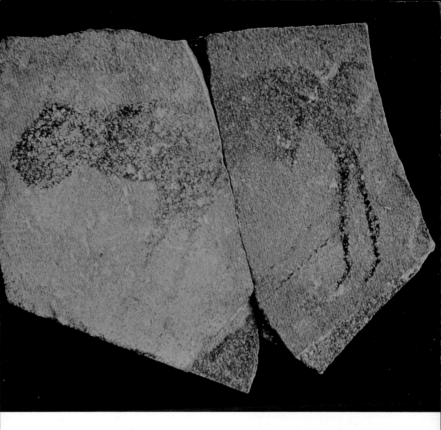

Above: (11) From the 'Apollo II' rock shelter in Namibia, this cat (or possibly bovid) may be the earliest evidence of representational painting in the world, dated to 40-60,000 years ago.

(12) One of the Sunghir burials, an old man, found near Moscow (dated to 24,000 years ago) with perforated fox canines in his cap, 20 ivory armlets and bracelets, and draped in thousands of ivory beads, a dramatic early example of personal ornamentation.

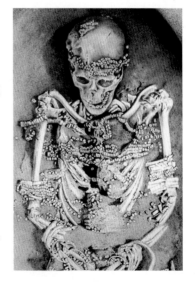

(13) Early Gravettian figurines made from (from left to right) fired clay from Moravia, mammoth ivory from France, the Willendorf Venus in limestone from Austria, and ivory from the Ukraine.

(14) Late Upper Palaeolithic reindeer carvings – on the tip of a mammoth tusk from Montastruc, France (above) and on a bone spear-thrower from Laugerie Basse, France (below).

been preserved. A curious point about Chauvet Cave, the earliest of European artistic canvasses, is that it represents the best we know of Palaeolithic art. With its extraordinarily realistic and imaginative action paintings, some of which exploit pre-existing physical features such as rocky outcrops for dramatic effect, Chauvet does not look like the first faint glimmerings of symbolic consciousness. What we see is a fully mature style, a confident peak from which later cave painting could only go downhill.[27]

However, the first clear evidence of representational painting was not found in Europe but in a cave in Namibia, in southern Africa, dated by its Middle Stone Age context to between 40,000 and 60,000 years ago, thus preceding European painting (see Plate 11). Haematite 'pencils' with wear facets have also been found in various parts of southern Africa, dating from more than 100,000 years ago. This sort of evidence in itself again contradicts the European location for the 'Human Symbolic Revolution'. As McBrearty and Brooks point out, painting could have an even greater antiquity in Africa, but the direct evidence has now perished or remains to be found when the same intensity of European research is applied to African sites.[28]

Recognizable pictures of people, animals, and things need not be the first evidence for symbolic representation in any case. Regular scratches, cross-hatching, and notching of pieces of stone or mineral pigment blocks are likely to have had some symbolic purpose. Such artefacts appear in the African record from 100,000 years ago. Arguably the earliest evidence of such deliberate patterning of stone comes from sandstone caves in India around the Lower–Middle Palaeolithic transition, anywhere between 150,000 and 300,000 years ago. Australian archaeologist Robert Bednarik argues, controversially, that a number of meandering scored lines and cupules (shallow depressions on a rock face) in the Bhimbetka caves near Bhopal are the earliest evidence of symbolic art anywhere.[29]

African ornaments

Personal ornamentation, for instance with beads and pendants, is claimed by archaeologists to show the novel sophistication of ritual and symbolic practices in the European Upper Palaeolithic. There is evidence for body ornamentation in Europe used by fully modern humans from about 40,000 years ago, but it was a particular feature of the Gravettian cultures that emerged about 30,000 years ago although there is evidence for it from 40,000 years ago. One of the most dramatic examples of such body decoration was found in a grave site 200 km (125 miles) east of Moscow at Sunghir. Here, 24,000 years ago, very close to the approaching ice sheets of the imminent glacial maximum, two graves were dug for three occupants, an old man and two children. They were all dressed in garments richly decorated with thousands of ivory beads (see Plate 12). Ivory bracelets, wands, animal figurines, and pendants completed the adornment.[30]

McBrearty and Brooks have shown that personal ornamentation in Africa predated that in Europe by tens of thousands of years. They cite a perforated shell pendant, buried with an infant, dated to 105,000 years ago in South Africa, and other decorations and drilled pendants dated back to at least 130,000 years ago in the African Middle Stone Age. Ostrich-shell drilled beads are a feature of the African Late Stone Age and may go back to 60,000 years.[31]

As we can see from Figure 2.5 (which summarizes the evidence for the rather gradual acquisition of the elements of 'modern' culture over the past 300,000 years), using pigment, making symbolic marks on rocks, and fashioning blades and points were not actually inventions of modern humans at all. These skills and symbolic behaviours originated over 250,000 years ago – rather early on in the history of our archaic ancestor. More perishable evidence of complex culture, such as painting and beads, are still found in Africa from tens of thousands of years before the first such signs in Europe.

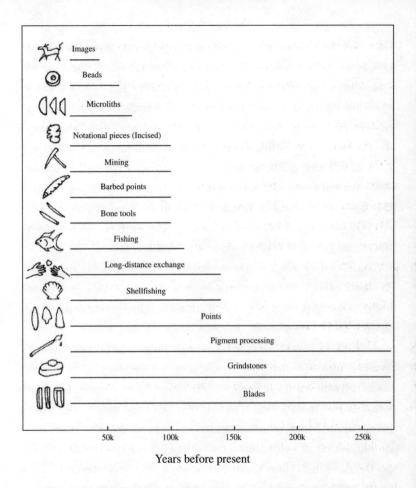

Years before present

Figure 2.5 Modern behaviours and evidence of their time depths of acquisition in Africa over the past 300,000 years. Four out of fourteen are present before modern humans, and the majority before the European Upper Palaeolithic.

Mining, bone tools, and bone harpoons appear from 100,000 years ago. In all these later instances the skills were chronologically and clearly associated with moderns.

African fishers

These 'modern' innovations were all things people made. When we look at what they did, we find an even more fascinating horizon of behaviour apparently starting between 110,000 and 140,000 years ago – just after the period of our emergence in the fossil record as a modern African species. While we should still not fall into the trap of automatically attributing new skills to any unique genetic change, it is worth looking at new behaviours that might have given us the edge over our large-brained ancestor, *Homo helmei*. Adapting to new and varied foods such as fish and shellfish may have been the key 150,000 years ago. Not to be outdone, Neanderthals also practised beachcombing 60,000 years ago on the Mediterranean.[32]

Arguably the most important animal behaviour is obtaining food. The last 2 million years have seen more and more of Africa turn into desert, making it increasingly difficult to find food. Humans had to become more ingenious in order to stay alive, and moulded themselves into the highly evolved savannah hunter-gatherers that we became. Archaic humans were capable of hunting large and dangerous herbivores from the early Middle Stone Age.[33] A severe glacial period lasting from 130,000 to 170,000 years ago nearly wiped out the game on which human populations depended for calories and protein. It may therefore be no coincidence that from 140,000 years ago the African Middle Stone Age shows a new subsistence type – beachcombing – gathering shellfish on the seashore to supplement game as a source of protein.

Beachcombing was also seen in South Africa, at Klasies River mouth, but it is the Eritrean Red Sea coastal beachcombing site of Abdur that is most interesting for our story. This is, after all, where the Australian beachcombing trek may have started (see Chapter 1). Here, around 125,000 years ago, at the sea-level high-point of the last interglacial we see Middle Stone Age tools and shellfish remains jumbled together with the butchered remains of large African game (see Plate 8). McBrearty and Brookes argue that extension from beachcombing to actual fishing had occurred in Africa by 110,000 years ago.[34]

I recently had the privilege of being shown the famous Abdur reef by its discoverer, Eritrean geologist Seife Berhe. Driving down steep escarpments, we left the cool watered highlands surrounding the capital, Asmara, 2,200 metres (7,200 feet) above sea level, and soon came to the baking coast of the Red Sea at the war-scarred, Arab-flavoured port of Massawa. Stopping briefly for water and ice, we travelled south for three hours along a ribbed, dusty, all-weather coastal road. Stunning young volcanic scenery and high folds of mountains alternated with dry, silted alluvial plains. We were held up only briefly, by a puncture caused by a sharp volcanic rock.

This was the end of the dry season, and stunted bushes, mainly acacia, were the only green. The occasional gazelle, jackal, hare, bustard, or eagle were the only remnants I saw of the larger game that abounded here before the recent war. Everywhere we saw herds of camels, goats, cattle, and fat-tailed desert sheep. Apart from some nomadic herdsmen, the Afars are the only indigenous population on this part of the coast, and they stretch right down to Djibouti. Living in simple airy brushwood huts, the Afars were mutually dependent on their herds, and drew water for the entire flock every day from wells dug in dry river beds. We camped on the edge of one of these dry estuaries on a flat sandy plain, raised 10 metres (about 30 feet) above the beach.

I soon discovered that we were in fact camped on the famous raised 125,000-year-old reef. When the climate had started to worsen 120,000 years ago, the sea level had dropped, leaving this reef dry with all the different types of coral and shells beautifully preserved right up to the surface of the ground under our feet. A steady tectonic uplift had continued to raise the entire coastal reef another 5 meters (15 feet), creating a cliff that runs along the coast for 10 km (6 miles). This extra uplift had protected the reef from the erosional effects of another high sea level 5,500 years ago.

The day after our arrival, we went down the cliff to the dry estuarine plain and found some friendly Afars watering their herds. To preserve the natural well, they drew up water in buckets and deposited it in large, dish-like mud basins they had built into the sand. While the cattle, goats, and sheep waited in single file for their turn to drink from these improvised troughs, the herders chanted a water-song.

Immediately above this ancient scene, Seife Berhe showed me the 125,000-year-old shell middens, the remains of meals of oysters looking as if they had been left behind only yesterday. Clearly visible, sticking out from but cemented in among the fossilized shells of the midden was an obsidian flake tool. From its shape it had clearly been worked, but it must have been brought to the reef because the nearest source of obsidian is 20 km (12 miles) away. The shell midden, butchered animal bones, the flake, and other obsidian artefacts completed the picture of a mixed diet eaten by the humans who lived by this reef so long ago.

Pieces of coral block were in the process of breaking away from the cliff, otherwise we would not have been able to climb and squeeze in so close. In the coral debris in the sand around these great blocks of coral were numerous small obsidian bladelets, 10–40 mm (0.4–1.6 inches) long, some very bright and sharp. I could have shaved myself with them. I remembered that the *Nature* paper reporting this important archaeological site had told of obsidian blades in the reef, but these were microliths. The puzzle was that 125,000 years ago should have been much too early for such small tools, unless they had been put there much later. The fact that they were loose, showing no clear association with the midden, made this an alternative possibility. Microliths start appearing in the African archaeological record only from 80,000 years ago. They were present all over the sand above the cliff, so maybe that was the case. Interestingly, the earliest microliths outside Africa have all been found to the east of the Red Sea in Sri Lanka.[35]

Last among the key elements of the 'modern human' behaviour package we find long-distance exchange – in other words, some form of trading or movement of important objects such as tools and raw obsidian over distances up to 300 km (200 miles). Again, we see in the African record that this most human of behaviours started at least 140,000 years ago.[36]

Two million years of human know-how

McBrearty and Brooks' composite picture of the first 'Anatomically Modern' Africans shows that soon after their first appearance, by around 140,000 years ago, half of the fourteen important clues to cognitive skills and behaviour which underpinned those that eventually took us to the Moon were already present. Three of these (pigment processing, grindstones, and blades) had been invented by the previous species of modern humans 140,000 years before that. By 100,000 years ago – just after the first exodus to the Levant – three-quarters of these skills had been invented; and the remaining three were in place before the first moderns stepped into Europe (see Figure 2.5). With such a perspective of cumulative increments in culture over the past 300,000 years, the concept of a sudden modern 'European Human Revolution' 40,000 years ago pops like a bubble. We begin to see instead our essential humanness as 'adaptation and invention followed by physical evolution' stretching right back into the 2-million-year story of our genus *Homo* – hunters, inventors, and tool-makers from the start.

In spite of this deconstruction of its evolutionary importance, the European Upper Palaeolithic remains a unique record of a most glorious period of local self-discovery. But what does it tell us about ourselves? Well, there are some hints, from the distribution and dates of the earliest Upper Palaeolithic stone cultures that were clearly associated with modern humans' invasion of Europe – the Aurignacian and its successor, the Gravettian – that there was not one invasion, but two. In the next chapter we shall find out why, where from, and how the genetic trail reinforces this view.

3

TWO KINDS OF EUROPEAN

As WE HAVE SEEN, the teasing issue of European origins is not just a matter of whether the future Europeans migrated out of Africa separately from the future Asians and Australians, or of just burying the myth that they were the first humans to show modern behaviour. It is more than that. Where did their extraordinary flowering of culture originate? Was it entirely home-grown, or was it imported? Why do some archaeologists argue for several different early cultural inputs to Europe in the period between 20,000 and 50,000 years ago – even one from the East? In this chapter we shall see that there are precise male and female genetic markers which parallel two different cultural waves that flowed in succession over the European archaeological record of the 25,000 years leading up the Last Glacial Maximum. These reveal that an 'Eastern' origin was no wild guess.

In Chapter 1 we saw that the ancestors of Europeans, the N (or Nasreen) clan, belonged to one of the first branches off the single exodus shoot which arrived in southern Arabia perhaps 80,000 years ago. In spite of this secure position at the root of the Asian maternal genetic tree, the Europeans' ancestors had to wait tens of thousands of years in South Asia. They waited until after 50,000 years ago, when a moist, warm phase greened the Arabian Desert sufficiently to open the Fertile Crescent and allowed them to migrate north-westwards towards Turkey and the Levant. Such constraints had not affected their cousins – the vanguard of beach-combers who pressed on round the Indian Ocean coast to Southeast Asia and Australia. They arrived in Australia over 60,000 years ago, long before Europe was colonized.

From an Asian point of view, Europe is an inaccessible peninsula jutting out north-west from the Old World, a geographical cul-de-sac. Genetically as well as geographically, Europeans are, similarly, a side-branch of the out-of-Africa human tree. Because the first non-African modern humans were Asians, 'peninsular Europe' was more likely to have been a recipient and beneficiary of the seeds of the earliest Upper Palaeolithic cultural innovations rather than their homeland. From this perspective the last chapter was devoted to deconstructing the archaeological/anthropological myth of a major human biological revolution defined in Europe and the Levant, with everyone else in the world following the European lead.

The first modern Europeans

We saw in the last chapter that our cousins the Neanderthals had already started to learn the smart new Upper Palaeolithic technology before their demise around 28,000 years ago. This partial blurring of the cultural distinction between Neanderthals and modern humans does not mean that archaeologists *cannot* detect the very clear cultural trails that mark the movement of the earliest modern humans into Europe. On the contrary, starting before 30,000 years ago, several such cultural traditions, specifically associated with modern humans, spread rapidly and successively across Europe. The dates and directions of spread of these traditions were different, and they have been given a number of names, based on the styles of tools and where the tools were found. The nature of the early modern cultures in Europe was diverse, and some archaeologists classify them more broadly into two waves. The concept of movement can be taken even further than cultural diffusion to suggest two different human migrations with their associated cultures. The first of these waves, which commenced as early as 46,000 years ago, is called the Aurignacian, after the village of Aurignac (Haute-Garonne) in southern France, where typical artefacts were initially found. The later one, mainly from 21,000–30,000 years ago, is called the Gravettian after the French site of La Gravette in the Perigord region, and is characterized by backed blades (where one edge is blunted, like a penknife) and pointed blades.[1]

It is tempting to attribute the spreading of ideas to mass migrations of people. However, as more recent history shows us, the movement of ideas and skills through populations can be more rapid and comprehensive than the movement of the people themselves. But for the first modern human colonizations of Europe there really does seem to be genetic evidence for at least two separate migrations corresponding to the new cultural traditions brought in by the moderns.

The Aurignacians

The Aurignacian Upper Palaeolithic culture first appeared in Europe in Bulgaria, presumably arriving from Turkey, after 50,000 years ago. Fairly soon after this, the new style of stone tools moved up the Danube to Istállósko in Hungary and then across, still westward along the Danube, to Willendorf, in Austria. The apparently relentless movement of Aurignacian culture, upriver and west from the Black Sea, eventually brought it to the upper reaches of the Danube at Geissenklösterle, Germany. Long before this time, however, the Aurignacian culture had also moved south from Austria into northern Italy. From there it spread rapidly, westward along the Riviera, across the Pyrenees, and through El Castillo in northern Spain, before finally reaching the Portuguese Atlantic coast by 38,000 years ago.[2] (Figure 3.1)

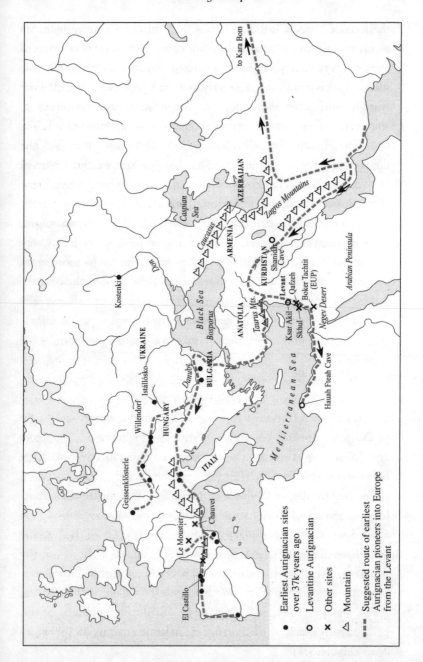

Earliest Aurignacian sites over 37k years ago

Levantine Aurignacian

Other sites

Mountain

Suggested route of earliest Aurignacian pioneers into Europe from the Levant

The Aurignacian cultural tradition persisted in some form or another until much later and in due course became more unequivocally identified with modern human skeletal remains; but this early, rapid spread into regions which had previously hosted only Middle Palaeolithic cultures suggests a real colonization event. There is no clearly dated archaeological source for the Aurignacian tool styles outside Europe from earlier than 47,000 years ago, but the Near East is a strong candidate. Belgian archaeologist Marcel Otte has suggested the Zagros Mountains (part of the Fertile Crescent) as a core homeland for the Aurignacian stone-crafting techniques, which is consistent with my view of the Fertile Crescent as a Palaeolithic corridor into the Levant. The route of entry of the first modern humans into Europe was most likely via the Bosporus (which at that time was dry, with the Black Sea a freshwater lake).[3]

Matching genes to the dates on the stones

The tantalizing question is whether there are any genetic traces of this first entry into Europe. Astoundingly, there is in fact just one single mitochondrial line that has anything like that antiquity in Europe, and 'she' has an ancestor in the Near East. In other words, there is a fit, and most likely indicates that Europe was initially colonized by a single group. This insight does not come from opening a 'genetic history book' and looking for the right gene line with the right date – such books do not exist.[4] The tangled genetic prehistory of Europe is only just beginning to be teased apart. For a start, in the past 50,000 years Europe has seen multiple population movements and suffered massive extinctions in the ice age. Wars, invasions, and later migrations to and fro between Europe and the

Figure 3.1 Map of the suggested routes of spread of Aurignacian pioneers into Europe before 37,000 years ago. Only the earliest Aurignacian sites are shown (filled dots) – the dashed line represents natural routes along rivers, lowland and coast joining the dots. A parallel route from the Zagros to Karabom in the Russian Altai is shown.

Near East may have churned the human melting pot on several occasions.

A major international team of thirty-seven collaborators, headed by evolutionary geneticist Martin Richards, now of Huddersfield University, England, collected all available mtDNA data and recently showed us how it can be done. They reviewed nearly all existing prehistoric mitochondrial research on Europe, and using a carefully crafted set of rules to detect and eliminate errors, such as effects of back-migration, they identified eleven founder lines in Europe and eighteen potential source lines in the Near East.[5]

Using the genetic clock, Richards and his colleagues dated both the source lines in the Near East and the founder lines in Europe (Figure 3.2). Four of the source lines (J, T, U5, and I in the figure) in the Levant could be dated to between 45,000 and 55,000 years ago, suggesting that the Near East had itself been colonized around that time by lines that were daughters and granddaughters of Nasreen. As can be seen from Figure 3.3, these were of course great-granddaughter and granddaughter lines from L3, our single Out-of-Africa Eve. Given the quite wide error margins for mtDNA dates, 45,000–55,000 years ago still brackets the earliest Upper Palaeolithic dates, so the time of the colonization of the Near East seems to fit.[6]

The fifth daughter of Europa

Perhaps the most stunning conclusion of many reached in this comprehensive review of European maternal genetic prehistory is the identification and dating of Europe's first founder line, U5. Initially it was only U5, a genetic great-granddaughter of one of the four main Levantine founders, who moved into Europe (Figure 3.4). The Europa clan is characteristic of the Near East and Europe. In spite of its antiquity, it is not found in East Asia, being confined to the Levant and the Gulf, western Central Asia, countries round the Mediterranean, and Europe, with an ancient daughter branch, U2i, in

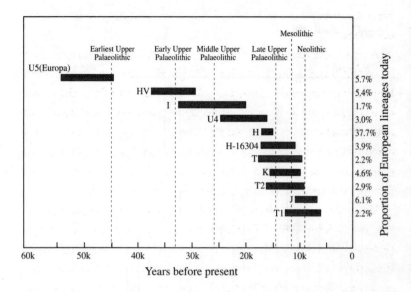

Figure 3.2 Estimated dates of intrusion (95% confidence range) of modern human mtDNA lines into Europe from the Near East, using founder analysis.[5] The earliest line is from Europa (U5), corresponding with the Earliest Upper Palaeolithic in Europe, followed by 'HV' corresponding with the Early Upper Palaeolithic, and 'I' corresponding with the Middle Upper Palaeolithic.[1]

India. The clan as a whole has an antiquity of over 50,000 years in the Near East. According to the molecular clock, our fifth daughter of Europa, U5, also dates back 50,000 years and represents by far the earliest line to enter Europe, 15,000 years before the next European founder line. But how is it that Europa's genetic signal spread to the Near East and, through her daughter U5, on to Europe, from 54,400 to 50,000 years ago, when the archaeological dates for the Upper Palaeolithic first appearing in the Levant, and then the earliest Aurignacian in Bulgaria, are respectively only 47,100 and 46,000 years? This difference can be explained by a systematic under-recording of radiocarbon dates for any age over 40,000 years, giving a ceiling effect.[7]

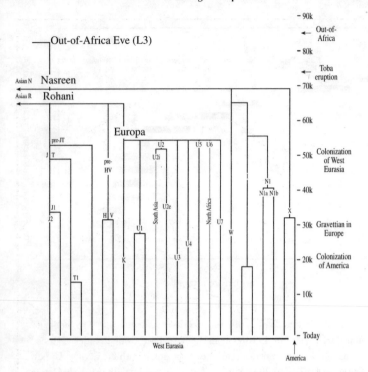

Figure 3.3   The West Eurasian mtDNA tree. As can be seen, Manju does not feature and, although Nasreen and Rohani date to between 65–70,000 years, expansion of West Eurasian lines only occurs after 55,000 years ago, corresponding with north-west movement from South Asia. Links with India[10], North Africa[9] and America (see Chapter 7[47]) in paler shade. Dating based on complete mtDNA sequence analysis (see Chapter 1[22]).

Although U5 apparently had her origins in the Near East at roughly the same time as her entry into Europe, her descendants are found there now only in a restricted area in minorities living mainly

Figure 3.4   Suggested routes of spread of gene lines into Europe. Grey line corresponds with the Earliest Upper Palaeolithic, remaining concentrated round the Mediterranean (Figure 3.1), black line with the later 'Early Upper Palaeolithic' entering from Eastern Europe and found more in north and western Europe.[3,5,8,14–19,28–37] (Y-chromosome lines are in italic – less securely dated than mtDNA.[29])

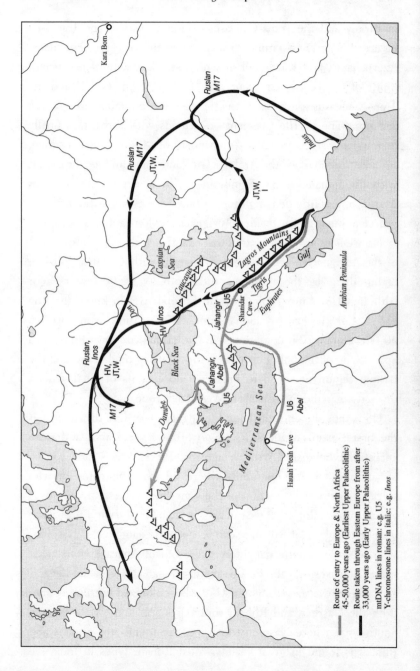

Kara Bom.

Ruslan
M17

Ruslan
M17

JT,W,
I

JT,W,
I

Indus

Zagros Mountains

Caspian
Sea

Gulf

Caucasus

Arabian Peninsula

Don

Inos

Tigris

Shanidar
Cave

U5

Euphrates

HV

Ruslan,
Inos

Jahangir

HV,
JT,W

Black Sea

Jahangir,
Abel

M17

Danube

U5

U6
Abel

Mediterranean Sea

Hauah Fteah Cave

Route of entry to Europe & North Africa
45–50,000 years ago (Earliest Upper Palaeolithic)

Route taken through Eastern Europe from after
33,000 years ago (Early Upper Palaeolithic)

mtDNA lines in roman: e.g. U5
Y-chromosome lines in italic: e.g. *Inos*

in Turkey and the Trans-Caucasus region of Turkey and Iran (see Figure 3.4). These minorities include the Turks, Armenians, Azerbaijanis, and Kurds, all of whom still live within the ancient limits of the Fertile Crescent that stretches from Turkey and the Trans-Caucasus south-east along the Zagros Mountains through Iraq and Iran. The Fertile Crescent co-extends with Kurdistan, finally forming a corridor parallel to but north of Mesopotamia, running towards the coast of the Arabian Gulf and thus linking the Levant with the Indian Ocean. Significantly, U5 is almost absent from Arabia, apparently denying those peoples' ancestors as the primary source population for the first Aurignacian colonization of Europe.

Do we have any genetic trail that exactly fits the rapid movement of the Aurignacian tool-makers, westward within central Europe, taking them to the Pyrenees and Spain by 40,000 years ago? Although U5 is now ubiquitous in Europe, we do know that the oldest Europa great-granddaughter, U5a, dating from around 40,000 years ago, is commonest in the Basque country of northern Spain. One of the only European refuges during the last ice age, the Basque region managed to preserve more of its original genetic diversity than did other parts of Western Europe.

U5 is thus the one surviving Europa daughter line that identifies the first European ancestors up to 50,000 years ago, and is an ancestral type shared with Armenians, Turks, Azeris, and Kurds. What do we know of her family, where did she come from, and who were her sisters? Inspection of the gene-line tree (see Figure 3.3) gives us a genealogy that we can recount in biblical style: Europa was genetic daughter of Rohani, who was genetic daughter of Nasreen, who was the genetic daughter of the out-of-Africa L3. By what route, however, did the Europa maternal clan arrive in the Levant, and where was her daughter U5, who colonized Europe, born? Both the Nasreen and Rohani root types are unknown except in South Asia, where Nasreen root types are found at low rates and Rohani is found in great variety. Most Rohani types in India are found nowhere else, and the great diversity of Rohani in India allows us to estimate when her line began to expand. This was at least 55,000 years ago, thus predating the arrival of Rohani's daughter Europa in the Levant and making a strong case for South Asia as the ultimate ancestral home of European lines. Even this expansion date is likely to be an underestimate of the age of the Rohani clan. Rohani may well be older than 55,000 years in Asia: much older estimates of the ages of two Asian subgroups of Rohani have been obtained in China.[8]

The first three of the seven Europa daughters were all 50,000 years old

The fifth genetic daughter of the Europa clan did have other sisters: there were seven Europa daughters, but only two of them were anything like the same age as U5. These were U6 and U2i, and neither was characteristic of Europeans. We have already come across U6 in North Africa. A unique identifier of Berbers, she has the same age as U5, 50,000 years, suggesting that as U5 moved north-west out of Turkey into Europe, U6 moved west round the southern shore of the Mediterranean to North Africa. We even have possible physical evidence of those North African pioneers arriving from the Levant. Early Upper Palaeolithic tools have been found at the Libyan coastal site of Haua Fteah probably starting from 40,000 years ago, and possibly reflecting this early invasion.[9]

The third of the Europa clan's three 50,000-year-old genetic daughters seems to have been born a quarter of the globe away from the Berbers of Libya, somewhere along the coast of the Indian Ocean. Accounting for 9.5 per cent of all Indian maternal lines and a massive 78 per cent of all Indian Europa lines, U2i is clearly home-grown in that region, with an age of 53,000 years in India. U2i is absent from the Levant and Europe, where we find a small European branch version, U2e, at half to two-thirds of her age.[10] (See Figure 3.3.)

Another pointer to the South Asian region as the ancestral source of the Europa clan is the finding of the ancestral root Europa type there and the origins of another Europa branch, U7, that subsequently spread in a small way to the Near East and Europe.[11]

The Fertile Crescent corridor opens

Our maternal gene tree thus suggests ultimately a 50,000-year-old South Asian origin for our oldest European founders. To arrive further north in Anatolia over 50,000 years ago they would have had to skirt the Libyan and Arabian Deserts, using the Fertile Crescent as a corridor. Given the rather generous margins of error on the molecular clock, for that trek up from the Zagros Mountains and Gulf marshes in south-west Iran, we should look at their migration from the perspective of climatic opportunity which, like the rings on a tree, gives us the most accurate dating. As I pointed out in Chapter 1, the Fertile Crescent corridor was dry, and was closed during much of the last 100,000 years, opening only briefly during climatic improvements called 'interstadials' (see Figure 1.7).

Between 55,000 and 65,000 years ago the world went through a period of almost unremitting cold and dryness. During this time the Fertile Crescent corridor was shut. Then, from 56,000 years ago onwards, there followed in quick succession a run of four warm and wet periods. The last of these, 51,000 years ago, was the warmest and most prolonged, lasting nearly 5,000 years. In fact, so warm and wet was this interstadial that the Indian monsoon was even wetter than it is today, and so, apart from the opening of the Fertile Crescent corridor, dry areas of the Levant such as the Negev Desert became potentially habitable for our Upper Palaeolithic toolmakers. If there was ever a time for us to multiply in South Asia and spread up to the Levant, this was it. The climatic and archaeological clock timings converge on the lush period between 45,000 and 50,000 years ago. So it looks as though the molecular clock's timing for the arrival of the earliest daughter lines of Nasreen and their families in the Levant is not far off.[12]

Adam's story

So, we have the story of the female Europa clan originating somewhere in South Asia over 50,000 years ago. The complete absence of the dominant Indian Manju clan in Europe and the Levant suggests that Europa, by contrast, may have been born to the west of India, even at the base of the Fertile Crescent near the ancient city of Ur on the Arabian Gulf. But of course, where there are mothers so also are there fathers. In Chapter 1, I briefly described the single Out-of-Africa Adam line and his three sons, Cain, Abel, and Seth, who left Africa by the southern route to people the world. All three genetic sons came from that single exodus.[13] Is there a similar story of the three sons of Out-of-Africa Adam, mirroring the tale of the two daughters of Out-of-Africa Eve in this particular trek from South Asia? Well, there is, and the geographical story of the descendants of at least one Y line, Seth, is even more specific than for the tale of Europa – although it is hard to date. (For another line, the Abel or YAP type, the argument may resolve one of the greatest puzzles in male genetic prehistory; see Chapter 4.) As with the story of Europa's daughters, we need to trace back from the twigs down to the branches to know in which direction the menfolk moved.

The descendants of Seth, son of Out-of-Africa Adam (Figure 3.5), are the most numerous in the world, let alone outside Africa. Along with Seth's root type, one of his five sons dominates the Middle East, accounting for between a quarter and half of all males in the region between Iran and the Mediterranean. According to a recent consensus reclassification this son is known as J, but I shall call him Jahangir, to reflect his putative South Asian origin. In West and South Eurasia he follows the Europa clan's distribution. The north-east coast of the Mediterranean Sea has the highest European rates of this genetic line. The Jahangir line reaches high frequencies

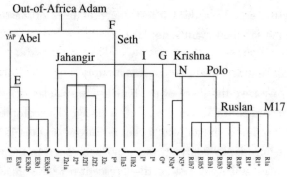

	Abel	Jahangir	M89	Inos	G	TAT/N	Ruslan	M17
Western Europe	0	0	0	3	0	0	4	0
Eastern Europe	0	0	1	2	0	3	0	3
Mediterranean Coast	2	2	0	1	1	0	1	2
Turkey and Levant	2	3	0-2	0	0	0	0	0
Southern Caucasus Region	0-1	1-3 (4 in Zagros)	0	0	2	0	1-3	0-2
Kurds & Turkmens (West Central Asia)	0	1-2	1-3	0	0	0	2-3	1
India & Pakistan (South Asia)	0	1	0-2	0	0	0	1	3

Key: 0=<7%; 1=7-20%; 2=20-30%; 3=30-50%; 4=>50%

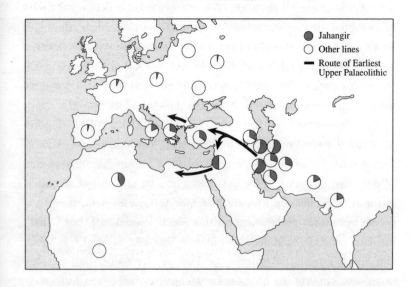

in the Levant (30–60 per cent). The highest European frequency is in Anatolia, at 40 per cent, followed by the Balkans and Italy at 20–30 per cent. While Jahangir is found throughout Europe, such high frequencies are concentrated around the Mediterranean. There are also high frequencies in North African countries, such as 41 per cent in Algeria.[14]

Such a Mediterranean distribution mirrors the spread of U5 and U6 50,000 years ago, so it is tempting to look back further south and east for the origins of Jahangir. When we do, the trail down the Fertile Crescent through Kurdistan becomes hotter the further south-east we go. Mostly above 35 per cent throughout Iran, the Jahangir male clan reaches frequencies of 55 per cent in the southern Caspian region and 59 per cent in the Zagros Mountains region further south. Jahangir is also found further south still, in Pakistan and India, and also in Central Asia and Siberia, but at lower frequencies.[15]

Clearly, frequency alone cannot tell us where a clan homeland is, but the diversity of genetic lines can help. Paris-based geneticist Lluís Quintana-Murci and colleagues argue for the ultimate origin of the Jahangir clan in the Zagros Mountains in south Kurdistan – the ancient land of Elam on the north-east bank of the Gulf. They have good reason, for the Zagros region has the greatest diversity of Jahangir types anywhere in the world. As I mentioned earlier, there is little agreement on calibration and methods of Y-chromosome dating, and most tend to underestimate dates; but one method gives

Figure 3.5 The West Eurasian Y-chromosome tree, geographical distribution and routes of entry. The tree is a subset of the eight main Y groups in West Eurasia (Consensus codes at end of each branch[13]). The table gives crude frequency of the same eight groups in three regions of Europe and four potential route locations en route from South Asia: e.g. Ruslan and M17 clearly enter through Eastern Europe, and high rates in Turkey and Mediterranean indicate southern entry to Europe – as shown in the map, where Jahangir has high rates and decreasing diversity from Pakistan to the Mediterranean.[14–16,19,29–37]

an age for Jahangir of around 42,000 years in Europe, 55,000 years in Iran and 49,000 years farther south in India. Clearly these dates would be consistent with the maternal genetic story, but, as with other Y lines, some other methods give much younger estimates.[16]

We have seen how the archaeological, climatic, and genetic stories of the first entry of modern humans into the Levant, and thence to both Europe and North Africa from around 50,000 years ago, can be drawn together. This South Asian origin for Europeans contrasts with the conventional view of a trail leading from North Africa round the Eastern Mediterranean into Europe, for which such combined evidence is scant.

We can instead trace dates and locations up the Fertile Crescent along the flanks of the Zagros range from the Gulf. A climatic opportunity to migrate up the Fertile Crescent through Kurdistan was provided by a prolonged interstadial warm spell. There is archaeological evidence for a homeland of the Aurignacian culture in the Zagros Mountains. The earliest Aurignacians in Europe appear in Bulgaria, not far from the Bosporus, around 47,000 years ago. When we look for genetic equivalents for such a migration, we find an early colonization of the Near East by multiple maternal lines, originating in the South but now characteristic of West Eurasia, around 50,000 years ago. There is no ancestral genetic provenance for these lines in North Africa, so the evidence points logically to the South Asian exodus. Three daughter lines of the Europa clan appear, around the same time as the colonization of the Levant, respectively as founders to India, North Africa, and Europe. Finally, a supporting trail for the maternal lines can be seen in the male line Jahangir, who also originated in South Asia, although there is less agreement on the date.

A second invasion of Europe: the Gravettian

From the Middle-Eastern tangle of Nasreen's line, Martin Richards and his colleagues teased out a second European migrant thread, and another stunning but different story. They called this second clan migrating into Europe HV, after the two daughter branches, H and V, which are found throughout Europe today (see Figures 3.2, 3.3 and 3.4). The second daughter line, V, did not appear until much later, in south-west Europe. The H descendants were to provide half of all western and northern European maternal lines, Slav, Finn, and Germanic in particular. This is clearly different from the very early U5 story. The expansion of HV has been dated to around 33,500 years ago – over 15,000 years later than U5, and 7,500 years before the next entrant. What is really interesting is that HV is considerably younger in the Near East (26,500 years) than in Europe (over 33,000 years), and much of her presence there may have been down to back-migration from Europe. This tends to rule out the Levant, Anatolia, and Bulgaria as homeland or source regions for HV, so we need to look for a route of entry into Europe for HV other than the Levant and Anatolia.[17]

A team of Estonian geneticists led by Richard Villems and Toomas Kivisild, whose seminal mtDNA work has brought Indian Palaeo-lithic genetic prehistory to the fore, have much to say on the origins and spread of HV. They point out that the earliest roots of HV are found in South Asia (in north-west India and Kashmir, perhaps 40,000 years ago), but that the Trans-Caucasus was the site of her first West Eurasian blooming.[18] (See Figure 3.4.) The Estonian work has suggested that the region around the Caucasus Mountains locked between the Black Sea and the Caspian was the Palaeolithic genetic starting point for several important early European migrant maternal clans, of which the most important was HV.

To many people, myself included, the word 'Caucasus' conjures up images of fierce and independent peoples in the south-west of the former Soviet Union, a region whose famous mountain range, the Caucasus, gives us the name 'Caucasian' – which for some obscure reason is used to describe Europeans as a whole. A tight patchwork of Caucasian languages certainly bears out this sense of ancient diversity. Hemmed in by a mixture of Indo-European and Altaic languages to the north and south, the Caucasus has two unique and ancient language families of its own, North Caucasian and Kartvellian. The region, bounded on the west and east by two inland seas and spanned by the Caucasus Mountains, forms the only usable corridor between Armenia and Azerbaijan down in the Levant and European Russia to the north (see Figure 3.4).

Can the male chromosome help any in tracing a second migration to Europe? To make up for the limited accuracy of dating with Y chromosomes, they are much more illuminating in their intra-regional specificity than mtDNA. Notable is an enigmatic male clan (see Figure 3.5) which I shall call Inos, after Seth's son Enos. Inos is almost exclusively European. According to the Leicester-based geneticist Zoë Rosser and colleagues, the relatively even distribution of this male clan indicates an early entry to Europe. Italian geneticist Ornella Semino and her colleagues from America are more specific, pointing out that the predominance of Inos in Ukraine and the Balkans suggests an association with the HV maternal clan and with the Gravettian culture. Like HV, Inos does not have a clear origin in the Levant, so a Trans-Caucasus route is a possibility. [19]

A gap in occupation of the Near East?

Before we get too carried away with such genetic speculation, we need to be clear on what the archaeological record tells us about the earliest modern human occupation of the Caucasus corridor. In the last chapter we saw that, at least in West Eurasia, the arrival of modern humans was associated with a change from the Mousterian (Middle Palaeolithic) tools used by Neanderthals to the Upper Palaeolithic tools used by Modern Europeans. In the Levant, the earliest changes from Mousterian to transitional Upper Palaeolithic industries have been found to the south, in what are now the Negev and Sinai Deserts, between around 45,000 and 47,000 years ago (see Figure 3.1). There was then a long gap in habitation of around 10,000 years before the south was re-occupied by humans making

Early Upper Palaeolithic tools of the so-called Ahmarian type, a culture which lasted until 20,000 years ago. This hiatus coincided with a climatic worsening characterized by two cold, dry snaps climaxing 45,000 and 40,000 years ago.[20]

Between 34,000 and 40,000 years ago, the world remained dry and cold, and there was no significant Indian monsoon. The prolonged warming that began again 34,000 years ago invited reoccupation of the drier parts of the Levant.[21] This time there was another reoccupation, of a famous cave far to the north at the top of the Fertile Crescent in the northern Zagros Mountains. Shanidar Cave nestles at the southern gate of the Caucasus corridor.

Shanidar Cave (see Figure 3.1), near where the modern-day borders of Turkey, Iran, and Iraq come together in northern Kurdistan, just south of Armenia, was made famous at the end of the 1960s by Ralph Solecki, an archaeologist who discovered what he regarded as evidence of Neanderthal burial with flowers. The Neanderthal occupation lasted from over 50,000 years until about 46,000 years ago. Then, after a climatic gap of 10,000 years, another human species became its new tenant. A transitional Upper Palaeolithic industry known as Baradostian appeared in Shanidar Cave around 35,500 years ago and lasted until 28,700 years ago. This is presently the best evidence for modern human occupation at the southern entrance to the Caucasus around that time.[22]

Also about this time, 36,400 years ago, the first Upper Palaeolithic colonization of European Russia appeared high up the river Don, at Kostenki, due north of the Caucasus.[23] The so-called Spitsynians made tools from flint imported from 150–300 km (100–200 miles) away. The Kostenki location later became famous for its extraordinary complex mammoth-based culture, between 24,000 and 33,000 years ago, but the pioneer Spitsynians showed nothing of this.

Several archaeological experts on Europe before the ice age see European Palaeolithic prehistory as having several distinct early phases of increased occupation corresponding to climatic improve-ment. The first of these, the Earliest Upper Palaeolithic between 33,000–45,000 years ago, was characterized by the spread of the earliest Aurignacian technology, which we have already discussed. The second phase, the Early Upper Palaeolithic between 24,000–33,000 years ago, heralds the start of the high cultural peaks of the Upper Palaeolithic. Cultures taking off from around 30,000 years ago, during this phase, are known collectively as 'the Gravettian technocomplex', although local name variations add confusing variety. Although the Gravettian really constitutes a third phase of high occupation and new culture in Europe, Palaeolithic expert Clive Gamble argues that the important cultural threshold of this second era in Europe as a whole started in north-eastern Europe around 33,000 years ago, for example at Kostenki on the Don, and not with the Gravettian, farther south-west, 30,000 years ago.[24]

The main cultural innovations of the Gravettian were the system-atic mining of high-grade raw materials, high-grade cave art, elabor-ate burials, large bone tool sets, the use of bone – particularly mammoth – for houses (see Plate 22), and highly specialized mammoth-hunting. In summary, the Early Upper Palaeolithic cul-tures not only reveal an accelerating advance in European repre-sentational art, use of exotic materials, and burial practice, but may also have represented an intrusion of peoples carrying the seeds of such cultural practices from Eastern Europe. This invasion of culture and people did not remain in Eastern Europe, finding some of its highest artistic expression in southern France and northern Spain.[25]

Can we reconcile the HV genetic signal of modern human expan-sion into Northern and Western Europe with the arrival of the Early Upper Palaeolithic around 33,000 years ago? The short answer is yes: there is a clear, single female genetic signal at the right date, there is an obvious route for her to have taken, and there is a male counterpart. The HV clan may thus represent the earliest movement of modern humans into northern Europe via the Trans-Caucasus.

Where did she go next? Probably everywhere. As we have seen, HV is the commonest clan in Europe, but her descendants are still commoner in northern and south-western Europe than around the Mediterranean coast. She had a daughter – the European V clan – much later, around the Pyrenean area, but recent studies show an older pre-V type in the Trans-Caucasus, the northern Balkans, southern Spain, and Morocco, suggesting an early westward progression across Europe from the Ukraine.[26] (See Figure 3.4.)

Could the ancestors of the Early Upper Palaeolithic people have come from farther east?

There is, however, just the possibility that HV's homeland before she moved into Europe was not the Trans-Caucasus but further east, across the Central Asian steppe. In this scenario the north Caucasus region would have received migration from Central Asia, east of the Caspian Sea, rather than from Armenia in the south. Essentially this means moving north into Russia via a route to the east of the Caspian Sea rather than to the west of it.

Much has been made of a group of perfectly preserved Caucasoid mummies found in Urumchi, Chinese Turkestan, and dated to about 3,000 years old, and others in Central Asian locations along the Silk Road. Whether these represent a Neolithic spread of Indo-European-speaking tribes towards the East or descendants of some more ancient local population, there is actually archaeological evidence for the occupation of Central Asia by modern humans from before 40,000 years ago. Early Upper Palaeolithic technology has been found in two sites in the Russian Altai, spreading to south-east Siberia by 39,000 years ago. This does mean there were modern humans in Central Asia early enough to have provided the base for an invasion into Europe through Russia.[27]

A third of today's Central Asian genetic stocks are West Eurasian 'Nasreen' maternal lines. Half of these consist of HV stock. The usual explanation for this 'Europe in Asia' presence is a recent

eastward European emigration along the Silk Road. The problem
with this argument is that HV's common European daughter V, who
might be expected to have joined such a movement, is absent from
Central Asia. Furthermore, most of the other West Eurasian
Nasreen lines in Central Asia look more like they have come directly
from India than from Europe. In other words, HV could have
originally come from South Asia, round the east of the Caspian Sea,
and then gone the other way, westward into Europe (see Figure
3.4). There is Y-chromosomal support for this view of an alternative
east-west route for South Asian genetic clans entering Europe via a
Central Asian detour.[28]

Asian men in Europe

The Y chromosome, being so much larger, should hold far more
secrets of our past than does mitochondrial DNA, that tiny trace of
our ancient microbial invader. But geneticists are only beginning to
unravel it, and have yet to fully master the trick of Adam's genetic
clock. Dates of branches vary enormously from one research group
to another, and are generally anything from twice to five times
younger than the equivalent dates on the mtDNA tree. In other
words, there is a good Y trail but researchers often underestimate
how old it is. Luckily, the careful analysis of founder lines and
mtDNA dating carried out by Martin Richards and his colleagues,
and others such as Toomas Kivisild, provide a framework of genetically dated routes on which to fit the Y trail. Here for the moment
we can use the Y tree to look much more closely at the geographical
routes of spread.[29]

Stanford geneticist Peter Underhill's extraordinary achievement
at the end of 2000 of building a world tree with 150 Y markers was
quickly followed by a more detailed look at Europe by Ornella
Semino and colleagues in Underhill's team.[30] This showed even
more clearly than the mtDNA story that Europe must have had
several routes of colonization.

We have seen how, in parallel with the daughters of Europa, Jahangir, a grandson of the out-of-Asian founder line through Seth, may have spread up the Fertile Crescent from the Gulf, thus making the first southern entry through Turkey and into Europe. Can we see any other male lines – apart from Inos – to parallel HV, who came out of the Caucasus, or even further east in Russia, and travelled through the Ukraine to western Europe? The answer is yes, and with much clearer trails. I have already mentioned Inos as type who could mirror HV in the north Caucasus. There are three more candidate genetic lines for an eastern entry to Europe that tease geneticists with their distribution, age, and origin. Like Inos (and Jahangir), they are all ultimately descended from Seth, the third son of Out-of-Africa Adam. Two of these lines very clearly come from the East, probably Central Asia, but how recently did they arrive, and where did they ultimately come from?' They are both descendants of the most prolific of Seth's five genetic sons, 'K, whom I shall call Krishna after the Indian deity of the same name.[31] (See Figures 3.4 and 3.5)

One of these two eastern genetic lines is called TAT, after its signature mutation, and by remarkable coincidence echoes the name of the Oxford-based geneticist Tatiana Zergal, whose name is most associated with him. In Europe he is confined to the eastern fringe, where he is most evident among eastern Baltic Finns and Russians. His origin is most likely to be Central Asian, although his genetic father and grandfather derive ultimately from Kashmir and South Asia. He is found in low frequency in the Far East as well. Again the dates are vague because we are looking at Y chromosomes, but the very local distribution (mainly among Uralic speakers) and low diversity in Europe suggest a migration from Central Asia.[32]

The other European intruder from Krishna's line is defined by the M17 mutation. The Hungarians achieve the highest frequency of this M17 line, at 60 per cent. The M17 line dominates Eastern Europe, and although he spread to all parts of western and southern Europe and the Levant, he is always found at low frequency in those places.

His low frequency in the Levant tends to undermine that region as a route into Europe. Lluís Quintana-Murci, Peter Underhill and their colleagues see Central Asia, especially the Altai, as the most likely source of the European M17 line. This is a necessary argument for Underhill and co-workers since they see the whole Seth clan as coming separately out of North Africa into the Levant and proceeding directly to Central Asia.[33] (See Figure 1.3.)

For me and for Toomas Kivisild, South Asia is logically the ultimate origin of M17 and his ancestors; and sure enough we find highest rates and greatest diversity of the M17 line in Pakistan, India, and eastern Iran, and low rates in the Caucasus. M17 is not only more diverse in South Asia than in Central Asia, but diversity *characterizes* its presence in isolated tribal groups in the south, thus undermining any theory of M17 as a marker of a 'male Aryan invasion' of India. One estimate for the age of this line in India is as much as 36,000 years while the European age is only 23,000. All this suggests that M17 could have found his way initially from India or Pakistan, through Kashmir, then via Central Asia and Russia, before finally coming to Europe. As an aside, these and similar observations for other Seth lines in South Asia form an important part of my counter-argument to the view of Seth entering Central Asia from North Africa and the Levant (rather than by my preferred single, southern out-of-Africa route).[34]

To return to Europe, while the origins of the European M17 line to the east of Europe in the Altai or beyond seem clear, the dates of that east–west migration are anything but. Semino and colleagues dispense with genetic dating and instead have both M17 and his father, M173, as part of an archaeologically dated Palaeolithic movement from the east to the west 30,000 years ago. Which brings us to M173, the other strong candidate male Asian line in Europe. He belongs to a very large clan that I shall call Ruslan, after a Russian folk hero.[35]

Ruslan: Asian progenitor of half of Europe's men

Spread throughout the Old World from England to South and Central Asia, Siberia, and beyond – even to Australia and America, the Ruslan clan is well travelled, and his root type is the commonest single Y type in the world according to one study. Yet Ruslan's genetic father, P, whom I shall call Polo after the family of Silk Road explorers, is confined to India, Pakistan, Central Asia, and America. Study of the geographical distribution and the diversity of genetic branches and stems again suggests that Ruslan, along with his son M17, arose early in South Asia, somewhere near India, and subsequently spread not only south-east to Australia but also north, directly to Central Asia, before splitting east and west into Europe and East Asia (see Chapters 5 and 6).[36]

Unlike his son M17, Ruslan does not lurk at the threshold in Eastern Europe. In fact he is very much commoner in the west, reaching 86 per cent in Basques and similar high rates in the British Isles. This back-to-front distribution of father and son suggests that the former may have arrived in Europe earlier. As we shall see in Chapter 6, this can be explained by the ice age. Suffice it to say here that although M17 may be a relative newcomer to Europe, his father Ruslan is possibly the strongest male marker line for the original Early Upper Palaeolithic invasion of western Europe from the east around 33,000 years ago. Between them, this father-and-son team account for 50 per cent of extant European male lines today.[37]

Europe's Asian roots

This trip through genetic and human time has suggested two extraordinary conclusions: first, that the Europeans' genetic homeland was originally in South Asia in the Pakistan/Gulf region over 50,000 years ago; and second, that the Europeans' ancestors followed at least two widely separated routes to arrive, ultimately, in the same cold but rich garden. The earliest of these routes was the Fertile Crescent, which opened 51,000 years ago as a corridor from the Gulf, allowing movement up through Turkey and eventually to Bulgaria and Southern Europe. This seems to coincide with the Aurignacian cultural movement into Europe. The second early route from South Asia to Europe may have been up the Indus into Kashmir and on to Central Asia, where perhaps more than 40,000 years ago hunters first started bringing down game as large as mammoths. Some of these hunters with their elaborate technical skills may then have moved westward across the Urals to European Russia and on to the Czech Republic and Germany. A more conservative view of this eastern invasion might be that the Trans-Caucasus, rather than Central Asia, was the earliest route of modern human entry into Russia.

4

FIRST STEPS INTO ASIA, FIRST LEAP TO AUSTRALIA

IN CHAPTER 1 WE SAW EVIDENCE for a single out-of-Africa genetic line, L3, whose two daughter lines, Manju and Nasreen, jointly peopled the rest of the world. This single genetic line is central to the logic of a single southern exodus. As we saw in Chapter 3, the fact that, uniquely, Europeans are descended solely from the Nasreen clan fixes the origin of their branch to a colony early on the route out of Africa, probably near the Gulf. The absence of any of the root daughter genetic branches of either Manju or Nasreen in North Africa or the Levant, and their abundance in India, excludes the northern route into Europe and confirms the southern route across the mouth of the Red Sea. We shall now look in more detail at the genetic and other evidence for the earliest primary colonization of South Asia and the coastline of the Indian Ocean beyond. The Y chromosome now enters the story more fully, along with some genetic markers other than the Adam and Eve genes. South Asia includes all the countries initially found along that pioneering beachcombing trail round the northern shores of the Indian Ocean.

Survivors of the great trek: place and time

If all non-Africans share one ancestral origin, the date of exit for the ancestors of aboriginal Australians is the same as for Europeans, Indians, and Chinese. All their trails should lead back to one point in space and time; and all the colonies, left behind en route, should hold genetic and even physical keys to who went that way. This is the case. We can look at the mtDNA or Y chromosomes from anyone outside Africa, and find them a place on their respective single branch of the out-of-Africa genetic tree. Exactly where they are on their out-of-Africa branch very often tells us how they got there and even, sometimes, when.

We should not be tempted into trying to draw firm conclusions from genetic dates in isolation. The exact branching *structure* of the tree and the geographical distribution of the branches are often much more revealing than are dates for them derived from the molecular clock.[1] Those dates are rather approximate and should always be weighed against of the rest of the evidence, namely the climatic record, which tells us when there were windows of opportunity for or constraints against migration, and of course the archaeological record, where present.

The archaeological beach trail is inevitably very faint. Between 60,000 and 85,000 years ago the sea level fluctuated between 40 and 100 metres (130 and 330 feet) below its present level, so the beaches and even the hinterlands our ancestors wandered along and frequented are now mostly deeply submerged. But there are exceptions to the effects of this watery blanket, as we shall see.

Along the coastline of the Indian Ocean we still find small colonies of so-called aboriginal peoples who may be descended locally from those first beachcombers. Long before the study of mtDNA, the first reasons for calling these groups aboriginals were that their cultures and appearance marked them out from the people surrounding them: some had features in common with Africans, such as frizzy hair and very dark skin. I shall discuss the more objective genetic and physical evidence to support these impressions here and in the next chapter, but it is worth first naming some of the groups in question.

Such peoples are often called by controversial and presumptive terms such as 'Australoid', 'Negroid', and 'Negrito' to indicate how they differ from surrounding peoples. Starting from the South Arabian coast in the west there are the Hadramaut, who have been described as Australoid but almost certainly contain an element of much more recent African admixture. On the coast of Pakistan around the mouth of the Indus are found the Makrani Negroid ethnic groups. Again, there is genetic and historical evidence to support a major recent African admixture as a result of the slave trade. This may not be the case for other so-called Negroid types, such as are found in India, including the Kadar and Paniyan. There are also a number of other South Asian aboriginal groups including the so-called Proto-Australoid ethnic groups, such as the Korava, Yanadi, Irula, Gadaba, and Chenchu of India, and the Veddas of Sri Lanka. Recent work on two of these groups, the Chenchus and Koyas, has strongly suggested not only that their ancestral mtDNA and Y chromosomes were uniquely shared with other South and West Asians, but that they are characteristic of the earliest genetic heritage of the region. Their beach-settling ancestors from Africa would have provided the genetic seeds for the subsequent differentiation of the distinctive East and West Eurasian gene pools, and they would have received only limited gene flow from other regions since then.[2]

The Andaman Islands, situated between India and Southeast Asia in the Bay of Bengal, include several groups with preliterate traditional cultures and a very distinctive, so-called African appearance. The groups least affected by outside intrusions are the Jarawa and the Onge, who live in the most southerly Andamans. Recent genetic studies still being analysed may help to elucidate their maternal and paternal origins. On the maternal side, the Onge and Jarawa feature two distinct mitochondrial groups which nevertheless both place them in the Manju super-clan, thus confirming fellowship of the single out-of-Africa migration. These genetic lines show connections to the base of two ancient and unique Indian Manju clans, M2 and M4. M2 is the oldest and most diverse Indian Manju group and is also the commonest mtDNA component among the Indian aboriginal groups mentioned above. On the paternal side, the Onge and Jarawa possess only the Abel clan (the rarest of the three out-of-Africa Y lines, and known as Group D or Asian YAP). This is all consistent with the view that the Onge and Jarawa have remained as isolated groups since the early beachcombing sweep round the Indian Ocean. The other aboriginal groups in these islands, known as the Greater Andamanese, are slightly different culturally and physically. Genetically, while they share branches of the same two unique Manju genetic lines, significantly their Y chromosomes all come from another of the three sons of Out-of-Africa Adam, Seth (see Figures 4.2–4.4).[3]

Farther along the trail are the so-called Negrito peoples of the Malay Peninsula, known generally as the Semang (see Plate 16), and perhaps the best known of the candidate remnants of the old beachcombers. Another relict group possibly left over from the beachcombers in Indo-China and the Malay Peninsula are the so-called Aboriginal Malays, who are physically intermediate between the Semang and Mongoloid populations (see Chapter 5). Crucially, they hold clues to the earliest branches of an mtDNA line now characteristic of Mongoloid populations, known as the F clan. This founder East Asian maternal pre-F line in Malay aboriginals is also shared with groups across the water in the Greater Andamans, discussed above, as well as with people in the Nicobar Islands a little farther south.[4]

I shall have more to say, in this and the next chapter, about the various peoples and colonies thought to be left over from that first great trek along the coastline of the Indian Ocean. As always, what is most important to bear in mind is that the genetic tree tells us this was not an earlier out-of-Africa venture, as has been thought by some archaeologists and palaeontologists. It was the vanguard of colonization of the entire Old World.

Curiously, some of the best, if not the only archaeological evidence for dating the beachcombers' trek along the coast of the Indian Ocean comes not from India, South Arabia, or Africa, but from the later parts of the trail – the Malay Peninsula, New Guinea, and Australia. So we shall take a trip there first to look at those who travelled farthest round the Indian Ocean, the New Guineans and the Australians.

The first Australians

Perhaps more academic heat has been generated over *which* humans first got to Australia, and *when*, than over any other question on the archaeology of the region. The 'which?' question, a rallying call for multiregionalists with their repetitive arguments about different regional skull shapes derived from earlier humans (see Chapter 1), is looking less and less relevant in the face of increasing genetic evidence that all modern Australians and New Guineans belong to either the Nasreen or the Manju clan.[5] In other words, they are not a special case, nor are they an earlier type of human or modern humans mixed with local *Homo erectus*. The mounting evidence has not stopped rearguard, Spielberg-like attempts by multiregionalists to use extremely ancient DNA to resuscitate their case. However, the evidence now available comes down on the side of antipodeans belonging to the same single out-of-Africa L3 migration as everyone else (for a discussion of recent developments on this thorny issue, see note [6]). The 'when?' question is now coming much more to the fore. Historians like to peg events on dates rather than be satisfied with a simple chronological order, so I shall deal with dates first, although they will probably be the last issue to be finally resolved.

The earliest generally accepted archaeological evidence of modern human colonization outside Africa has, until recently, been Australian – but this is a rapidly changing field. Until the 1990s, there was no clear evidence for humans in Australia or New Guinea before 40,000 years ago. It now seems that, as with datings for Europe, this was largely due to the limitations of the radiocarbon method of dating. But then new methods of dating began to be applied. One approach, the so-called luminescence dating of silica, enabled researchers to probe beyond the radiocarbon limit of 40,000 years. In 1990, the Australian geologist-cum-archaeologist team of Richard Roberts and Rhys Jones reported dates between 50,000 and 60,000 years ago for the first occupation of a rock shelter (see Figure 4.1) on the coast of Arnhem Land, in northern Australia. Arnhem Land is directly opposite Timor, the nearest island of the Indonesian archipelago and therefore the most likely casting-off point for the first Australians.[7]

Then Australian 'dates' took a rather more dramatic turn and, as it were, came off the wall. In 1996, archaeologist Robert Fullagar examined the rock art site of Jinmium. The wall of this shelter is covered in artefactual dents known as pecked cupules, and Fullagar reported that a fallen fragment of engraved sandstone, buried in sediments, had been dated in two independent estimates to 50,000 and 75,300 years ago. He even recovered stone artefacts from levels dated by thermoluminescence to between 116,000 and 176,000 years ago, which would have made it the oldest known human occupation site on the continent, and two to three times as old as the Arnhem Land shelters mentioned above. These new dates caused a furore. But the problem appeared to be solved when it was shown that contamination by sand grains from fallen rubble had produced the wildly old dates for the earth surrounding the arte-facts. In other words, the dates were wrong, and analysis of individual grains of sand helped to detect and overcome inaccuracies caused by contamination. The oldest dates of human occupation in Australia have therefore remained around 60,000 years.[8]

Controversially, human occupation dates as old as 62,000 years ago were also recently published, based on several different methods applied to earth surrounding the skeleton of a gracile Anatomically Modern Human found at Lake Mungo in the Willandra Lakes region of south-east Australia. One of these reports pointed out that, to have been there so long ago, the first Australians must have crossed earlier at a previous low sea level. The low-sea window of opportunity to get to Australia 70,000 to 60,000 years ago suggests that the anatomically modern Lake Mungo people really were among the oldest on that continent, since the previous low sea level was another 80,000 years before, and near the dawn of our species.[9]

Only one window of opportunity

Whatever the academic claims and counter-claims, there seems now to be a convergence of evidence from a variety of sites that points to a human presence in Australia as far back as 60,000 years ago. This date followed a very deep lowstand of the world's oceans caused by an increase in water locked up in the northern ice caps, and took Australia's shores to around 100 metres (330 feet) vertically below today's levels. Although the date of lowest sea level of that glacial period was 65,000 years ago, the world's oceans only fell below 100 metres briefly at that point, and then rose rather rapidly.[10]

The presence of humans on the north-west coast of Australia from 62,000 years ago does not necessarily date their actual arrival from overseas at that time, since the sea-level was at its lowest 3,000 years earlier. There would have been more difficulty in getting to Australia if 62,000 years ago really was the date of arrival. The actual depth of the lowstand makes a big difference to the chances of successfully crossing the sea from Timor to Australia. From a contour map of sea-level depths off the north coast of Australia, we can see that the distance between Australia and Timor increases from

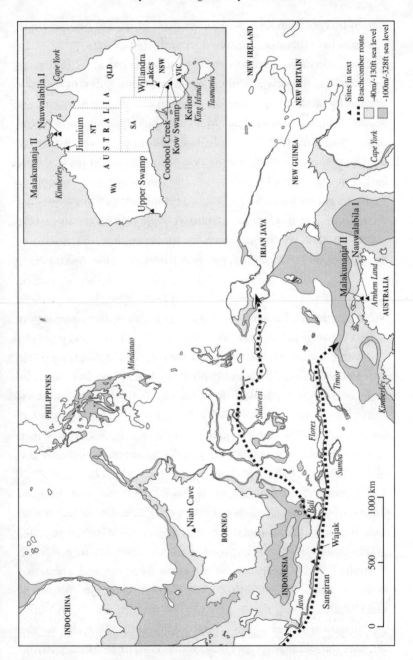

160 km at −100 metres, and 220 km at −40 metres, to 470 km at −20 metres (100 miles at 330 feet, 135 miles at 130 feet, 290 miles at 65 feet). (Figure 4.1.) The difference between 160 and 220 km may seem small but, until 6,000 years ago, 180 km (110 miles) was the absolute limit of inter-island sea crossings anywhere in the world. The oldest instance of this length of crossing, for which there is archaeological evidence, is the colonization of Manus Island, north of New Guinea, by about 20,000 years ago. So, unless there was a single long-drift colonization of Australia, the window of opportunity to get to Australia was at 65,000 years ago − in order to be visible in the Australian archaeological record from the period 55,000–62,000 years ago. In any case, colonization of Australia solely by random accidental drifts is an unlikely scenario in view of the genetic evidence for multiple founding Australian maternal lines. Such a date of arrival is consistent with a 68,000-year-old genetic date estimated for the expansion of Australian populations.[11]

We also have to put evidence of occupation 60,000 years ago into another context: there is evidence of shell middens from some of the earliest Australian sites. Presumably, then, the first people in north-west Australia were still beachcombing when they arrived. If they were, we would not expect to find any dated evidence of their initial presence on the seashore, since the Timor Sea has now advanced up to 500 km (300 miles), covering those first beach habitations. The first datable evidence in north-west Australia following a lowstand entry 65,000 years ago would naturally be from above the next highstand. This highstand occurred between 50,000 and 60,000 years ago and took the sea level to only

Figure 4.1   Last leap to Australia. Shows Southeast Asia (Sundaland) and Australia/New Guinea (Sahulland) as they would have looked 70,000 years ago with the low sea stand of −80m. Beachcombing as far as Bali was dry-footed, but after that there were two routes to Sahul involving island-hopping. Up to Timor this was always easier in the south; thereafter the sea-level window was crucial.

40 metres (131 feet) below today's, and the beach nearer to its present location. A beach close to the Arnhem Land rock shelters 50,000–60,000 years ago is consistent with projected sea levels and with geologist Richard Roberts' dates of 50,000–60,000 years ago for the occupation of those sites. With this sea-dependent lag period between colonization and archaeological evidence of occupation, the next available lowstand 47,000 years ago would clearly have been too late for sea-crossing and an archaeologically visible presence any earlier than 45,000 years ago.[12]

Although Australia's neighbour, the giant island of New Guinea, appears to pose an identical seafaring problem for would-be colonists, there are significant differences. There is a distinct possibility that New Guinea was colonized even earlier than Australia. First of all, there are two stepping-stone routes across the islands of eastern Indonesia (see Figure 4.1). As we have seen, the direct route to Australia from Timor requires a very low sea level for any chance of survival across the long last leg, across the Timor Sea. The natural route to New Guinea via Sulawesi and the Moluccas, however, has shorter inter-island distances and is virtually unaffected by changing sea levels. From each island along the way the next was visible. The islands have steep shorelines, and the voyage to New Guinea passed across very little continental shelf. As a result, sea-level changes made little difference to inter-island distances, and it was an equally easy (or difficult) trip at any time after our ancestors arrived in Borneo overland.[13]

One could ask whether there is any evidence that the Australians did not take this alternative but slightly longer northern route, since Australia was actually connected to New Guinea throughout this period. The genetic picture tells us that there are no shared clans between Australians and New Guineans, and that New Guineans are as genetically distant from Australians as they are from any other non-African peoples. Not only that, but estimates of the times of expansion for indigenous New Guinea mtDNA clans are around

77,000 years, much older than for Australians. This suggests that New Guinea may have been colonized before Australia, and also that Australian clans were not descended from New Guinean ones; in other words, the first Australian colonists may have found it easier to follow an unoccupied island trail, albeit the more challenging one.[14]

This tempting genetic story, which is consistent with the extreme antiquity and independence of the colonization of Australia and New Guinea, is not matched by much dated archaeological evidence from the islands of eastern Indonesia or New Guinea. Until recently there was no evidence for human presence along either of these two island trails across eastern Indonesia much more than 40,000 let alone 65,000 years ago. Exciting new evidence from Flores, one of the largest islands on the southern route, now could change all that. A deep (7 metres, 23 feet) pit excavated in Liang Bua cave on Flores has revealed a continuous archaeological record spanning 840,000 years. Liang Bua could play a significant role in providing cultural and palaeontological evidence for much of that period, including the date of arrival of modern humans. Two human species occupied the cave over that period. The first human occupants were probably not modern. Estimated dates for modern human occupation are still under review, but may be the best evidence yet for dating the early arrival of modern humans in East Asia.[15]

Now, if, following the window-of-opportunity argument, the actual colonization of Australia was 65,000 years ago, and Flores and even New Guinea were colonized 75,000 years ago, we have to start asking how long before that would modern humans have had to leave Africa in order to trek all the way to the South Seas. Short of a guess, that question is remarkably difficult to answer. For a start, we cannot tell how long it took our beachcombers to literally eat their way right down to Timor or Sulawesi unless they left some evidence as they went. As is clear from the sea-level record, however, the beaches our ancestors combed over 60,000–85,000 years ago are now well beneath the sea, so that we should not expect to find much of the evidence – unless we go diving.

Oldest relics of the beachcombing trail?

There is also the problem that if our forefathers left Africa over 70,000 years ago, they could initially have been making and using old-fashioned tools that were largely similar to the ones used by archaic *Homo sapiens*, who may have left Africa at least 100,000 years earlier (see the Prologue). Such Middle Palaeolithic tools are abundant in India from as long ago as 160,000 years, and are therefore not very helpful as markers for the arrival of Anatomically Modern Humans. Middle Palaeolithic tools also abound in the sands of the southern coast of the Arabian Peninsula, but they have not been dated with much certainty. The Yemen, my suggestion for the landing point of the single exodus, has not received much recent archaeological attention, but stone tools similar to those of the African late Middle Stone Age have been found there.[16]

The early Australian archaeological dates and the suggestion of even older colonization of New Guinea have been reinforced by an extraordinary reappraisal of the Kota Tampan Palaeolithic culture found in Lenggong Valley, in Perak on the Malay Peninsula, two-thirds of the way from Africa to Australia. This culture first identified by the find of large, curious, and rather crude pebble tools, fashioned on one side only, was thought by archaeologists in the 1960s to be the work of an earlier human species. When the geological layers surrounding the tools were reassessed, it became clear they were more recent. Wider interest was sparked in 1975, when Tom Harrison, the colourful curator of the Sarawak Museum, tried to relate the tools to the great eruption of the Sumatran volcano Toba. His suggestion, based on examination of the volcanic ash that surrounded the tools and the site, set off a hare which has only recently slowed down enough for others to get a good view.[17]

No one has done more research into Kota Tampan and the Lenggong Valley culture than archaeologist Zuraina Majid, of the Universiti Sains Malaysia in Penang. Her extensive work at a number of sites in the Lenggong Valley suggests that a local pebble-tool culture may have existed from the days of that great Toba volcanic eruption right up until 7,000 or even only 4,000 years ago.[18] If that is so, it may provide the answer to one of the most nagging questions about the unifacial oval pebble tools: who made them? On the face of it, these are by no stretch of the imagination sophisticated tools. Better-looking tools were made long before in Africa and Europe by archaic humans, so why should anyone think that the unifacial pebbles encased in volcanic ash had been made by modern humans living at the time of Toba?

Two of the highest authorities on the Southeast Asian Palaeolithic, Australian archaeologists Peter Bellwood and Sandra Bowdler, agree with Zuraina Majid and Tom Harrison to the extent that these tools were most likely made by Anatomically Modern Humans. For a start, the dates for most of the pebble tools found in the Lenggong Valley are too recent for them to have been made by anyone else. Second, no pre-modern humans have ever been found in the Malay Peninsula, let alone the Lenggong Valley. Zuraina's trump card in this respect is the much publicized finding by her team of 'Perak Man' in the Gunung Runtuh cave in the Lenggong Valley in 1990. Surrounded by the same class of pebble tools, this complete skeleton of a modern human was described by experts as having Australo Melanesian characteristics. He was about 10,000 years old. This clear recent association of pebble tools with modern humans undermines the argument that the Kota Tampan pebble tools were too crude to be the work of moderns. The same locality also provides a continuity link with the older tools, which Zuraina argues is supported by technical comparisons. So, for the moment at least, Perak Man is the best local evidence that the older pebble tools encased in ash were made by the same (modern) human species.[19]

Another venerable expert on the archaeology of Southeast Asia is Richard Shutler. He makes the more general point that these kinds of tools were first brought to Island Southeast Asia by *Homo sapiens* about 70,000 years ago. (Island Southeast Asia, or ISEA – as opposed to Mainland Southeast Asia – means all the islands of Indonesia and the Philippines, excluding West New Guinea but including all of Borneo.) Shulter cautions against the view that such tools reflect cultural backwardness, agreeing with others that the quality of the available raw material determined what could be used for tools, and that for more sophisticated implements such as knives, bamboo was more likely to have been used.[20]

So how old was that Kota Tampan ash? When it was first dated, several decades ago, the result came out at 31,000 years old. This date for ash from the Toba volcano has always worried geologists, and even archaeologists such as Peter Bellwood.[21] The trouble is that Toba did not undergo a massive explosion at that time. Toba's last big bang, the largest explosion in the world in the past 2 million years, came much earlier, 71,000–74,000 years ago. More recently several geologists, including the one who did the original dating, have agreed that the ash surrounding the tools was indeed 74,000 years old. The dating is critical. If the Kota Tampan pebble tools were made by modern humans, they would be the oldest precisely dated evidence for modern humans outside Africa. It therefore looks as though the ancestors of the Australians could well have left Africa and arrived in Malaysia on their beachcombing trail before the great Toba explosion.

Perhaps more important than the precision of the dating, this connection between stone tools and ashes in Malaysia puts the first Indians and Pakistanis in the direct path of the greatest natural calamity to befall any humans, ever. The Toba explosion was that disaster, the biggest bang in 2 million years. Carried by the wind, the plume of ash from the volcano fanned out to the north-west and covered the whole of the Indian subcontinent (see Figure 4.3). Even today, a metres-thick ash layer is found throughout the region, and is associated in two Indian locations with Middle and Upper Palaeolithic tools.[22] An important prediction of this conjunction of tools and ash is that a deep and wide genetically sterile furrow would have split East from West; India would eventually recover by recolonization from either side. Such a furrow does exist in the genetic map of Asia, as we shall see.

In spite of the proximity of Toba to Perak, the Toba ash plume only grazed the Malay Peninsula. The occupants of Kota Tampan were the unlucky ones – others on the peninsula escaped. Some argue, on the basis of comparing skull morphologies, that the Semang aboriginal 'Negrito' hunter-gatherers, who still live in the same part of the dense northern Malaysian rainforest, are descendants of people like Perak Man. The continuity of the Kota Tampan culture as argued by Zuraina Majid provides a link back to the 74,000-year-old tools in the Toba ash. In the next chapter we shall look at the physical evidence that links the Semang to the first modern human explorers along the coast of the Indian Ocean.[23]

For a film documentary, *The Real Eve* (*Out of Eden* in the UK), with which this book is associated, Discovery Channel helped to fund a genetic survey of the aboriginal groups of the Malay Peninsula which I conducted in collaboration with English geneticist Martin Richards and some Malaysian scientists (see Plate 16). This survey was part of a much larger ongoing study of East Asian genetics. The mtDNA results were very exciting: three-quarters of the Semang group (i.e. the 'Negrito' types) have their own unique genetic Manju and Nasreen lines with very little admixture from elsewhere, which is consistent with the view that their ancestors may have arrived with the first beachcombers. Their two unique lines trace straight back to the Manju and Nasreen roots (the first two daughters of Eve outside Africa – see Chapter 1). Their Manju line is not shared with anyone else in Southeast Asia or East Asia (or anywhere else) and, although it has suffered severe genetic drift through recent population decline, retains sufficient diversity to indicate an approximate age of 60,000 years. Their unique group on the Nasreen side, R21, comes from Rohani, Nasreen's genetic daughter. This lack of any specific connection with any other Eurasian population is consistent with the idea that after arriving here so long ago, they have remained genetically isolated in the jungles of the Malay Peninsula.[24]

Another piece of evidence from the region may help place Anatomically Modern Humans in the Far East over 70,000 years ago. This is the famous southern Chinese Liujiang skeleton. Consisting of a well-preserved skull (see Plate 19) but few other bones, Liujiang was discovered in a small cave at Tongtianyan in the Guangxi Zhuang Autonomous Region in 1958 by people collecting fertilizer. There is no doubt that this person was anatomically modern, but from the start there has been controversy over its age. A uranium date of 67,000 years was reported, but has been questioned on the basis of its exact location in relation to dated geological strata. In December 2002, a Chinese group headed by geologist Shen Guanjun reported their reinvestigation of the stratigraphy of the cave and dating of the skull (extending to several neighbouring caves) and claim it should be placed in a time bracket between 70,000 and 130,000, and not less than 68,000, years ago. The skull was found in a so-called intrusive breccia, a secondary flow of debris containing jumbled material of different ages. From their paper in the prestigious *Journal of Human Evolution*, the lower date bracket of 68,000 years seems solid, since it comes from multiple date estimates of the flowstone above and covering the breccia. (A flowstone forms when flowing water deposits calcite down a wall or across a floor.) Their preferred dating of 111,000–139,000 years ago based on unstratified fragments of flowstone and calcite within the breccia seems to me more speculative. Whatever the outcome, the safer lower bracket for the presence of an anatomically modern human in the Far East additionally tends to support the early exodus across the Red Sea before the Toba event of 71,000–74,000 years ago. This is because, to be in China by 68,000 years ago, their ancestors would still have had to expand across a quarter of the globe.[25]

Some are still convinced that Australian aboriginals represent an earlier migration out of Africa than that which gave rise to Europeans, Asians, and native Americans. Yet again our genetic trail tells us otherwise. Several studies of Australian maternal clans have shown that they all belong to our two unique non-African super-clans, Manju and Nasreen, and large studies of Y chromosomes show that male Australian lines all belong to the same Out-of-Africa Adam clan as other non-Africans, and belong to the Seth and Cain lines. The same pattern is seen with genetic markers not exclusively transmitted through one parent. In other words, the combined genetic evidence strongly suggests Australians are also descendants of that same single out-of-Africa migration. The logic of this approach, combined with the archaeological dates discussed above, places the modern human arrival in the Malay Peninsula before 74,000 years ago and Australia around 70,000 years ago. It is also consistent with the date of exit from Africa predicted on beach-combing grounds. As we saw in Chapter 1, the motivation for leaving the African continent may have been the failure of the beach harvest on the shores of the Red Sea caused by sharply rising salinity 85,000 years ago. My date estimates for the trek around the Indian Ocean en route from Africa suggest that the beachcombers could have taken as little as 10–6,000 years to eat their way down the coastline to Perak and another 10–4,000 years to reach Australia. Such a time requirement is fulfilled by the difference between leaving Africa around 85,000 years ago and arriving in Australia 65,000 years ago. The former date is consistent with a date of 83,000 years estimated for the African L3 cluster expansion using the molecular clock (see also Chapter 1).[26]

To gaze upon the face of the mother who launched a billion families
A question which has obsessed journalists and film-makers ever
since *Newsweek*'s 1988 Mitochondrial Eve story is what she and her
companions looked like. It is likely that they all looked very different
from one another, more varied than any random selection of people
from any non-African country might look today. They were, after
all, the stock from which all non-Africans developed, and all the
evidence suggests that the variation *within* individual groups
decreases the farther away from Africa one goes, even today. Yet, it is
also the case that differences between one group and another,
between, say, Chinese, Native Americans, Polynesians, Melanesians,
and Australians, increase the farther we move from Africa; so the
total diversity *between* the so-called races might seem to increase
with distance from Africa. Let me put this another way. My late and
very dear mother-in-law, who was Chinese, once told me – and she
wasn't joking – that Europeans all looked the same to her. Europeans have said the same about the Chinese. There is a paradox here,
which we need to resolve before we can continue to chart the
genetic diaspora out of Africa.

It is all a question of how the diversity is split up. What appears to
be a paradox is actually the result of multiple unequal group splits
followed by genetic drift in action. It can be explained thus: as the
explorers split into more and more branches, the original genetic
variation was parcelled into different groups which today live scattered around Eurasia and America. Over the past 50,000 years or so,
members of these individual splinter groups in the ex-African diaspora have drifted to become more like one another than like members of other groups. The splinter groups have diverged from one
another. While I shall argue later that many of these changes were
true evolutionary adaptations to new environments, some of them
were just down to the random and unequal way the cake was cut.

How is this? The answer lies in the same processes that operated when that first small group left Africa. Imagine – as we did in an earlier chapter – our stock of human diversity as a bag of marbles. Let us say that in Africa 75,000 years ago there were 10,000 marbles in the bag. When the exodus crossed the Red Sea, that diversity was reduced to 250 marbles in the founding colony. That reduction is known as a 'founder effect'. When that first colony had been living as an isolated colony for several thousand years somewhere in south Arabia, a number of marbles had failed to reproduce themselves and others became the dominant types. The bag of genetic variation became even smaller. As discussed in Chapter 1, that is genetic drift.

As the colony moved on there were unequal splits. When the group size became too large for the beach to sustain it, smaller groups, 'pioneers', broke off and ventured inland, travelling up rivers. Those smaller groups carried even fewer of the original genetic marbles that left Africa. They were undergoing further founder effects and drift.

Now we have to ask which was the tree and which was the stem. Were the beachcombers always in the majority, and the river explorers the minority, or did the main trunk veer inland at some stage? Which group kept most of the marbles? Such a question might seem academic, but if our journalists want to gaze upon the faces of a modern group which is as close as possible to the original exodus, this is the question we must answer: which modern non-African population has retained most varieties of the original ancestral African marbles?

Nuclear genetic markers: a bigger bag of marbles to look for older markers

To look at this question of diversity further, we cannot rely on our mitochondrial and Y-chromosome genetic markers. As far as they are concerned, only one original African marble from each single parent line ultimately survived to mother and father the rest of the world. As I have said, that is how we can argue there was only one exodus (see Chapter 1). There is no diversity in one line. No, if we want to compare ancestral African genetic diversity with the rest of the world, we need genetic marker types that survived the founder effect and genetic drift of the exodus in greater variety and larger numbers than one line each. So we have to look at the rest of our genetic make-up that resides in the nucleus of our cells and is not solely linked to one sex or the other.

For clarity's sake, my marbles analogy was grossly oversimplified. When we look at the surprisingly small proportion of our DNA that actually does anything useful, we find that for each gene there may be from one to a dozen slightly different versions. These versions can usually be linked together in a family gene tree. The base of each gene tree and its lower branches are usually predominantly African, whereas later branches and occasionally some of the earlier ones are found in different frequencies outside Africa. In addition, we can look at the non-functioning parts of our DNA that also progressively acquire extra packets of meaningless information which can, none-theless, be utilized by geneticists as tracer junk mail. These extra packets may accumulate to the point where they constitute as much as 10 per cent of our entire DNA. The absence of specific extra packets in an individual generally means that they have retained the ancestral or African type.[27]

When we look at which populations have preserved most of our original African genetic heritage, we come back to Australia and New Guinea. These two landmasses together make up the huge, remote, and partially submerged Sahul Continental shelf and have retained more original African gene types than any other part of the non-African world.[28] Today, however, New Guineans and Australians do not look alike (see Plate 17), and superficially the only population in the region who look at all like modern Africans are Melanesians, with their very dark skin and tightly frizzy hair. Even then, New Guinean highlanders, who are regarded as the 'least diluted' Melanesians from the original Pleistocene populations, are much more robust-featured (heavy-boned with strong supra-orbital ridges – see Chapter 5) than present-day Africans. But this begs the question as to what Africans looked like at the time of the modern exodus around 80,000 years ago. Almost certainly they did not look exactly the same as the gracile (fine-boned) Bantus, Nilotics, Pygmies, or !Kung look today. The fossil Qafzeh and Skhul skulls, dated to between 90,000 and 120,000 years ago, are much more robust than those of modern African populations, suggesting that Africans may have changed more than New Guinean highlanders in this respect. Having lived for a number of years both in New Guinea and Africa, it is my guess that the reconstruction of one of the Qafzeh skulls commissioned for our documentary would today pass unnoticed in New Guinea, but might be harder to place in Africa (see Plate 18).

Genetic traces of the exodus among relict populations nearer to Africa

What of other peoples who may be genetically closer Africans as a result of their position on the old beachcombing trail – what can comparing the frequencies of retention of ancestral gene types in African and non-African peoples tell us? Two regions stand out. The closest (along with Australians and New Guineans) are those in Pakistan and the southern Arabian peninsula, followed by Europeans and Indians. Trailing a long way behind, with the least retention of African diversity and the most drift, are the peoples of East Asia and the Americas.[29]

The root position of Pakistanis and southern Arabians in retaining ancient African genetic diversity is certainly what we would expect from our proposed southern route out of Africa, and there are other pieces of evidence to support this. Along the south coast of Arabia are the isolated Hadramaut peoples, described by some as Australoid. Their maternal genetic make-up includes 40 per cent of

African genetic lines; but although some of these markers could be related to the founding Out-of-Africa Eve, the majority of such lines have arrived from Africa more recently. Farther along the Indian Ocean coast the peninsular Indian populations also group genetically closer to the African root than do more easterly Asian peoples. Indian ethnic groups, both caste and tribal, were included in a large study of nuclear autosomal (non-sex-linked) markers. They were found to retain a higher rate of the African ancestral types than do Europeans and other Asian groups. [30]

There are other signs that the ancient African genetic diversity has been preserved in Pakistan. While the population of Pakistan in general shares some ancient mtDNA links with India, Europe and the Middle East, they also possess unique markers that are found nowhere else outside Africa. There are indeed populations that hark back to that ancient connection. One aboriginal so-called Negrito group, the Makrani, is found at the mouth of the Indus and along the Baluchistan sea coast of Pakistan. It is speculated that they took the coastal route out of Africa. They have an African Y-chromosome marker previously only found in Africa which is characteristic of sub-Saharan Africa. The same marker is found at slightly lower frequencies throughout other populations of southern Pakistan, Saudi Arabia, and the United Arab Emirates, and at higher rates in Iran. Another unique Y-chromosome marker appears outside Africa only in this region (see Note 31). One other ancient Y-chromosome marker points specifically to Pakistan as an early source and parting of the ways. This is an early branch off the Out-of-Africa Adam that is present at high frequency in Pakistan and at lower frequencies only in India (especially in tribal groups) and further north in the Middle East, Kashmir, Central Asia, and Siberia. The fact that this marker is not found farther east in Asia suggests that the only way it could have arrived in Central Asia was by a direct early northern spread up the Indus to Kashmir and farther north. [31]

The origins of Europeans: where was Nasreen born?

The prime position of South Asia in retaining African genetic diversity brings us to discuss the South Asian site of the parting of the ways. And we can now focus on the power of our maternal and paternal gene trees to leave trails of their ancient movements. Although the finding of roots and early branches of the Nasreen and Manju lines along the South Arabian and Baluchistan coastlines is strong evidence for the idea that a single southern out-of-Africa exodus continued first to South Asia, it does not necessarily identify the exact site of origin of Nasreen or her six Western daughters, including Rohani, or of Rohani's own West Eurasian daughters (U, HV, and JT) (Figure 4.2). Although Rohani clearly derives from somewhere in South Asia (see below), the birthplace of her West Eurasian daughters is less clear but of great interest. However, when we look at the mitochondrial genetic make-up of the whole of the Near East (including the Levant, Anatolia, Armenia, Azerbaijan, northern Kurdistan, as well as more southerly regions such as the Yemen, Saudi Arabia, Iraq and Iran) as revealed by the European founder analysis of Martin Richards and colleagues we find the greatest genetic diversity of Rohani's western daughters in the Gulf state of Iraq (see Chapter 3). Notable in Iraq are the high rates of unclassified root genetic types and the absence of other non-Rohani western daughter groups of Nasreen, such as W, I, or X. So it may be that Rohani's western daughters were born farther south, in Mesopotamia or near the Gulf, either before or during the first northward migration up the Fertile Crescent.[32]

Such questions can be sorted out only by a formal founder analysis, such as that used by Martin Richards and colleagues to trace the European founders, but this time comparing South Asian regions with the Levant. My own view is that for Rohani's Indian granddaughter U2i to be of a similar age, around 50,000 years, to her sister U5 in Europe, it is simplest for both Rohani and her daughters

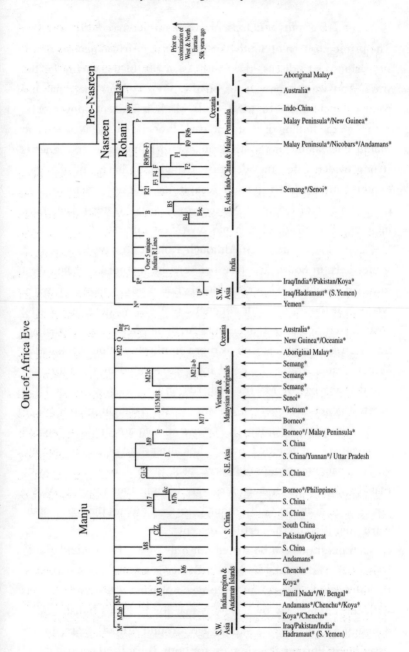

(Europa, HV, and JT) to have been born down south in the Gulf region, halfway between India and Europe. Certainly, as we saw in Chapter 3, a strong argument can be made for several early non-African Y-chromosome groups having their roots in southern Asia rather than up in the Levant.[33]

South Asia: fount of all Asian lines?

While little has been published on genetic markers for the southern Arabian peninsula, there is a magnificent body of information on the Indian subcontinent. For mitochondrial DNA we have an Estonian genetics team, with Asian collaborators, to thank for much of this, and several European and American groups are now collaboratively working on the Y chromosome. While this may bias our attention to India and Pakistan, the focus is deserved. Pakistan is the source of the Indus, the main route for direct access from South Asia to Central Asia west of the Himalayas. India, Bangladesh, and Burma also harbour the great southern Asian rivers, the Ganges, Brahmaputra, and Salween, draining the south and east of the Himalayas.

With the diversity of its inhabitants' physical appearance and their cultures, peninsular India is a rich transitional ethnic and geographical zone between West and East Eurasia. To the north and west we see only a very gradual change in people's appearance, including pigmentation (see Chapter 5), as we move from Pakistan, through Afghanistan and Iran, and west into Europe. The similarities between many South Asians and Europeans are striking.

Figure 4.2   The beachcomber mtDNA tree. Shows mtDNA branches found along the Indo-Pacific coast, Oceania and the Antipodes. In each, genetic continuity of spread can be seen from South Asia to Japan and to the south-west Pacific. Horizontal lines are for regional representation, vertical arrows for specific local representation; names with a star ('*') indicate putative relict populations from the trek.

This gradual east–west transition across northern India and Pakistan is paralleled in the relative frequencies of the two genetic daughter super-clans, Nasreen and Manju of the Out-of-Africa Eve founder line (L3). (Figure 4.3.) When we look at the Hadramaut in the Yemen, these frequencies are in the ratio 5:1 Nasreen to Manju, consistent with the view that Nasreen originated farther west than Manju, in the Gulf region. Between the Red Sea and the mouth of the Indus in Pakistan, West Eurasian genetic descendants of Nasreen continue to outnumber those of our Asian super-clan Manju. As we move east across the mouth of the Indus in Baluchistan and on towards India, the picture begins to change. The ratio of Nasreen to Manju lines decreases to 1:1 in the far-western states of Rajasthan and Gujerat. By the time we get to Bengal and Bangladesh, the ratio has reversed and Manju dominates. We thus find that the dominant clan in India is Manju, with an increasing frequency as we move from west to east.[34]

To the north and east of India, however, the changes are even more abrupt. In Nepal, Burma, and eastern India we come across the first Mongoloid East Asian faces. These populations generally speak East Asian languages, contrasting strongly with their neighbours who mostly speak Indo-Aryan or Dravidian languages. By the time we get to the east of Burma and to Tibet on the northern side of the Himalayas, the transition to East Asian appearance and ethno-linguistic traditions is complete, as is the rapid and complete change of the mitochondrial sub-clans of Manju and Nasreen. In Tibet, for instance, the ratio of Manju to Nasreen clans has evened back to 3:1, and there is no convincing overlap of their sub-clans with India (see Figure 4.2). Instead, Tibet shows 70 per cent of typical East and Southeast Asian Manju and Nasreen sub-clans, with the remainder consisting of as-yet unclassified Manju types of local origin. The north-eastern part of the Indian subcontinent therefore shows the clearest and deepest east–west boundary.[35] This boundary possibly

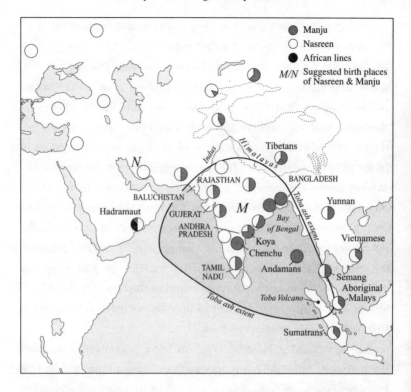

Figure 4.3   Distribution of Nasreen and Manju in South Eurasia. In West Eurasia there is only Nasreen; in most of East Eurasia there are even mixtures of Nasreen and Manju, but on the east coast of India there is nearly all Manju. The latter is consistent with near local extinction following the Toba explosion with recovery only of Manju on the east coast.

reflects the deep genetic furrow scored through India by the ash-cloud of the Toba volcano 74,000 years ago.

To the south of the Indian peninsula, the main physical type generally changes towards darker-skinned, curly haired, round-eyed so-called Dravidian peoples (see Chapter 5). Comparisons of skull shape link the large Tamil population of South India with the Senoi, a Malay Peninsula aboriginal group intermediate between the Semang and Aboriginal Malays (see above).[36]

*Manju born in India, Nasreen possibly a little farther west
in the Gulf*

Manju, who is nearly completely absent from West Eurasia, gives us many reasons to suspect that her birthplace is in India. Manju achieves her greatest diversity and antiquity in India. Nowhere else does she show such variety and such a high proportion of root and unique primary branch types. The eldest of her many daughters in India, M2, even dates to 73,000 years ago. Although the date for the M2 expansion is not precise, it might reflect a local recovery of the population after the extinction that followed the eruption of Toba 74,000 years ago. M2 is strongly represented in the Chenchu hunter-gatherer Australoid tribal populations of Andhra Pradesh, who have their own unique local M2 variants as well as having common ancestors with M2 types found in the rest of India. Over-all, these are strong reasons for placing Manju's birth in India rather than further west or even in Africa.[37]

The spectrum of Nasreen types in India is also different from further west. Although her granddaughter Europa types are present in 13 per cent of all Indians surveyed, these are nearly all accounted for by two Europa sub-branches, U7 and U2i (the Indian version of the U2 clan), along with a scattering of other Europa clans also found in the West, with virtually no root Nasreen types. This sug-gests that although U7 and U2i are both very ancient South Asian clans, they entered from further west at the time of the first colon-ization of Europe from South Asia 50,000 years ago – well *after* the initial out-of-Africa trek. There is also no evidence which would place the origin of Nasreen in India proper, although a scattering of her first-generation daughters, who have West Eurasian counter-parts, is found there.[38]

The real surprise among Nasreen's clan representatives in India is her daughter Rohani. If we recall, Rohani is Nasreen's most prolific daughter, being mother to most Westerners including Europa, not to mention two Far Eastern daughters with very large families (see Fig 4.2). In India, Rohani makes even that fecundity look like family planning. Estonian geneticist Toomas Kivisild has identified numerous other Rohani daughter branches, apparently all originating in India and none of them shared any other region. So rich are these new branches that he has been able to date their expansion to around 73,000 years ago.[39]

Nowhere else, west or east, do we find such deeply branched diversity in the Rohani genetic line. On this basis alone there is a strong case for identifying South Asia as Rohani's birthplace. It would seem more logical for Rohani and her European daughters to have been born in the Gulf than in India; but there is no genetic evidence as yet for that. Given the short distances and great time depth, however, either scenario is possible. One thing seems extremely unlikely, and that is that Rohani was born in the Levant or Europe. No Rohani roots are found anywhere in those regions to support that possibility, thus again slamming the door shut on any early northern migration out of sub-Saharan Africa.

What is perhaps most interesting about the unique Indian flowerings of the Manju and Rohani clans is a hint that they represent a local recovery from the Toba disaster which occurred 74,000 years ago, after the out-of-Africa trail began. A devastated India could have been recolonized from the west by Rohani types and from the east more by Manju types. Possible support for this picture comes from the recent study by Kivisild and colleagues of two tribal populations in the south-eastern state of Andhra Pradesh.[40] One of these populations, the Australoid Chenchu hunter-gatherers, are almost entirely of the Manju clan and hold most of the major Manju branches characteristic of and unique to India. The other group, the non-Australoid Koyas, have a similarly rich assortment of Indian type Manju branches (60 per cent of all lines), but have 31 per cent uniquely Indian Rohani types. The Chenchu and Koya tribal groups thus hold an ancient library of Indian Manju and Rohani genetic lines which are ancestral to, and include, much of the maternal genetic diversity that is present in the rest of the Indian subcontinent. Neither of these two groups holds any West Eurasian Nasreen types. The presence of Rohani types in the Koyas but not in the Australoid Chenchus might fit with some component of a recolonization from the Western side of the Indian subcontinent. As evidence of their ancient and independent development, and in spite of their clearly Indian genetic roots and locality, there were *no* shared maternal genetic types (i.e. no exact matches) between the two tribal groups thus indicating deep antiquity.

The first Asian men: three roots

Can we trace a similar route and history along the coast of Arabia and through Pakistan into India for the founder Out-of-Africa Adam? It would be easier if there were any representatives of Out-of-Africa Adam left, but like Out-of-Africa Eve, Adam's root line is effectively extinct outside Africa and is best represented by his three immediate sons, Cain, Abel, and Seth, the three male lines which encompass all non-African peoples (see Chapter 3).[41]

One of these three root branches, C (or RPS4Y), which I have called Cain after Adam's first-born, is an exclusively non-African line and is found at generally low rates throughout South and East Asia, Oceania, and the Americas. Cain is present at an even rate of around 5 per cent throughout India, including among the Proto-Australoid Chenchus. Seth's line, F (or M89), is nearly exclusively non-African, with the exception of several root types which, like a branch of the maternal Manju line (M1), appear to have found their way back into North Africa, in particular Morocco. Seth is by far the commonest of the three branches and is found throughout the non-African world (see Figure 4.5), with high rates in Australia and New Guinea, demonstrating clearly that he joined the other two genetic sons of Out-of-Africa Adam on that initial epic beachcombing trip. He accounts for 95–98 per cent of Indian male lines and has deep splits in his branches there.[42]

Three of the commonest Seth branches in India are found hardly anywhere else in the world (except in nearby Central Asia, just to the north) and thus echo the pattern of the local flowering of Indian maternal lines. Two of these are offspring of Group K, or Krishna, Seth's most prolific son (see Figure 4.4), while the third is a first-degree branch from Seth that has been found not only in nearby parts of Central Asia to the north but, significantly, further east in Cambodia. All these three types feature strongly in tribal populations of South India, especially the Australoid Chenchu. The Koya tribespeople *in addition* feature a rare root Seth type in a quarter of their population. This type is largely restricted to the Indian subcontinent and neighbouring parts of Central Asia, thus supporting the idea that India was the first major port of call on the southern route for Seth.[43]

In another view of out-of-Africa, derived from Y-chromosome data, the initial beachcombing party featured only Cain and Abel; Seth came much later, through North Africa and the Levant, directly to Central Asia and thence to India and Southeast Asia. As should be clear from this chapter and elsewhere in the book, I disagree with this view, arguing for a number of reasons – including the tight geographical and genetic coincidence of the founder lines – that a single southern route best explains the findings. As far as Seth in Central Asia is concerned, the commonest Indian Y-chromosome type holds the clue to the question of whether the numerous Y lines shared between Central Asia and India had their roots in India or vice versa. This type is M17, which I described in Chapter 3 as a major European player that had come in from Central Asia. M17 has an overall Indian frequency of 27 per cent but reaches 47 per cent in the Punjab. M17 achieves its highest diversity in Iran, India, and Pakistan, much higher than in Central Asia or Europe. This points to South Asia as its original homeland. The clincher is to find M17 at

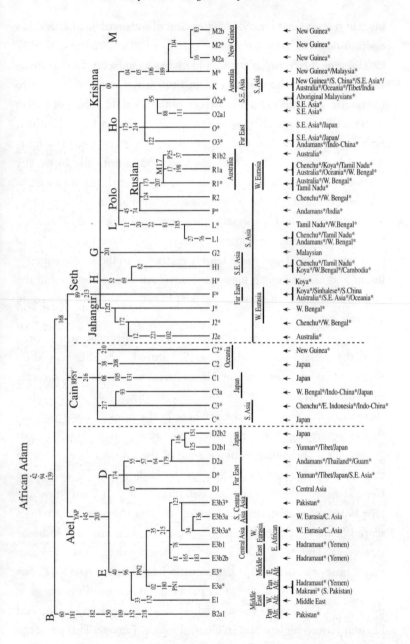

both high rates *and* high diversity among the tribal populations of South India, including the Australoid Chenchu and Yadhava. If M17 had been intrusive rather than indigenous among such tribal populations, the diversity would have been low.[44]

The YAP controversy: African or Asian?

The third primary line, often called YAP, I call Abel after Adam's second-born. This line has a small, deep, early Asian branch found in a patchy distribution nearly exclusively in the Far East (of which more below). The other, western YAP, branch split again and mainly peopled northern parts of Africa and the Middle East, although he spread in small numbers into Pakistan, India, and Central Asia. Some derived YAP lines are commonest back in Africa, while others are characteristic of the Middle East.[45]

There is a biblical analogy here: in the Book of Genesis, Shem and Ham were two brothers who peopled, respectively, the Middle East and northern Africa. Sadly for our story, the original root male Abel line from before the east–west YAP+ split does not seem to have survived, only his two sons. All he left us is the enigma of his birthplace: Ethiopia or Arabia? This question – 'African or Asian?' – persists into the name 'Hamito-Semitic' used for the language family spoken by of most of YAP's descendants. Whether we use that older, biblically inspired family name or the more modern term 'Afro-Asiatic', the dispute over whether the language family's origins are African or Asian remains. Given the young age of most large language families, any such spread, whether west–east or east–west across the Red Sea, is likely to have happened within the past 12,000 years or so.

Figure 4.4 The beachcomber Y-chromosome tree. Shows Y branches found along the Indo-Pacific coast, Oceania and the Antipodes. In each, genetic continuity of spread can be seen from South Asia to Japan and to the south-west Pacific.

One American geneticist, Mike Hammer, has insisted that YAP was born outside Africa and one of his two sons then returned, while Peter Underhill's group insist upon an African origin.[46] I am inclined to side with Mike Hammer and argue that YAP evolved in the first out-of-Africa colony, wherever that was, and then went back into Africa, but the ambiguity of the origins of the Afro-Asiatic language family perhaps carries more than an analogy. The non-African genetic lines that have crept back into Ethiopia and North Africa[47] may well have done so after the Last Glacial Maximum as peoples spread back to re-occupy green lands that were former desert. Quite how soon after the last glaciation the re-expansion occurred is an interesting question. Some linguists and archae-ologists see the enlargement of the world's major language families as having accompanied the Neolithic agricultural revolution of the last 5,000–7,000 years.[48] The genetic dates, however, suggest a re-expansion during the Mesolithic (i.e. 12,500 years ago), in other words much earlier than the Neolithic.[49]

A puzzling aspect of the Abel trail is the big gap in his distribution between West Eurasia and the Far East and, notably, his complete absence from India (Figures 4.4 and 4.5). That he was on the beachcombing trail is evident from the presence of Asian YAP in the Andaman Islands, Cambodia, and Japan (see Chapter 5). Recent evidence shows Asian YAP at rates of 3–6 per cent alongside western YAP at similar frequencies farther north from the beach trail in Central Asia (Uzbekistan). This mirrors the picture for Cain, who although not completely absent in India, has much lower rates there than in Central Asia to the north. Given that, although rare, Asian YAP is present beside the trail and farther along it, it is possible his absence in India – and indeed Cain's low rates in South Asia – could also be explained by the devastating effect of the Toba blast on the Indian subcontinent, as suggested by the geology and the maternal genetic story (see above). Toba could have created a genetic bottle-neck in India which was followed by a predominant local recovery of

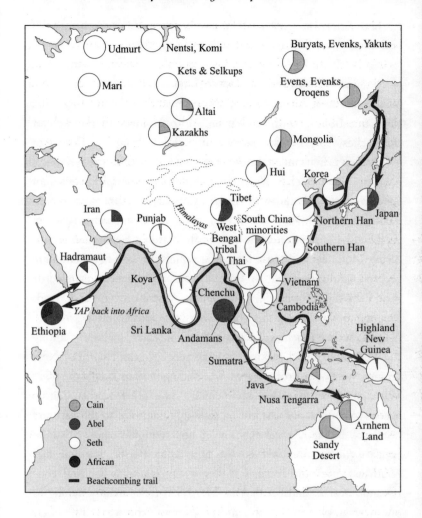

Figure 4.5 Distribution of the three male founders Abel, Cain and Seth in ethnic groups of Eurasia. Seth predominates overall, but reaches c. 100% in India possibly resulting from the Toba explosion. The latter is consistent with near local extinction following Toba with recovery only of Seth on the east coast. Extreme drift to Seth also occurs in north-west Asia. High rates of Cain in north-east Asia and Australia and of Abel in Tibet, the Andamans and Japan may result from drift.

the Seth line at the expense of his two beachcombing brothers, Cain and Abel.[50]

The three Asian male founder lines: beachcombers all

With our three primary out-of-Africa male lines, can we ask the same questions as with nuclear and mitochondrial markers about the earliest route of spread out of Africa? I think so. Dating of Y branches is in its infancy, but we can get a view of the geographical sequence of branches if we look for the geographical sites of ancestors and descendants. This is the phylogeographic approach. Taking Cain first, at 60 per cent of all Y-chromosome types in Australia he is the dominant line. In the Eastern Indonesian islands of the Moluccas and Nusa Tenggara, which the first beachcombers had to island-hop to get to Australia, we find the least changed or root Cain type, from which the unique Australian type is derived. The only other place in the world where this root Cain type is found is India, where it achieves a low rate throughout, including among the Australoid tribal groups. On the neighbouring island of New Guinea we find a brother group to the Australian Cain type, C2. When we look for other early colonies we see first that Cain is absent from West Eurasia but increasingly common to the east and north of India. A breakdown of Cain frequency shows that he appears most commonly on the East Asian Pacific coastline and Southeast Asia, and much less frequently inland in Central continental, North, and South Asia. The Asian types mainly belong to one derived clan which later moved over to America as a founder, although there is some greater diversity in Japan.[51]

The East Asian coastal distribution of Cain and his offsprings' strong regional differences in Southeast Asia and Oceania (see Figure 4.5) suggest that he was numerically the main male founder along the initial coastal beachcombing route round Asia, although clearly not the only one since his other two brothers also made it round the coast to East Asia and Japan. Only one of the two remaining founding male types got as far as Australia *as well as* Southeast Asia and round the East Asian coast – Seth. This is shown by the presence of Seth at low frequencies in his ancestral or root form in all these areas. Australia has two main local ancestral Y types: one comes from Cain (see above), and is the commonest at over 60 per cent; the other is from Seth's Asian genetic son Krishna, at around 30 per cent. This 30 per cent rate for Krishna persists, with variation, more or less throughout Southeast Asia and up the Pacific Rim to Korea. Seth's ancestral line, however, persists at a couple of per cent throughout Southeast Asia and Australia and also on the Pacific coast in Korea. These patterns strongly suggest that the first beach-combing route not only went to New Guinea and Australia, but continued round the coast to China, Japan, and Korea. The third root Y line, the Asian YAP, got as far as Cambodia but apparently did not cross to Australia, instead continuing round the Indo-Pacific coast to appear at low rates in Southeast Asia and at higher rates in Tibet, southern China, and Japan.[52]

This picture of the first male beachcombers mirrors that of the maternal mtDNA lines and tells us much, albeit indirectly, about the identity and ages of the first male founder lines. A prediction of our southern route is that somewhere near the beginning of the trail, and before the parting of the ways, we should find these three oldest non-African lines all together. Southern Arabia and the Gulf region are still under study, but when we look for the three male founder lines in Pakistan and India as a whole, there they all are. We can find root and branch for Cain, Seth, and Seth's genetic sons and grandsons. We can even find several unique YAP types from a YAP branch normally only found in Africa and West Eurasia.[53]

Nowhere else outside Africa do we find such a diversity of deep Y roots and branches except, to a much lesser extent, in Central and North Asia. This picture of Central Asia as another transition zone between East and West is borne out in the rich mixture of European and Asian maternal mtDNA lines also found in that region,[54] suggesting that one of the primary splits after the arrival in India was to travel north up the Indus to Central Asia. This early inland route is one of the main topics of the next chapter.

In summary, the South Asian region, the first homeland of that single, successful southern exodus, shows the presence of the genetic roots of that expansion not only in the so-called aboriginal peoples around the Indian Ocean, but among the bulk of the modern populations. Among these roots we can detect genetic base camps for the most westerly of the subsequent pioneer treks inland to the vast Eurasian continent. These treks set off, after a pause, for Europe, the Caucasus, and Central Asia. It seems that the vanguard of the beachcombing trail retained a surprising proportion of the original genetic diversity left in the out-of-Africa group and moved rather faster round the shores of the Indian Ocean. So fast, in fact, that they travelled right round to Indonesia and on into Near Oceania, arriving in Australia long before their first cousins made it to Europe.

The exact chronological relationship of the exodus and the subsequent arrival in Southeast Asia to the massive Toba volcanic explosion of 74,000 years ago is critical. First, Toba is one of the most accurately and precisely dated events of the Palaeolithic, and its ashfall acts as a time datum for the whole of southern Asia. Second, the effects of Toba's direct ashfall followed by the inevitable 'nuclear winter' would have been disastrous for any life in its path, and pretty bad farther afield. The presence of tools thought to be made by modern humans found with Toba ash in the Malay Peninsula suggests that the beachcombing vanguard had arrived in the Far East before the eruption. Triangulation of this anchor date with other pieces of evidence supports this scenario. Other clues include new dates for the Liujiang skull, luminescence dates from Australia, the date of the lowest sea level enabling passage to Australia at 65,000 years ago, genetic dates of the expansion of the L3 group at 83,000 years ago, and the onset of significant salinization of the Red Sea dated to 85,000 years ago. The best evidence for early modern humans in Asia should come from real fossils and their dated context. Such work is in process at the site of Liang Bua in Flores.

Now, if Toba really did blow its top after India was first colonized, we would expect a mass extinction event on the Indian Peninsula which affected the eastern side more than the west. This is certainly one interpretation of the paradox of the Indian genetic picture, in which the genetic trail of the beachcombers can be detected, but the bulk of Indian subgroups of Manju and Rohani are unique to the subcontinent, especially among the tribes of the south-east. This is what we would expect for a recovery from a great disaster. The oldest of these local lines have been dated to around 73,000 years ago.

In the next chapter we shall see what those pioneers did on the North and East Asian mainland after they arrived, and how they got to those places.

5

THE EARLY ASIAN DIVISIONS

WE ALL HAVE A TENDENCY to see differences. 'Mummy, why does that person look like that?' is a question we hear on children's lips from an early age. So why is it that people from different parts of the world all look so different? Why are children and adults so interested in these things? To many people the issue of physical difference is loaded with that ugliest and most destructive form of human group behaviour, racism. But we get nowhere by shutting our eyes. Differences will not fade away, and open-minded enquiry should help us to understand 'why that person looks like that' and why differences in physical appearance can be such a sensitive issue.

A common argument, introduced in the last chapter, is that after the various groups which are now spread over the huge Asian continent split up, they somehow drifted apart and 'evolved' in isolation from one another. As with the evidence for the unity of the original dispersal, there is genetic support for these ideas of isolation and change, but the archaeological and fossil support for the details of the story is less clear. The truth is that there is very little archaeological, let alone fossil evidence for where and when the ancestors of different modern Asian groups have been for most of the past 80,000 years, so, to a certain extent, any answer is speculative. Even with the uncertainty of fossil evidence, however, dates from archaeological sites, combined with knowledge of past climate and the evidence from genetic markers, do allow us to reconstruct the routes taken by the first Asians. The pioneers penetrated their vast continent from three widely separated parts of the Asian Indo-Pacific coast. The choice of those routes had profound consequences for the subsequent physical differentiation of the explorers, resulting from isolation and adaptation to new environments.

Why is the question so fascinating – and anyway, what do we mean by 'different'? The answer to the first is probably in our nature in that humans have evolved an extraordinary capacity for recognizing and remembering a large number of different faces. We need this skill partly because our extended social groups are large.[1] They are larger, and the interactions between their members are far more complex, than those of even our nearest living relatives, the chimpanzees. We *have* to be able to recognize many people. Failure to identify people you should know is embarrassing and is quickly noted as a weakness.

Along with the social advantages it provides, our ability to recognize faces enables us to classify what we see, and identify shared physical similarities within groups, and differences between one group and another. Clearly this can and does feed into our inclusive and exclusive group behaviour, and is what can lead us to discriminate against 'outsiders' who look 'different'. Luckily our insight into our own innate tendency to 'group and exclude', and the terrible crimes against humanity that can result from organized racism, have led us to take statutory and voluntary steps to control and proscribe such behaviour. Tragically, these checks are not always successful, and old lessons of the evils of pogroms and group persecution are ignored, even by former victims of racism.

The limited power of words

A by-product of the fight against racism has been to render discussion of race taboo. Even the word 'race' itself, tainted forever by the

Nazi era, is outlawed by many anthropologists as unscientific, derogatory, meaningless, and giving the misleading impression that races are discrete entities when in fact variation, gradation, and admixture occur everywhere. This is all very worthy, but the fact remains – as children are quick to notice – that people from different regions can look dramatically different from one another. In the end, proscription and regularly changing euphemisms do not help; most alternative terms for race such as 'population' or 'ethnic group' are so vague as to be just as misleading. In this book I use terms such as 'Caucasoid', 'Mongoloid', and 'Negrito' to describe physical types, not because they are accurate but because they have common usage. Many anthropologists will object that they are derogatory and imprecise. From Figure 5.1, readers who share this view will be able to interpret my terminology in terms of their preferred emphasis on the geographical area of indigenous populations who appear broadly related on a wide range of biological attributes.

Terminology used in this book	Terminology focused on regions of geographically related indigenous populations
Africans	Sub-Saharan Africans
Negritos	Andaman Islanders, Semang, Philippine 'Aeta'
Caucasoids	Europeans, Middle East, North Africans
Australoids	Aboriginal Australians including Tasmanians
Melanesians	New Guinea, Bismarck Archipelago, Vanuata, New Caledonia
Southern Mongoloids	Southeast Asians (excluding Negritos), Polynesians, Micronesians
Northern Mongoloids	Northeast Asians (excluding Ainu), New World populations

Figure 5.1   Table of rough terminology for ethnic groups and names/apparent racial differences.

With my choice of terminology I am not intending to derogate people who do not look like me – on the contrary, I know that the rest of the world has a distinct advantage in not looking like me. Equally, however, I believe that politically correct euphemisms are just as imprecise and misleading as the older terms. Inevitably, a well-known word such as 'Mongoloid' is often useful as a shorthand description of a general physical type, but we should always remember that the 'traditional' terms are imprecise descriptions of a complex biological reality that varies enormously within groups as well as overlapping between populations.

The most obvious physical difference between peoples of Eurasia is their skin colour, which tends to be darker in the sunnier tropical regions. This is no coincidence. Skin darkness, which depends on the pigment melanin, is controlled by a number of poorly under-stood genes and is also under evolutionary control. For those who live in tropical and subtropical regions, the risk of burns, blistering, and the likelihood of death from skin cancer induced by ultraviolet light is dramatically reduced by having dark skin. There are other, less dramatic advantages: for example, the melanin in pigmented skin allows it to radiate excess heat efficiently, as well as protecting against the destruction of folic acid, an essential vitamin. So in sunny climes, over many generations, people with dark skin live on aver-age longer and have more successful families.[2] In North Asia (i.e. Asia north of the Tibet-Qinghai Plateau and east of the Urals) and Europe there is less sun and a lower risk of skin cancer, but there is the ever-present risk of rickets, a bone disease caused by lack of sunlight that was still killing London children even at the beginning of the twentieth century. I know this because I once did research on rickets while I was based at the Royal London Hospital's pathology department. Rickets, or osteomalacia, came back in a small way to Britain in the second half of the twentieth century, but affected the children of families from the Indian subcontinent. Part of the reason for this was their darker skin colour, which filtered out some of the already meagre sunshine.

So there are at least two evolutionary selection forces working in concert, tending to grade skin colour according to latitude. The sun-driven change in skin and hair colour evolves over many generations. From the available genetic evidence, Africans appear always to have been under intense selective pressure to remain dark-skinned. Outside Africa, though, we can see gradations of skin and hair colour as we move from Scandinavia in the north of Europe and Siberia in the north of Asia down to Italy and Southeast Asia in the south of those regions. The darkest-skinned groups of non-Africans still tend to live in sunny and tropical countries. Clearly, if change in skin colour takes many generations, we shall sometimes find people whose recent ancestors have moved to live in sunny countries and who are still fair skinned (and vice versa). A good example is Australia, a sunny country where the majority of today's inhabitants are pale-skinned descendants of recent immigrants. Australia has one of the world's highest rates of skin cancer, and this has already started it on the slow evolutionary path that will eventually lead to descendants of Europeans becoming generally darker-skinned. Conversely, the first visitors to the north of Europe and Asia probably started their journeys looking very dark skinned and evolved to become paler later. Apart from exceptions such as Australia, the average skin colour around the world is thus tuned to the relative amount of ultraviolet light (Figure 5.2).[3]

Since this evolutionary trend continuously affects people of all latitudes at all times, our colour may have more to say about where our ancestors lived over the past 10,000–20,000 years than about their genetic divergence over the previous 60,000 years. So, the skin colours of today's people are of limited value in tracing ancient routes of migration after the African exodus. In other words, colour is not the most useful marker for the understanding of human

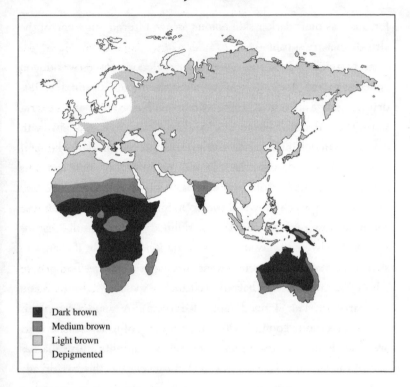

Dark brown
Medium brown
Light brown
Depigmented

Figure 5.2   Original distribution of skin colours in the Old World. With a few obvious exceptions such as Australia, the darkest-skinned groups still tend to live in sunny and tropical countries.

prehistory between 80,000 and, say, 10,000 years ago. It may come as a surprise that skin colour is so evanescent, since it is the most obvious and divisive of all 'racial' characteristics. The key to human discriminatory behaviour is not in logic, however, but in the need to find an easily recognizable feature or pretext which unites our own group and excludes competing groups. The difference may be trivial. We regularly choose even more absurd differences, such as between closely related varieties of religion, to justify persecuting or killing our neighbours.

Changing face

Other, more solid differences, such as the shape of our face, are determined by the underlying skull bones. These do vary between different parts of East, Southeast, and South Asia, and imply a rather long period of separation between the populations of these regions. Throughout East Asia we see the Mongoloid type (see Plate 17) with an extra, so-called epicanthic fold protecting the upper eyelid, and broad cheeks and skull. This type is often further divided into Northern Mongoloid and Southern Mongoloid, with the latter showing a less marked eye-fold and including southern Chinese and darker-skinned Mongoloid types in Southeast Asia (see Figure 5.3).[4]

A great variety of peoples is found in South Asia, particularly in India. The majority of Indians, although dark skinned, are more similar physically to Europeans and Middle Easterners than they are to East Asians. Europeans, with their long, narrow heads, round eyes, and pale skin are sometimes called Caucasian. The farther north in India and Pakistan we go, the closer is the physical resemblance to 'Caucasoid' Levantines and Middle Easterners. In southern India, darker-skinned, curly haired, round-eyed peoples predominate. In eastern India, Assam, and Nepal there are peoples with a more Mongoloid appearance.

In Chapter 4 we looked at another category of Asian peoples who may represent remnants of the original beachcombing trek to Australia. Scattered around the coast of the Indian Ocean, in Pakistan and India, and in the Andaman Islands, the Philippines, and Malaysia, are several so-called aboriginal groups who are superficially more reminiscent of Africans and New Guineans, because of their very dark skin and frizzy hair. These minorities have been called respectively Negroid, Negritos, and Melanesians.

Although they are just a tiny minority among the other Asian Old World peoples I have mentioned, such aboriginal groups have long been regarded by scholars as physically somewhat nearer to the first out-of-Africa people than are the other Asians. This generalization effectively suggests that it is the bulk of the rest of Asia that has changed. A parallel dental study of the same aboriginal populations that I sampled for genetic markers (Chapter 4) has produced physical confirmation of this view. Another piece of evidence in favour of these aboriginal groups being relicts of the beachcomber trail is that the earliest fossil skulls from Europe and from East and Southeast Asia from before the last glaciation are not typically Caucasoid or Mongoloid in shape. Instead, we see forms closer to the oldest African and Levantine skulls of 100,000 years ago.[5]

Earlier people were bigger and more rugged

How do we know what that first group of emigrants from Africa looked like in any case? The simple answer is that we do not. The reasonable and most parsimonious speculation, that they were dark-skinned and frizzy-haired, is based on the appearance of modern Africans,[6] although it is unlikely that Africans of 80,000–100,000 years ago looked quite like those of today. There are, however, some clues.

A few fossilized skulls of Anatomically Modern Humans have survived intact from around 100,000 years ago. One that is frequently referred to as characteristic of the period is from the failed first exodus to the Levant. It is named Skhul 5 after the cave where it was found. A number of other skulls were found in the same location – Skhul 5 was just one of the best preserved. A Skhul type was used to reconstruct the 'face of Eve' (see Plate 18) in our documentary film *The Real Eve*. Anatomically Modern Human skulls of this period show great variability, but they also share a few general characteristics that have changed in later populations, including modern Africans. Most obvious are the two closely related features of large size and 'robusticity'. Robust features include large, craggy skulls, thick bones, and heavy brow-ridges when compared

with all today's populations. The opposite of robust, 'gracile', is used
to describe individuals with a flat, high, vertical forehead, smoother
brow-ridges, and thinner long bones and skull bones. Other ancestral features of the time before the southern exodus include a
relative narrowness of the skull (narrow breadth side to side compared with length front to back) and a broad upper face.[7]

Size and robusticity of the skeleton are closely linked (especially
in the skull). This presents us with a problem when we try to use
bones to reconstruct prehistory, because the most marked change
since the time of the African exodus has been a progressive reduction in size and robusticity in *all* peoples of the world, *including
Africans*. Although some of the long-term change is probably
genetic, the most dramatic size reductions have occurred within the
past 10,000 years and may, paradoxically, be nutritional rather than
genetic.

How did we get to be smaller?

Early hunter-gatherers led a tough, roaming life and therefore had a
low population density, but their diet was rich in protein and minerals and varied in vegetables. Conversely, although the cereal
farmers of the past 8,000 years may have had a high per-hectare crop
yield and large families as a result of early weaning, their diet was
monotonous – high in carbohydrate, and low in protein, vitamins,
and calcium. Early weaning with high-carbohydrate, low-protein
foods resulted in growth-stunting persisting into adult life. Consequently, although populations *expanded* with the advent of farming,
child and adult size *decreased* dramatically. This effect is particularly
marked in peoples eating rice without much animal protein, as in
the Far East.

Today we can see the effect of reversing this form of cultural
malnutrition. When East Asians migrate from a rice-eating culture
to the USA and take on the low-bulk, high-calorie, protein-rich diet
there, within two generations we see Asian children approaching the

size of American children. American and European populations, with their improved diet, have also seen a steady increase in adult size since the Second World War.[8]

So, if robusticity depends partly on size, and the average size of today's regional populations depends on their present diet, then the value of these two important determinants of our appearance in tracing the differentiation of non-Africans over the past 70,000–80,000 years is reduced. Also, many of the changes in robusticity, size, and general appearance of modern humans since the out-of-Africa migration could actually be reversible with a good diet and a healthy lifestyle. The rugged 'Neanderthal' look of some large players of contact sports can now be explained.

A couple of permanent changes can be observed over time, though: namely, in skulls and teeth. Reduction of skull size, to take that first, was caused by slightly different mechanisms in different regions.

Changing skulls

Although Australian aboriginals, and to a lesser extent some New Guineans, have undergone size reduction, they appear to have retained more of their skeletal robusticity than have nearly all other groups. The Australian skull reduction was both in length and breadth. Australian aboriginals are sometimes cited as the best examples of retention of the ancestral form, but, for several reasons, a better case could be made for New Guineans. A few details about the Australian aboriginals, past and present, remain unexplained – one is that the earliest fossil skulls from Australia were actually gracile, not robust. Another reason to regard the Australians as somewhat 'changed' from the ancestral type, perhaps as a result of admixture, is that most Australians today have curly rather than frizzy hair.[9]

Only one other modern group has retained a similar degree of robusticity to Australians and New Guineans, namely the Tierra del

Fuegans of South America, and they are now practically extinct. In Japan another rather robust skull type is represented in the fossil record by the famous Minatogawa fossil skulls from Okinawa, a subtropical Japanese island, dated to the height of the last glaciation (see Plate 20). These skulls group by shape with the pre-Neolithic ancient Jomons of Japan, who are regarded as the ancestors of the modern aboriginal population of northern Japan, the Ainu. Among the ancestors of Europeans and Middle Easterners there was a limited and variable reduction in skull length and robusticity, leaving some degree of long skull shape (dolichocephaly) and also a variable retention of robusticity, which helps to explain my own beetle-brows.[10]

It is in the peoples now called Mongoloid that the most marked changes occurred. The size reduction happened mainly by a marked shortening of the skull from back to front while retaining breadth and height. A further change that was characteristic of Mongoloid peoples was an exaggeration of facial flattening. This is most pronounced in Neolithic populations on the east coast of Lake Baikal in Siberia and around Mongolia (Figure 5.3). It is referred to as an exaggeration since facial flattening is not a new feature to the normal range of human variation. Facial flattening is also seen to a lesser extent in some early African skulls, in modern-day Khoisan hunter-gatherers, and in the revered founder-father of post-Apartheid South Africa. These changes resulted in the high, fine-featured, rather broad (brachycephalic) head shape now prevalent in East Asia, which is almost certainly genetically determined. East Asians are also among the most gracile of modern populations.[11]

When and where did the physical changes characteristic of today's Mongoloid populations occur? The date of the first modern human arrival in China is disputed, but may be around 70,000 years ago. It is important to remember that the first modern human inhabitants of China did not have a typical Mongoloid appearance, and that the few fossil skulls surviving from before the last ice age

20,000 years ago in lowland China and Southeast Asia had a robust, more ancestral form. In fact, the earliest undisputed Mongoloid remains anywhere in the world are dated only to within the last 10,000 years. Although these come from the Far East, the earliest human remains in Asia to have claims made for Mongoloid characteristics come from much further west at the site of Afontova Gora II on the Yenisei River in southern Siberia, to the west of Lake Baikal, and have been dated to 21,000 years ago. Since this is an isolated find of disputed significance, and there are no other preglacial skulls in southern Siberia to indicate a sequence, all that can be inferred from this scanty fossil record without reference to other evidence is that the location of the change towards Mongoloid features need not have been China.[12]

The story of the teeth

Another, less striking but no less significant change was in tooth shape. The retention of several ancestral skeletal traits in modern Europeans is echoed in recent detailed dental research (Figure 5.4) which shows that Europeans can be grouped with the chain of remnant beachcomber populations around the Indian Ocean (including southern Indians, the Negrito Semang of Malaya, and New Guineans), who have retained more African ancestral dental and cranial features than other non-Africans. This remarkable long-distance dental link between Europeans and the other 'least changed' non-African groups of the Indian Ocean would be expected from a single southern exodus. To my mind, it is also another nail in the coffin (if any were needed) of racist stereotyping of Europeans as *advanced* and aboriginals as *primitive*.[13]

Those 'dentally undifferentiated beachcomber' peoples are followed closely in the dental analysis by another cluster. It includes the non-Semang (non-Negrito) aboriginals of Southeast Asia, such as the Aboriginal Malay peoples of the Malay Peninsula, various remnant Pacific Rim populations such as the aboriginal Ainu in Japan,

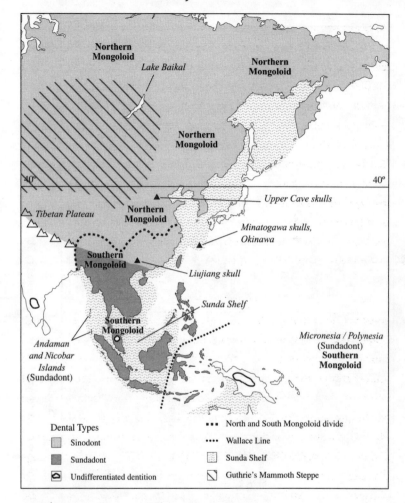

Figure 5.3 Map of Mongoloid types and dental differentiation in East Asia. Sundadont and Sinodont dental types occupy roughly the same areas as Southern Mongoloid and Northern Mongoloid, respectively, except in South China, where the Yangtzi River divides Northern from Southern Mongoloid. The islands of Sakhalin and Japan are excluded since the aboriginal group, the Ainu, and their Jomon ancestors show partial Sundadonty.

and the Polynesians. These groups all share some features of an early, derived form of dentition, Sundadonty, so called after the Southeast

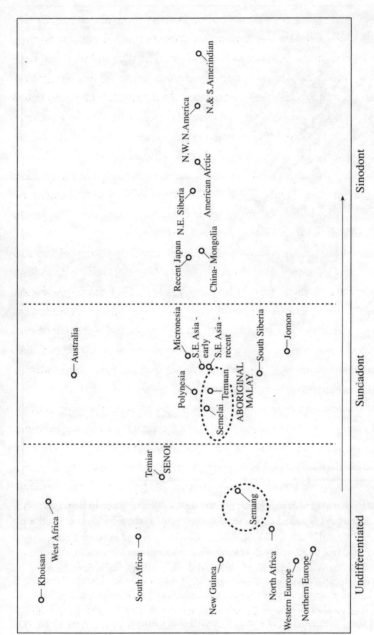

Progression of dental type from undifferentiated to Sinodont

Asian geological region of the Sunda shelf (Sundaland) where the type is proposed to have arisen. Sundadonty is not found any farther back west on the beachcombing trail, for instance in India. Importantly, most Sundadont populations also show some Mongoloid features and are classified as Southern Mongoloids. The Palaeolithic Minatogawas and Neolithic Jomons of Japan, who may be ancestral to the present-day Ainu, also share some dental features of Sundadonty with Southeast Asian and Pacific peoples.[14]

Australian aboriginals occupy an interesting position in this spectrum (see Figure 5.4) in that they show some features of Sundadonty, unlike their neighbours the New Guineans. This tends to confirm the possibility of some admixture.[15]

Second of the two important derived dental groupings of Eurasia after Sundadonty is Sinodonty (literally, 'Chinese teeth'). Sinodont people are characterized by an exaggeration of certain tooth shapes already present in Sundadonts and also, generally, a reduction in tooth size. Sinodonty is characteristic of mainland Asian Northern Mongoloid peoples, increasing in degree towards the north and extending to include the Americas (see Figure 5.3). Sinodonty is uncharacteristic of Southeast Asia, even today.

As an oversimplification, Sundadonty represents the earliest dental change from the out-of-Africa beachcombers, and combinations of its features are found both in Southern Mongoloids of Southeast Asia, Polynesia, and Micronesia, and, to a lesser extent, in some non-Mongoloids such as the Jomon of Japan and the isolated Andaman Islanders. Sinodonty represents a further divergent trend in the same morphological direction as Sundadonty and is found in

Figure 5.4 Two-dimensional plot of the spread of dental morphology. The spectrum runs from undifferentiated (Africa, Europe, relict aboriginal Semang and Senoi groups and New Guinea) through Sundadonty (Aboriginal Malay, Southeast Asians and Pacific Islanders) to Sinodonty (Northern Mongoloid and Native American groups). Narrowing of plot indicates reduction of diversity away from Africa. Jomon and South Siberians are notable outliers.

Northern Mongoloids, including most Chinese, and in an even more exaggerated form in Northeast Siberians and Native Americans.[16]

The enigma of Mongoloid origins

What is clear, whether one looks at skull shape, teeth, or genetic markers, is that of all the groups outside Africa, Mongoloid populations have changed or drifted the most since the exodus. This differentiation from the ancestral type and loss of group diversity increases in today's populations as we go northwards in East Asia and then east into Arctic America. What is not at all clear is how, when, and where the features that distinguish Mongoloids from all other Eurasians developed. These are not idle academic questions. Mongoloids are, after all, the world's most numerically successful and widespread physical type. They arrived in America before the last glaciation 20,000 years ago (see Chapter 7), yet they do not definitely appear in lowland China until well after that icy bookmark in human history. We can summarize the rather complex story so far as follows:

1 The very first Asians (who were also the ancestors of the Europeans) looked rather like the Africans of that time and probably had similar teeth.

2 Those first undifferentiated robust South Asians, starting from 85,000 years ago, spread out all along the South Asian coastline from the southern Arabian coast, through India, to Southeast Asia, also reaching New Guinea at the end of the arc in the south-west Pacific. The present-day relict descendants along that route have retained ancestral tooth features.

3 From Indo-China, these undifferentiated types also spread north to China, moving round the western rim of the Pacific Ocean between 35,000 and 70,000 years ago.

4 At some time *before* the last glaciation, a new complex of tooth shape called Sundadonty developed among 'pre-Mongoloid'

people living in Southeast Asia. These new dental types subsequently spread, in modified form, north-east along the Pacific coast to Japan (the prehistoric Jomon and modern Ainu) and south-east to Polynesia (see Figure 5.3).

5 A second dental complex, Sinodonty, is probably much more recent and is derived from Sundadonty. The evolution from Sundadonty to Sinodonty does not seem to have happened in Southeast Asia or along the west Pacific coastline among the Jomon or Ainu of Japan; but the degree of Sinodonty increases as we move north through the modern Mongoloid populations of mainland East Asia, and it reaches its extreme in the Americas. So, it appears that Sinodonty originated with Sundadonts from the south. Due to lack of fossils, Sinodonty has not been detected from any earlier than 10,000 years ago in South China or in Japan.

6 The Mongoloid skull shape is characterized by delicate gracile bones, marked facial flattening, and length shortening. Nasal flattening is found in one skull from just before the LGM, in the region around Lake Baikal. Facial flattening is still most marked in that region.

7 Like Sinodonty, Mongoloid features have not been detected in Chinese fossils from before the LGM. More recently they have spread widely in North and East Asia and are characteristic of Sinodonts – in other words Northern Mongoloids – as well as of most Native Americans.

The progressive change in skull features thus appears to have been paralleled by the change from Sundadonty to Sinodonty. If the ancestors of Sinodonts were Sundadonts from the south, then at least some of the other physical features that characterize Northern Mongoloids may also have originated in the south. If the first characteristically Mongoloid ancestors of Northern Mongoloids came from the south, they would share ancestors with peoples, such as the Aboriginal Malays, who still live there. As we shall see later, there is good supporting evidence that at least some of the major gene lines in East and Northeast Asia derive ultimately from Indo-China, with ancestral types still found among aboriginal Southern Mongoloids of the region.

It is worth pausing to review the various implications and consistency of this south–north as opposed to north–south model of movement and change in teeth and bones. Of the two East Asian dental types today associated with Mongoloid peoples, Sundadonty probably originated rather early in Southeast Asia, representing the earliest dental change, still being found in some non-Mongoloid relict populations. Sinodonty, on the other hand, is commonest over most of East Asia and the Americas but is, even now, not found in indigenous Southeast Asians. This latter observation favours the south–north view.

What about admixture from the north? If this is how Southern Mongoloids arose, we would expect, merely by association and carry-over, to find Sinodonty massively intruding into Southeast Asia – which we do not. Simple observation of degree of change also backs up the theory that dental types evolved first into Sundadonty in the south, and then drifted towards Sinodonty as the Mongoloid peoples moved into Central Asia.

As with the progression and exaggeration of Sundadont features resulting in the Sinodont type, some Mongoloid features, such as facial flatness, are more exaggerated in Northern Mongoloids than in Southern Mongoloids. So, whatever evolutionary force was driving those specific changes must have continued to apply somewhere farther north, perhaps in the interior. Fossil evidence (or rather, lack of it) suggests that the region of 'further development' of Mongoloid features was not China, Japan, Southeast Asia, or India – which leaves somewhere in Central Asia north of the Himalayas, such as Mongolia or the Lake Baikal region in southern Siberia. Furthermore, there is one particular southern Siberian group which features a cluster of Sundadonts among its people, unlike the rest of that region, suggesting a local retention of ancestral type (see Figure 5.4).

Why did Mongoloid peoples come to look different?

There have been a number of theories of how and where Mongoloid skeletal features developed. The first thing to say is that all these theories are highly speculative and even contentious. The 'where' theories are speculative mainly, as I have pointed out, because of the overall lack of early Mongoloid fossil evidence. The 'how' theories are speculative because at present there is no way of linking particular skeletal changes to specific controller genes. However, this should not prevent us from at least looking at the theories.

Unfortunately, as with many scientific debates, controversy usually ends in a split between two opposite views, when the truth probably lies somewhere in between. For origin theories we are left having to choose between southern homeland and a northern one, and for the 'how' theories we have adaptive physical evolution in response to cold versus simple isolation and genetic drift. (There is some linkage between the two proposed mechanisms of change, since the adaptive theories specify a cold northern zone of adaptation.)

The north–south geographical division has been etched even deeper by physical (and genetic) evidence, old and new, that the Northern and Southern Mongoloid populations can indeed be separated. Studies of child growth curves in China, for instance, have shown that Hong Kong children in the south, although well nourished, are smaller than those from Beijing in the north. The fact that the better-nourished Hong Kong children are still a different size from those in Beijing, even after generations of booming development, suggests that there is a systematic genetic difference between north and south.[17]

Do Mongoloid features result from drift or selection?

The main alternative 'how' solutions to the origins of Mongoloids are fairly easy to state. The simplest answer (discussed in the last chapter) is that a small founder group isolated from other groups will drift randomly toward one genetic or physical type. These combined founder and drift effects can be exaggerated by sexual selection. To take an absurdly oversimplified example, imagine that the founder Mongoloid group, in this instance coming from the south, has by chance a higher proportion of smaller rather than larger noses. As a result of group identity, or maybe of preference in choosing a sexual partner, retroussé noses (small and turned up at the tip) may then become the preferred physical type in the group. That will reinforce drift towards small noses, and the descendants of the group will all end up having very small noses. Other features genetically associated with small noses, such as flat faces, also get drawn into the drift.

The other theory, older and perhaps most contentious, is that Mongoloid founders somehow adapted to cope with a changed and hostile environment, in this case the much colder and windier conditions of the Asian Steppe north of the Himalayas. This idea has a long pedigree, but is perhaps best articulated by American biologist Dale Guthrie. Guthrie has persuasively described what he calls the Mammoth Steppe of Palaeolithic Asia. The Mammoth Steppe was in reality a vast, high grassland whose heartland was in the region north of the 35th parallel, the Himalayas and the Tibetan plateau. Also known to biologists as the Palaearctic biome, the whole complex cold habitat disappeared from 10,000 years ago, as a paradoxical result of global warming, taking with it a whole range of large and small fauna and flora for ever.[18]

According to Guthrie, the southern heart of the steppe was occupied by early modern humans spread across Singkiang, Mongolia, and the Lake Baikal region of Siberia. These are areas that now contain large expanses of desert. At its greatest extent the Mammoth Steppe stretched from the Atlantic coast of Europe in the west to Hokkaido in the east. It was the greatest grassland the world had ever seen, and it supported almost limitless herds of large herbivores. Some of these herbivores still survive in a severely reduced range and mostly in small numbers – they include wild horse, reindeer, musk-ox, and saiga antelope – but the large ones – woolly mammoth, steppe bison, and woolly rhinoceros – became extinct.

Clearly, the Mammoth Steppe would have been paradise for hunters who could cope with the intense cold, dry winds. Guthrie suggested that the Palaeolithic peoples who preyed on the herds of the steppe tended to inhabit the warmer southern fringes around the 40th parallel, where there were more islands of forest shelter (see Figure 5.3). It is certain that people living in such cold conditions would have needed clothing. Guthrie and others have suggested a number of physical adaptations which would have helped Mongoloids to cope with this harsh environment. They include the double upper eyelid, or fatty epicanthic fold, to reduce heat loss from the eye; more insulating subcutaneous fat padding around the eyes on the cheeks, jaw, and chin; a smaller nose profile to reduce the risk of frostbite; a rounder head with fewer angles which loses less heat; a shorter, stockier body with relatively shorter limbs; a more even distribution of fat which, with the changes in limb proportion, gives an overall reduction of 10 per cent in surface-to-volume ratio; a pale skin like that of Europeans, allowing adequate vitamin D production against rickets; and an enhanced response of blood vessels in the limbs to avoid frostbite.

Personally, although the overall argument is attractive, I find the rest of Guthrie's list over-inclusive and I am not at all convinced by the argument about small nose size. In Europe, both modern Europeans and Neanderthals seem to have selected for large noses as air conditioners to warm and moisten air about to enter sensitive lungs.

This seems a convincing enough reason for big noses and, if correct, would clearly have happened independently twice. How can small noses then also be good for the cold? Eskimos and, to a lesser extent, the Chuckchis of north-east Siberia have what has been referred to as a 'pinched' nose' – a projecting nose set in a very flat upper face.[19] This further adaptation in extreme northern Mongoloids suggests that the small nose was not a particularly good air conditioner in the first place and required modification in the Arctic.

Perhaps the strongest pieces of internal evidence (by which I mean consistency of degree in actual observations based on predictions of the theory) for the adaptations occurring to the north, where Guthrie said they did, are the relatively paler skin found in Northern Mongoloids, and the most extreme physical changes, such as facial flattening, having occurred around Lake Baikal in both ancient and in modern populations.[20]

Guthrie also speculates on how long these adaptive changes took and when they started. Reasonably, he views the last glacial maximum 20,000 years ago as the climax of cold stress that produced most change, but he suggests that the whole process started as long ago as 40,000 years. What might support this longer timescale is that, as already mentioned, Mongoloid changes such as facial flattening are known from the west of Lake Baikal from before the last glaciation (see Figure 5.3).

Although I am tempted by Guthrie's story as far as the evolutionary pressures are concerned, I have a problem with the scarcity of hard physical evidence in the fossil record. There is also the major question of how the Southern Mongoloids of tropical Southeast Asia gained their characteristic features in the first place if they are supposed to be descended from the stay-at-homes. If the whole package of features common to both Northern and Southern Mongoloids is primarily due to cold adaptation, then, according to the south–north theory, it should not be present in Southern

Mongoloids. As an anecdotal aside, I can record that my dear wife, whose ancestors are all from the south coast of China and who in the classification I am using here is therefore Southern Mongoloid, is far less tolerant of cold than I am, consistent with an ultimate southern origin!

If the south–north and cold-adaptation theories are both correct, we have to concede that the initial physical changes may have resulted from an evolutionary mechanism other than adaptation to cold, and that some of those changes were later serendipitously amplified by cold selection.

Neoteny in humans

I am drawn to Guthrie's explanation of evolutionary pressures in the north, but also favour an initial south–north movement on the basis of dental and genetic evidence. There is another evolutionary phenomenon that may bridge the two. An interesting hypothesis put forward by palaeontologist Stephen Jay Gould many years ago was that the package of the Mongoloid anatomical changes could be explained by the phenomenon of neoteny, whereby an infantile or childlike body form is preserved in adult life. Neoteny in hominids is still one of the simplest explanations of how we developed a disproportionately large brain so rapidly over the past few million years. The relatively large brain and the forward rotation of the skull on the spinal column, and body hair loss, both characteristic of humans, are found in foetal chimps. Gould suggested a mild intensification of neoteny in Mongoloids, in whom it has been given the name 'paedomorphy'.[21] Such a mechanism is likely to involve only a few controller genes and could therefore happen over a relatively short evolutionary period. It would also explain how the counterintuitive retroussé nose and relative loss of facial hair got into the package.

There are several evolutionary mechanisms by which paedomorphic individuals could produce relatively more offspring over time, which could operate through drift or selection, and which are not mutually exclusive. One could be through an association with thrifty genes, useful for the cold steppe (decrease unnecessary muscle bulk, less tooth mass, thinner bones, and smaller physical size); this follows the selective/adaptive model of Mongoloid evolution, which could have made use of pre-existing traits that just happened to arise among Sundadont populations migrating up the coast from the south. Equally, paedomorphic women may have been more highly prized for looking cuter: this is more of a sexual selection and drift hypothesis and, again, while further exaggerated drift or selection may have occurred in the north, the pre-existing traits could have ultimately come from the south.

I would argue that both mechanisms came into play in Mongoloid development. Southern Mongoloid features could have developed initially as a result of sexual selection and/or drift. Then, as some of those peoples moved north into Central Asia, there would have been further 'development on the theme' in response to the evolutionary pressures Dale Guthrie so vividly describes. In a sense, therefore, there were two homeland platforms for the development of Mongoloid features. This armchair theory has no immediate scientific support since geneticists are, as yet, only on the threshold of understanding the genes that control growth and body moulding, let alone detecting meaningful differences within our own species. On the other hand, genetic tracking may be able to help with the direction of migration.

Four routes into Central Asia

As with all previous explorations, by both modern and archaic humans, geography and climate decided the newly arrived occupants of Asia where to go next. The rules would have been simple: stay near water, and near reliable rainfall; when moving, avoid deserts and high mountains and follow the game and the rivers. We have seen circumstantial evidence that the beachcombing route round the coast of the Indian Ocean to Australia was the easiest and earliest option. Why should this have been? It was not that easy: for a start, every few hundred kilometres our explorers would have had to ford a great river at its mouth. Yet this is just what they must have done to get to Australia, so it is possible they did the same along the East Asian coast. At each river there was the option for some people to turn left and head inland, harvesting river produce and game as they went.

As one of the earliest European explorers, Marco Polo, found out, mountains and deserts present formidable barriers to those trying to gain access to Central Asia; apart from a few trails, the only routes of entry are along the river valleys. We have seen that our first successful exodus from Africa took the ancestors of all non-Africans south along the Indian Ocean coast perhaps as long ago as 75,000 years. They may also have beachcombed as far as eastern China and Japan rather early on. They would thus have skirted the whole of the Central Asian region. They could have tried to head upriver and inland at any point on their journey.

North of India, with the Himalayas in the way, it was not as straightforward as that. The raised folds of mountains caused by India's ancient tectonic collision with Asia extend either side of Nepal and Tibet well beyond the highest Himalayas. A vast band of mountains, all over 3,000 metres (10,000 feet), blocks Central Asia to access from the Indian Ocean coast for a distance of 6,500 km (4,000 miles) from Afghanistan in the west to Chengdu, in China, to the east. This band is rucked up like a carpet in the east, thus extending the mountain barrier south as a series of north–south ridges over a distance of about 2,500 km (1,500 miles) from the beginning of the Silk Road in northern China south to Thailand.

The Silk Road, first made famous in the West by Marco Polo, is a long trading route, parallel to and to the north of the Himalayas, connecting West with East. It passes right through Central Asia, directly along the southern edge of Guthrie's Mammoth Steppe heartland. The Silk Road was then, as it is now, one of the few links between China and the West, if the long coastal route round south via Singapore was to be avoided.

East along the Silk Road from the west end of the Himalayas   Today the Silk Road skirts both the southern and northern edges of the Taklamakan Desert of Singkiang. During the Palaeolithic, what is now desert was mostly lush grassland, and farther north a series of waterways, including the Tarim and Dzungaria rivers, provided easy west–east access for hunters from the western Central Asian regions of Tajikistan, Uzbekistan, Kirghistan, and Kazakhstan into Singkiang and Mongolia. These waterways may have been used by earlier humans to get to Central Asia.[22]

To look at Stone Age practicalities, let us take the first access route to Central Asia up the Indus, 8,000 km (5,000 miles) to the west of China at the western end of the Silk Road. Assuming for the moment that we are talking about an offshoot of the first Indian beachcombers, their first task after moving up the Indus would have been to negotiate the mountain barriers to the north of India and Pakistan. These extend as far west as Afghanistan. Bypassing the mountains and moving through Afghanistan too far to the west would have been difficult if not impossible, since it was near-desert. Marco Polo crossed these deserts, leaving from Hormuz at the mouth of the Gulf and passing through Afghanistan to Kashmir, crossing a high pass directly into China and the city of Kashgar, to arrive well along the Silk Road and directly in the heartland of the former Mammoth Steppe (Figure 5.5).

Marco Polo could have followed a much easier route to Kashmir, however. From the coast of Pakistan a little further to the east, the great Indus snakes northward to a point where there is a water connection through to Kashmir. Another lower-altitude route into Central Asia, also via the headwaters of the Indus, would have been

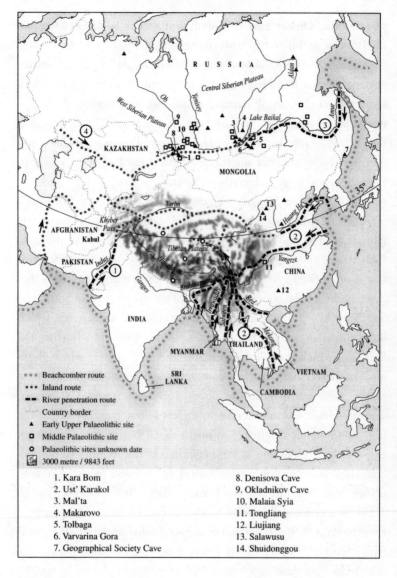

Figure 5.5 Four Palaeolithic routes into Central Asia. Access to Central Asia has always been limited by the Himalayas, their flanking ranges and various deserts. The possible routes of entry, mainly via the great Asian rivers, are shown here and apply to the following maps in this chapter and the next. Earliest human settlements also shown.

to cross the Khyber Pass to Kabul, and thence to Uzbekistan and Kazakhstan, and then east towards Singkiang.

West along the Silk Road from China   Equally, during all of human history, the Silk Road has been the only route west from China into Central Asia. So, an alternative route into the Mammoth Steppe would have been from the East Asian Pacific coast. The vanguard of the earliest beachcombers could have gone all the way to China and then moved west from northern China along the Silk Road into Mongolia, Sinkiang, and southern Siberia.

North into Tibet from Burma   The third access route to the Mammoth Steppe, not much used by traders today, is just to the east of the Himalayas. The eastern edge of the Himalayas consists of multiple folds where the edge of the Indian plate rucked up the Asian continent on collision. We can see from the map (see Figure 5.5) that these rucks are the conduits for most of the great rivers of South and Southeast Asia. From west to east, these are the Brahmaputra, which flows into Bangladesh, the Salween, which flows into Burma, the Mekong, which flows into Vietnam, and the Yangtzi, which flows into southern China. As they flow out of south-east Tibet these four major rivers run parallel for about 150 km (around 100 miles), separated from one another by only a few kilometres. The last of the four, the Yangtzi, originates in north-east Tibet near the northern edge of the plateau and at the beginning of the Mammoth Steppe. I mention these multiple river routes not because many legitimate traders use them today, but because they allow direct access to Tibet, Mongolia, and Central Asia from any of four widely separated river mouths in Southeast and East Asia discharging on to the Indo-Pacific coast. Also, as we shall see, Tibet shares much genetically with Indo-China and Southeast Asia.

East from Russia   Finally, there is another, more northerly route of migration from the West into East Asia to be considered: via Asian Russia, known as the Russian Altai. The easiest direct land access from the Russian Altai to Central Asia during the milder parts of the

Late Stone Age 30,000–50,000 years ago would have been to cross the steppe directly. Travelling east through southern Siberia via a series of lakes and waterways, our ancient explorers could have reached the Lake Baikal region by a route passing north of Singkiang and Mongolia. At that time the steppe covered the whole region in greensward and open woodland. Clearly, for modern humans to have taken this route they must have got to the Russian Altai in the first place. As we shall see, they had reached both the Russian Altai and Lake Baikal in southern Siberia by 40,000 years ago.

*   *   *

We have now seen that there are four possible access routes into Central Asia: three from the Indo-Pacific coast (west, south, and east) and one from Russia (north-west). Once in Central Asia, there were three parallel routes along water bodies between East and West Asia which the pioneers could have followed: two southern ones, through Singkiang and Mongolia, and a northern one across Southern Siberia. The northern route would have been accessible only during the milder periods of the Palaeolithic 30,000–50,000 years ago, during the interstadials (see Chapter 3).

When did modern humans first roam the steppe?

At present, it is along the last and most northerly of these three corridors that we find the clearest archaeological evidence for modern humans north of the Himalayas over 40,000 years ago. Southern Siberia is right at the northern reaches of Guthrie's favoured Mammoth Steppe heartland of Singkiang and Mongolia. Exciting recent excavations in the caves of U'st-Karakol and Kara-Bom in the Russian Altai (see Figure 5.5) indicate that the new Upper Palaeolithic stone technology had arrived there by 43,000 years ago. These Altai dates are closely followed, farther to the east, by a 39,000-year-old Upper Palaeolithic site at Makarovo on the western side of Lake Baikal. By 30,000–35,000 years ago, more such sites appear at Varvarina Gora and Tolbaga on the eastern

side of Lake Baikal, and at Malaia Syia, much farther north near the
Yenisei River. This means that the Upper Palaeolithic transition
across southern Siberia was at least as early as that in Europe.[23]

Belgian archaeologist Marcel Otte has recently suggested a centre
of origin for the Upper Palaeolithic technology in the northern
Zagros Mountains of Iran and Iraq from where it spread both north-
west to the Levant and Europe, and north-east into Central Asia and
the Russian Altai, presumably either along the route just described
for Marco Polo or through the Caucasus first.[24]

Can stone tools tell us which human was the first in Central Asia?
The appearance of Upper Palaeolithic technology has been accepted
as the definitive signal of modern humans' first entry into Balkan
Europe further to the west, and has been used to distinguish their
movements from Neanderthals who had been making Middle
Palaeolithic tools there for several hundred thousand years (see
Chapter 3). This could suggest a parallel arrival of modern humans
sharing the same Upper Palaeolithic technology into the Altai by at
least 43,000 years ago from the Zagros region to the south.[25]
However, if Upper Palaeolithic technology is not a *sine qua non* for
moderns in Asia, then modern humans might actually have arrived
even earlier in the Russian Altai.

There are several reasons for this caution in dating modern
arrivals anywhere in Asia. First, although the Upper Palaeolithic
stone technology uniquely confirms the presence of modern
humans in Europe, as we have seen for the Levant and Southeast
Asia, it was not the only technology used by moderns so it cannot
help us to define their first arrival elsewhere. The Upper Palaeolithic
was a collection of innovations, the first of which appears in the
archaeological record 45,000–50,000 years ago and is particularly
associated with North and West Eurasia. Early modern humans
used several different older techniques, including similar Middle
Palaeolithic traditions to those of the Neanderthals. The caves in

the Russian Altai, in particular Kara-Bom, also show a Middle Palaeolithic tradition underlying the Aurignacian Upper Palaeolithic layers and dating back as far as 62,000–72,000 years ago. These lower layers are difficult to assign to either modern or archaic humans (such as Neanderthals), since they could have been made by either and there are no fossils available to identify their makers. No Neanderthal remains have ever been found as far north as the Russian Altai, although they have been found much farther to the south-west, in Teshik Tash in Uzbekistan, Central Asia. A key issue is whether the older Middle Palaeolithic layers show a continuous indigenous graded change towards the later technology, or the Upper Palaeolithic is intrusive. The latter seems to be true, at least for the Aurignacian technology. So the possibility remains that the earlier Middle Palaeolithic, going back 60,000–70,000 years in the cave of Kara-Bom, represented an even earlier modern human occupation of the Altai.[26]

The second reason for caution is that, until recently, the timeline of the Palaeolithic record of Singkiang, Tibet, and Mongolia to the south has hardly been studied. This is not for lack of Palaeolithic remains, but at least partly because many of them have not been datable. A recent field report from Mongolia suggests a Middle Palaeolithic tradition going back perhaps 60,000 years. Another report suggests two separate Upper Palaeolithic (microlithic) traditions in Tibet, a northern and a southern one, which were linked respectively with peoples and stone-tool traditions of northern and southern China. Dating was uncertain, since many finds were on the surface (surface finds lack context and stratification, which are essential in the process of archaeological dating).[27]

So, there is very clear archaeological evidence for an Upper Palaeolithic technology spreading parallel but farther north right across southern Siberia, starting from the Russian Altai 43,000 years ago. On the other hand, there was an earlier human occupation of Central Asia and the southern heartland of the Mammoth Steppe, but there is as yet no clear fossil evidence for their identities. As we shall see shortly, the genetic evidence from North Asia supports the 40,000-year date for the arrival of modern humans in north-west Asia. The North Asian Upper Palaeolithic eventually shared the rich Mammoth-based Gravettian culture of Central and Eastern Europe farther west, as can be seen from art discovered at Mal'ta near Lake Baikal from 23,000 years ago (see Plate 21).[28]

Genetics

I have reviewed archaeological evidence which supports the presence of early modern humans in Central Asia and for their presence at the three entry points from the coast to the only corridors into Central Asia, the Silk Road and Guthrie's Mammoth Steppe heartland. These three entry gates were in north-west Asia, Indo-China, and north-eastern China. So far I have mentioned little about the genetic evidence – and there is a reason for this. The tree structure of the mtDNA and Y markers is better at signalling ancient migrations of molecules than it is at dating movements or identifying so-called 'races' or ethnic groups. It is therefore safer, where possible, to identify what migration routes are allowed by geography, archaeology, and climate before testing how these are supported by the genetic story.

A clear north–south division in East Asia

I said in Chapter 2 that after the initial modern human dispersals out of Africa, each region of the Old World and the south-west Pacific became settled, and little if any further inter-regional gene flow happened until the build-up to the last great glaciation 20,000 years ago. Asia, in spite of its history of mass movements, is no exception to this rule. Certain broad genetic divisions within Asia became clear to geneticists before the focus on mtDNA and Y markers. As expected, the Caucasoid regions of West Eurasia were found to group together, with some overlap on the Indian subcontinent.

There was a clear separation from East Eurasia, which in turn split north–south, consistent with the Northern and Southern Mongoloid division. In terms of human provenance, we can thus distinguish between Southeast Asia (including the south coast of China: Guandong, Guangxi, and Fujian provinces) and Northeast Asia (including northern China, the east coast of China, Korea, Mongolia, Tibet, and parts of Siberia), with one group in the extreme north-east of Asia intermediate between the Caucasoids and Northern Mongoloids.[29]

Such studies have not helped much to trace origins, but they do serve to show that there are still marked regional differences, even among the majority so-called Han ethnic group in China, who also show a clear north–south difference. These studies also bury some myths that have grown up about Chinese genetic origins. For example, it had been widely accepted that there was a massive population expansion of Han Chinese from north to south during the past several thousand years of Imperial rule, overlaying, displacing, and replacing the bulk of indigenous minorities in the south. Recent historical research has shown, however, that Han identity in the south of China was, for pragmatic political reasons, adopted or even synthesized by southern indigenous peoples over the past few hundred years.[30] This suggests that much of the historic population migration in China was apparent rather than real, and supports the view that regional populations may have been more stable over the past few thousand years than was previously assumed.

Another approach to the question of whether Mongoloids originated in the north or the south is to consider diversity. On general Darwinian principles, a new species (or, in this instance, new ethnic group expanding from a small founder population) should have one centre of origin, which should retain the greatest diversity of types (e.g. genetic) within that group. Now, whichever genetic system one uses, Southern Mongoloids always show far greater genetic diversity than do those in the north. Y-chromosome evidence has already been used to justify placing the Mongoloid homeland in the south.[31] Although it is useful, we face two potential pitfalls if we take such a simplistic diversity approach. First, none of the gene lines or markers used has been clearly identified as 'Mongoloid': they are simply Mongoloid by implication because of where they have been found, so the argument is in danger of becoming partly circular if it is crudely applied. Second, North Asia, unlike tropical Southeast Asia, would have suffered depopulation, great extinction, and genetic drift during the last glaciation, so the low diversity would be expected in the north today and thus may not necessarily reflect the original picture.

An extreme hypothetical view of the effect of the last glaciation on Central and North Asia is that the entire Asian region extending north of the Himalayas was completely cleared of people, so that today's populations are merely re-entrants from South China and Southeast Asia and from Europe. That would of course mean that we can never know the original genetic composition of Northern Asia. This view is not tenable. First, palaeoclimatological studies show that during the ice age extensive steppe tundra regions persisted in Central Asia which could have supported hunters. This is backed up by archaeological evidence for continuous occupation through the last glacial maximum (see Chapter 6). Dale Guthrie certainly argues against such a complete extinction in the south of the Mammoth Steppe heartland. Second, as we shall see, this picture fails to explain the deep genetic diversity of south-west Central Asia (Uzbekistan and Kirghistan), or the marked geographical difference in deep genetic branch lines between north and south Asia. In particular, as I shall show, there are a group of lines still shared uniquely between northern Europe, northern Asia and northern America that have no links at all with south China or Southeast Asia.[32]

Mapping the spread of the gene tree

As with the out-of-Africa story, the answer becomes clearer when we look at the Adam and Eve markers. The great advance that came with the mapping of the mtDNA and Y-chromosome trees was the ability to trace individual molecular branches and their twigs, like a vine, from one region to the next. The fancy name for this tracking game is phylogeography, but at its simplest it consists in following twigs back to their branches and connecting points on a map.

The rules are simple, although their application can be complex. To detect a migration from one region to another, we need to find the source branch type in both regions and a new unique twig in the target region that is not present in the homeland. For a homeland with multiple migrations in different directions, we need to identify common branches in the homeland that have *different* unique twigs in the other regions. Perhaps one of the best known and earliest examples of this approach was published by Italian geneticist Antonio Torroni and his colleagues in 1993. They identified four American founder mtDNA lines, which they labelled A to D. Each of these four bushy twigs, although showing unique new sprouts in America, could be traced back to the equivalent source branches, A, B, C, and D, in Asia (see Chapters 6 and 7).

We can apply this process to the much more difficult task of identifying the Mongoloid homeland in Asia. Taking East Asian mtDNA first, we find that at present there are nine well-described deep branches (haplogroups; see Figure 5.6), which have been designated A–G, X, and Z. With the exception of the sister groups C and Z, none of the nine groups can be derived from any other; they each arise more or less directly from the two Eurasian founder lines Manju or Nasreen. Several other minor groups (M7/M10, and N9) have recently been described, but their existence doesn't alter the argument. (For details of the phylogeny of and sources for mtDNA haplogroup distributions in East Asia, see note [33].)

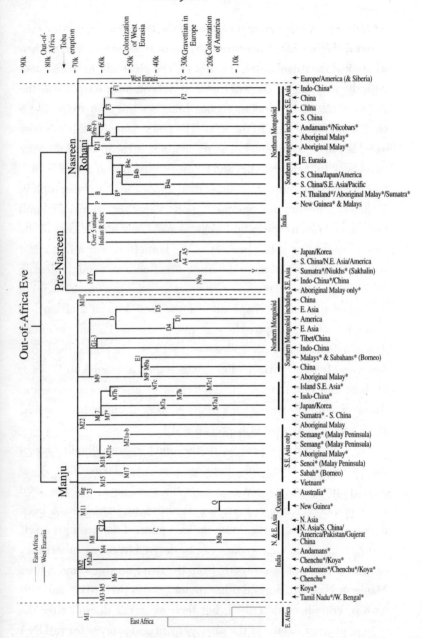

Of the nine better-known East Asian mtDNA branches, three (C, X, and Z; Figure 5.6) feature only north of an east–west line drawn below the Himalayas, while the other six (A, B, D, E, F, and G) are found in *both* Northern and Southern Mongoloids. At first these unique northern branches might appear to favour a Mongoloid homeland north of the Himalayas, but there is a simpler explanation. This is that C, with her closely related sister Z and the mysterious X group, were not part of early Mongoloid history and had intruded among Northern Mongoloids from somewhere else, such as Siberia or Central Asia. As we shall see, there is evidence to support this view. the distribution and tree structure of the other six branches appears to favour a genetic homeland south of the Himalayas, particularly for the oldest branches of B and F. So we appear to have several genetic sources among Southeast Asians that have also spread north. In contrast, there are several branches among Northern Asians which have no roots in Southeast Asia. In crude branch terms, therefore, the idea of a southern homeland with subsequent migration to the north would seem to be supported by the maternal genetic evidence, and would be consistent with Sundadonty-became-Sinodonty (see Chapter 5).

In order to focus on that possible secondary northern region of 'further development on a theme', we have to look for geographical areas possessing all the six mitochondrial branches – A, B, D, E, F, and G – that are common to both Northern and Southern Mongoloids. So, moving from west to east, we find Central Asia with five (lacking just G), Tibet with all six, Mongolia with five

Figure 5.6 The Asian and Pacific mtDNA tree. Note: 1) no overlap in subbranches of M and N between India and East Asia except for the M8/CZ clan which went to North Asia; 2) Oceania and Southeast Asia have unique local diversity associated with their aboriginal groups; 3) extensive overlap between lines in Southern and Northern Mongoloid groups, but the Southerners, including aboriginals, have a complete set while the North has fewer and more derived lines.

(lacking E), China with four (lacking E and G), and Korea with five (lacking E).[34] Perhaps it is not too much of a coincidence that the countries with the highest proportion of lines generally associated with Mongoloid peoples – Central Asia, Tibet, Mongolia, and Korea – straddle Dale Guthrie's 40th parallel of the Mammoth Steppe (see Figure 5.3).

On this basis, we could start to ask for how long those branches have been present around the 40th parallel. Toomas Kivisild has estimated the local age of four of these lines in Mongolia and they look fairly consistent: A at 35,500 years, B at 40,500 and 33,500 years (see below), D at 44,500 years, and F at 42,000 years. These dates are mostly younger than the overall ages of the same lines farther south in China. But again, they are consistent with dates for the start of the Central Asian colony, and after the Asian climatic amelioration that set in from 52,000 years ago (see Chapter 3), which could have allowed the early Asians to penetrate far into the Mammoth Steppe.[35]

By what routes, then, did modern humans first make their way up into this region? Returning to two of the oldest Southeast Asian lines, B and F (from Nasreen's descendants), which appear to have spread north from Southeast Asia into Tibet, Mongolia, and northeast along the Pacific coast, we find that they stopped inland short of Siberia in Northern Asia.[36] In this respect, the distribution of Groups B and F mirrors the ancient distribution of Sundadonty. Both B and F reach their deepest and greatest diversity among the aboriginal ethnic groups of Thailand, Vietnam, and Cambodia, thus pointing to Indo-China as their homeland.

Strong supporting evidence for Group F having originated in the south is provided by our newly identified 'pre-F' group (R9), which is common in the Aboriginal Malays of the Malay Peninsula (at the base of the Sundadont radiation – see Figures 5.6 and 5.7). This pre-F is also found in South China (Yunnan and Guangxi), Indo-China (Thailand and Vietnam), Sumatra, and the Andaman and Nicobar

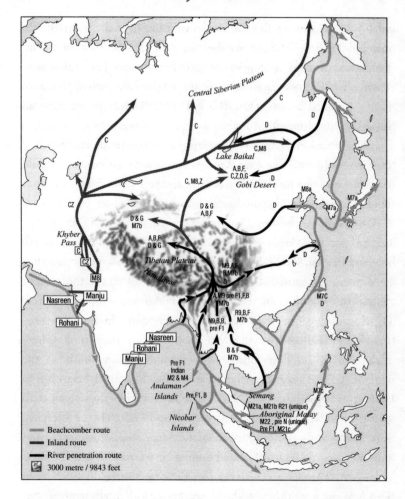

Figure 5.7 First entry of mtDNA lines into Central Asia from the Indo-Pacific coastline. The entry routes mainly correspond with rivers shown in Figure 5.5 and along Silk Road branches once in Central Asia. With the exception of lines M8/C/Z which enter west of the Himalayas, all other lines originate from Southeast Asian beachcombers.

Islands, suggesting possibly the oldest link with the first beachcombers in Southeast Asia.[37]

Knowing whether Group B originally spread west from China

into Mongolia along the Silk Road or moved north from Burma through Tibet would tell us the route of that first colonization, which was perhaps as long ago as 50,000 years ago. There are clues. Toomas Kivisild estimated the ages of the two common subgroups of B in Mongolia as 40,500 (B1) and 33,500 (B2) years. This all suggests that although Mongolia and parts of western Central Asia may have received both B types during the Palaeolithic, the older of the two could have come up through Tibet, while the younger could have moved west into Central Asia from the Pacific coast, where it now predominates.[38]

We also have the three partly related Manju lines D, E, and G, whose distribution in East Asia increasing from south to north mirrors that of Sinodonty. The genetic evidence suggests that they came from the south. There is still the puzzle of where those other 'intrusive' founders of the Mongoloid Mammoth Steppe colony (C, X, and Z) came from in the first place, and which of the three possible corridors into the Mammoth Steppe they took. These three North Eurasian lines are very uncommon south of the Himalayas. The sister branches C and Z reach their highest rates in Siberia and Northeast Asia, and are hardly found farther south at all except in India, Mongolia, Central Asia, and Tibet. They stretch in a broad east–west continuum across the Asian Steppe, achieving significant rates in Central Asia and even as far west as Turkey. Group C even got to America via Alaska, yet their northerly distribution in East Asia suggests they could not have moved up north from Southeast Asia via China. Rather, they are more likely to have arrived from farther west in Asia, along with the eastern spread of the Upper Palaeolithic technology that appeared in Kara Bom in the Russian Altai 43,000 years ago. They belong to the Manju group, and their ultimate ancestors appear to come from Pakistan or India, having moved up the valley of the Indus via Kashmir or Afghanistan round the *western* end of the Himalayas (see Figures 5.5 and 5.6). This all suggests that they moved into the Asian Steppe between

40,000 and 50,000 years ago from west Central Asia (see Figure 5.7). Consistent with the concept that C and Z spread east across the steppe with Upper Palaeolithic technology, Toomas Kivisild has estimated the age of C in Mongolia at 42,000 years.[39]

The last of the northern lines, X, is found only among Europeans and Native Americans, with a single report from southern Siberia, but the link between the Old and New Worlds is up to 30,000 years old. This suggests that X must originally have spread right across Central and Northeast Asia with the mammoth-hunting culture, but she was all but extinguished in Asia during the last ice age, surviving only at the extremes of her distribution in America and Europe (see Chapter 7).[40]

The complicated mitochondrial picture described above suggests that Mongoloids derive primarily from the south, while Central Asian peoples came mainly from a West Asian source, but combined with additional East and Southeast Asian sources in Central and Northeast Asia. This genetic evidence then supports the geographical theory of a three-pincer colonization of Central Asia from the Indo-Pacific coast about 40,000–50,000 years ago. The dissection of the various admixed genetic contributions to Northeast Asia clarifies and is consistent with the concept of an ultimately Southeast Asian origin of Mongoloid peoples.

Adam's story

Now, having looked at the mtDNA evidence, when we study the same Asian story in the Y-chromosome tree the picture of several inputs to Central Asia takes on more contrast. Adam's tree is in many respects a scientific newcomer. As yet, it lacks the vast number of unique twigs sprouting from Eve's tree of life, and the Y-chromosome branch dates are still very unreliable. So why should I keep turning to Adam, merely to back up the same story told much better by Eve? Because where the Y chromosome comes into its own is in clearly marking regional patterns. We saw a good example of this with the peopling of Europe (see Chapter 3), where different paternal clans have greater regional clarity within Europe than do Eve's maternal clans. The latter, although regionally structured, seem more blurred in their distribution. The same is true of East Asia. The Adam and Eve trees both suggest that Central Asians and Americans have Northwest, East, and Southeast Asian origins, but the separation of these three strands for the founding peoples of the Mammoth Steppe is much clearer in the Adam tree. To understand this better, we need to remind ourselves briefly of the three main out-of-Africa Adam founding lines: Abel (YAP or M145), Cain (or RPS4Y), and Seth (or M89).[41] (See Figure 5.8.)

Cain was the line that travelled rapidly south-east along the Indian Ocean coast to become the first male founder in Eastern Indonesia, Australia, and New Guinea. The beachcombers did not confine themselves to the Antipodes but moved on around the Indo-Pacific coast to Japan and Korea, where they formed the earliest colonies there. Somewhere along the Palaeolithic coast-ride, most likely towards the end of the trail in Japan, Cain had a unique progenitor Asian son whose descendants spread throughout Northeast Asia, then west along the Silk Road into Mongolia and Central Asia. They also eventually went east into the Americas.[42]

We saw in Chapter 4 that Abel's western sons contributed respectively to the peopling of Europe, the Middle East, and Africa, but there was another, uniquely East Asian branch of Abel's line. Just like Cain, this Asian Abel followed rapidly round the coast road, south-east to Indonesia, and then north to Taiwan and Japan, but no farther north than Korea. Asian Abel's descendants cannot now be

Figure 5.8 The Asian Y-chromosome tree. Note the almost complete separation between South Asia and Southeast Asians, except for overlap in tribals from West Bengal and shared root lines among all relict groups; also, unlike mtDNA, the near total separation of Northern vs. Southern Mongoloids, with latter dominated by Ho and former sharing lines extensively with South Asia and west Central Asia, particularly Polo derivatives.

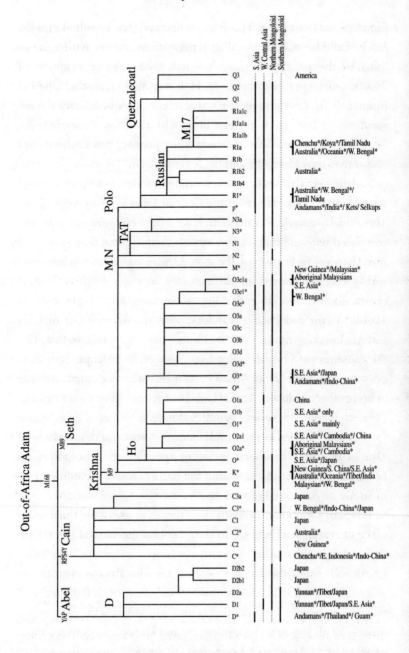

found en route in India. This may be because they travelled rapidly, but it could be that their Indian representatives were wiped out in India by the ash cloud from the great Toba volcanic eruption of 74,000 years ago (see Chapter 4). However, there is now a high Abel frequency in Tibet, suggesting that some of his ancestors were survivors of Toba from eastern India who took the river route up from Southeast Asia onto the high Asian plateau, from where they also spread into Mongolia and the Russian Altai.[43]

So, the first two male beachcombing founder clans used both of the eastern corridors to enter the Central Asian Steppe (Figure 5.9). Their final numerical contribution to world colonization was tiny compared with the third Adam branch, Seth, whose dominant seed spread to every corner of the non-African world and whose off-spring eventually used all three routes to enter Central Asia. A recent survey showed Seth's line accounting for 93 per cent of 12,127 Asians and Pacific islanders, with the descendants of Cain and Abel making up the rest. It is important to appreciate that, like the daughters of Out-of-Africa Eve, Nasreen and Manju, Seth trav-elled the coast road from Africa in company with *and at the same time as* his brothers Cain and Abel. He did not come out at a later time or by another route, as several geneticists have suggested. The evidence for this may be seen in the simultaneous presence of descendants of each of the three brothers, including specific Seth types, in relict beachcomber populations around the Indian Ocean, including those in Southeast Asia (see Figure 5.9).[44]

It is Seth's trail that confirms the alternative use of the third route – the northern trail into Central Asia round the west of the Hima-layas (along with the more southerly beachcomber trails to Indo-China and round the eastern edge of the Himalayas). We can see where he started. Two-thirds of the world deep-branch diversity of this major founder Eurasian line is found in India. Seth represents a quarter of all Indian Y chromosomes, and his sons account for most of the rest.[45] Another 10 per cent of the Seth node is found in

Central Asia and, correspondingly, all four of his first-generation sons have significant Central Asian representatives, again suggesting the potential for direct spread north at the same time as the North Eurasian mitochondrial groups C, X, and Z around 40,000 years ago (see pp. 234–5).

We have seen that three of Seth's sons were responsible for the colonization of much of India, Europe, the Middle East, and Mediterranean lands.[46] In this part of the story, however, we are not so much concerned with Seth and his three West Eurasian sons as with his fourth genetic son, Krishna, and the latter's role in fathering the bulk of Eurasians not to mention nearly all Native Americans.

Krishna accounts for about 40 per cent of Y-chromosome types discovered so far. His wide distribution in Europe, Asia, the Pacific, and the Americas suggests that he was born in India very soon after the initial out-of-Africa dispersal. In spite of his early birth and the wide dissemination of his line, Krishna's immediate sons have very discrete geographical distributions. Several are local to Pakistan and India, with some minor spread north to the Levant and Central Asia; another is found only in Melanesia (New Guinea and the surrounding islands); yet another (TAT) is exclusive to Central Asia and north-eastern Europe.[47]

The two most prolific genetic sons of Krishna, however, are also by far the most dominant in terms of territory covered. They each illuminate the separate trails of the Palaeolithic peopling of Eurasia and America. One of these branches, Group O, is found nearly exclusively in East and Southeast Asia. I shall call this branch Ho, after both the Chinese explorer Admiral Cheng Ho and the revered Vietnamese nationalist hero Ho Chi Minh. If we imagine that this branch was born, like the maternal lines B and F, when a beach-combing Krishna arrived in Burma from India, then Ho splits easily into three branches. All three branches now have representatives in China, Indo-China, and Southeast Asia, but they differed in their degree of northern spread. One remained in southern China, Indo-

China, and Southeast Asia and still makes up 65 per cent of Malaysian aboriginal types. The second spread up the Pacific coast into southern China, although concentrating on Taiwan. The third spread much farther into China and north along the Chinese coast right up to Japan, Korea, and Northeast Asia, with a small amount of spread west along the Silk Road into Central Asia.[48] Notably, none of these three related East and Southeast Asian male branches ever made it to the Americas (see Figure 5.9).

In contrast to the East and Southeast Asian dominance of Ho, North and Central Asia and the Americas were to have their Y chromosomes supplied almost exclusively by the other major Asian son of Krishna – Polo (M45). The structure of Polo's origin from Krishna in India (Figure 5.8) shows an early branch giving rise to Y markers and their offspring, who are still found among the former inhabitants of the Lake Baikal region (the Kets and Selkups). What is most exciting historically about this root is that it is the same son of Krishna who also gave rise to the westward influx into north-east Europe through Russia, thought to be associated with the Gravettian culture (see Chapter 3). We can now put all this together with the Upper Palaeolithic record of the Altai from 23,000 to 43,000 years ago, and with the story of the mitochondrial lineages of North and Central Asia. Polo would have arrived in Central Asia from Pakistan 40,000 years ago, and spread out in a giant 'T' formation, both east and west across the steppe – east to Lake Baikal and much later to America, and west into Russia and eastern Europe (see Figure 5.9).[49]

We also have confirmation of this extraordinary twin distribution in the mitochondrial X marker in the Americas and Europe, and we have a genetic basis for the North Eurasian origins of the Native American mammoth culture, so eloquently implied by the title of a 1990s book, *From Kostenki to Clovis: Upper Paleolithic – Paleo-Indian Adaptations.*[50]

A picture emerges of peoples moving north out of India and

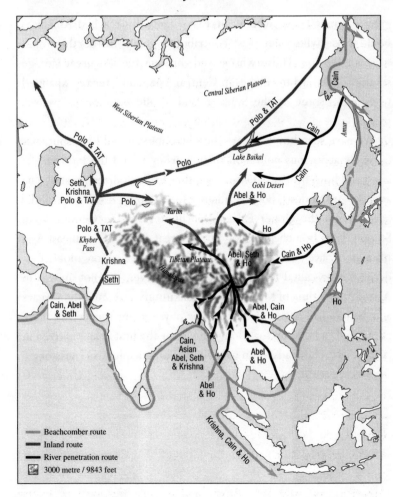

Figure 5.9 First entry of Y-chromosome lines into Central Asia. As with mtDNA (Figure 5.7), the entry routes correspond with major Asian rivers. Seth's grandsons Polo and TAT entered to the west of the Himalayas, dominating North Asia. The rest of East Asian Y lines entered from the Indo-Pacific coast, with Ho dominating China and Southeast Asia, and Cain further north.

Pakistan to occupy the Russian Altai, coping with extraordinary environmental stress but reaping the rich rewards of big game. This North Asian founder population split east and west to occupy the great steppe. Those who went east eventually reached America, while those who went west contributed greatly to northern and western Europe. Those who stayed through the last great ice age shrank southward to refuges in Central Asia, and later re-expanded to become some of the Siberian and Uralic populations we see today.

We have seen how the early beachcombers could have split successively at various points on their journey round the Indo-Pacific coast and how, by 40,000 years ago, they had colonized most of Asia and the Antipodes. The first inland branch going north from India gave rise to the Upper Palaeolithic hunters of the Central Asian Steppe; later branches forging up the great rivers of Southeast Asia ultimately gave rise to a populations we now call Mongoloid. Evidence for so-called Mongoloid types, however, did not appear in Asia until the time of the last glacial maximum, around 20,000 years ago. So the forces that produced this physical divergence may have continued to build up for a long time after the first Asians arrived in North Asia. This leads us on to the next climatic phase of our story – the Great Freeze.

6

THE GREAT FREEZE

IN THE LAST CHAPTER we saw how East and Central Asia as a whole was peopled by a three-pronged pincer style of genetic colonization, starting originally from India. The oldest settlers followed the ancient beachcombing route right round the coast, from India through Indo-China and up north to Japan and Korea, leaving colonies as they went. From these coastal Asian colonies, pioneers penetrated the Central Asian heartland up the great Asian rivers through gaps in the huge east–west wall of mountains that flanks the Himalayas. South-east Tibet and the Qinghai Plateau may have been the first part of Central Asia to be breached 60,000 years ago, from Burma and Indo-China, while those who went up the Indus from Pakistan to the Russian Altai farther west settled during a mild period around 43,000 years ago. People who had reached northern China by the coastal route could have gone west up the Yellow River (the Huang He) into Central Asia around the same time or later.

The map of Northern Asia was now starting to fill up. By 30,000 years ago, a large swathe of the wooded southern part of the former Soviet Union (see Figure 6.1a), from the Russian Altai through Lake Baikal in southern Siberia to the Aldan River in the east, had been colonized by modern pioneers carrying a technology similar to that of the contemporary European Upper Palaeolithic. Even the Arctic Circle was penetrated north of the Urals nearly 40,000 years ago. There is some evidence that the Upper Palaeolithic technology of North Eurasia may have travelled south to Inner Mongolia on a northern bend of the Yellow River, but on present evidence it seems that at this time such cultural influences spread no farther south into China.[1]

Dale Guthrie's vision of the hunter-gatherers wandering the great Asian Mammoth Steppe, stretching from eastern Siberia right across to Europe (see Chapter 5 and Figure 6.1a), takes shape in the archaeological record of around 30,000 years ago. His prediction of the incipient 'Mongoloid' homeland in the southern Steppe is, however, highly speculative for this period and for Siberia. For a start, as mentioned, no indisputably Mongoloid remains have been found from such an early date. For all we know, those early southern Siberians could have looked like the Cro-Magnons of Europe. They shared a similar culture and, at least according to the story told us by the Y-chromosome lines, they shared genes with North Europeans (see Chapter 5). As evidence perhaps of a Western cultural centre of gravity, the first flowering of the mammoth culture at this time seems to have taken place much farther west, in Central and Eastern Europe (see Plates 13 and 14). Evidence for the mammoth culture seems to have reached Mal'ta near Lake Baikal only by perhaps 23,000 years ago (see Plate 21). This is just 2,000 years earlier than the first possible evidence of Mongoloid features from a little to the west of the same region of southern Siberia, at Afontova Gora.[2]

The Big Freeze: ice, lakes, and deserts

As the Palaeolithic clock rolled on towards 20,000 years ago, however, events in the Earth's spin axis and influences on its orbit hundreds of millions of kilometres away from our planet took tighter hold. Three great heavenly cycles of the solar system moved into a conjunction that ensured a minimum of the Sun's heat reached the northern hemisphere during summer.[3] The weather became colder, and the recurrent brief warm periods, or interstadials, which had characterized the period of 30,000–50,000 years ago, just stopped. It was these warm periods and their summer sunshine that had helped to melt the accumulated northern ice and prevent the ice caps from advancing across Scandinavia into Northern Europe. Now, the ice caps were able to expand in the north. The sea level started to fall again, eventually by 120 metres (400 feet). In short, the Earth was approaching its most recent ice age, or glaciation. (There had been quite a bit of ice on and off for the previous 100,000 years, and archaeologists tend to call the height of the Big Freeze the Last Glacial Maximum, or LGM for short, rather than an ice age.)

The LGM and its aftermath saw far more dramatic disruption and movement of northern human populations than at any time since. A glance at the world climate map 18,000 years ago begins to give us the reason why (Figure 6.1b). Huge areas of land became totally uninhabitable. For a start, the ice caps, some of them 5 km (3 miles) thick, clearly prevented the land they covered from being occupied. These white sheets were not laid evenly across the northern hemisphere. In Europe they mainly affected the central and north-western regions. The British Isles, then part of the European mainland, were frozen down as far as Oxford in the south. Scandinavia will for ever bear the scars of the glaciers in its lakes and fjords and in the crustal depression now known as the Baltic Sea. Northern Germany, Poland, and the Baltic states bore the southern edge of the ice sheet, which extended north-east around the Arctic Circle across Finland and Karelia, into Archangel, and as far as the northern Urals. Farther south in Europe, mountainous regions such as the Pyrenees, the Massif Central, the Alps, and the Carpathians were ice-bound (sse Figure 6.2). As we shall see, however, Eastern Europe came off rather more lightly than the west.

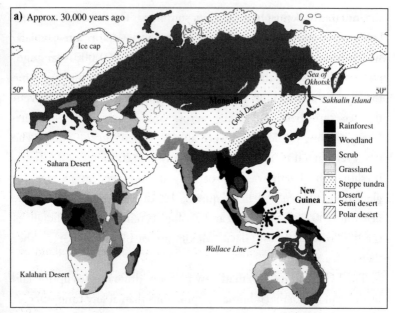

a) Approx. 30,000 years ago

Ice cap

50°   50°

Mongolia

Gobi Desert

Sea of
Okhotsk

Sakhalin Island

Sahara Desert

New
Guinea

Kalahari Desert

Wallace Line

Rainforest
Woodland
Scrub
Grassland
Steppe tundra
Desert/
Semi desert
Polar desert

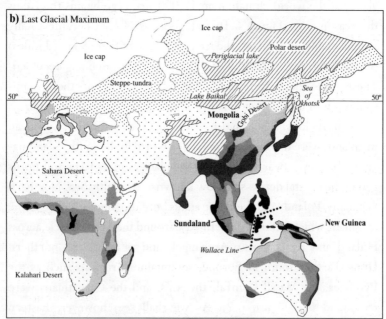

b) Last Glacial Maximum

Ice cap

Ice cap

Periglacial lake

Polar desert

Steppe-tundra

50°   Lake Baikal   50°

Sea
of
Okhotsk

Mongolia

Gobi Desert

Sahara Desert

Sundaland

New Guinea

Wallace Line

Kalahari Desert

Asia fared rather better than Europe. Most of North and Central Asia remained ice-free (see Figure 6.1b). Just to the eastern side of the Urals, a large cap covered the Tamyr Peninsula and spread some way to the south. The other part of the continent which could have sported an ice cap was the huge Tibetan Plateau much farther south, its great elevation making it a very cold place. Even here there is some doubt of the extent of ice cover, since surprising forensic evidence of the presence of humans in Tibet dates back to the LGM.[4]

North America was particularly severely affected, with Canada, the Great Lakes, and the north-eastern states – in other words the entire northern two-thirds of the continent – weighed down by two massive ice sheets that connected on the east with the Greenland ice cap. Alaska, on the other hand, was then connected to Siberia by a huge ice-less bridge of now submerged land, Beringia, and to some extent shared Asia's freedom from ice. The largest of the two American ice sheets, the Laurentide in the east, left its vast imprint as a deep dent in the Earth's crust in the form of the great inland sea now known as Hudson Bay (see Figure 7.4).

In some places, in both Eurasia and America, huge lakes (known as periglacial lakes) surrounded the ice caps. The best-known remnants of these lakes are the Great Lakes of North America. The ice sheets themselves were not static, but flowed like the glaciers they were. Not only did these frozen rivers grind out new valleys and fjords, they also obliterated much evidence that humans had ever lived in the north.

Ice was not the only barrier to human occupation during the big freeze. The world's deserts expanded to an even greater extent.

Figure 6.1   World habitat changes at the LGM. Around 30,000 years ago (a), a huge open conifer woodland stretched from the Pacific to the Arctic and Atlantic coasts, allowing hunters to expand. At the LGM (b) this was reduced to a thin tongue of steppe tundra still occupied by hunters. While most of the world saw loss of habitable land Southeast Asia or Sundaland saw a dramatic increase.

Around the ice caps, huge regions of North Eurasia and America
became polar desert in which only the hardiest of plants and animals
could survive. In Europe, the polar desert stretched east from the
southern edge of England and due east across northern Germany, to
the south of the Finno-Scandinavian ice sheet. The whole of the
region from the Levant and the Red Sea to Pakistan, normally pretty
dry, became a continuous extreme desert. Southern Central Asia,
from Turkmenistan and Uzbekistan by the Caspian Sea in the west,
through Xinjiang (north of Tibet), to Inner Mongolia in the east
became continuous desert either side of the 40th parallel. This
desert, which effectively replaced Guthrie's Mammoth Steppe
heartland, also split North and northern Central Asia from the
whole of East and Southeast Asia.

Ice-age refuges

Africa's human population suffered, as their forebears always had
during every big freeze of the previous 2 million years. The Sahara
expanded to cover the whole of North Africa; the Kalahari spread
over most of south-west Africa; dry, treeless grasslands covered
most of continent south of the Sahara. The great rainforests of
Central and West Africa shrank into small islands in Equatorial
Central Africa and the southern parts of the West African Guinea
coast. In East Africa, the expansion of the dry savannah again
separated humans in East Africa from those in South Africa. Only
scrubby refuges surrounded by dry grassland were left as islands for
the hunter-gatherers (see also Figure 1.6).

   With North and Central Europe taking the lead along with
America in building ice castles, we might wonder what happened to
anatomically modern Europeans. Did they all leave or die, to be
replaced later with another batch from the Middle East? Our cousins
the Neanderthals had already disappeared 10,000 years before the
LGM (see Chapter 2). Well, the archaeological record tells us that
the pre-LGM Europeans hung on in there, but as happened in

Africa, their range contracted southward to three or maybe four ice-age temperate zones. The genetic trail also tells us an enormous amount about the origins and human composition of these glacial refuges, but first we shall go into the archaeological record to paint in some background.

Most of Northern Europe was unoccupied at the LGM. There were three main refuge areas of Southern Europe to which the Palaeolithic peoples of Europe retreated (Figure 6.2). From west to east, the first consisted of parts of France and Spain either side of the Pyrenees, in the Basque country, characterized by the finely

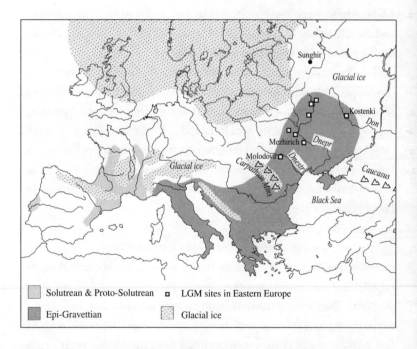

Figure 6.2   European refuges at the LGM. Cold and loss of habitat forced humans down to refuges in south-west France and Spain, Italy and parts of the Balkans, Slovakia and Moldavia. The Ukraine, in Eastern Europe, paradoxically continued to thrive. (Shaded areas show maximum extent of cultures between 15–20,000 years ago.)

knapped stone 'leaf points' of the Solutrean culture (named after a French village called Solutre). Receiving, perhaps, their technologies from north-west Europe, this south-western refuge was culturally distinct from other southern refuges, whose stone technology is described more generally as Epi-Gravettian. The second refuge area was Italy, with more or less continuous local occupation. The third was the Ukraine, a large area north of the Black Sea defined by two great rivers, the Dnepr and the Don, and separated from the rest of Southern Europe by the Carpathian Mountains, which were partially glaciated at the LGM. Two other regions of Central Europe have some claim to small-scale occupation at the LGM. These were western Slovakia, just south of the Carpathians, and the Dnestr River basin of Moldavia, just east of the Carpathians on the north-west coast of the Black Sea.[5]

The Eastern European sites were home to the final flowering of the Upper Palaeolithic mammoth culture. As the LGM reached its climax, one focus of activity shifted away from western Slovakia, mainly eastward towards Moldavia and the Ukraine, but also south into Hungary. It is in the Ukraine and farther north up the rivers Dnepr and Don into the Russian plain, however, where we find the best record of continuous human occupation – even expansion – in Eastern Europe during the Big Freeze.[6]

Genetic continuity and the last glaciation

Can the genetic record tell us more about the ebb and flow of populations in the real human sense of where they *came from* and *went to*, rather than the inferred cultural picture of what they *were doing*, as the cold grip of the ice took hold? Genetic tracing can and does fit the archaeological record of that time rather nicely, but it also tells us something much more relevant and general to European roots: that 80 per cent of modern European lines are essentially derived from ancestors who were present in Europe before the Big Freeze.

In Chapter 3 we saw how the important European maternal clan

HV spread from Eastern into Northern and Western Europe, perhaps heralding the beginning of the Early Upper Palaeolithic 33,000 years ago. The HV clan is now widespread and fairly evenly distributed in Europe. H is the single, commonest line of all. It was not always so, and a specific sister cluster of the H clan, V, who were probably born in the Basque country, tells us why.[7]

The archaeology shows us how the south-western refuge of the Basque country drew cultures and presumably people down from north-west Europe during the lead-up to the LGM. Since Western Europe is separated from Italy by mountains, we would expect the reverse process after the ice age as people re-expanded again from the Basque country and north along the Atlantic coast. This is exactly the picture left by the post-glacial spread of the maternal subgroup V, which has its highest frequency, diversity, and age in the Basque country, falling off as one goes north and only present in rather low frequencies in Italy. V arose in the Basque country shortly after the LGM. Her pre-V ancestor has been dated to 26,400 years ago, long before the LGM. Pre-V is still found farther east in the Balkans and Trans-Caucasus, consistent with her ultimate eastern origin. Even the post-glacial dates of expansion of V (16,300 years in the west) fit this scenario. Exactly the same pattern was seen for the Y-chromosome marker Ruslan, who we saw had moved into northern Europe from the east and found his home in Northern and Western Europe (Chapter 3). The present-day picture shows Ruslan at his maximum frequency of 90 per cent in the Spanish Basque country, with the next-highest rates in Western and Northern Europe.[8]

Italy, on the other hand, capped as it is by the Alps, was less a refuge for northern populations than a temperate region of continuous occupation by Mediterranean folk present from before the LGM. This is reflected again in the high proportion (over one-third of the total) of persisting preglacial mtDNA lines found in that region. We can see from these examples that the refuge zones are characterized by dramatic expansions of lines born locally in the refuge zones during the LGM, and also by high rates of persisting lines left over from the preglacial period. The latter pattern is certainly a feature of the Ukraine refuge, which as predicted by the archaeology retains 31 per cent of its preglacial maternal lines. A slightly less convincing case can be made for south-eastern Europe and the Balkans, which retained 24–26 per cent of preglacial lines.[9]

I should clarify that just because 20–34 per cent of modern European mtDNA lines have been retained from before the LGM, that does not mean that the rest of the lines found today had to have entered Europe from outside after the LGM. No, they were mostly locals. Of all modern European lines, 55 per cent originated in the period just after the ice age (the Late Upper Palaeolithic) but these, like the V haplogroup, probably derived from pre-existing European lines and simply reflect the post-glacial re-expansions from the refuges – in other words, new shoots off an old stock. Real fresh immigration into Europe from the Near East during the Neolithic period (from 8,000 years ago onwards) perhaps accounts for only 15 per cent of modern lines.[10]

An interesting recent discovery about the genetic make-up of the south-eastern European region has to do with Adam's markers in Romania. The Carpathian Mountains were glaciated at the LGM and thus formed an effective, jagged barrier between south-eastern Europe and the regions bordering the Black Sea. This barrier splits Romania in two from top to bottom. Without their ice, the Carpathians hardly constitute an insurmountable physical barrier today, but they still mark a clear genetic boundary. This is revealed by Y-chromosome markers characteristic of north-eastern Europe and the Ukraine occurring at higher rates to the east of the Carpathians, while the markers more characteristic of Central Europe are found to the west. But this micro-regional boundary is very much obscured by the great dominance of the main Eastern European Y lineage M17, which may characterize the original preglacial

Eastern Gravettian intrusions from the east. This lineage is found at very high rates throughout Eastern Europe – from Poland, through Slovakia and Hungary, to the Ukraine. M17 is still found at high frequencies among the Slavic peoples of the Balkans, which could support the existence of the Balkan ice-age refuge.[11]

Northern Asia in the cold

The Himalayas grew an ice cap, and deserts expanded in the band round the 40th parallel and to the south, in Central Asia, during the LGM. The population of southern Central Asia was severely reduced, although probably not completely wiped out – at least in Tibet if not elsewhere. This may have effectively separated South, East, and Southeast Asia from Central and North Eurasia, but it does not mean that life stopped in the centre and the north. During the LGM, the permafrost boundary extended down to about the 50th parallel. Permafrost did not prevent human occupation of the steppe tundra. There is even evidence of human activity north of the permafrost line at the LGM, particularly in the Russian plain and also further north-east in Talitskogo, Siberia. Hunter-gatherers of southern Siberia continuously occupied some sites, especially Afontova Gora on the Yenisei River, developing their own unique southern Siberian culture. Strips of steppe tundra and forest steppe, rich in large herbivores, still stretched eastward from the Russian plain through to north-eastern Siberia (Figure 6.3). In spite of the severe weather extremes, there were rich pickings for those hunters who could adapt. And they did, as is shown by evidence from scattered archaeological sites in those areas that date to this period.[12]

Again, the genetic record tells us that these hardy hunters of the permafrost retained some of their ancient maternal lines from before the LGM, and that there were subsequent expansions of certain subgroups after the thaw. As I mentioned in Chapter 5, A, C, and Z are characteristic of North Asia, while D also extends farther

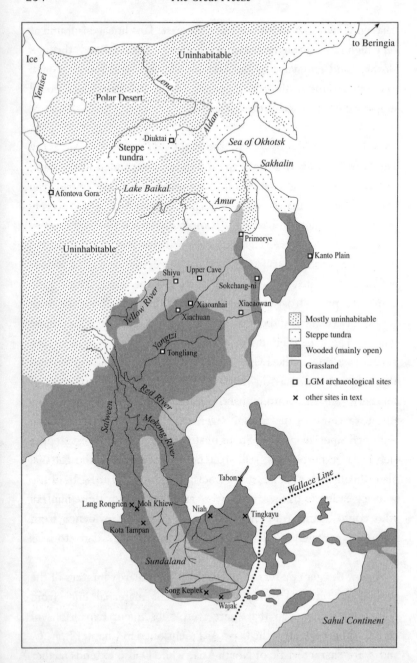

south in China. Of these lines, A clearly survived from well before the LGM, as did various Manju and Nasreen lines. Then there was a gap of 10,000 years until about 17,000 years ago, before the re-expansion of lines such as variants of D, A, C, and finally Z.[13]

The genetics of North and Central Asia has simply confirmed what we might expect from the archaeology: when it got cold, the hunters of the Mammoth Steppe shrank in range and hunkered down, and when it got warm again they bounced back and re-expanded. The more interesting questions are what they looked like, and who their closest local descendants are today. Why and when did Mongoloids become the dominant types throughout most of Asia and the Americas? Does the genetic story tell us anything that cannot be inferred from the archaeological record?

Driven off the high cold steppe

In the last chapter I started to scratch away at several of these questions, particularly the genetic origins of the Mongoloids. I showed how several pieces of evidence point to southern Siberia, the Upper Yenisei River, and the Lake Baikal region as possible sites for further physical specialization of the Northern Mongoloid peoples during the Palaeolithic. The earliest Eurasian skeletal evidence for the Mongoloid physical type was claimed for part of a skull found in Afontova Gora, in southern Siberia, dated to 21,000 years ago, just before the LGM (see Chapter 5). Even this evidence is weak though, and no other place in the Old World, including East Asia, shows such types from before the LGM or for a long time afterwards. Admittedly, human skeletal evidence of *any* description

Figure 6.3   East Asian refuges at the LGM. Most of Northeast Asia was uninhabitable save for narrow corridors of steppe tundra, but some hardy hunters stayed on there. In contrast, Japan, China and Sundaland increased their habitable areas. As the refugees left the northern steppe, intrusive Upper Palaeolithic technology appeared in East Asia at the peak of the LGM, particularly in Japan and Korea.

from the Far East before 11,000 years ago is scanty. This gap in
the record leaves the impression – sometimes taken as dogma –
that there were no Mongoloid types in East Asia until around
7,000–10,000 years ago, and none in Island Southeast Asia until
well after that.[14]

The big problem with the fossil gap is how to explain that the
Mongoloid physical type accounts for 99 per cent of peoples living
in these regions today. Not only that, but they are the most numerous type in the world. In fact, since most Native Americans are
generally also regarded as Mongoloid and are, with a couple of
exceptions, extreme Sinodonts, they were geographically the most
widespread physical type before Columbus reached America and
changed its history irrevocably.

It takes no real stretch of the imagination to view the Northern
Mongoloid peoples as evolving a specialized physique adapted to
hunting in harsh, windy, and cold conditions in a geographically
isolated region of southern Siberia. But hunting and gathering was
what all humans did at that time. So how did these hunter-gatherers
come to rapidly occupy and dominate more than half the world after
the ice age? An extraordinary story waits to be unlocked, perhaps by
our genes. Another problem we face, if we accept this late dispersal
of Mongoloids, is posed by the date of colonization of America by
Mongoloids. In the next chapter we shall look at both the archaeological and the genetic evidence for the date of their first entry, and
shall find that the latter suggests that all the main founder genetic
lines had entered America before the LGM.

With the American pioneers in mind, I think the concept that
Mongoloids dispersed to East and Southeast Asia only within the
past few thousand years is also likely to be wrong, mainly because
most of the gene lines that are characteristic of Southern
Mongoloids appear to have their origins in that region. But there is
no obvious reason why a Central Asian group of highly specialized
hunters should disperse so rapidly to dominate East Asia at the

beginning of the Neolithic less than 10,000 years ago. I think that the Mongoloid presence, expansions, and dispersals started much earlier and continued in pulses up until recently. But before going into detail, let me sketch in the next two paragraphs what I think happened in East Asia. In the absence of a strong archaeological record, much of my speculation is based on the genetic trail.

Throughout the Upper Palaeolithic period, from 40,000 years ago up to the LGM, there was a huge partly wooded hunting ground between the Tibetan Plateau and southern Siberia. It was occupied by skilled hunters who derived their genetic heritage from widely separated parts of Asia (see Chapter 5). First, I think Dale Guthrie is partly right in that the Northern Mongoloids overdeveloped the Mongoloid physical type in adapting to the extreme cold and wind at high altitude in the southern and eastern part of this homeland. But farther to the west, at lower altitudes, the hunters may have looked more like Europeans. As the glaciers began to take their grip, all the hunters on the high steppe were squeezed. Those in the south of the homeland in south-eastern Tibet were forced off the high, cold, and dry Tibetan Plateau and down the great Asian rivers to China and Indo-China. They escaped down the Brahmaputra, to Assam, down the Mekong to Indo-China, and east down the Yangtzi to southern China. Those on the Qinghai Plateau to the north-east of Tibet were squeezed down the Yellow River to northern China. Those who had hunted farther north at the 40th parallel in the uplands of Xinjiang and Mongolia were forced even farther north by the rapidly expanding Taklamakan and Gobi Deserts of southern Central Asia and into the lowland refuges of southern Siberia, such as Afontova Gora on the Yenisei River (Figure 6.4).

The problem with the hunters going north to find warmer lowlands was, of course, that the nearer they got to the Arctic Circle, the more chance there was of it getting colder and windier. There was one escape from this northern cold trap – to the north-east.

They could have moved along a narrow tongue of steppe tundra either side of the Lena River to Yakutsk, then east to the Sea of Okhotsk, where the coastal climate was more temperate. Low sea levels at the time exposed a wide lowland strip creeping out into the Sea of Okhotsk. Another north-easterly escape route from the Lake Baikal region to the Pacific coast lay a little farther south down the great Amur River. This temperate north-west Pacific coastline was the route to America. Such dispersals from Central Asia, to three points of the compass, would in several instances have taken Mongoloids back to East Asian coastal regions from which their ancestors had originally trekked inland 20,000 years or more before.

South China may have had an expanding Mongoloid population as refugees left the high steppe, but judging from the genetic story, most of the mtDNA lines in Southeast Asia were local and had always been there. Groups such as B and F, which are regarded as typical of Mongoloid populations, have great local antiquity in the south.[15] This time round, however, those coasts looked very different.

More land on the coast

The period around the LGM was not just a time of territorial contraction and humans seeking refuge. Paradoxically, more land was opened up for human colonization by the lowering of the sea level than was closed off by the freeze-up. Large parts of the Asian coastline from India to Siberia now extended hundreds of kilometres farther out towards the edge of the continental shelf. Siberia joined with America to create the new landmass of Beringia. The East China Sea and the Yellow Sea were drained. Japan became connected with the Asian mainland through the island of Sakhalin. These northern coastal regions were warmer than the Central Asian steppe. Australia and New Guinea joined to form the continent of Sahul. The Indian subcontinent acquired new land, and joined up

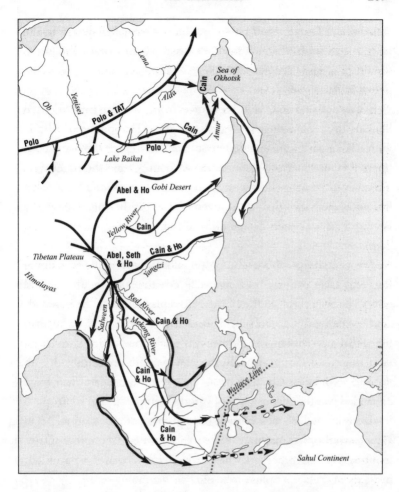

Figure 6.4 Centrifugal migrations from Central Asia at the LGM. The LGM forced Central Asians back down the same rivers they had come up 20–40,000 years before. This meant Siberians mainly going to Northeast Asia and America (Polo and Cain). People from Xinjiang and the Tibet-Qinghai Plateau went to China and Indo-China and the latter on into Southeast Asia (Cain and Ho). Only a few Cain and Ho genes would have crossed the Wallace Line to form colonies. The mtDNA picture is similar.[21–24]

with Sri Lanka. The region that gained most out of the LGM was Southeast Asia, where the South China Sea, the Gulf of Bangkok, and the Java Sea all dried up to link Indo-China, Malaysia, and the largest islands of Indonesia into one great patchwork of woods and savannah, a vast continental landmass called Sundaland, twice the size of India (Figure 6.3).[16]

It was not just coastland reclaimed from the sea that beckoned humans to recolonize as the ice sheets grew. The joining of Siberia with Alaska gave humans their first chance to enter the great continental landmasses of the Americas without getting their feet wet. This they did during the last stages of the build-up to the LGM. That fits with the view that the movement across Beringia (now the Bering Strait) at such a cold time was in response to worsening conditions in Asia.

The centrifugal dispersal of Mongoloid hunter-gatherers down the great Asian rivers to the long Pacific coastline (see Figure 6.4) did not necessarily result in the immediate replacement of the descendants of the beachcombers who were living there. It is more than likely that a patchwork of colonies was established which lasted for a long time, and that eventually the new genetic pool merged with the old. Northern China, Korea, Japan, and Sundaland had huge expanded coastlines consisting of wooded temperate and subtropical lowlands into which new refugee immigrants from the Central Asian steppe would most naturally have expanded. So, the initial settlement by the newcomers may have partially flowed over, or avoided, pre-existing relict peoples of the old beachcombing route.

When the sea returned like a huge tide after the ice had melted, however, much of the archaeological evidence of such coastal occupation would have been washed away. We would expect to see such ice-age archaeological evidence only in regions with a steep coastline and continental shelf, such as Japan, and some of the Indonesian islands. Remnants of preglacial beachcombing populations would also be found only in regions that have remained isolated by geography or rising sea levels, such as Japan.

I should stress that the Mongoloid dispersal view I am presenting here differs from orthodox archaeological reconstruction not just in dates and timescale but also in the movements of people. Some prehistorians of the Southeast Asian region, such as Australian Peter Bellwood, favour a recent one-off Mongoloid replacement of older Australo-Melanesian hunter-gatherers in Island Southeast Asia by Taiwanese from farther north along the Pacific Rim. In this view, the Australo-Melanesian hunter-gatherers would have corresponded most closely to the Semang 'Negritos' (see Chapter 5). Bellwood argues, moreover, that the expanding population of Mongoloids were Neolithic rice farmers from southern China who arrived by sea via Taiwan and the Philippines only 4,000 years ago. I have presented the evidence against this theory elsewhere.[17]

What I am saying is first that Mongoloid expansions and re-expansions in East and Southeast Asia *started earlier*, around the LGM at least 18,000 years ago. They mainly used land routes, and have continued on and off ever since. In fact, possibly the largest population expansion in Island Southeast Asia before the present era may have occurred as recently as the arrival of the Metal Age in the islands, around the last few centuries BC, when rice agriculture greatly expanded.[18]

The second point is that there were not just two groups, the Mongoloids migrating down from the north and the Semang-like hunter-gatherers, who were vying for the landmass of Southeast Asia. There was another indigenous expanding group, the Southern Mongoloids, who may have occupied the Southeast Asian continental shelf and much of the Pacific coastline from very ancient times, and may indeed have been ancestral to all Mongoloids themselves.

This indigenous Southern Mongoloid group is identified best by its unique and associated southern genetic markers, which dominate the region.[19] They probably looked rather like some minorities of south-eastern Indo-China today, and in particular like one of the groups of Malaysian aboriginals farther south in the Malay Peninsula, known as the Aboriginal Malays. The latter also resemble the

majority Malay population in having some Mongoloid features.
From this perspective, aspects of the so-called Southern Mongoloid
appearance may have been around for a much longer time. As we
shall see, their ancestors can be identified by more than just their
genes and teeth.

In common with the great majority of other Southeast Asians, the
Aboriginal Malays have been identified as Sundadonts. The Aboriginal Malays are even closer dentally to the Pacific Rim populations,
including the Polynesians, and on a dental basis could be regarded
as ancestral to the Sinodonts further north (see Chapter 5 and
Figures 5.3 and 5.4).[20] In short, Southern Mongoloids could have
been around in the South since before the LGM.

Post-glacial Asian invasions of Southeast Asia and Oceania

As I have said, my reconstruction is based more on the genetic
record than on the scanty skeletal and archaeological record. In fact,
my own interest in genetic prehistory was first awakened by medical
genetics, while I was working in the south-west Pacific in the early
1980s. My findings suggested that *early* migrations of local genetic
types out of Southeast Asia to New Guinea and Island Melanesia
were more likely than huge *late* Mongoloid migrations from China
replacing Australo-Melanesians throughout Australasia and the
Pacific, as previously thought.[21] So I shall start with genetic evidence for the dates of Mongoloid expansions into Southeast Asia and
Oceania.

In Chapter 3 we saw how the some of the best combinations of
archaeological, physical, and genetic evidence for the early route
out-of-Africa come from intermediate and end points of the trail in
Malaysia, Australia, and New Guinea. I also described how the deep
branching genetic lines for the Australia and New Guinea were
different from each other, indicating the antiquity of their colonization. The unique genetic identity of such early arrivals allows us to
measure and clearly identify all latecomers and to see where they

came from. Equally useful is the ability to date and estimate the size of later migrations.

By taking this approach, the English geneticist Martin Richards and I were able to suggest that while, in agreement with current views, the ancestors of the Polynesians – the great Pacific pioneers of 3,500 years ago – were mostly different from the oldest inhabitants of the New Guinea region, they did not come from Taiwan, farther north, as generally believed but from Southeast Asia. Furthermore, although the Polynesian lines were newcomers to the Pacific, their own forebears had probably already arrived in eastern Indonesia from Indo-China by 17,000 years ago.[22] The lines carried by the Polynesians were branches of those found on the Southeast Asian mainland, and one ancient line in particular (mtDNA Haplogroup B4) was shared with the American dispersal via the northern Pacific Rim. Apart from genetically linking the Americans with the Southeast Asian dispersals, this also suggests a date near the LGM for the earliest migrations out of mainland Southeast Asia. Richards and I have continued to explore other markers of Southeast Asian migration, leading up to the work on the aboriginal peoples of the Malay Peninsula described in this book.

Several other geneticists have also dated local clusters of Asian lines, male and female, that had found their way from mainland East Asia into Southeast Asia and the Pacific. Cambridge geneticist Peter Forster has dated several such colonizing clusters, which may reflect a local population increase in the south-west Pacific. One of these was a local version of the East Asian Haplogroup E, now also found in Malaysia and Sabah (north-east Borneo). He dated the Southeast Asian E cluster to 12,100 years. Another was a sub-clan of major Southeast Asian Haplogroup F, found in Vietnam and Malaysia, which he dated to 9,100 years. Forster also found that one version of Haplogroup B4 had arrived in New Guinea from Asia by 12,500 years ago. All these findings support my view that such East Asian population dispersals in Southeast Asia and to the south-west

Pacific were going on continuously from around the time of the LGM and long before the Neolithic revolution. In other words, typically East Asian lines were expanding in the region of Southeast Asia and farther east into Melanesia long before farming could have provided an impetus to the colonization of these regions. Similar post-glacial dates of dispersal are found for intrusive Y chromosomes from East Asia.[23]

The dates on their own fail to show the extent of gene flow from Indo-China, through Island Southeast Asia, to Melanesia after the ice age. In 1994, Italian geneticist Antonio Torroni and colleagues made a significant breakthrough by identifying seven East Asian maternal clans, labelled A–G, all present in Tibet and to varying degrees on other parts of the mainland (for A–G, see Chapter 5). Together with a recently identified deep East Asian line, M7, these seven East Asian genetic groups were found in 85 per cent of Koreans, 79 per cent of southern Han Chinese, 75 per cent of Vietnamese, 25 per cent of Malays, 44 per cent of people from Sabah, and 20 per cent of New Guineans in the survey.[24]

Such a steady decline in Southeast Asian maternal lines as we go from East Asia to New Guinea implies a progressively higher proportion of indigenous lines the farther we go from Asia. The groups in Torroni's study that had the least identifiable typical East Asian lines, however, were back in mainland Southeast Asia. These were the Orang Asli, the aboriginal peoples of the jungle interior of the Malay Peninsula.

Martin Richards and I, with Malaysian colleagues, were recently able to confirm this picture in a much more detailed study of the Orang Asli (see also Chapter 5). The two key aboriginal groups least affected by recent immigration are the Semang and the Aboriginal Malays. The former have only 22 per cent typical East Asian genetic lines in their make-up. This is consistent with the view that the Negrito Semang are a very isolated relict people. However, there was an unexpected surprise when it came to the Southern Mongoloid Aboriginal Malays. While only a quarter of the latter have typical East Asian lines, another half were composed of two major ancestral Asian branches. One of these two (accounting for a quarter of lines) arose just before, but on the same branch as, the Eurasian ancestral Nasreen supergroup. In other words, she was a twin sister to Nasreen, one of the two daughters of Out-of-Africa Eve. This ancestral 'pre-Nasreen' had never been found before. Another surprise was that a further quarter of lines belonged to a pre-F branch. Since F is a major maternal founder line for East and Southeast Asia, this strongly supports the idea put forward in Chapter 5 that such Southern Mongoloid populations represent the ultimate geographical and genetic Mongoloid homeland.[25]

Coming back to the period around the LGM, these exciting new genetic findings are consistent with the view of today's isolated Aboriginal Malays and Semang being the least admixed, and hence closest to Malay Peninsular types before the Mongoloid expansions from farther north. Just how much real Northern Mongoloid intrusion of maternal lines actually occurred more recently among Southeast Asian populations remains to be seen.

As a demonstration of a tendency for higher male intrusion across international boundaries, typical mainland East Asian Y-chromosome markers as defined by the single marker Ho (see Chapter 5) completely dominate Indo-China and Island Southeast Asia, ranging from 54 to 97 per cent, in different parts of the region, with a sharp fall-off across Wallace Line (the Wallace Line marks the south-eastern limit of the Sunda continent dividing it, and the rest of Asia, from the islands of Eastern Indonesia, New Guinea and Australia – shown in Figures 5.3 and 6.4). However, since Ho probably originated in Southeast Asia, there is no reason to suppose that his dominance reflects Northern Mongoloid intrusion rather than simply re-expansion from Southeast Asia after the LGM.[26]

The genetic evidence thus supports the idea that East Asian lines expanded south within Southeast Asia, starting from 18,000 years ago (the LGM) and continue to do so even today. This goes a long way to explaining the varying mixtures of Mongoloid and non-Mongoloid features among the present numerically dominant Southern Mongoloid peoples of Southeast Asia right up to the limit of the Wallace Line.

The non-Mongoloid 'Negritos', with their undifferentiated dentition (the Semang – see Chapter 5) of the Central Malaysian jungle would then represent isolated, relatively unmixed relict populations derived from the original beachcombers before the Mongoloid expansions. The Semang were presumably left as central genetic islands in the dense jungle, as the invaders flowed around them.

The other isolate, the Aboriginal Malays of the Malayan jungle, give dental and genetic clues to the ancestral relationship between the Sundadonts of Southeast Asia and the Sinodont populations farther north.

Physical evidence for the earliest Mongoloid dispersals in Southeast Asia

The most recent archaeological development of note is the discovery of Mongoloid skeletal remains in Song Keplek, a cave in Gunung Sewu, Java, dated to 7,000 years ago. This was a time long before rice began to be cultivated in Indonesia, and thus challenges the orthodoxy that Mongoloid intrusion to Island Southeast Asia coincided with the arrival of rice agriculture. From the LGM up until about 10,000 years ago, there was no sea barrier to Mongoloid spread until they reached the Wallace Line at Bali. When the Mongoloid intruders reached Bali and Borneo, having walked all the way from Asia, they would have faced a sea crossing. This was not an insuperable barrier, as we know from the exploits of the early Australians, but it surely must have slowed the flow of population and genes (see Figure 6.4). Accordingly, Eastern Indonesia, on the other side of the Wallace Line is a boundary zone, with some groups showing Negrito features and others Mongoloid. By the time we cross to New Guinea, on the other side of a transition zone formed by the Moluccas and the other scattered islands of Eastern Indonesia, most local inhabitants possess characteristically Melanesian frizzy hair and dark skin (see Plate 17). The people of New Guinea are by several measures morphologically similar to the Negritos of the Malay Peninsula, thousands of kilometres to the west.[27]

Despite the picture I have painted so far, there is an orthodoxy that until recently Southeast Asia was inhabited only by Australo-Melanesian hunter-gatherers. Given the shortage of human remains of any description on the remaining landmasses after the post-glacial rise in sea level, this assumption remains the view of many. What evidence there is does not support the Australo-Melanesian view. At the moment, the oldest documented skeletal legacy of Anatomically Modern Humans anywhere in Southeast Asia is the famous 'deep skull' from Niah Caves in Borneo. Carbon-dated to around 42,000 years ago, this skull has in the past been described as 'gracile Australo-Melanesian', more particularly as being like the now extinct Tasmanians. But as Australian physical anthropologist-cum-archaeologist David Bulbeck points out, the relatively gracile Tasmanians were not typically Australoid or Melanesian, and the Niah skull, like Tasmanians, shows instead a similarity with the aboriginal Ainu of Japan. Bulbeck drew a similar conclusion for another ancient skull, this time a partial skull from Tabon Cave in the Philippines, dated to around 20,000 years.[28]

Two famous human skulls found at the end of the nineteenth century at Wajak in Central Java have provided a focus for a number of different reconstructions of the human prehistory of the region. For more than a century, these skulls were thought to predate the LGM and to have represented an early proto-Australian type. However, a complete reverse of this Australo-Melanesian view has been put forward by a number of anthropologists who have pointed out that the Wajak skulls show no similarities to Australians of any antiquity. Instead, the skulls have been claimed to be early Mongoloid, or even identical to but more robust than modern (Mongoloid) Javanese. Most convincingly, David Bulbeck argues that they too are like the Ainu and are part of a Pacific coast/Sundaland continuum. While early reports insisted that the Wajak skulls were Pleistocene – older (or much older) than 10,000 years, two recent carbon dates suggest that they are either 10,560 or 6,560 years old, which puts them more in the pre-agricultural early Holocene.[29]

Clearly, the possibility that the Niah, Tabon, and Wajak skulls may be evidence of the early presence of early Mongoloid or pre-Mongoloid types in Island Southeast Asia might have a bearing on the date of such a presence. There may not be a single date at all, if the transition to Southern Mongoloid was a gradual local evolutionary process. This could be a problem for the orthodox view of a late Mongoloid replacement. While this does not prove that Mongoloid features appeared in Island Southeast Asia at the time of the LGM, it does suggest they may have reached Java well before the Neolithic period, which is normally put forward as the date of their arrival. In summary, from both physical as well as genetic evidence, Aboriginal Malays may turn out to be descendants of the earliest Southern Mongoloids, as their original name, 'Proto-Malays', was intended to imply.[30]

Mongoloid replacement in China?

Turning now to the north, a similar picture of post-glacial, local genetic expansion clusters of mitochondrial DNA may be seen along the Pacific coastline from South China up to North Asia, reflecting refugee flow east from the Central Asian plain and subsequent expansion along the coast. Of these genetic expansions, the closest to the LGM is part of the common Asian Haplogroup D, with an age of 16,800 years. One D subgroup characteristic of the Chukchi aboriginals of the far north-east of Siberia is dated to

14,900 years ago. Others include A2 (11,200 years) and a C type (10,800 years).[31]

In China and on the Pacific coast we find again relict aboriginal coastal groups from before the arrival of the Mongoloids, isolated this time not by jungle but by the sea. One of these groups is the well-known Ainu of northern Japan. The Ainu are descended from the original Jomon peoples of Japan, who 12,500 years ago made some of the world's first pots. Later Mongoloid immigration from the mainland by the Yayoi of Korea all but replaced the original population, and the modern Ainu represent varying degrees of admixture. There are sufficient similarities between the prehistoric Jomon skulls, the ice-age Japanese Minatogawa 1 skull from Okinawa (dated to between 16,600 and 18,250 years ago; see Plate 20), and the modern Ainu for them to be regarded as lying on the same continuous line of descent. As mentioned above, these Pacific Rim groups may represent a pre-Mongoloid substratum.[32]

As a result of its isolation, Japan probably received its last Mongoloid immigrants, the Yayoi, starting 2,300 years ago. This event is thought to have left its genetic trace. Studies conducted in different parts of Japan suggest that the YAP+ marker, Abel, one of the oldest out-of-Africa beachcombing lines, would have characterized the Jomons. In Okinawa, the rare Asian YAP+ marker achieves frequencies of 55 per cent. The other beachcombing Y marker, Cain, is also found among Japanese at rates of up to 10 per cent.[33]

The Minatogawa 1 skull shows similarities with two other famous ancient skulls of China, the Upper Cave 101 and Liujiang (see Plate 19). The former is from the Zhoukoudian or Dragon Bone Hill in northern China and although poorly dated is certainly more than 10,000 years old and probably preglacial. The Liujiang skull is from southern China (see Chapter 4). Australian physical anthropologist Peter Brown has argued against the view that these three rather robust skulls show proto-Mongoloid features. On his plots they are closer to Australian aboriginals than to modern East Asians, although they are not even particularly close to the former.[34]

This evidence is consistent with the idea that the preglacial population of China and the Pacific coast may still have resembled the first beachcombing settlers, before the Mongoloid expansions took place, and that their genetic heritage may still persist. The other ancient beachcombing Y marker, Cain, is also found in Northeast Asia, but this time on the mainland and coast in peoples of the Amur River, Okhotsk, Mongolia, and central and southern Siberia (see Figure 6.4). In these regions Cain, normally only present as a tiny minority, is found at rates of 50–90 per cent.[35] The fact that this ancient Northeast Asian beachcombing marker persists is entirely consistent with the evidence from the skulls, which suggests that the ancestral non-Mongoloid population survived in that region until at least the LGM.

Cultural evidence for an Asian dispersal

Is there any archaeological evidence, apart from the Wajak skulls, to support the presence of antique Palaeolithic societies throughout North and East Asia who were infiltrated, or replaced by, Mongoloid dispersals from the Central Asian Steppe 20,000 years ago? There is, but with caveats. The interpretation of the archaeological record from Northeast Asia, China, and Korea (and also Southeast Asia) between 5,500 and 25,000 years ago is hampered by lack of coastal archaeological evidence. This is because today's high sea level now covers the coastal sites that would have preferentially been occupied by the invaders (see above and Figure 6.3). What is left is a number of inland and island cave sites that could easily have been the refuges of the original indigenous peoples rather than those of the invaders.

At this stage I would like to present a highly simplified interpretation of East Asian archaeology of the glacial period. This will serve as a background against which changes from the LGM onwards can be viewed. As we have seen (Chapter 3), Europe underwent a replacement of the Middle Palaeolithic technology of the Neanderthals by the more sophisticated Upper Palaeolithic technology of the first Anatomically Modern Humans there. We also saw that the Middle Palaeolithic technology of the Neanderthals was by no means primitive, but represented a tradition parallel to styles of Middle Stone Age tool-making by Anatomically Modern Humans in Africa before 50,000 years ago.

It is therefore a surprise to find a low level of stone technology being used by modern humans in East and Southeast Asia at the time of the Neanderthals' final competition with Cro-Magnons. Tools associated with Anatomically Modern Humans in Southeast Asia and Australia seem to have been less sophisticated than those used by the Neanderthals.[36] The contrast is so great that in some cases archaeologists who have concentrated on the African and European Palaeolithic traditions cannot believe that some of the tools attributed to modern humans by their Asianist colleagues were artefacts at all.

This contrast of styles and 'quality' was first pointed out by an American archaeologist, Hallam Movius, in 1948. What became known as the Movius Line separated off the Far East, including Southeast Asia, from the rest of the world as an area of cultural 'backwardness' and 'unstandardized tools' more or less right up to the last ice age. To make things even more confusing, the East Asian Palaeolithic tool-making tradition which produced what are called 'chopper-chopping' tools stretches from the time of modern human occupation back into the Middle Palaeolithic period, at least a million years ago. This was a time when East Asia was occupied by *Homo erectus*, and long before modern humans had even evolved. There is some dispute about when chopper-chopping tools were first made in Island Southeast Asia, with several archaeologists claiming, with reason, that they were first introduced by modern humans possibly around 70,000 years ago (see Chapter 4).[37]

Several archaeologists have pointed out that the lack of sophistication of the chopper-chopping tools reflects the poor knapping quality of the types of stone available, for example quartzite and basalt. It has been surmised that people then were making (as they still do today) much more sophisticated implements from perishable materials such as hardwood, bamboo, and plant fibres.[38] The fact that people of Oceania managed to colonize the Northern Solomon Islands by boat 30,000 years ago, and tens of thousands of years before evidence of European sailing, is ample evidence – if any were needed – of the level of early technical sophistication in the Far East.

A tale of two rivers

Whatever the reasons for the persistence of the distinctive chopper-chopping industries in the Far East, they do provide us with a simple background on which to record the intrusions of other cultures into China and Southeast Asia from Central Asia at the height of the last ice age. On top of this general background is a geographical and chronological structure that we might call 'a tale of two rivers'. Northern Chinese Palaeolithic cultures are geographically clustered around the Yellow River and, well before the LGM, under the increasing influence of Upper Palaeolithic innovations from Central Asia. First flakes, then blades, and finally the characteristic bifacial points reminiscent of the Diuktai cultures of eastern Siberia during the LGM, could have moved to places as far east as Japan to replace the older tools and weapons. Southern China, on the other hand, dominated as it was by the Yangtzi River and shielded both geographically and environmentally from the cultural influences of the Central Asian steppe, seems to have had a separate and rather slower evolution.[39]

Other potential western influences on China and Southeast Asia at the LGM, which may have developed in parallel with the Siberian Upper Palaeolithic, are a flaked stone industry in the Tarim River basin on the southern margins of the Taklamakan Desert of Xinjiang province and a microblade industry on the Qinghai-Tibet Plateau (a microblade is a small prismatic parallel-sided flake struck from a prepared core).[40]

Some western Upper Palaeolithic technical influences appeared in northern China and southern Inner Mongolia even before the ice age. Perhaps the earliest, between 35,000 and 50,000 years ago, have been uncovered near a loop of the middle Yellow River known as the Ordos Plateau. The famous Upper Cave near Beijing yielded sophisticated bone, shell, and stone artefacts from around the LGM, including an eyed needle and a complex necklace of bone, shell, and stone dated to around 18,000 years ago. Even more sophisticated Upper Palaeolithic cultures, featuring three-eyed needles and bone-and-antler tools, continued to develop after the LGM along the lower reaches of the Yellow River towards the coast.[41] But much of the east coast of China which was most habitable during the LGM now lies under the sea, inaccessible to the archaeologist.

Farther to the north and east, the Russian Far East, Japan, and Korea showed dramatic changes in technology at the time of the LGM. In the Russian Far East, the earliest carbon-dated Upper Palaeolithic macroblade site is what has become known as the Geographical Society Cave, on the Amur River. (Any blade longer than about 50 mm (2 inches) is classified as a macroblade.) Microblades first appear in this region around the LGM (19,350 years ago) but nearer the coast of the Sea of Japan, in Primorye.[42]

Japan has one of the most detailed sequential records of events around the LGM anywhere in the world. Before 20,000 years ago, Japan shared the East Asian predominantly core tool and chopper-chopping tradition. Between 18,000 and 20,000 years ago this gave way to a rich new stone technology, reminiscent of the Western Upper Palaeolithic, with flakes and blades (the latter becoming more and more frequent with time) and a profusion of other derived products. Finally, from 12,000 to 14,000 years ago, microblades and bifacial points became common. Korea remains rather less intensively researched, although the same sequence of core tools giving way to flakes then blades around the time of the LGM has been found. In both of these sequences we see the period around the ice age as a time of expansion and technological change, with old East Asian traditions being swept away, presumably by an influx of skills and hunters coming in from the freezing Asian steppe to the west.[43]

The regions around the Yangtzi River in southern China appear to have been shielded to a certain extent from the full impact of Western Upper Palaeolithic technology, but the preglacial, quartzite-based chopper-chopping industry was modified (although not replaced) at the LGM by new tools and materials. The new tools were smaller and more varied, including flakes, and were also fashioned from other materials such as chert, bone, and antler. As in the north, the coastal regions of southern China at the LGM now lie deep beneath the waves, hiding any possible evidence of LGM technical change on the seafront.[44]

Southeast Asia: a gap in occupation, or just the effects of sea level?
In contrast to the clear technological changes that took place around the LGM farther north, Southeast Asia has very little to show from around the climax of the last ice age. In fact, there are few remains of material culture of any description. Whether this dearth of evidence reflects a lack of people or an absence of evidence in the right places, it cannot be used to support the idea of immigration from the north. The masking effect of low sea levels during the LGM is nowhere so great as in Southeast Asia, where the present land above the water is but a meagre remnant of the former continent of Sundaland (see Figure 6.3). David Bulbeck has pointed out that the reason why there is so little evidence of occupation at the time of the LGM may be that people generally lived on land less than 100 metres (330 feet) above sea level. They thus simply followed the sea, moving down from the hinterland as the sea fell to occupy land which is now beneath the waves. When the sea rose again after the

LGM they moved back inland, and this is the point where their cultures reappear in the modern archaeological record.[45]

Whatever the reason, the result is an apparent gap of occupation in inland Indo-China and the Malay Peninsula from around the LGM until about 14,400 years ago, when inland caves were reoccupied by people making pebble and chopper-chopping tools. In some cases the old lithic traditions continued right through the Neolithic period until 2,000 to 3,000 years ago. Since these regions were clearly habitable during the LGM, it is more likely that their occupiers had simply moved back from lower altitudes as the sea level rose.[46]

The interesting question is who these cave-dwelling, pebble-tool-using people were. It is generally thought that they were the ancestors of the nomadic Negrito forest hunter-gatherers who still occupy the same regions today. Archaeologist Zuraina Majid argues further that the post-glacial technology of the Lenggong Valley in Malaysia was really a continuation of traditions that locally go right back to the valley site of Kota Tampan, now tentatively dated to 74,000 years ago (see also Chapter 4). There is some genetic evidence that the ancestors of the Aboriginal Malays could have been living on the Indo-Chinese coastline as well over the same period. Again, the sea would have covered their traces.[47]

The picture of changes around the LGM is only slightly more revealing in Island Southeast Asia, where a flake-and-blade technology lasted to within the last 2,000 years. There are clues that there was an expansion into Island Southeast Asia during the ice age, as implied by the first evidence of colonization of the Philippines from 17,000 years ago. American archaeologist Wilhelm Solheim, doyen of Southeast Asian prehistory, sees the flake-and-blade tradition as a late Pleistocene intrusion to Island Southeast Asia from South China rather than as being home-grown.[48]

Perhaps the only star find that could signal an intrusion of really smart new technology, as it were from another planet, is in eastern Sabah on the shores of the extinct Lake Tingkayu. Beautifully, bifacially worked lanceolate chert knives have been found here with a date inferred to be between 18,000 and 28,000 years ago. ('Lanceolate' means shaped like the head of a lance or leaf.) The latter date would suggest an arrival before rather than after the LGM. In Peter Bellwood's words, these knives are 'unique in the whole of Southeast Asia, except for one apparent lanceolate found . . . in a tin mine in Kedah in Peninsular Malaysia.' If the Tingkayu knives from Borneo really were an introduced style, Bellwood's comment may be a clue to a route taken by the technology from China, since he also mentions the two other preglacial sites on the same peninsula, but on the Thai side: Moh Khiew and Lang Rongrien. At each site there is some evidence for similar bifacial technology, but overlain by the 'cruder' Hoabinhian tools.[49]

Bellwood also finds technical echoes of the Tingkayu lanceolate points in Northeast Asia – specifically in the Diuktai of northeastern Siberia (since 18,000 years ago) and several regions of Japan from the same time.[50] Although Bellwood feels that the Tingkayu culture is an independent local event, the cultural echoes he describes would be just the same as those suggested by the genetic model I have put forward. In other words, the dispersal of the hunter-gatherers from the Central Asia steppe around the time of the LGM took high-grade grassland hunting technology east and south-east to regions of China and Sundaland with expanding temperate grasslands. Curiously, the other technical link made with the Diuktai technology is with the New World – the subject of the next chapter, and the last leg of our journey with the first people to arrive at the farthest corners of the globe.

The extraordinary regional specificity of the paternal and maternal gene trees persisting today has made it possible to trace ancient migrations. It shows us that, as they were filling up the Old World, once people got to where they were going they tended to stay put and, at least until the last five hundred years, were mostly able to repel newcomers. What disturbed this conservatism the most was the LGM. In the northern hemisphere, vast areas of the Old and New Worlds were rendered uninhabitable by ice, glacial lakes, and polar desert. For the formerly highly successful hunter-gatherers of the North Eurasian steppe there were few choices, and these, as usual, were determined by geography and climate. In the peninsula of Europe, locked in by sea, mountain, and desert, the only chance of survival was to be found in refuges in the more southerly temperate zones bordering the Mediterranean and Black Seas. After the LGM, the refugees re-expanded in number and territory, mostly back to where they had come from.

In Central and North Asia, formerly covered in grassland and roamed by huge herds of large herbivores, the increasing cold and desiccation forced the Upper Palaeolithic hunter-gathers off the high steppe in several directions to warmer and more temperate regions. These would have included the Ukraine to the west, China to the south and east, and Japan, Korea, and north-east Siberia. As always, the great rivers of Asia could have played a role as highways, but this time the traffic was downstream. The archaeological evidence for this migration of Upper Palaeolithic steppe hunting cultures towards the Pacific coast at the LGM, is best seen in Japan, but is echoed elsewhere. In South and Southeast Asia huge areas of continental shelf opened up for colonization as the sea level fell. How much of the population expansion in Sundaland (greater Southeast Asia during the LGM) resulted from local people, and how much from refugees from farther north, is not clear, but the genetic and dental evidence suggests mostly the former. The drop in sea level also opened a new continent, 'Beringia', to the north-east. This provided a land-bridge to the Americas, where our story reaches its final chapter.

7

THE PEOPLING OF THE AMERICAS

THAT THE AMERICAN INDIANS came across the Bering Strait from Asia has been a natural solution to an obvious shared ancestry. As Thomas Jefferson noted in 1784, 'the resemblance between the Indians of America and the Eastern inhabitants of Asia, would induce us to conjecture, that the former are the descendants of the latter, or the latter of the former . . .'. This even-handed but ambiguous idea had already been given direction 200 years earlier by the Jesuit scientist and traveller José de Acosta, who had suggested that the Asians had come to America 2,000 years before the Spanish. There has not, until recently, been any serious rival to this view.[1]

With the exception of the colonization of Polynesia, it is likely that the entry into the Americas was the last of the great expansions of humankind into unexplored territory. With the great recent technical advances in the study of prehistory, intense local interest, and the enormous resources of the world's richest nation, we might well expect the story of the peopling of the Americas to be wrapped up. We might expect to know approximately when the first entry occurred, how many subsequent migrations there were, who they were, and where they came from, and how and when. We might even expect to have a clue about what sort of languages they spoke.

Discord in academia

Nothing could be further from reality. Scientists cannot agree about dates of first entry, having offered estimates ranging from 11,500 to 50,000 years ago. They cannot agree on how many migrations there were, some suggesting one, others many. They cannot even agree on how many Native American language families there have been during historic times, let alone how many entered America. Much of the problem lies in the nature of the evidence and with entrenched, polar academic opinions which have made rational agreement impossible. But, as we shall see, American observers of American prehistorians are becoming increasingly bemused by the very free-enterprise approach to influencing scientific decision-making.[2]

Formal scientific method should allow for, even insist upon, the uncertainty of theories. Crudely speaking, a theory (or 'model') sets out to provide a logical explanation of something not previously understood, in the best way allowed by the observations. We have to accept that some observations may be inaccurate or even misleading, and that more and better observations may allow a new and better theory to be constructed. Observations which call the new theory into question may well turn up, in which case it will give way to another new theory. The hope is that, sooner rather than later, we can get as close as we can to some ideal reality or truth. It is misleading to assume that we can ever get to that absolute truth. Above all, we should always be open to the possibility of being wrong.

The reality of academe is rarely like this. Bright young academics make their names with a new theory or some work that breaks the mould, and then spend the rest of their professional lives consolidating and defending their position from attack. Their students, their financial sponsors, and, of course, the public expect much more certainty than is available. This all encourages inflexibility. The gap between reality and credibility has always been filled with that thick, all-purpose glue of society – authority. Senior academics in each field have authority invested in their positions and defend both like high priests. When their authority is threatened by outsiders they perceive their positions to be under threat too, and they close ranks, form alliances, and chase off the pretenders. It is irrelevant whether the threat – some new interpretation which runs counter to a cherished, established view – actually gets closer to the Holy Grail of truth, or merely gives another angle on an opaque subject: the big guns still come out.

When two 'authorities' turn on each other, then we have civil war. The academic ground shakes as the great grey elephants thunder and charge. Neutral and objective colleagues are coerced to take sides, and juniors are advised to beware. Obviously there is a reverse side to such anti-establishment views of academe. Society abounds with adventurers who like to make capital from the unwary masses by exploiting their fascination with mystery. Some writers make large amounts of money, to the disgust of the archaeological establishment, questioning what they choose to label 'dogma', for instance whether humans invented their own ancient cultures, rather than the more exciting possibilities of Martian influence. Who could argue that accredited experts should not be there to defend our weak and ignorant minds from such charlatans? The problem of course is for the observer to know who is defending what in each situation.

The Clovis-first orthodoxy

What has all this to do with the peopling of the Americas? The answer is, much. The most contentious issue in American archaeology is the so-called Clovis orthodoxy or Clovis-first theory. The history of this orthodoxy goes back perhaps to the end of the nineteenth century, before which time it was a heresy. In the 1890s, William Henry Holmes of the Smithsonian Institution's Bureau of American Ethnology and Thomas Chamberlin of the United States

Geological Survey chased off many dubious claims for Pleistocene (ice-age) occupation of the New World. The mantle of authority for this gatekeeper role was passed in the 1920s to the physical anthropologist Ales Hrdlicka, also of the Smithsonian. Long after, in 1995, Hrdlicka was singled out by American author Vine Deloria in his book *Red Earth, White Lies* as a heavy-handed zealous defender of the academic status quo who quashed research proposals designed to explore alternative theories. [3]

In 1926, Jesse Higgins of the Colorado Museum of Natural History found a pointed stone artefact at a site near Folsom, New Mexico, which also yielded the skeleton of an extinct bison. Hrdlicka refused to accept this as evidence of Pleistocene human occupation since no archaeologist had checked the association with the bones before the point was removed. Another stone point was found in 1927. It was left on site, examined, photographed, and verified by outside experts. Higgins found more and larger points, with the same fluting (fluting is where flakes have been struck from the base, presumably to facilitate hafting), first in 1932 in Colorado, in association with mammoth skeletons, then five years later, again with mammoth bones at Clovis, New Mexico. These larger points, now known as Clovis points, lay beneath representatives of the other type, now known as Folsom points, which were associated with bison skeletons. [4]

Thus was it 'proved', by the criteria of the time, that humans had entered the New World before 10,000 years ago. The old theory, of a more recent colonization, was overturned, and 'the rest is history' as far as many American archaeologists are concerned. But all was not quite as it should be in a nicely rounded drama. In the cycle of theories, this was the 'good guy' phase: authoritative dogma overturned by careful observation and persistence after frustration and denigration. In due course, the wheel would turn.

Subsequently, Clovis points were turned up throughout the continental United States. The conviction grew among American archaeologists that these stone tools were the signature of the first human colonization of the Americas. After all, surely these first explorers were expert Upper Palaeolithic big-game hunters who had followed the mammoth trail across Beringia from Asia in the waning years of the last glaciation?

In 1964, American geochronologist C. Vance Haynes collected and linked together the dates of various Clovis-point sites using the new technology of carbon dating. These dates bracketed the earliest Clovis points to 11,000–11,500 years ago, and none was more than 12,000 years old. This latter age was significant for geologists, since they believed this was after the time when a corridor opened up between the two great melting ice sheets of North America and allowed passage from Alaska through Canada to the rest of the Americas (about 12,000–13,000 years ago). These two ice sheets, the Laurentide lying over Hudson Bay to the east and the Cordilleran covering the Rockies to the west, were so large that, on the evidence available in the 1960s, they seemed to span the continent.[5] (Figure 7.1.)

The Clovis-first theory had now matured into a complete and established orthodoxy. The argument went that humans could not have come into America before the Clovis points made their appearance because the way through was blocked by ice. All the Clovis dates pointed to a beginning that coincided with the opening of a vast corridor through the ice running from north-west to south-east from 13,000 years ago. Before this corridor opened, went the argument, no-one could have traversed the ice-sheets. Never mind that, even when it was open, the ice corridor was several thousand kilometres of barren Arctic desert and a lake requiring many packed lunches to traverse – this was the grand theory into which all elements could be fitted. The architects of the theory now became its high priests, and the theory was ripe for the next phase in the cycle of attack and defence of the new status quo. That attack and the fierce defence have now lasted over thirty years.

The strength, and at the same time the chief weakness, of the Clovis-first theory was that the earliest Clovis point had to be just after the opening of the ice corridor, and the ice corridor had to be just before the earliest Clovis point. Like a house of cards, nudge a key structural element and it will fall down. The key element was the insistence on the dates limiting the earliest entry to the Americas to after the opening of the ice corridor. If the occupation of North or South America could be pushed back just a few thousand years to a time when the corridor would have been closed, the theory would fall. In that case, the first entry would have to have been much earlier – before the Last Glacial Maximum (LGM), and probably before 22,000 years ago.

Pretenders, heretics, or scientists?

Seen in this light, new pretenders bearing dates more than 1,500 years before Clovis would in effect be suggesting entry to the Americas before the ice age rather than after, a radically new theory. Although it would be marginally less persuasive, any evidence of occupation in South America, even slightly before Clovis and with different adaptive technology, would also make it unlikely that Clovis points identified the entry of the first Americans.

There have been plenty of new pretenders over the past few decades, whether we are talking about new archaeological sites with pre-Clovis evidence, or their advocates. In one review from 1990 I counted eighteen contender sites. This is a conservative estimate, perhaps half, of the total challenges mounted over the past two decades. Most of these pretenders have been routed by defenders of the Clovis-first orthodoxy in skirmishes characterized by attacks on

Figure 7.1   Theories of entry to America. At the LGM, access to the Americas was blocked by ice. Two window periods existed, one just before and one just after the LGM, when the Beringian land bridge was open and access was possible through the ice corridor or along the west coast. Also shown are other theories and sites mentioned in text. For clarity, present-day coastline shown.

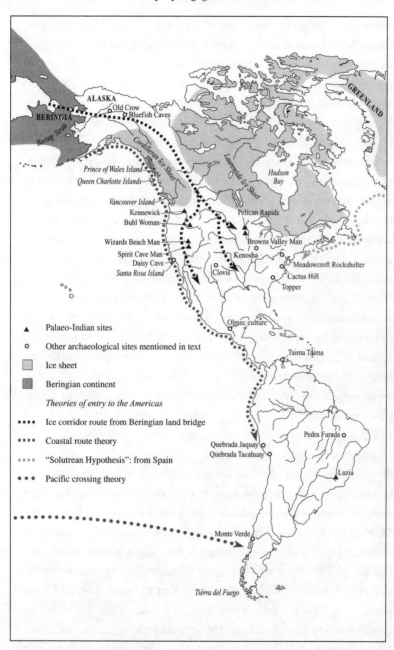

Palaeo-Indian sites ▲

Other archaeological sites mentioned in text ○

Ice sheet

Beringian continent

Theories of entry to the Americas

•••• Ice corridor route from Beringian land bridge

•••• Coastal route theory

∗∗∗∗ "Solutrean Hypothesis": from Spain

••• Pacific crossing theory

scientific method, context, and observation. Only a few have survived the 'critical' broadsides fired by defenders of the orthodoxy,
but they are still embattled. The most persistent and serious
pretenders are the sites of Monte Verde in northern Chile and
Meadowcroft Rockshelter in south-western Pennsylvania (see
Figure 7.1). New recruits have joined their ranks, namely Cactus
Hill in Virginia and Topper/Big Pine in South Carolina.[6]

The history of these claims and refutations is revealing of academe. The weapons of argument used by the defenders certainly
appeal to scientific method, careful observation, avoidance of
known sources of error, balanced logic, and reason; but the tactics
of appeal are clearly biased, selective, petty, personal, and confront-
ational. In other words, the method of defensive attack is 'sling
enough mud in the form of possible errors or what if's, and the good
evidence all becomes tarred with the bad and can be dismissed'. This
is reminiscent of a stock courtroom drama, where the witness is
discredited by the clever, aggressive lawyer. That is, however, an
adversarial, not a scientific approach. Furthermore, unlike the
judge, archaeologists are not required to come to closure of a case
or theory. They can and should remain open to different interpretations of the evidence. The 'truth' – whatever it is – is not on
trial. Clovis-first and its defenders, however, may well be.

There is no particular a priori reason to think that America was
first colonized after the last ice age rather than before, since sea-
locked Australia, New Guinea, and even the Bismarck Archipelago
and the North Solomon Islands were all colonized well before the
LGM. On the other hand, there is every reason to assume that
evidence is generally clearer the more recently it was set down, and
that the global effects of the ice age destroyed much good evidence
in North America. The fact, therefore, that there are a lot of Clovis
points lying around from a few thousand years after the LGM, in
good context, as opposed to the less well-provenanced evidence
from before the LGM, does not *prove* that Clovis was first. It merely

disproves the preceding orthodoxy of the nineteenth century, that America was not colonized until 10,000 years ago. We should expect the preglacial evidence (if any) that questions Clovis-first to be weaker than Clovis itself.

MonteVerde

We can illustrate some of these points with the history of the Monte Verde controversy. Tom Dillehay of the University of Kentucky has been involved in the excavation of Monte Verde site in southern Chile since 1977, and he and his colleagues have amassed a considerable arsenal to use against the Clovis-first citadel. While there is some evidence for a very early occupation of MonteVerde, with split pebble tools dating to around 33,000 years ago, the 'best' evidence is dated much more recently. The site is a peat bog and has preserved a number of organic and other remains suggestive of human occupation: a footprint; wooden artefacts; structures that may be parts of huts; hearths; the remains of palaeo-llamas and mastodons, including cut bone; and seeds, nuts, fruits, berries, and tubers. Radiocarbon dating of the organic remains has yielded dates from 11,790 to 13,565 (average 12,500) years ago. Simple stone tools such as flakes and cobbles were also found.[7]

Monte Verde lies 12,000 km (7,500 miles) south of the Alaskan ice corridor and, with an age of around 12,500 years, appears to antedate any Clovis site by a millennium. This raises the logical question of how anyone could have passed through the ice corridor after 13,000 years ago and still had time to travel so far south and then change culture.[8] This looked like powerful ammunition to use against the Clovis-first orthodoxy. Predictably, the Clovis-first camp fought back. To break the resulting deadlock, an independent set of referees was brought in.

In 1997 an invited group of the foremost Palaeo-Indian specialists, including sceptics such as Vance Haynes, gathered in Kentucky to hear Dillehay's presentation, and then visited Chile for a site inspection and further presentations. Each member of the group was handed a detailed site report published by the Smithsonian Institution. The group's consensus report, published later that year in the academic journal *American Antiquity*, concluded that the site was an archaeological site and that the dates of occupation were around 12,500 years ago. A further article in *American Antiquity* by dating specialists, including Vance Haynes, confirmed the dates, freeing them from any suspicion of contamination with older carbon sources.[9]

Then something happened which revealed the dispute in its true colours. This was now an academic turf war, with no place for the open-mindedness, objectivity, and reason expected of scientific peer review. Just when the Dillehay camp thought that the matter was closed, the wall of scepticism broken, and Monte Verde finally accepted by the establishment, a private archaeological consultant, Stuart Fiedel, published a long and stinging critique of the entire site report. Media drama intensified. Unconventionally, Fiedel chose to make his attack not in a peer-refereed academic journal but in a popular magazine, *Discovering Archaeology*.[10] The journal also ran responses from Dillehay's group and supporters, as well as further sceptical comment and what amounted to a partial retraction by Haynes. This time the reaction came not just from the Dillehay supporters but from the establishment, in particular from *Archaeology*, the high-profile, high-circulation organ of the Archaeological Institute of America. The strength of the reaction is evident from the following extracts from both publications. First, from *Discovering Archaeology*:

> If the case for the new idea or theory is deemed convincing, then the old paradigm quietly dies and the particular scientific field is better for it. In point of fact, however, and particularly in archaeology, it seems this admittedly idealized sequence of events rarely comes to pass. Instead, the whims of personality and pride are

frequently injected into the process, acrimony and *ad hominem* attacks set the tone of the debate, and objectivity is submerged in personal polemics. For these reasons, paradigms, especially old ones, die harder than Bruce Willis. This is clearly the case with the 'Clovis-first' or 'Clovis primacy' model, which is now more than 50 years old. (James Adovasio, 'Paradigm-death and gunfights'[11])

[Fiedel] blankets the whole in a patina of almost-conspiratorial mistrust and accusations, layered with all too-frequent snide remarks (e.g., 'Dillehay's Hamlet-like agonizing'). In that, he does his critique no favors. More to the point, the most useful, productive, and constructive procedure (and certainly the most open and fair minded) would have been to first send Dillehay a draft of the criticism for comment and clarification of what were the trivial/editorial problems, and then once the minor problems were dispersed with and the major issues clarified, submit the piece to a rigorously peer-reviewed academic journal. Fiedel did not do so. (David Meltzer, 'On Monte Verde'[12])

And from *Archaeology*:

Fiedel's review is clearly biased and negative in tone. He ignores material that does not support his critical thesis and takes the more negative or improbable of alternative views of each case that he discusses. (Michael Collins, 'The site of Monte Verde'[13])

I'm irked at the carping tone of Fiedel's commentary, and the ferreting out of meaningless conflict in interpretation over two decades of reporting on Monte Verde. Fiedel cops an attitude which, in my opinion, is entirely inappropriate. For my money, the Monte Verde research team should be celebrated, rather than henpecked, for their willingness to publish their findings in great detail and to share their misgivings about their own data . . . I think its [sic] a cheap shot to dredge up preliminary assessments and press reports to attack the Monte Verde project. I still think its [sic] a good thing to change your mind (so long as you're honest about it). I question Fiedel's decision to rush his manuscript into print without first passing it by Dillehay and his colleagues for comment. Picking up on my earlier theme of self-criticism, its clear that the mishmash of Fiedel's shotgun criticism could have been winnowed down through frank person-to-person communication with the Monte Verde principals. Once this interchange had occurred, we could have been presented with a concise summary of the real issues, unclouded by the chaff and attitude . . . Ambushing the Monte Verde team in this way inevitably raises questions over Fiedel's motivations. Was the critique primarily concerned with clarifying the pre-Clovis possibilities at Monte Verde? Or was this just another carefully timed headline-grabber? Handled the way it was, who knows? (David Thomas, 'One archaeologist's perspective on the Monte Verde controversy'[14])

Other reviews of Fiedel's critique were approving. But the furore it caused left the big question mark hanging over Monte Verde.

For the interested lay person, or even an archaeologist unfamiliar with the sites, trying to assess what was going on here is rather like having to choose a doctor when all the doctors are accusing one another of professional misconduct. One clear conclusion from that hypothetical situation would be to distrust doctors' opinions of one another. Perhaps the shrillness of the defenders of the Clovis-first orthodoxy is a measure of how much they perceive Monte Verde as a threat. Their response also serves as a baseline for assessing objections to other sites that are claimed to be pre-Clovis. If the objections come from well-known defenders of the Clovis-first orthodoxy, distrust them. If the objections (or confirmations) come from neutral experts or from the whole profession, take them seriously.

Meadowcroft

Another veteran high-profile site under siege is Meadowcroft Rock-shelter. For thirty years, Pennsylvania archaeologist James Adovasio has led work on this site (see Plate 24). He and his colleagues have dug through eleven floor layers, unearthing 20,000 stone flakes and objects and a huge quantity of animal and plant remains. Fifty-two radiocarbon dates have been published for the Meadowcroft finds, the oldest at the bottom in sterile clay 31,000 years ago and the youngest at the top, just 1,000 years old. Dates unambiguously associated with Palaeoindian occupation go back to 16,225 years ago, while dates in excess of 19,000 years have been claimed for the deepest occupation layer.[15]

As soon as these old dates were published they drew a storm of protest. No prizes for who has been the fiercest critic: Vance Haynes. Years of criticism focused on details of stratigraphy, documentation, dating anomalies, and possible contamination by a coal seam a kilometre away. Adovasio is reported as regarding such criticism as pathological scepticism. Thousands of pages have been written answering specific questions. The contamination issue was buried by an independent geomorphologist in 1999, but Haynes still wants to get carbon dates on a few remaining items, a nutshell and some seeds. Adovasio has had enough, however. He is reported to have informed Haynes three years ago at the Monte Verde meeting that, 'I will never run another date you have asked me for, because since 1974, we've addressed every criticism anyone has raised. I have spent half my life on this.'[16]

If professional sceptics such as Haynes and Fiedel are right, then they are to be congratulated for maintaining their integrity in the face of a massive synthesis of false evidence. If they are wrong and/or biased in their approach, on the other hand, then they would have successfully and vaingloriously held up the progress of American archaeology for three decades and artificially prolonged the life of the obsolete Clovis-first orthodoxy to around seventy years. With the ever-accelerating pace of scientific discovery, that would be an extraordinary achievement. Even Hrdlicka did not achieve that length of filibuster at the beginning of the last century.

Two other, more recently discovered North American pre-Clovis sites now vie for immediate attention – Cactus Hill and Topper. Cactus Hill, on the East Coast near Richmond, Virginia, now has a full site report, written by two competing private archaeological teams, waiting for the sceptics to tear into it.[17] Joseph and Lynn McAvoy of the Virginia Department of Historic Resources run one team, while Michael Johnson of the Archaeological Society of Virginia runs the other. Cactus Hill is an ancient sand dune, so-called after the prickly pears that cover it in the summer.

The original find at Cactus Hill was made, as often happens, by a perceptive farmer; he noticed a stone point in a pile of sand dumped some way from the hill and traced it back to its source. Digging through the layers of time, the teams have uncovered stone points of progressively greater antiquity including some of the fluted Clovis type. At the lowest level they found flaked tools, a scraper, a quartzite core, and some small blades. Radiocarbon dates from this bottom layer are in the 15,000–16,000-year age range – earlier than the opening of the ice corridor. In one of the deep layers, unusual stone points suggested an antecedent to the full Clovis style. Together with the other tools, these finds constitute even more evidence for a pre-Clovis culture. Needless to say, Haynes and Fiedel have been here too, to doubt the age of the artefacts. They have not, of course, suggested that they are older, rather that they are younger.[18]

The other new site is Topper, in South Carolina, named after David Topper, the forester who discovered it. The site research is directed by Al Goodyear, a state archaeologist with the University of Carolina. Five years ago Goodyear and his team were forced off another site by floods and re-excavated Topper instead. Only this time they dug deep, deeper than the Clovis level. Formerly an uncontroversial card-carrying Clovis-first archaeologist, Goodyear was converted by the shock of what he found. Below the Clovis level were small blades of chert, chiselled burins, a scraper, and micro-blades. The technology was more reminiscent of the Upper Palaeolithic in Siberia than anything previously found in the American south-east. Luminescence dating puts the age of the artefacts at 13,000 years.[19]

Have the sceptics chimed in again? Of course. This time their beef is not with the dates but with the tools. Were they made by humans? Another objection: most Clovis sites do not have pre-Clovis tools beneath them. According to the journal *Science*, Vance Haynes finds it hard to accept that this is just 'a coincidence'. Such an argument seems rather like rejecting the Roman occupation of England because not every house in England has Roman remains beneath it. 'I've been looking at this for 40 years', says Haynes. Hmm.[20]

Two more recent sites with pre-Clovis dates are playing out their cycles of claim and criticism: Schaefer and Hebior, in south-eastern Wisconsin. Both sites have been radiocarbon dated to around 12,500 years ago. At one of them, Hebior, near Kenosha, flakes, a chopper, and two flaked stone bifaces have been found among butchered mammoth bones.[21]

With archaeologists such as Dillehay, Adovasio, the McAvoys, Johnson, Goodyear, and their colleagues going to extreme lengths to document their evidence, warts and all, and the persistent 'what if' responses from the critics, there has been a sea change in discussions on the pre-Clovis issue. The critics are at last being viewed less as the careful counsel of the establishment, and more as those who 'doth protest too much'.

The Clovis-first mindset has, at last, been weakened. There is now a rash of recycled, new, or alternative explanations of the early colonization of the New World. The debate is moving from asking whether there was a pre-Clovis movement into and throughout the

Americas, to which, and how many, exotic routes were taken. These 'big arrows into America',[22] which, if all valid, would have to imply multiple entries from elsewhere, including a west coastal land route, a west coastal sea route, a North Atlantic route from Europe, a South Pacific route from Australia, and a South American re-entry after the ice age (see Figure 7.1). There is, however, less secure archaeological evidence for any of these scenarios than for Monte Verde and Meadowcroft.

The language story

Before I discuss those possible routes and what the genes can tell us about them, I would like to bring in another discipline that has always offered promises of great insight into the past: language history. Sadly, academic temperament has again helped to inject more confusion than clarity.

Comparative or historical linguistics has as hoary a role in speculations on the first Americans as does archaeology. In each case the nation's most revered founding father and well-meaning polymath played a part. In 1784, Thomas Jefferson directed the controlled excavation of an ancient mound in Virginia, the first scientific excavation in the history of American archaeology. Four years earlier, he had begun pioneering efforts to collect standardized vocabulary lists for Native Americans. He wanted to trace their origins through comparative linguistics. By 1809 he had several dozen lists, but they were stolen and almost totally destroyed while his possessions were being transported. Jefferson recovered the surviving fragments and sent them to the American Philosophical Society. America thus had a head start on most nations in gazing through this promising yet opaque window onto our past.[23]

What was it Jefferson wanted to do with language? His idea itself was simple in concept but well nigh impossible to apply in reality. It goes like this: over time, languages split and branch. If this represents expanding peoples splitting into bands, then we should be able to date the splits and place them on a map. This should then give us a family tree of migrations. For example, European languages such as German, French, Spanish, and English all come from a common Indo-European stock. By comparing them using certain rules, linguists can show that they have branched progressively from that stock via dead ancestors such as Latin and proto-Germanic. If the whole European language tree could be reconstructed – which, though there are certain areas of contention, is possible – the hope is that it might then be possible to trace geographic population splits.

So, if we then lay out the language tree on the map, we find, for example, that French and Spanish come from Latin and, before that, from proto-Italic. English and German came from some proto-west-German root. All the languages from this European family eventually join up with a proto-Indo-European root thousands of years ago. Now one can start drawing big arrows on the map from A to B and C, from C to D, and so on, and write the history of European colonization as told by the languages.

The trouble is that it does not work quite like that. Languages do not change only as a result of population splits and random change. For example, the roughly 15 per cent of English that is not Germanic comes from French. That French vocabulary was imported by a very small number of Norman nobles a thousand years ago, after the Norman conquest – a phenomenon called language borrowing. The French intrusion into English came about via the dominance of a small Norman elite, not through massive Norman migration. French is an Italic language, but no one would suggest on that basis that the French are all direct descendants of Roman invaders. The French language changed from Celtic to a Romance language under the influence of the Roman Empire. That is called language shift. Language borrowing and shift can take place with only a minimal movement of people, which spoils simplistic models of language migrating synchronously with people.

Of course, Europe might not provide the best linguistic comparison with the USA. It has been occupied by modern humans for
45,000 years or more, and there has been a lot of complex internal
population movement. But there are a few good examples of people
moving and taking only their own language with them in such a way
that the language tree can trace the migration history and indicate
the source of the migration. These good examples are almost always
of migrations into previously unoccupied territory, such as the
Polynesians' spread through the empty islands of the deep Pacific.
The small subfamily of Polynesian languages really does look like a
tree and does recapitulate their spread as tracked by the archaeological record. What is more, the genetic picture fits the linguistic
trail very well within Polynesia.[24]

The colonization of the Americas could actually be regarded as
similar to the conquest of the Pacific, in that people would have been
moving into a huge virgin territory – a New World – and spreading
out and separating like rays from a star. The trouble is that the
Americas were colonized a long time before Polynesia, which was
occupied progressively only between 800 and 3,500 years ago.

Great time depth has critical effects on language change and
limits the possibility of reconstruction. Not only is it extremely
difficult to date the splits in languages, but also most linguists feel
that because of the inevitable decay in detectable relationships
between words, language families cannot be reconstructed or traced
further back than about 6,000–8,000 years.[25] This is only slightly
over half the time since Clovis, so reconstructing a unified New
World language tree back to its base is a major problem. If Native
American language families can be traced back only 7,000 years,
their tree will be missing all its roots and lower branches: we would
be looking at a mess of prunings, with little chance of fitting them
together as a tree. And indeed this is the case with North, Central,
and South America, which are characterized by many language
families, over a hundred in all, consisting of about 1,200 languages.

(15) Just visible in a faded mulberry colour, to the left of the lens cap, is the oldest dated rock painting of a human figure, 17,000 years old from the Kimberley region of Australia.

(16) The author conducts a genetic survey among the Semang, who are most likely to be relics of the first beachcombing trek out of Africa.

(17) Faces of our time: (from top, left to right) a Chinese grandmother and grandchild, a boy from the Highlands of New Guinea, an English man, and an Australian aboriginal from Arnhemland.

Facing page: (18) The image of Out-of-Africa Eve, used in the documentary 'Out of Eden'/'The Real Eve'. Reconstructed from one of the best-preserved Skhul remains from the Levant exodus, her features reflect a robust build typical for that period, a relatively narrow skull and a broad upper face.

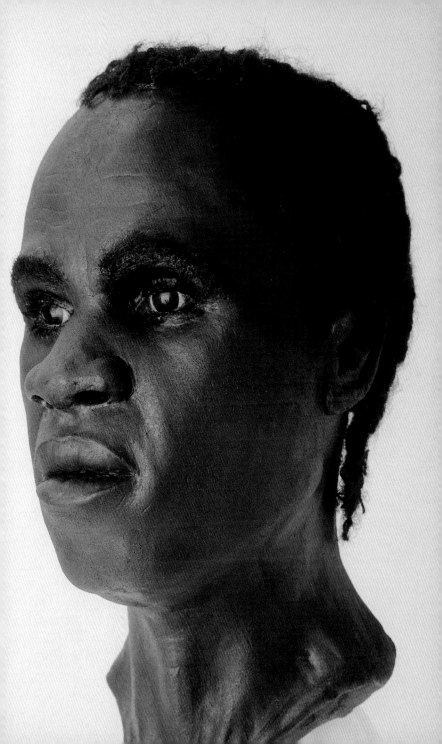

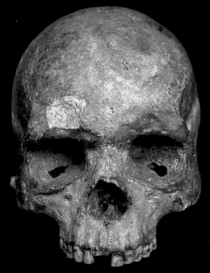

(19) China's Liujiang skull, with its clearly robust but modern features, recently re-dated to at least 68,000 years ago, suggests very early spread of Anatomically Modern Humans out of Africa, before the Toba explosion.

(20) The Minatogawa 1 skull from Okinawa, dating to the Last Glacial Maximum, may ultimately be an early ancestor of Japan's modern aboriginal Ainu population.

(21) This female figurine from Mal'ta near Lake Baikal, carved from mammoth ivory and, dated to around 23,000 years ago, evidences the far spread of mammoth-based hunting culture.

Below: (22) Paleontologists try out for size a reconstruction of a mammoth-bone hut, first unearthed during excavations at Mezin in the Ukraine.

(23) Now virtually extinct, the Tehuelche of Tierra del Fuego (photographed here in 1905) are the only modern group with features as robust as Australians and highland New Guineans.

Below: (24) Archaeologist James Adovasio surveys the numerous layers showing occupation of Meadowcroft Rockshelter, one of the most important potential pre-Clovis challenge sites in America.

(25) A Native American from the Cree tribe takes his own DNA sample during the research associated with *The Real Eve* project.

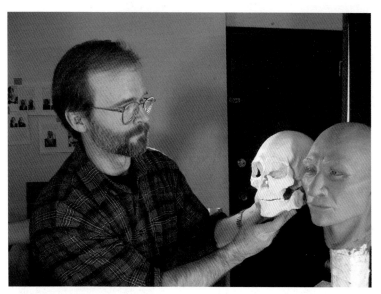

(26) James Chatters with the reconstruction and skull model of Kennewick Man, showing the mysterious jutting chin and possibly Caucasoid features.

Above: (27) The forensic reconstruction of Luzia, the twenty-two-year-old woman from over 11,500 years ago, whose skull was found in Minas Gerais, Brazil.

(28) Carved Olmec head from Mexico – do Luzia's facial features hint at a forgotten link?

To most linguists, these cannot be drawn together into any semblance of a single tree, and even a few trees would be ambitious. Attempting to find out how many individual language branches entered America on this basis would thus be an educated guess at best. That has not stopped some people from trying.

The Australian linguist Robert Dixon has estimated that about a dozen separate groups speaking different languages entered the Americas between about 12,000 and 20,000 years ago. American linguist Johanna Nichols, known for her deep-time analysis of world language change, reckons that about 35,000 years of occupation of the New World, based on multiple separate original entries from Asia into America, is necessary to explain the present diversity of American language families. The English linguist Daniel Nettle, in contrast, sees the Americas as having reached their climax of family diversity within the last, say, 12,000 years.[26]

There is a big problem in using numbers of language families to estimate time depth. This is because, apart from the lack of agreement on time calibration, not all historical linguists are agreed on how to define a family of languages. The result is that numbers of families vary from linguist to linguist and country to country. Historical linguists can generally be divided into 'splitters' and 'lumpers', the former generating large numbers of families of a few languages, and the latter favouring small numbers of super-families containing large numbers of languages. At one extreme is the veteran American linguist Joseph Greenberg, who has famously gone much further than most other American linguists find acceptable by claiming that he can divide all Native American languages into three founder groups. At the other extreme we find classifications with over 160 families. The majority of American linguists tend to the higher rather than the lower figure.

In calculating the overall age of American languages (mentioned above), Johanna Nichols has estimated that there are 167 American language 'stocks' (groups of languages that can be reconstructed or related back to a common node or branching point) using the strict rules of comparative linguistics. Nichols' estimates of the number of American language stocks are intended for comparison with language diversity in other countries. She argues that in a region such as a continent or subcontinent which is isolated from outside influences, the number of stocks increases as a simple function of time.[27]

There are difficulties with all these analyses based on subclassifications. First, there is no fully agreed approach to reducing numbers of languages to stocks or families, and even Nichols' definition of 'stock' is likely to be subjective in its application. Second, the numbers of individual languages per stock varies from country to country and continent to continent, for reasons that are themselves contentious.[28]

Still, whichever way one looks at it, in terms of stocks or languages, South America has far greater linguistic diversity than North America. From a statistical point of view, when exploring unknown mathematical relationships it is generally safer to use the simplest raw measurement for analysis rather than some derived value, which may carry further unknowns. The raw data in this instance are the numbers of languages rather than numbers of stocks.

I have taken the liberty of expressing the data used by Nichols and Nettle as a simple 'numbers and time' graph (Figure 7.2). I have plotted numbers of the world's languages per region (grouped by subcontinent/continent, as in Nichols' original dataset) according to estimated dates of occupation, using an intermediate dummy average age of 16,000 years for each of North, Central, and South America. The result is rather straightforward: as Nichols found, there is a simple straight-line relationship between age of occupation and numbers of languages in each region. The exception is Australia, which has always been recognized to have a lower than expected diversity for its age of occupation, being dominated by one language family. This relationship is so clear that we can put Nichols' regions

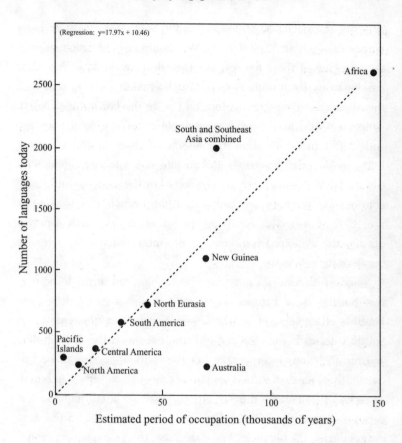

(Regression: y=17.97x + 10.46)

Figure 7.2 Plot of regional language numbers in the Americas and worldwide. Note how the points for the Americas are as predicted by regression equation. The two outliers can be explained on basis that Australia has only one main family, and South and Southeast Asia should really have separate entries but are shown together as in Nichols' original data-set.[26–28]

of North, Central, and South America back into the equation and predict their respective approximate ages of occupation. The result is interesting, almost a caricature, because the crude linguistic age in North America comes out at a Clovis-like 13,000 years, in Central

America at a glacial 20,500 years, and in South America at an Early Upper Palaeolithic 32,500 years. We should not put much store in the accuracy of these figures, but they do provide us with a clear ranking in age from south to north. Such a ranking is consistent with the Americas having been colonized before the last ice age. North America would have been largely depopulated during the ice age and would therefore show the effects of re-expansion after the LGM, with fewer languages and an inferred date coincident with Clovis. South America, largely unaffected by the ice age, would have continued to generate new languages right through, thus looking its age. Central America, receiving migrations from North America during the re-expansion, would be intermediate in diversity between the other two.[29]

Since South America must have been colonized through the narrow bottleneck of Panama from North America (see below), the South is effectively yet another New World. So a first entry into South America before the last glaciation seems to be the simplest and most obvious interpretation of the south appearing to be linguistically older than the north. The low language diversity in North America, particularly the far North, may be a consequence of depopulation at the LGM, followed by re-expansion of a few languages during the big melt. As we shall see, this re-expansion model has resonance in the genetics.

A northern enclave

While very few American linguists recognize Greenberg's largest American language family, Amerind, which he claimed encompasses 97 per cent of all American languages, there is little dissent about the other two groups which are found in the far north of America, namely Na-Dene and Inuit-Aleut. Thereby hangs a long-running tale. In 1986 Greenberg got together with a geneticist and a specialist on dental variation. The three of them published a theory which came to be known as the 'Greenberg hypothesis',[30] which was that the synthesis of the three disciplines told of three separate migrations into the New World, distinct in dental morphology, genes, and language. The first of these migrations carried the ancestors of those Native Americans who speak the huge number of languages Greenberg classified as Amerind. The second, Na-Dene, carried a conglomerate of north-western and coastal languages such as Athapascan, Haida, and Tlingit, while the third carried the languages of the Aleutian islands and the Arctic – Inuit and Aleut. The Greenberg synthesis was conservative as far as dates were concerned, suggesting that these three linguistic groups arrived respectively 11,000, 9,000, and 4,000 years ago.

Greenberg's neat, simplistic reductionism appealed at the time to geneticists thinking and working on the peopling of the Americas. Not so to most American linguists, who long before had rejected almost unanimously Greenberg's 'lumping' methods. Some linguists argued that the diversity of American languages and their stocks means separate migrations, while the more cautious have just disputed the integrity of the Amerind group and any conclusions based on the assumption of its reality.[31]

How many founding genetic lines? How many migrations?
The gulf between linguists and geneticists has widened rather than narrowed since the late 1980s as more has been learnt about the genes carried by Native Americans. Rather than accept that the Americas were colonized by several migrations, geneticists have tended to reduce Greenberg's magic number of three to two, then to just one migration. They also parted company with both Greenberg and the archaeologists on the dating of the first migration, initially coming up with estimates of as long ago as 50,000 years, which had even some of the pre-Clovis archaeologists and 'deep-time' linguists gasping. A multidisciplinary synthesis is difficult enough if the disciplines are singing different songs, but if they are in different auditoriums . . .

We need to go look at some of the developments in Native American genetics since 1990 to understand how this divergence of views came about. In 1991, New Zealand geneticist, the late Ryk Ward, sequenced a small number of mitochondrial DNA types from the Nuu-Chah-Nulth (Amerind-speaking peoples from the American north-west) and identified four clusters or lines of sequences. Ward calculated that they came together as one line between 41,000–78,000 years ago. With foresight, he correctly inferred that this original branch point must have been long before in Asia. This meant that multiple lines must have entered America. Ward's interpretation of four founding lineages started geneticists speculating on numbers of migration events, which they continue to do to this day.[32]

In 1993, the Japanese geneticist Santoshi Horai argued that four lineages could mean four migrations.[33] This symmetrical 'one line equals one migration' view has been regarded by some as too simplistic an interpretation of founder effects and American genetic diversity, but that is not the last word on the matter. By this time, however, other geneticists were already suggesting that even three migrations was one too many.

Genetic geography and the Americas

Their early mtDNA results suggested to American and Italian geneticists Douglas Wallace and Antonio Torroni and colleagues that, while the Amerinds had arrived around 20,000 years ago, the Na-Dene speakers of the north-west coast and Alaska arrived later, around 6,000–10,000 years ago. The next year (1993), Torroni and Wallace further clarified the mtDNA types that had been present in the colonization of America. They performed a high-resolution analysis on a sample of 527 Native Americans from twenty-four ethnic groups throughout America (excluding only Inuit), 404 Siberians from ten ethnic groups, and 106 other East Asians.[34]

This was the first attempt ever at drawing up formal 'phylogeographic' rules to identify original 'founder genetic types'. Torroni and Wallace argued that:

1 True founding mtDNA types should be at the root of their own particular branch, because all subsequent types in that branch would have originated from them.

2 It should still be possible to detect the founding mtDNA types in the region that was the source of migration, in this case East Asia.

3 Subsequent or daughter mtDNA types in a founding American cluster should be unique to America and should not be found in Asia.

Torroni and Wallace identified four main founder clusters throughout Amerind populations, each of which seemed to have been founded by a single mtDNA type. These clans (strictly, haplogroups), designated A–D, overlapped with three of Ward's groups. Just one of these clusters, A, was found in the northern Na-Dene speakers. Also, the identifying mutations of the founder types were the same for the sister clusters found on the other side of the Bering Strait, in East Asia. (In Chapters 4 and 5 we came across these four groups in Asia – but more of that later.) Although the Americans and East Asians share these four genetic groups in general, the specific daughter American types of the four founders were not found in Asia. In other words, they had probably evolved further in America. These findings were consistent with the three rules given above, and meant that the four clusters had come across from Asia as founders already possessing their A, B, C, and D identities.[35] (Figure 7.3)

Torroni and Wallace also argued that mtDNA sub-types were specific to and typical of particular Native American groups. This suggests that tribal isolation had begun early, since when gene-flow between tribes has been limited. The four groups could all be found in Siberia, except for Group B, suggesting that this region might be

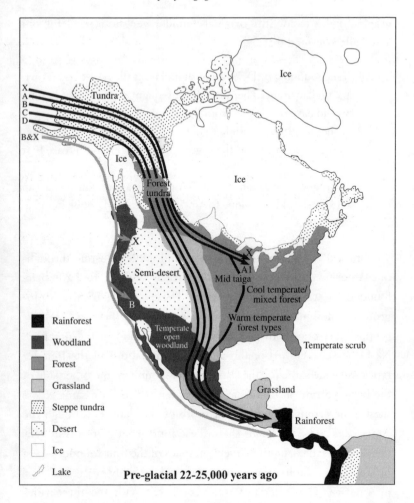

Figure 7.3   Suggested pre-glacial entry of mtDNA founder lines into North America. The genetic evidence suggests entry of all five founders via Beringia during this period. I have suggested dual coastal/corridor routes for groups X and B, although B may only have been coastal.[36–44]

the original source, or at least that eastern Siberia and America had a common source.

With the likely founder types identified, it was then possible to use the molecular clock to estimate the founding date for each founder cluster. There were surprising results: Groups A, C, and D appeared to be very old (20,000–41,000 years old in America), certainly much older than Clovis, while B appeared to be nearer the age of Clovis. At the time, Torroni and Wallace took these results to mean an early pre-Clovis entry of Amerinds, with a possible later entry of Group B. They suggested a distinct origin for the Na-Dene and the Inuit-Aleut. Although they were careful this time not to specify an exact number of migrations, they gave the impression that there were three.[36]

Torroni and Wallace's findings seemed to fit Greenberg's three-entry model quite well. The immediate problem seemed to be the timescale. The young age of Group B even suggested that B might be independently signalling the post-glacial Clovis expansion in North America.[37] The oldest ages of colonization suggested by the molecular clock, however, were supported by only minimal archaeological evidence and by very few archaeologists, but most of the younger dates were still older than Clovis. Taken as a whole, the new genetic evidence seemed to be moving even further away from a consensus with archaeologists and linguists.

As it turned out, the pre-Clovis genetic dates were the more durable conclusions of this major study. Subsequent re-estimates for the age of Group B in Amerinds have also tended to be pre-Clovis rather than post-Clovis. Research published since Torroni and Wallace's 1993 results has produced similarly old genetic dates for the other three groups, A, C, and D, thus supporting a growing genetic perspective that all the main mtDNA lines had already entered America before the LGM. The older genetic dates have even raised the possibility that the Americas could have been colonized during a previous glaciation 30,000 or even 40,000 years ago.[38]

What has changed our perspective of American colonization more is detailed knowledge of the branching coming out of those founding branches, and advances in the methods used to date them. The insights and new methods that developed from this extensive and expensive enquiry into American genetic prehistory laid the ground for all the analytically much more difficult studies on Africa, Asia, and Europe that have provided much of the new body of knowledge of ancient migrations discussed in this book.

Greenberg's three groups are related to one another within America
As more markers came to be used, the inner structure of the American mtDNA branches revealed a genetic link between the Na-Dene, the Inuit, and the Amerinds that Torroni and Wallace did not uncover in their earlier work. Initially they had thought that both Inuit-Aleut and Na-Dene speakers had only Group A markers and that this somehow indicated that they were descended from a separate migration event. It was also soon realized that Inuit-Aleut speakers had both A and D groups. Their D group was identified as a new subgroup of Asian D which had not previously been recorded in Asia or America: D2. The main American founder D type, D1, was partly related to D2 but unique to Amerinds.[39]

A much more convincing argument that Na-Dene and Inuit-Aleut speakers shared a common source with Amerinds came with the discovery that the American A cluster was actually composed of a unique founder, A1, and her daughter, A2 (and other daughters). A1 was a first-generation daughter of the Asian root A type, and A2 was A1's daughter by one mutational event. While A1 was found only in Greenberg's Amerind group, A2 was found in all three language divisions but was the only type in the Na-Dene and Inuit-Aleut. These complex inclusive and exclusive founder relationships carried a simple message: they bound together the three Greenberg groups as a 'family' in that they had at least one founding genetic source in common – the American founding line A. Neither A1 nor A2 are found in Asia, with the exception of Siberian Inuit and Siberian Chukchi. (The Chukchi language belongs to Chukchi-

Kamchatkan, a unique group of Paleo-Siberian languages spoken in the far eastern tip of Siberia and the Kamchatka Peninsula.)[40]

These two Siberian peoples share a further unique subgroup of A2 with all other Inuit populations in both North America and Greenland, thus still keeping their family together, as it were by a network of related A types. This again seems to point to a single entry into the Americas. A similar network of subgroups related to one founder seemed at first to bind D subgroups throughout America. D2 was a feature of the Inuit-Aleut, while another related but unique subgroup, D1, was found almost only in Amerinds, who constitute the majority of Native Americans.[41]

These genetic findings appeared to strengthen the links between the three Native American groups, the two in the Arctic and Sub-arctic and the rest (Greenberg's Amerind group) farther south. This seemed to be leading back to the reductionist idea of a single migration, but several puzzling questions remained. For a start, the most convincing link between the three language divisions, the A1/A2 family network, although it arose after the exit from Asia, still shows a very deep and ancient division. This split separates the Arctic and Subarctic groups from the rest of the Americans to the south. Not only that, but the A2 subgroup in the Inuit-Aleut and Na-Dene is much younger than in the rest of America.

Why so little diversity in the north? Must be the ice age

Another continuing difficulty that faces those trying to link the colonizations of the American Arctic and Subarctic with the peopling of the rest of the two continents, as a single migration from Asia, is the imbalance in distribution of the founder groups. According to the principles of founder analysis – and an evolutionary rule of thumb – the nearer you get to the source of a migration, the more likely you are to find all the founders. Conversely, the farther you travel from the start of migration, the lower the diversity becomes. In the Americas, we have just the reverse. Up in north-west Alaska, where the migration into the Americas must have started, there is now only one of the founder lines, A, present only as the derived type A2. Furthermore, B and C are completely missing from the whole of the Arctic and Subarctic. Conversely, in the rest of America, the founding Groups A to D are widely distributed and diverse. This seems all wrong. How could A, B, C, and D all be at large in the Americas when all we can find at the portal of entry in Alaska and neighbouring parts of Canada is a rather young A2 maternal clan?

In many ways, the high genetic diversity in the southern half of North America, even more diversity in South America, and the lowest diversity in the extreme north (Canada and Alaska) mirrors the upside-down distribution of language numbers. If Clovis-first was correct, and the first colonization occurred after the LGM, we would find the opposite. As I argued for the languages, if the primary colonization had occurred before the ice age, extensive parts of North America would have been depopulated during the LGM. If the North American population had re-expanded during the 'big melt', northern peoples would show lower diversity and consequently younger time depths than those farther south.

The idea of an expansion phase in North America after the ice age, which would explain some of the upside-down genetic findings, had already been put forward in 1993.[42] Alaskan geneticist Gerald Shields and colleagues had noticed that all the circum-Arctic populations in Asia and in the Americas appeared to be genetically young, similar to one another, and different from populations farther south in both continents. In particular, the Group B was completely absent north of the 55th parallel. They argued that the circum-Arctic peoples could have originated in a more recent expansion of a single northern population lacking in genetic diversity. They also argued that this expansion had happened after the Americas had been colonized by a more diverse population. This view of populations with low genetic diversity expanding in Canada and Alaska, after the ice age and after a previous colonization of the Americas, appeared to go a long way to answer some of the genetic and linguistic conundrums posed by those regions.

A refuge on the lost continent of Beringia

There was still the problem of where these re-expanding far-northern groups came from – was it Asia or America? The new genetic evidence of the A1/A2 link seemed to point to America, while the presence of A2 in Siberian Inuit and Chukchi suggested a possible Asian source. Anyway, if the Na-Dene and Inuit-Aleut were from the same original genetic stock as all other Americans, how come there was such a difference in age, and such a deep genetic, physical, and linguistic split?

In 1996, the Anglo-German geneticist Peter Forster and an international team drew these problem strands into a coherent explanation. It was like a chess problem which had had a number of people puzzling over it for a long time: the answer, when it came, was so simple. Forster's collaborators included Antonio Torroni and a German mathematician/polymath, Hans-Jurgen Bandelt, who has been the creator and inspiration for much of the analysis necessary to create the real gene trees I have used in this book. The answer to the Americas conundrum was that the ice-age homeland of the northerners was neither Asia nor America, but another continent – Beringia.[43] (Figure 7.1.)

Between 11,000 and 25,000 years ago, sea-levels were so low that the Bering Strait was then a land bridge between Asia and North America. But Beringia was more than that: it was a huge continent in its own right, 1.3 million square kilometres (500,000 square miles) at its maximum extent. Not only was it ice-free, but its grassy tundra supported herds of herbivorous mammals. The summers were for sure cooler than today, but the winters were, paradoxically, milder. For most of the period in which the land bridge existed, the ice caps persisted farther south and, as we saw earlier, the ice corridor was closed between 15,000 and 22,000 years ago, presumably preventing contact between the far north and the rest of America. The Siberian hinterland could hardly have been more inviting than North America, being an Arctic desert at this time, so Beringia and the western part of Alaska effectively became an ice-age refuge, cut off from both continents (Figure 7.4). With the Beringian refuge holding remnants of the original genetic founders of America, we can now see why the Na-Dene and Inuit-Aleut who, with their low diversity, seemed so different from the rest of the Americans, were yet linked to America through their A1/A2 group gene tree.[44]

Do the dates fit entry before the ice age?

So far, so good. The high-resolution mtDNA analysis seemed to be saying that a collection of founding mitochondrial lines had arrived in Beringia before the LGM and spread throughout the Americas. Then along came the ice age, cutting off the Canadians and Alaskans from the rest of the population farther south. In the process, the genetic diversity of those far northerners was severely reduced by the extreme privations and near-extinction resulting from trying to survive the ice age in Beringia. So, what about the genetic dates? Do they fit this new theory of one entry to the Americas before the ice age, with secondary re-expansion afterwards?

The answer is that they do, and surprisingly well. For the regions south of the ice caps, Forster and colleagues calculated the ages of A1, A2, B, C, and D1 in Amerinds from North America, Central America, and South America. Ten of the twelve groups analysed were all older than Clovis. To increase the precision of the estimate they then averaged the ages of all four groups (A–D) together in each of the three regions. North American Amerinds came out at 23,000 years, Central Americans at 16,000 years, and South Americans at 21,000 years. So there was a case for the founding lineages

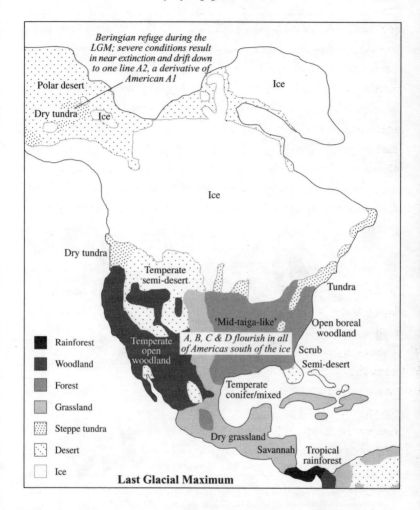

Figure 7.4 North America during the last glacial maximum. At the LGM, no further movement was possible and the ancestors of sub-arctic Americans were locked into a Beringian refuge with drift down to one line A2. South of the ice, people carrying groups A, B, C and D could continue to develop diversity in language, culture and genes.

A1, A2, B, C, and D1 arriving before 21,000–22,000 years ago, the time when the ice corridor closed. When Forster and his team

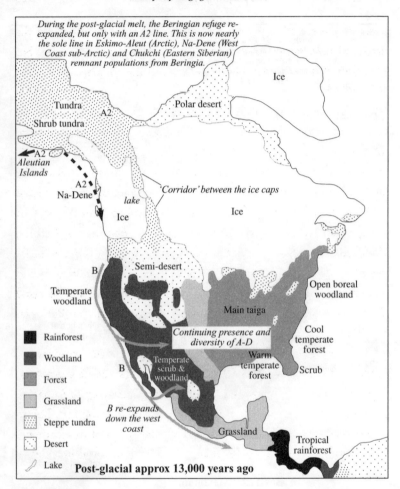

During the post-glacial melt, the Beringian refuge re-expanded, but only with an A2 line. This is now nearly the sole line in Eskimo-Aleut (Arctic), Na-Dene (West Coast sub-Arctic) and Chukchi (Eastern Siberian) remnant populations from Beringia.

Ice

Tundra   A2

Polar desert

Shrub tundra

A2

Aleutian Islands

A2

Na-Dene

lake   'Corridor' between the ice caps

Ice   Ice

B   Semi-desert

Temperate woodland   Open boreal woodland

Main taiga   Cool temperate forest

Continuing presence and diversity of A-D

B   Warm temperate forest

Temperate scrub & woodland   Scrub

■ Rainforest

■ Woodland

■ Forest   *B re-expands down the west coast*

░ Grassland

▒ Steppe tundra   Grassland   Tropical rainforest

∴ Desert

⟋ Lake   **Post-glacial approx 13,000 years ago**

Figure 7.5   Post-glacial mtDNA re-expansions in North America starting from 13,000 years ago. In Beringia, the tundra area has increased and access to the Aleutians and south along the west coast has opened, allowing group A2 to re-expand among the Inuit-Aleuts and Na-Dene. The ice corridor is not quite open. Group B can also expand along further down the west coast and into the south-west.

looked only at the derived A2 types in the Inuit-Aleut and Na-Dene, the expansion age came out at 11,300 years, suggesting a re-expansion around the time of Clovis (see Figure 5.5). The other insights these studies give us add to the strong impression that the Inuit cultures and peoples are a relatively recent phenomenon, but that they still owe their genetic heritage to the ancient founders of America.[45]

For my money, the results obtained by Forster and colleagues are among the most important in clarifying dates in the complex story of American colonization. They also contained the first clear genetic evidence for the Beringian re-expansion as previously suggested by archaeologists. It is worth summarizing the conclusions. The first is confirmation that there were four main American founder mtDNA types arising from the four Asian groups A–D identified by Antonio Torroni and colleagues in 1993: A1 (leading to A2), B, C, and D1. Second, these four founders probably arrived in America before Clovis and before the LGM 18,000 years ago. Third, the homeland for the movement of these founders into the Americas was Beringia, not Asia.

This last point may sound like splitting hairs (or continents), since Beringia must ultimately have received its people from Asia, but this is not a fine point. What Forster and his colleagues are saying in effect is that from some time after it was first colonized, before the last ice age, until maybe the last thousand years of its existence, Beringia was effectively cut off from Asia and received no further Asian founders. The importance of this distinction will become apparent shortly. Beringia was the source of American lines both before the LGM (Amerinds) and during the Arctic/Subarctic re-expansion by the Na-Dene and Inuit-Aleut. The post-glacial re-expansion from Beringia only included A2 presumably because the ice age caused a near-extinction in the north, and a so-called genetic bottleneck that resulted in only one genetic line surviving.

Others have since come up with essentially similar scenarios or variations on the theme of an early migration(s) into the Americas taking in most if not all the founders before the last ice age.[46]

The X line

Before we look at what the evidence has to tell us about whether this preglacial invasion was single or multiple, there is one more maternal founder line to consider. The fifth founder had an enigmatic identity, which has only fully emerged in the last few years. Appropriately, the name chosen for this extra founding line was X.

In 1991, Ryk Ward came up with four clusters. Two years later, Torroni and colleagues identified their own groups A, B, and C in three of Ward's clusters and resolved the remaining types partly into their new D group; but they left the rest of Ward's fourth cluster in an unresolved 'others' bin. Over the next couple of years, more research groups came to see that this other group was, as Ward had originally suggested, another cluster with a single origin – in other words, a fifth American founder line. Among them were Argentinian geneticist Graciela Bailliet and collaborators, and also mathematician Hans Bandelt and colleagues, who noted the likelihood of a fifth founder in connection with his new method of genetic tree-building. Forster's re-analysis of American founders in 1996 defined and renamed this new American clan the X group. This confirmed that the fifth American founder and the European X group which Torroni identified in the same year had the same common X ancestor.[47]

The American X group had a limited, northerly distribution, mainly in two separate Amerind-speaking cultural regions around the 50th parallel. The first of these cultural groups, in the Pacific north-west, were the Yakima of Washington State and the Nuu-Chah-Nulth. The latter is a fishing culture found on the western coast of Vancouver Island (and also on the Olympic Peninsula of Washington State) with a cultural continuity of 4,000 years. These groups had rates of 5 and 11–13 per cent X, respectively. The other northern groups holding X types were the Sioux and the Ojibwa of the eastern woodlands around the western edge of the Great Lakes. The latter had rates of 25 per cent.[48]

Could these X types in Native Americans have come from European female lines entering the tribal populations recently? Almost certainly not, since X was already present in pre-Columbian peoples of these regions. Ward's original study had carefully excluded the possibility of significant European admixture in the Nuu-Chah-Nulth. In the case of the eastern woodlands Native Americans, direct evidence of X in pre-Columbian populations was provided by an analysis of ancient mtDNA from the prehistoric Oneota population of the nearby Illinois River region.[49]

Kennewick Man: a pre-Columbian European connection?

This transatlantic DNA cross-match between Europeans and Native Americans has helped to fuel a chronic, rather dubious debate on who got to America first. The bone of contention is the problem of skeletal resemblances between ancient Americans and Europeans. Skulls of ancient Americans dating from 5,000–11,000 years ago have been studied for decades, and are known to be different from the skulls of later inhabitants, but it is not clear *why* they are different.

In 1996, the same year as the X founder was given her name and was linked with Europeans, two young men found a skull in the Columbia River at Kennewick, Washington State. American physical anthropologist James Chatters was called in by the coroner and was able to retrieve more of the skeleton. Embedded in the pelvis was a stone spear tip typical of the location and the period 4,500–8,500 years ago. The obvious antiquity of the leaf-shaped serrated stone point prompted the coroner to order radiocarbon and DNA studies.[50]

From the start, it was obvious that the skull did not look like a typical modern Native American. This man, who had died aged between forty and fifty-five, had a long narrow skull with a narrow face with a jutting chin, and looked more like a European than the broad-faced, broad-headed individual that might have been expected. James Chatters' professional reconstruction (see Plate 26) looks strikingly like Patrick Stewart of *Star Trek* fame, although maybe it is the baldness of the reconstruction that enhances this impression. The trouble is that Kennewick Man was not Caucasoid. Some of his features can be described as Caucasoid, and others as Asian. The features that make Kennewick Man look like a European were seized upon by the press – and by white supremacists eager to claim that America had been colonized by whites a long time ago.

Kennewick Man's teeth were Sundadont, suggesting Southeast Asian origins, and his eye sockets were also unlike those of Europeans or modern Native Americans. Intensive studies of combinations of his skull features revealed that the extant modern populations he most resembled were the Ainu and South Pacific peoples, including Polynesians.[51] Most striking of all was how unlike any peoples of the past 5,000 years he was. A lot of other things were learnt about Kennewick Man. He had suffered many injuries and bone fractures, and had enjoyed a diet rich in marine protein, such as salmon.

Radiocarbon dating confirmed the age of the skeleton to be 8,400 years.[52] The skeleton was then impounded by the US Army Corps of Engineers and became the object of a legal tug-of-war between different advocacy groups. In spite of this, several DNA labs attempted to extract DNA from the bones. For technical reasons, and contamination by modern DNA, they were unsuccessful, which is regrettable.

A successful DNA extraction and analysis could have provided us with any of several different results, most of which might not have answered everyone's questions. Mitochondrial DNA, although it is useful for tracing movements of peoples, is but a small fragment of our genetic heritage. It does not tell us what we should look like. But it can often tell us where our maternal ancestors came from. For example, if in the unlikely possibility that uncontaminated Kennewick mtDNA had shown him to belong to one of the typical

European clans and to have close type matches in modern Europeans, that *would* have been some evidence of direct European input into North America. Most other possible outcomes are more likely to have been generally confirmatory of a Native American maternal origin, but this would not have proved that there had been no European colonists over 9,000 years ago. The lack of numbers of successful uncontaminated extractions is one of the many problems of studying ancient DNA; if uncontaminated DNA can be extracted, it is still only a single sample which tells us little about the rest of the population or their history. For these reasons, large-scale mtDNA studies of modern populations are generally much more informative than one-off ancient DNA investigations.

As if to tickle up the link between Kennewick Man and Europeans, his location on the Columbia River in Washington State near the American north-west coast put him near one of the two regions where the X group had been found, in particular near the Yakima tribe.

The Solutrean hypothesis

The idea of Europeans and European technology crossing the Atlantic in prehistoric times is not new, and was around long before Kennewick Man was found. One of the best known of such theories is called the Solutrean hypothesis (see Figure 7.1). Denis Stanford, an anthropologist at the Smithsonian Institution, has been particularly identified with it.[53] The story goes that, at the height of the last ice age or maybe a little later, some hunters from the south-west European refuge area bordering France and Spain (see Chapter 6) took to their boats. They made it all the way from the European Atlantic coast, round the north Atlantic, to the east coast of America, where they became the Clovis people. The culture in the southwestern European refuge around the time of the LGM is known as Solutrean, and is famous for its beautifully worked bifacial points.

Solutrean points are argued to be a rare invention and similar to Clovis points or their precursors such as those found at Cactus Hill.

In support of the Solutrean theory is the habit, present in cultures both sides of the Atlantic, of driving herds of game over cliffs. This is hardly strong support since there is evidence for this practice even among pre-modern humans in China. It is also claimed that the highest concentration of the oldest Clovis points, which is said to be in the south-east USA, points to an Atlantic landing of immigrants. There certainly are problems with this theory, the most important of which are practical. The Solutrean cultures came before Clovis – and, as Vance Haynes so clearly demonstrated, Clovis did not appear until well after the LGM. If makers of Solutrean points had ventured round the northern Atlantic rim at the LGM, they would have to have skirted a coast that was ice-bound all the way round to New York.[54]

Unfortunately for such wishful theories of Europeans having an early stake the Americas, as opposed to the view of them as much more recently responsible for the rape of the beautiful New World, the genetic story has no supporting evidence to offer. Rather the opposite, according to Atlanta geneticist Michael Brown, of the Emory University School of Medicine in Atlanta. Confirming that the American X line was indeed a single fifth American cluster, Brown and colleagues estimated the age of arrival of the founder at 23,000–36,000 years ago, far too early for the Solutrean hypothesis or any other post-glacial entry. X was easily as ancient in America as were any of the other four founders. Five daughter X clusters had spread over North America into the different regions of the Great Lakes and West Coast both around the 50th parallel at around the same time.[55]

There is no doubt that the American and European X lines have a common X ancestor, but they may have split from this ancestor as long ago as 30,000 years. If there had been a recent but pre-Columbian European admixture in the Americas, it should reveal itself in Native Americans with typical European X subgroups or other commoner modern European lines, since X is quite rare in Europe. They are not to be found in America. The American X is therefore most likely to have arrived from Asia, the same way as the four other mtDNA founders (see Figure 7.3).

The power of mitochondrial DNA to trace such ancient relationships was demonstrated during the making of *The Real Eve*, the Discovery documentary film based on this book. The producers decided to take a small number of DNA samples at random from volunteer Americans of different ethnicity. The mtDNA was extracted and analysed by Martin Richards in his lab at Huddersfield, West Yorkshire. Towards the end of the film is a shot of the participants being told their results (with full consent). By rare coincidence, two of the them, an American of Greek ancestry and a Native American of the Cree tribe (see Plate 25), both belonged to the X mtDNA clan. For a moment they stared at each other across the lab, at first silently and in amazement, then finally able to express their emotion at the realization of an ancient link between them.

How many migrant groups, and where from?

The real genetic puzzle about the origins of X in the Americas is its rarity in Asia and the linked question of where in Eurasia it originally came from. That is part of the larger problem of deciding whether the Americas were populated by single or multiple immigrations, which must be addressed first. So, before we look at how X got to both Europe and the Americas, we must look again at what the evidence can tell us about how many migrations there might have been to the Americas. But haven't I already resolved that, by presenting the genetic evidence of all five lines entering America before the ice age, the so-called 'one-wave and re-expansion' hypothesis? Not so. The uncertainty associated with genetic ages is usually in terms of thousands of years. And while it is possible to use genetics to argue against Clovis-first, we cannot use genetics the other way round to show that that all five founders entered the Americas at exactly the same time.

Looking through the genetic research on the peopling of the Americas, we can see a clear tendency, as the 1990s progressed, to reductionism, with four migrations turning to three, three to two, and finally to a single colonization of the Americas followed by a re-expansion from the same founder types. This minimalist approach is not mirrored in a rationalization of the total number of maternal American founder lines, which started at four over ten years ago and is now at least five.

By simple analogy, the five mtDNA strands that colonized the Americas are five times as many as the single African mtDNA line that colonized the non-African world; so either there was a large founding group with no genetic drift, or there were multiple entries. This does not give strong support to a single band colonizing the Americas, for the following reasons. In Chapter 2, I argued that the single African exodus follows logically from the single paternal and maternal African lines that parented the rest of the world. To get down to just one line, the founding group must have gone through a period of isolation and drift. This unitary argument clearly cannot be applied to the Americas. Although it is possible that the Americas were colonized by a single large hunter-gatherer group, this cannot be inferred from any of the genetic evidence, including and not forgetting the Y chromosome. The weakness in the evidence has been tacitly acknowledged by geneticists Anne Stone and Alan Stoneking, who have recently argued for a 'single' entry. Three lines before they postulate a 'single wave of people', they state disarmingly that, 'Most likely, many small groups of people wandered across Beringia as they followed game . . .'[56]

But does it matter whether the single wave was composed of one or many small groups? I think it does, because one band implies, logically, there was only one geographical source. Several genetics labs have taken the idea of a single American entry one step back-wards into Asia by looking for a single Asian geographical source of Native Americans. So convinced are they that there must be one origin in Asia that they look for Asian regions that hold all five of the American founder lines.[57] The idea that there can be one part of Asia that had all the right gene lines and the right Palaeolithic technology is not only naive but, as we shall see, does not fit other observations.

In any case, the genetic story told by Peter Forster and others is not of an Asian homeland. They tell us rather of a homeland in the now partly submerged Beringia, an environmental refuge which straddled the two great continents and was continuously occupied through the ice age. It was Beringia, then, that received incoming migrations from, presumably, several parts of Asia, and acted as a staging post for onward migration. The climatic conditions leading up to the LGM cut Beringia off ecologically, first from Asia (by polar desert) and then from America (by ice). Before the Americas were colonized, and before the ice sheets finally blocked the route onwards into Canada, the maternal lines in the Beringian settle-ments had drifted down to the five that eventually did enter the Americas. Then, during the ice age and after the Americas had been colonized, Beringians dwindled further down to just one of the five mtDNA founder lines, Group A.

We shall come back to the possible Asian and other sources of those five lines. But first, what other evidence is there that could tell us whether the migrations to Beringia from Asia was single or multiple? We have just been looking at one clear piece of evidence that tells us that the first Americans were anything but – if I may be excused for using the expression – clones from a single Asian tribe. That piece of evidence is Kennewick Man. He physically breaks the mould with his non-Mongoloid, South Pacific, and Ainu character-istics. Obviously, we can never know his skin colour or whether his

hair was dark, curly, straight, or whatever, but he was clearly different from the majority of modern Native Americans, and he was not
the only early North American to be so different.

Spirit Cave Man, at around 9,400 years, is another famous
ancient American, this time from the Great Salt Lake (see Figure
7.1). He was also different from any modern population, including
Native Americans; uniquely in his case, his body had mummified and
his black hair could be seen for a while before it bleached red in the
light. The nearest source groups suggested for him were Ainu,
Polynesians and Australians. Three other atypical Palaeo-Indians
from the northern States include Pelican Rapids, or Minnesota
Woman (7,800 years old and found in 1938), Browns Valley Man
(also Minnesota and 8,900 years old), and Buhl Woman from Idaho
(10,800 years old). We should remember, however, that not all
North American Palaeo-Indians of that vintage were different from
modern Native Americans. Wizards Beach Man, at 9,200–9,500
years, did resemble modern Native Americans.[58]

South America has its own claims for extremely old dates of
colonization, and clearly was not going to keep quiet on the issue of
'unusual' palaeo-ancestors. Although they have been known about
for some time, these skeletal reminders of the southern past came to
public attention only quite recently. As with Kennewick Man, this
happened through media speculation over a rather dubious interpretation of an interesting discovery. In August 1999 a BBC documentary reported that Brazilian human evolutionist Walter Neves
had been studying so-called Negroid people from extinct tribes in
South America. The centrepiece was the skull of a twenty-two-year-
old Brazilian woman born over 11,500 years ago, nicknamed Luzia.
Initially discarded and donated to the National Museum of Brazil by
a French archaeologist excavating in Minas Gerais, Brazil, in the
1970s, her skull had features which suggested an Australian,
Melanesian, or even African origin. In 1999 the forensic artist
Richard Naeve, from Manchester University, reconstructed Luzia

and fleshed her out.[59] Reborn, she looked anything but modern Native American (see Plate 27). Judge for yourself – we all have a claim to be innate experts in such recognition. Negroid, Australian, Melanesian, Liujiang possibly, but to me she looks just like one of the 3,000-year-old great carved Olmec heads of Central America (see Plate 28).

Is Luzia a remarkable link to an unknown past, or is she just one of a kind? Human variation is such that one swallow does not make a migration. More numbers are needed. A time-depth study of several ancient skulls from Serra da Capivara in north-east Brazil indicated to Neves that there was a change in skull shape around 9,000 years ago from robust-featured skulls to more Mongoloid and modern types. He speculated on an earlier migration of robust non-Mongoloid people, similar to those I referred to in Chapters 5 and 6 as remnants of the beachcombing route. The beachcombers represented the least physically changed types outside Africa. Australian, Melanesian, Ainu, and Polynesians (and even Europeans) are all likely to be nearer to the original beachcombers than to the Mongoloid peoples of East Asia and America (see Chapters 4 and 5). So if there is a possibility that these non-Mongoloid types formed part of the migrations to America, appropriate comparisons have to be made. However, the best representatives of the Asian beachcombers of over 12,000 years ago are more likely to be the rather robust East Asian skulls of that vintage found in China, than today's admixed relict groups. Neves did actually find links between the Palaeo-Indians and Palaeolithic skulls in northern China as well as South Pacific peoples.[60]

Unlike the makers of the 1999 BBC documentary *Tracking the First Americans*, Neves apparently did not favour the theory that these Luzia-like people had sailed to South America across the South Pacific from Australia. In his view, these robust types were more likely to have taken the same route as everyone else – either through Beringia or along its coast. He also felt that they had been replaced or wiped out by a later influx of Mongoloid types in a separate migration into the Americas.

Are there any remnants of those beachcombers left in modern American populations? Well, there may have been until very recently. The first European explorers to reach the southern tip of the Americas noticed numerous fires burning on the land, hence the name given to that extreme region – Tierra del Fuego, the 'Land of Fire'. The people who kept these fires burning to counter the bitingly cold wind were hunter-gatherers entirely different biologically and culturally from their neighbours and from all other known Native American groups. In the maze of waterways to the south-west, around Cape Horn, were the so-called 'canoe indians'.

Slightly farther north were the so-called 'foot indians'. These included the Tehuelche of Patagonia and the Selknam of north-eastern Tierra del Fuego. Large, robust hunter-gatherers, their burning campfires were seen by Ferdinand Magellan and his crew as they sailed through what is now called the Magellan Strait. Many skulls of these people are in the possession of museums – the English ranchers who subsequently occupied the area placed a bounty on Selknam and Tehuelche heads when the indigenous peoples turned to sheep-raiding after their 'free-range guanaco' lands were taken over as sheep stations. There may only be a couple of descendants of these tribes still alive today (see Plate 23).

Cambridge-based Brazilian biological anthropologist Marta Lahr included a group of skulls from the historic period (twenty-nine, including Selknam and Tehuelches) in her classic study of human cranial variation.[61] This group shared several features with Australians, in particular their degree of robusticity. However, apart from robusticity and its associated features, the Selknam and Tehuelches did not share much else specifically with the Australian skull morphology (e.g. non-metric traits) – and were, in particular, much larger – indicating most likely simply a shared retention of a Pleistocene trait if not a more distant relationship. Lahr was of the opinion that these hunter-gatherers were unlike other modern Native Americans and East Asians, and more like Southeast Asians and South Pacific Islanders. She thought that these differences between Amerindians most likely indicated that there had been separate immigrant groups to America.

Recently, Walter Neves, of the University of Sao Paulo, and Joseph Powell, University of New Mexico, two of the foremost specialists in this field, joined forces in a major comparative analysis to see whether they could make sense of the accumulating evidence for Palaeo-Indians being different from, and more variable than, modern Native Americans.[62] Their findings confirmed that if there were multiple founding migrations (the alternative would have to be local differentiation), Palaeo-Indians would have been more like the undifferentiated Indo-Pacific beachcomber type, while modern Native Americans are more like Northeast Asians, and also have affinities with Europeans. Furthermore, they argued, North American Palaeo-Indians were different from South American Palaeo-Indians in that the former strongly resemble Polynesians, while the latter are more like early Australians. They did not accept the latter as evidence of a direct migration across the South Pacific. Instead, like Lahr, they argued that both Australians and Southern Palaeo-Indians derived from a common ancestral source on the Asian mainland.

Such a picture of multiple separate morphological affiliations between different American groups (ancient and recent) and different Asian/Oceanic types is consistent with at least two, and possibly three or more, separate migrations from different Asian regions, with the Mongoloid type eventually expanding largely to replace Palaeo-Indian types.[63] We can definitely fit this in with the emerging genetic consensus of Beringia as the homeland, acting as a staging post for inward migrations of different peoples from various parts of East Asia.

Are the various geographical sources of the first Americans suggested by the anthropologists consistent with those indicated by the genetic story? The stories told by mtDNA and the Y chromosome should have more power to resolve such questions. We can now look at all the American founder lines in terms of their individual Asian genetic homelands discussed in Chapter 6.

Two or three Asian sources?

In the last chapter I presented a tale of the Great Freeze driving Asians east, south-east, and north-east out of the increasingly inhospitable Mammoth Steppe, the Central Asian upland region north of the Himalayas. I also suggested that there were at least three different sets of peoples in East Asia, with different genes and technologies. First, already resident on the eastern coastline of Asia, and in particular in Japan, were the descendants of the old beachcombers. Second, there would have been the Mongoloids: the Southern Mongoloids in Southeast Asia, and the Northern Mongoloids to the north of the Yangtzi and most likely also inland on the Tibetan-Qinghai Plateau. Finally there were likely to have been North Eurasians spreading over from the Russian Altai and sharing gene types with North and Eastern Europeans. In terms of geographical locations of potential sources for migrations into America, there were correspondingly at least three (see Figure 7.6). In Central Asia there were two potential source regions. They overlapped extensively before the ice age, but were roughly represented in the south by the Tibetan-Qinghai Plateau and in the north by the Russian Altai and the southern Siberian steppe. So, there were two genetically, culturally, and physically different groups: mammoth-hunting Upper Palaeolithic West Eurasians to the north-west, and microblade-making, probably incipient Mongoloids to the south. As I mentioned in Chapter 6, the former would most likely have made their way east down the Uda River to the Sea of Okhotsk, and then and down the Amur River to Sakhalin, to the north of Japan. The latter might have moved down the two great rivers of China, the Yangtzi and the Yellow River, towards the coast.

These three Eurasian peoples, with their three sets of genetic markers, stone tools, and distinctive physiognomies, mingled or staked out their territory before the LGM in the relatively temperate Asian coastal region stretching from Japan and Korea north-east to Okhotsk. They were all candidates for the next step into Beringia, and thence to America, before the ice caps slammed the door shut. The question is whether the evidence of the genetic trail supports that sequence. We can take the story of the male line first because it is relatively clear cut.

A north Eurasian source for American males?

Is the picture of regionally diverse genetic origins supported by the Y chromosome story? The answer is no and yes. No, because as far as the Y chromosome is concerned, one line dominates all the Americas. And yes, because, when we look more closely, we shall find that line and its geographical origin injecting a strong element of Asian regional differences into the parallel mtDNA picture, thus supporting multiple sources (see Figure 7.6). Furthermore, there are several curious interlopers. The most striking aspect of the male line in the Americas is that over 90 per cent of all modern Native American Y chromosomes derive from one North Eurasian line, Polo (Figure 7.7), and that Polo's branch, as a whole, also accounts simultaneously for 50 per cent of Europeans, has a scattered Siberian tribal representation, and is virtually absent from East Asia and elsewhere.[64]

Not surprisingly, given the passage of time, most of the subtypes of the Polo line present in Europe are not the same as the American subtypes. This distinction is close to what is found with the mitochondrial X line, in that the split was a long time ago, maybe more than 25,000 years, and the two separated lines have each gone their way, generating more differences as time has gone on. The position

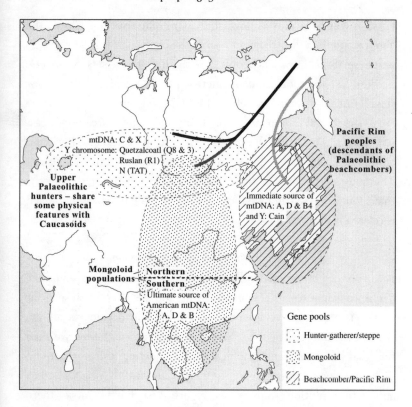

Figure 7.6   Possible Asian sources of American founder lines. The 'Venn' approach rather than precise mapping is used to emphasise the ultimate genetic sources of American lines from three overlapping ancient ethnic groups, the original Pacific Rim beachcombers, the Mongoloids and the Upper Palaeolithic Eurasian hunter-gatherers.

is not quite the same as with X, however, since the Polo line is still common in North Asia, was also the main American founder, and is also found in Europe. These findings support a common origin for European and American members of this male line somewhere in North or Central Asia, and a northern route of entry into the Americas. Having looked at the tribal distribution in Siberia, Russian geneticist Tatiana Karafet and colleagues suggested that the

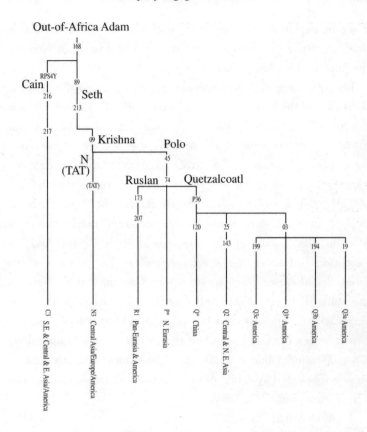

Figure 7.7 The American Y-chromosome tree. While the bulk of Native American Y chromosomes derive from Polo's son Quetzalcoatl, scattered other North Eurasian Seth offspring are represented. In contrast to the mtDNA picture, the solitary Cain founder is the only male hint of any provenance from further south or east in Asia.

Lake Baikal region is the homeland source of the American migration of this marker (although of course high frequency in itself does not identify a homeland). (Figure 7.6.) The European–American links do not stop there. The dominant European subgroup of the Polo line, Ruslan, accounting for 30 per cent of Europeans, is also found among Native Americans at a rate of 12 per cent, higher than could be explained by recent European admixture. North Asia also holds the Ruslan root type, and thus could have been the source of the American Ruslan founder.[65]

Far commoner in America than the Ruslan line is a direct branch derivative of the Polo root, Q – which I shall call Quetzalcoatl after the mythical feathered serpent. Quetzalcoatl and his sons account for 64 per cent of American Y chromosomes and are almost unique to the Native Americans. The only exceptions to this last statement found so far are three Siberian Inuits; and one individual each from a neighbouring Siberian group, the Chukchis; the 'Even' tribe, an isolated group farther south on the Siberian Pacific coast; the Manchu (of Manchuria); and the Uzbeks from Central Asia. The exceptions all share the special American Y-chromosome type Quetzalcoatl. Since Quetzalcoatl is found among the Na-Dene and the Inuit-Aleut, it is most likely that this American Y marker arose very early on, perhaps even before the founding colonists entered North America before the last ice age. In other words, Quetzalcoatl is a true founder line and not a first-generation derivative. Such a view is supported by dating of the Quetzalcoatl marker in America, which comes out at 22,000 years ago.[66]

Another North Eurasian Y line that is found very rarely in Native Americans is the TAT type. Although it could have been a post-Columbian European admixture, a North Asian source is still statistically more likely.[67]

This overwhelming dominance of North Eurasian Y lines in America might seem to point to a single southern Siberian source of Native Americans, and knock multiple migrations out of play. But we should remember that the Y chromosome is much more prone to drift than is mtDNA. Another way of putting this is to say that in many traditional societies, a few of the men tend to father many of the children, whereas the women tend to have more equal numbers of children. This enhanced drift effect is most likely why American Y-line types seem so lopsided.

There is, however, a remaining American Y founder who is more likely to have come from farther east than southern Siberia, and from a beachcomber rather than a Central Asian hunter source. This is the Cain beachcomber line, which spread round the Indo-Pacific coast soon after the movement out of Africa and is identified by an extra mutation, M217. While this Cain line is present throughout North and East Asia, his highest frequencies are found nearer the Pacific coast, in Manchuria and Okhotsk, around the lower Amur River. He is present at 10 per cent or more right down to Southeast Asia (see Figure 4.5). With his beachcombing history, this Cain could be the Y type that matches the B mtDNA marker in its more southerly Asian origin (see below).[68]

Maternal lines from other parts of Asia

The geographical origins of the maternal American founders are more diverse than the male lines, particularly with respect to the mtDNA B group, which is derived from Southeast Asia and is absent from the regions of North Asia most favoured for American Y sources. This spread of geographical sources of migrants supports the view that there were several founding sources for the New World.

In the last chapter I mapped the distribution in Asia of the five American maternal genetic founder lines. Group C is found north of the Himalayas in Asia, and A is far commoner in north-east Asia than further south, so we should look north of the Himalayas for source populations for the peopling of the Americas with these two lines. Group C is widespread in this region, extending from Tibet in the south nearly as far west as the Urals, where it has its highest frequency among the Sel'kups, hunters and fishers who live near the lower Yenisei River, within the Arctic Circle. On the Asian Pacific coast and farther south, C has a much lower frequency. As I explained in Chapter 6, the effects of the last ice age would have produced bottlenecks and re-expansions, so gene frequency on its own may not tell us the exact site of a homeland. However, given that the only parts of northern Central Asia we are certain remained occupied throughout the last ice age were Lake Baikal and the Upper Yenisei River areas of southern Siberia, this seems as likely a region as any for the homeland source of the American Group C (see Figure 7.6).[69] Group A, on the other hand, coming ultimately from South China, perhaps up the Yangtzi to the Qinhai Plateau, is uncommon in Central and North Asia, with the exception of the extreme north-east of Siberia, where it is the main type. Since this part of Siberia was also part of Beringia, and closest to North America, and since it was A that re-expanded in Beringia after the LGM, north-east Siberia seems to be the most likely immediate Asian source of American Group A. As we saw in Chapter 5, the ultimate origin of C was probably India and Pakistan, via the western end of the Himalayas. Group C is a key candidate for the eastern maternal marker of the Upper Palaeolithic peoples who ranged from France to Manchuria before the last ice age. Those hunters may have contributed their skills to the pre-glacial ancestors of the big-game, Clovis-point hunting cultures of North America, which expanded after the ice age.

Like C, the American X line is also likely to have a more northerly Eurasian origin (Chapter 5), but because of the large X-free gap between Europe and America, where she is absent, her actual source regions for the peopling of the Americas is a puzzle. The X line has recently been unambiguously identified in North Asia among Altaic peoples of southern Siberia, suggesting a possible homeland (see Figure 7.6). The 30,000-year-old link with Europe strongly suggests that X moved across the Asian steppe with Upper Palaeolithic hunters as a low-frequency shared Caucasoid component in the peopling of the Americas, and subsequently nearly became extinct in Asia. Group D is another of the five American maternal founder lines which is common in north-east Asia today. Group D's ancestor, on the other hand, could have come into North Asia from Southeast

Asia, south of the Himalayas. Its present distribution all along the East Asian Pacific coast, as far south as southern China, suggests a mainly coastal route north.[70]

In contrast to these four maternal lines, which have a more northerly distribution today, the B maternal group clearly has her origin and place in the south. Group B dominates Indo-China, Southeast Asia, and the Pacific, and has a very different world distribution from the northern lines. Although B is found in Japan, China, and Mongolia, she is absent from the Subarctic regions both in Eurasia and North America. This makes a strong case for the source population of American Group B having been very different from C or X.

There are further constraints on the origins of Group B. In Asia, B is represented by two main branches, B4 and B5, found side by side in most regions except the Americas and the South Pacific, where only B4 is found. B4 is the only branch that got to America, and she also dominates the South Pacific. The B4 branch in East Asia is so huge, varied, and widespread that it would be like looking for a needle in a haystack to search for an Asian match for the precise American founder type. But by coincidence, there is a near match from the recent results of two independent, complete mtDNA sequencing studies, one conducted by geneticists in Japan and the other by geneticists from Sweden and Germany. This laborious method, rather like a mini Human Genome Project, on just one stretch of DNA, goes for complete sequencing of the whole, circular mtDNA molecule. The result is the most precise and specific maternal genetic fingerprint possible. The match I found when comparing these two studies was between a Piman Indian Group B4 and a Japanese Group B4, thus pointing to the Asian Pacific Rim coast as the source for at least one American B type. The matches are strong, although as expected they are not like identical twins, but they do exclude the rest of the deep branches of Asian B4 and they do establish a link between Japan and America (see Figure 7.7).[71]

Rainbow coalition

Arguments based on finding individual near matches cannot accurately identify multiple different Asian homelands for the five American founder lines in Asia any more than the process of looking for a region, such as Mongolia, which harbours A, B, C, and D can identify a sole American homeland in Asia. They do, however, show us a more open-minded view of the possible events leading up to the peopling of the Americas and the potentially diverse sources of that colonization. We saw in Chapter 6 how the archaeology of the Asian Pacific coast bears signatures of new incoming Upper Palaeolithic technology from the Eurasian steppe in the west, and probably also microblade cultures from Tibet and the Qinghai Plateau, during the build-up to the last ice age. These may well have represented refugees from Caucasian populations to the west and from a Mongoloid source farther south. Arriving in north-east Asia, Korea, and Japan, they may have found themselves rubbing shoulders with the older coastal East and Southeast Asian peoples who were descended from the beachcombers (and represented today by the Ainu). So there were possibly as many as three different-looking groups that moved north-east along the coast, living off the rich marine life and game. They and their diverse cultures, genes, and physiognomies would all eventually have arrived in Beringia.

Wandering separately

What might Beringian communities have looked like on the eve of their entry into Alaska, 22,000–25,000 years ago? Were they like *Star Trek*'s Star-Base 9, polyglot, polymorphic, and polychromatic? In other words, were they completely mixed communities? I do not think so. Beringia was huge, with a variety of resources and locales to offer different cultures. It is more likely that, in spite of inevitable mixing, some of the cultural and genetic diversity was preserved in separate ethnic groupings.

When those groups ventured into the Americas and fanned out and multiplied, they did not proceed like some consolidated, multi-ethnic United Nations team. The cultures which sprang up when the newcomers put down roots in the New World preserved separate and unique physical, genetic, and cultural elements from the various Asian homelands. Is this picture supported by the archaeological evidence? I think so. The search for pre-Clovis artefacts turned up implements beneath the Clovis layers and in the early non-Clovis sites of North and South America which were from completely different traditions and had different analogues on the Asian side. This is just what we would expect from several parallel colonizations by different cultures.

We might expect, given the varied physical appearance of early American communities, to see clear genetic differences between them. Such differences are there in the marked tendency for tribal differentiation in mtDNA subtypes as noted by Torroni and Wallace (see above); yet one of the arguments for a single colonization of the Americas has always been the finding of A, B, C, and D major groups present in North, Middle, and South America. The Americas are huge, however, and there are marked differences in the relative frequencies of the five founders across different American peoples.

Present-day ethnic groupings are distinguished by particular tribal-specific mtDNA types. With certain exceptions, there is little sharing of individual mtDNA types between ethnic groups. This has been interpreted to mean that the single founding wave quickly split up into groups that remained separate and drifted to different frequencies of founders. But the evidence equally fits the alternative picture of the first wave of colonization containing multiple discrete genetic strands which can be traced all the way back, through Beringia, to different Asian sources. We have already seen the most extreme cases in the Subarctic region, where the Na-Dene speakers of Alaska and the north-west coast only have Group A2 American maternal types. As we have seen, the reason for the single American A2 line in the Na-Dene and Inuit-Aleut is thought to result from the near extinction of their ancestors causing drift down to one line.[72]

This extreme predominance of Group A extends throughout northern America north of the 50th parallel, and includes not only the Na-Dene and Inuit-Aleut but also the Amerind, Algonquian-speaking northern Ojibwa of Canada and the Great Lakes. Their Group A is characterized by three unique types not found anywhere else. Not only that, but the Ojibwa have the highest rates of the rare X type at 25 per cent (see Figure 7.3), and have the unique honour of having only the dominant Y founder rather than its commoner derivatives. Although they speak an Amerind language, the Ojibwa share their Subarctic location and even some northern cultural features with the Na-Dene speakers. Their unique but relatively diverse genetic make-up contains a high rate of true founding lines. This suggests that the Ojibwa and related groups, rather than being a population which nearly became extinct during the ice age, as happened to the Na-Dene, may through their northern isolation have preserved a particular genetic identity deriving from their Beringian source, and ultimately from north-east Asia.[73]

The two Native Americans who volunteered, along with others, to be sampled in the film (*The Real Eve*) associated with this book (see Plate 25) were from the Great Lakes region. By some extra-ordinary coincidence, each had one of these unique and uncommon local types. Our Ojibwa participant had the rare A1 type, while our Cree participant (Cree also belongs to the Algonquian language group) had an X type, which had previously been found only in Northern Ojibwa people.[74]

The overall distribution of the founding maternal group A shows a clear decline from near 100 per cent in Subarctic North America to generally low frequencies in South America. The more detailed picture of A in the rest of North America is one of great variability, between zero and high frequency. Several studies of ancient DNA in the Americas have revealed peoples completely lacking in Group A, suggesting that the older picture was one of even greater differences. A northern example was the Fremont cultures of Great Salt Lake, while another was in the extinct Fuegan tribes of the tip of South America (discussed earlier), who had only C and D.[75]

The distribution of X, as we have seen, is an exaggeration of the A picture in Amerinds, as X is confined to two ethnic groups in the far north of North America. Group D, however, is found at low frequencies in North America but very high frequencies in South America, in particular the equatorial region.

In summary, the extreme variation seen in the regional frequency of the five founder lines throughout America, could support a view of separate ethnic strands in the original colonization (although there are other explanations).

A west-coast route into America?

I have left the distribution of the most interesting mtDNA group, B, to the end. As we have seen, Group B is absent above the 55th parallel but present in North, Central, and South America. This odd southern distribution has often been put forward as proof that B arrived in the Americas along with the other lines and before the ice age. While I agree with these arguments, there is still a question mark over the exact age of Group B. Torroni found B to be significantly younger than A, C, or D; in Forster's re-analysis, B remained younger in Central America. She is old in South America, where she has a very variable frequency, from 0 to over 70 per cent. While these discrepancies in age and distribution may be just the effects of inadequate sampling, bottlenecks, or drift, there are several other intriguing possibilities. For example, Group B4 is extremely common and diverse in East Asia. So more than one B4 colonization at different times by related twigs might not be obvious in the American genetic record without more detailed sequencing.[76]

Alternatively, B4 may indeed have been a separate or last-minute entry to the Americas after A, C, D, and X. This is what the Russian geneticist Yelena Stariovskaya suggests. Her argument is that, apart from the younger age of Group B, she has high frequencies in Central America and in regions where Clovis tools are found, and is absent from the far south of South America. Group B is absent from Ne-Dene-speakers of the Subarctic west coast (see above), but present amongst Amerind speakers farther south. Perhaps to explain her absence from the Subarctic and the problem of the ice barrier, Stariovskaya also suggests that B came in separately along the west coast of North America. Given that there is at least one close B4 match for a Piman Indian B4 in Japan, further complete mtDNA sequencing studies on samples from both sides of the Pacific would be the way to answer these questions (see Figure 7.5).[77]

The idea of a coast-hopping fast migratory track from Beringia and down the west coast of the Americas has a respectable vintage and is coming back into fashion. First raised thirty years ago by Knut Fladmark of Simon Fraser University, British Columbia, the idea is an attractive explanation for the rapid colonization of South America. The problem has always been lack of evidence. Most of the beaches such a hypothetical migration would have used are now well beneath the sea. Only coastlines where there is a steep continental drop-off would be less affected by sea-level changes. Two sites on the southern Peruvian coast, Quebrada Jaquay and Quebrada Tacahuay, have just that. The bones of butchered birds and fragments of sea-shells (clams and mussels), crustaceans, and anchovies tell the story of sophisticated fishers and beachcombers exploiting the South American coastline 11,000 years ago at the same time as the Clovis hunters were valiantly trying to extinguish all northern big game. Evidence is also emerging from the North American west coast of human occupation and beachcombing at the same time.[78]

Some of the evidence for the viability of this now-submerged route soon after the LGM comes from another large mammalian omnivore, the bear. UCLA biologist Jennifer Leonard and Alan Cooper, New Zealand specialist in ancient DNA working at Oxford University, have been tracing North American brown bear mtDNA, both modern and ancient, to see what happened to bears in Alaska and the north-west coast at the time of the big freeze.[79] There are close mtDNA analogues between brown bears of parts of East Eurasia and the USA, suggesting that Eurasian brown bear mtDNA lines entered Alaska through a preglacial corridor via Beringia. Bears are known to have persisted both in Beringia and on Prince of Wales Island, off south-east Alaska, through the LGM, although like humans, their diversity became reduced.

Before the LGM there were no brown bears in southern Canada, but they had spread across there by 13,000 years ago. Their mitochondrial group suggests that they arrived there, not from Alaska through the ice corridor, or by re-expansion from Alaska after the melt, but from refuges on west-coast islands. As near extinction loomed, some bear clans must have moved from Alaska down the west coast, where they have survived to the present day. What is key about the brown bears now in the Canadian and US Rockies is that their particular mtDNA clan belongs to a line that was in Alaska 35,000–45,000 years ago and is now extinct there. In other words, they expanded from an ancient Beringian resident population. Since bears and coastal humans have an omnivorous diet that overlaps considerably, the bear story may be pointing us to the route that could have been taken by humans 12,000–15,000 years ago.

Human remains and artefacts on Prince of Wales Island have been dated to 9,300 years ago and earlier. Some 3,200 km (2,000 miles) to the south, Jon Erlandson has unearthed evidence of beach-combing dating to perhaps 11,600 years ago in Daisy Cave, on San Miguel Island in the Santa Barbara Channel, southern California (see

Figure 7.1). Clearly, to cross the 40 km (25 miles) from the mainland to the island, some form of craft must have been used. Radiocarbon tests from a woman's bones found on nearby Santa Rosa Island give her age as 13,000 years.[80]

How early was the coastal route free of ice and open? From 14,000 years ago, it seems. Daryl Fedje of Parks Canada. British Columbia, and Heiner Josenhans of the Geological Survey of Canada have used high-resolution sonar to make a detailed map of the ocean floor off the north-west coast of Canada.[81] The area they chose is around the Queen Charlotte Islands, just south of Alaska. Their map shows a new world of former rivers meandering down around flood plains and ancient lakes. The plains would all have been above sea level and free of ice from after 14,000 years ago for a few thousand years – that is, until the continuing sea-level rise drowned the land again. Armed with this new map of the drowned coastline, the researchers went out to collect wood from the flooded forests. They pulled up the stump of a pine tree and other bits of wood from the ocean floor, which they carbon-dated to 12,200 years ago; they even found remains of edible shellfish of the same age. From a slightly younger beach of 10,000 years at 60 metres (200 feet) below sea level they found a stone tool, the earliest tool on the north-west coast of America.

Putting this all together, it does seem that from 14,000 years ago there was a way for humans to move from Beringia and Alaska and down the west coast of America, completely bypassing the ice caps. There is also evidence that they were there at least 10,000 years ago. Furthermore, the evidence from the west coast of South America shows that the same beachcombers, with the aid of coastal vessels, could have made it all the way down from Beringia by 11,000 years ago.

The west-coast route gives one geographical explanation for the late spread of Group B as advocated by Yelena Stariovskaya. B4, the American founder line, was also spreading into the islands of eastern

Indonesia, presumably by boat and far to the south in the south-west Pacific, around 17,000 years ago (see Chapter 6). The coastal bypass route also has the unexpected potential of making the ice barrier and ice corridor dates irrelevant to the Clovis story. When I visited Knut Fladmark at Simon Frazer University, Vancouver, I was surprised to find he was a convinced Clovis-first conservative; but the Clovis-first position is to some extent shored up by the bypass.

Pre-Clovis only

Can we put this back into the larger genetic picture of the peopling of the Americas? I think we can. In spite of the sparse evidence, I find the story of the alternative west-coast trail compelling as a parallel route of colonization, but not the only one. For Group B4 to have been on the west coast of Canada 12,000–15,000 years ago, it seems to me more likely that – as with the ancestors of the west-coast brown bears – their ancestors were already resident in Beringia with the other lines (A, C, D, and X) before the LGM. The alternative, that B4 raced out of Asia along the coast only just after the LGM, would not have been feasible: there were major coastal barriers, such as the Aleutian ice sheet, to negotiate between the East Asian coast and British Columbia during the LGM and its immediate aftermath.

So, I still go for the entry of all the ancestors of the Native Americans to Beringia and the Americas before the LGM and before Clovis. The genetic picture for A, B, C, D, and X founders suggests multiple parallel entries into the Americas before the LGM via different routes, by pioneer groups coming ultimately from the north-eastern Eurasian steppe and the east coast of Asia. They may have looked variously like Europeans and like the Ainu and some Pacific islanders. Also at this stage, some, like the ancestors of Wizards Beach Man, looked more like Northern Mongoloids and recent Native Americans. They spread throughout the Americas, perhaps more rapidly via coastal beachcombing. The B4 line (or one particular B4 line) may have entered at this early point and made it down to South America, where, in contrast to her relative youth in North America, she is now as old as the other founders. Then came the ice age. Those left in Beringia north of the ice caps went through the most dreadful privations, but descendants of Group A survived the deep freeze to emerge as skilled fishermen, the ancestors of the Na-Dene and Inuit-Aleut speakers. The B4 group may have sat out the ice age on the west coast and then re-expanded inland, like the brown bears, or there might possibly have been a fresh introduction of Group B from Asia running up, round, and down the Pacific Rim coastline. As far as we know, however, America and Alaska (the remnant of the lost continent of Beringia) had no further significant Asian genetic input from the time of the LGM until the time of Leif Eriksson and the human tidal wave that followed Columbus and his 'discovery' of the New World.

EPILOGUE

SEVEN MILLION YEARS AGO, cool dry weather devastated the habitat of forest-dwelling ape species. Some time thereafter, the first evolutionary steps were taken towards the two-legged, large-brained creature we call *Homo sapiens*. Palaeontologists have yet to agree on exactly when anatomical evidence for bipedalism appears in the fossil record, and whether the split with the ancestors of chimps occurred 5 or 7 million years ago, but those steps clearly were taken. While the first walking ape to evolve, *Australopithecus*, had the same moderately large brain as chimps, this too changed as further genera evolved. With the intensification of the dry cool phase a little over 2 million years ago began a dramatic growth of the brain, which happened only in humans who appeared around that time and their sister-genus *Paranthropus*. The rapidity of that initial change was never to be repeated.

Biology and culture: coevolution

Something new these two new genera of hominids were doing gave them both a special advantage in this period of increasing aridity. The new behavioural resource did not seem to be linked to a specific diet since subsistence differed widely between the two genera, but it selected for, thus presumably benefiting from, a larger brain. During this phase of human evolution our brains grew rapidly while our bodies changed little. The rate of proportionate increase in brain size was at its maximum near the birth of the *Homo* genus, supporting the implication from *Paranthropus* that our pre-human ancestors already possessed that unique new behaviour which subsequently drove human evolution. The most obvious candidate 'unique behaviour' which would benefit from a large brain is the same one which still separates us from all other living species, namely *speech*. But, in the absence of prehistoric cassette recorders, the most obvious physical evidence of cultural change was that, from the start, humans fashioned stone tools.

In spite of the rapid brain enlargement, progress in tool-making was painfully slow for a million years and new technology did not automatically follow the appearance of each new human species. Acheulian-type stone tools were invented by African *Homo erectus* 1.4 million years ago, but this was long after the ancestor of Asian *erectus* had left the home continent. Acheulian technology therefore did not enter Eurasia until the next exodus.

Humans as mammals

The human story over the last 2.5 million years has been punctuated by great leaps in technology and world exploration separated by long periods of fallow. A common perception is that our ancestors were climbing an evolutionary stairway of achievement and ability, on which each new step had been unavailable to their immediate ancestors. From this Utopian standpoint we are merely the latest in a long line of ever-improving models. This view carries with it the implication that, all along, we have been the masters of our destiny, our limits of colonization set only by the intelligence and resource-fulness of whichever of our species was dominating the planet at any given time. Such an optimistic view of our intelligent self-determination is overstated.

One of the first humans, *Homo erectus*, made it rapidly out of Africa to colonize the whole of Eurasia. They were not, however, the first ape to do so, as can be seen from the orang-utans and gibbons that inhabit Southeast Asia. Nor were they the last humans to make the exodus before ourselves. Compared with earlier humans, our recent ancestors' only *additional* globetrotting exploits were to have reached the Americas and the Antipodes. Our recurrent expansions were also mirrored by other mammalian genera, and were determined mainly by climate and geography, following the two well-worn paths out of Africa. We differ from other large mammals, but not much from rodents, in the great variety of habitats we now occupy and in the population densities we have achieved. In this context, we differ from rodents only in that, being large, we consume vastly more resources per individual.

Human movements out of Africa via the northern and southern routes were always determined by the climate cycle and the availability of resources. The grinding glacial cycle not only opened and closed the gates out of Africa but also periodically squeezed local populations through the mangle of near-extinction to produce new, larger-brained humans to stay at home or leave their African birthplace to try their luck elsewhere.

Our brains stopped growing long ago

In Africa by 1.2 million years ago the brains of *Homo rhodesiense* had grown to within 6 per cent of the volume of modern humans. Around 300,000 years ago, the climate-driven brain-growth machine reached a plateau of size 11 per cent above that of today's people. Since then our brains and bodies have got smaller. The glacial cycles of boom, stress, and bust continued unabated; but except for cosmetic changes in limb proportions, eyebrows, and skull shape, the gross physical evolution of the human genus had by now slowed to a snail's pace. Perhaps, as with cars, there was a law of diminishing evolutionary return, and it was no longer economical to build models with ever larger engines.

As anthropologists Sally McBrearty and Alison Brookes argue persuasively, the real physical and behavioural threshold of *Homo sapiens* was reached at that point. Under this view, Anatomically Modern Humans are merely a later race which developed out of the older, so-called archaic *Homo sapiens* after another glacial near-extinction in Africa 150,000 years ago. There is evidence that archaic *Homo sapiens* types themselves also left Africa to colonize Eurasia long before we did.

Cultural evolution took over

In the picture McBrearty and Brookes draw, all the discriminating elements of behavioural modernity can be traced back to the African Middle Stone Age. That is not to say there was a technological big bang 300,000 years ago. Their evidence emphasizes the subsequent acceleration in human technology, first slow, then faster and faster. The early advances were individually rather minor and late to appear, but as more and more knowledge began to be transmitted and accumulated down the generations as compound interest, cultural evolution began to leave genetic evolution far behind. Looked at another way, if cultural evolution really took over from genetic evolution 300,000 years ago, then the differences between us and them are merely cultural and archaic *Homo sapiens* individuals could well have the intellectual potential to put a man on the Moon if they were living among us today.

The story of the genes: how it helps

What can the new genetic tools tell us about ourselves and our ancestors that such perceptive palaeoanthropologists and archaeologists have not already sketched out? The answer is much, as

I hope this book has shown. Genetic palaeontology brings clarity to a field of near-medieval confusion. The measurement of skulls and their shapes and the documentation of stone tools and their dates alone lead to an imperfect view of human prehistory. Apart from the paucity of Palaeolithic skeletal remains, there is enormous variation in human skull shape. The use of skull shape as a marker system to determine ethnic relationships has been further confused by the effects of under-nutrition and stunting in traditional agricultural societies and also by unknown proportions of admixture between different groups of humans. This all makes it quite easy to poke holes in reconstructions of the prehistory of human migrations based on such measurements. While stone tools are far more abundant than human bones, they are also a one-sided view and can only tell us about the received culture of their makers, not necessarily about their origins, migration routes, or biology.

The two best examples of controversies that rumble on among anthropologists as a result of these imperfect tools are, first, the multiregional versus out-of-Africa theories of modern human origins, and second, whether or not there was interbreeding between Neanderthals and the first modern Europeans – the Cro-Magnons. Classical population genetics using simple protein markers gave as blurred a picture as did studies of skull shape. The unadulterated direct transmission of the Adam and Eve genes down the generations has changed all that.

Clear genetic trees for both modern Y chromosomes and mtDNA point back to a recent common ancestor of all modern humans within the last 200,000 years and a migration out of Africa less than 100,000 years ago. This new line rather quickly replaced all pre-existing human genetic lines, including the Neanderthals. Admittedly there could have been interbreeding between archaic and modern *Homo sapiens*, but there is no convincing evidence for this in our male and female gene lines. So, if there was miscegenation it would have been rather small-scale, and the ancient lines would have become extinct. Some have suggested that traces of such past interbreeding could reside undetected in our vast nuclear genome, but the key word is 'undetected'. Because of their tendency to recombine and mix at each generation, it is difficult to draw unambiguous trees of nuclear genes, so there will always be questions.

The first exodus to South Asia

I argue in this book from the genetic evidence – with back-up from several landmark archaeological dates – that the first successful exodus was single, occurred 85,000 years ago, and took the southern route out of Africa, reaching the Malay Peninsula by 74,000 years ago and Australia by 65,000 years ago. The earlier exodus to the Levant had already died out 90,000 years ago. Although there remains the possibility of a later archaic human colonization of Australia from Eastern Indonesia, the earliest people there were modern humans, and *so far* there is no convincing evidence of archaic Adam and Eve gene lines in today's aboriginal Australians.

Explicit in all these predictions is the central role of South Asia (particularly India, Pakistan, and the Gulf) as the fount of all non-African dispersals. As far as the gene tree is concerned, the earliest branches of non-African gene lines are in South and Southeast Asia. The dates of first colonization of East and Central Asia by modern humans are problematic, because of uncertain skull dating and the evidence for a more recent Mongoloid replacement, but if the re-dating of the Liujiang skull at no less than 68,000 years is correct, South China could have been colonized at the same time as Southeast Asia. If modern humans had reached Southeast Asia before the great Toba volcanic explosion, the sharp genetic break between India and the Far East may be explained by the ash cloud that covered India around 74,000 years ago.

Trekking north

Europe and West Asia were colonized later, around or after 50,000 years ago, when the world warmed up, opening a land corridor from the Gulf region to the eastern Mediterranean countries.

Archaeological evidence suggests that Central Asia was first colonized at the same time as West Eurasia, 40,000–50,000 years ago. A group of genetic lines still found in North and Central Asia support this and suggest a direct movement north from the Indian subcontinent round the western edge of the Himalayas. Some of these North and Central Asian lines eventually moved west into Europe and east to the Americas. Other Central Asian lines seem to have come ultimately from the early beachcombing Southeast Asian pool, presumably taking routes round to the east of the Himalayas. The homeland of the so-called Mongoloid physical type, if there is such a single complex, remains unknown and contentious, although associated dental evidence again points to the south. The simplest view of the genetic and geographic evidence is consistent with the idea that somewhere in east Central Asia (i.e. north of the Himalayas) was a region where certain physical trends which had already begun to appear in Southeast Asian peoples, as a result of drift, were exaggerated either by drift or under selection to cope with a cold climate.

The last glaciation: refugees and pioneers

Following Toba, the most dramatic recent climatic event to have affected modern humans the world over was the Last Glacial Maximum (LGM), 18,000 years ago. For Africa it meant another great desert and a population crash. For Europe, the best-studied region, it meant people retreating south to a few refuges in the Basque country, Italy, and the Balkans, and to the Ukraine in Eastern Europe. The genetic picture supports the Western and Central European population crash implied by the archaeology. In one conventional archaeological account, the remnant Palaeolithic hunter-gatherers were more or less replaced within the past 10,000 years by farmers from Anatolia and the Levant. In contrast, the genetics reveal that most modern European paternal and maternal gene lines derive from the Palaeolithic ancestral lines already in Europe which re-expanded from their refuges in the south before the Neolithic period.

Much less is known of the effects of the LGM on Asia. Some suggest a near-total abandonment of the once vast Central Asian steppe, formerly inhabited by Upper Palaeolithic mammoth-hunters. The archaeology reveals that there was at least one refuge, in southern Siberia, which was inhabited right through the Big Freeze. The surviving genetic lines tell us that at least some people made it through the worst of the cold in those refuges.

One thing we can be sure of is that, even if a few remained, others would have tried to escape the increasing cold of the steppe while they had the chance. Unlike Europe, where escape to the south was bounded by the Mediterranean and the Syrian Desert, Central and North Asia offered several escape routes to more temperate climes: west to Eastern Europe, north-east to Beringia and America, east to Japan and Korea, and south-east to south China and Southeast Asia. The last destination would have proved the most attractive, because unlike the others its habitable area was increasing, thanks to the falling sea level, not shrinking under the encroachment of the ice. In Chapter 6, I speculated on these pre-glacial diaspora in the light of available genetic and archaeological evidence.

The peopling of the Americas remains a contentious field for American archaeologists. A die-hard old school hangs on to the post-glacial Clovis-first orthodoxy, while others are persuaded of a pre-glacial migration by more recent findings, and linguists are unable to supply live ammunition to either side of the academic battle. The genetics community, by contrast, seems mainly to agree that most, if not all, of the founding American lines entered North

America before the LGM, between 22,000 and 30,000 years ago. The former date would fit well chronologically and genetically with the preglacial refuges referred to in Chapter 5. Not all American founding lines came from north Central Asia: at least one genetic match can be made with Japan and multiple sources seem more likely. The much-maligned discipline of measuring heads also supports the view that the first Americans were not all derived from a single Asian homeland, rather from a mixture of Mongoloid, Caucasoid and the more robust Pacific Rim types.

As in Europe, there was re-expansion after the LGM – in Beringia and the far north of America – from the original Palaeolithic founder lines. This gave rise to the distinctive Arctic and Subarctic peoples found in Canada, on the west coast.

How much of this do I expect the reader to believe?

Presenting our genetic history before 10,000 years ago in fewer chapters than even Julian Barnes' *The History of the World in 10½ Chapters* is an ambitious aim. Inevitably there are regions, such as east and north-east Asia, where the trail left by the bones, stones, and even genes wears thin or is confused by overlaying evidence. With so many new reconstructions of Palaeolithic prehistory being offered, I could be accused less of speculation than of semi-informed guesswork. I am in good company, however. Several multi-author reviews published in the last couple of years feature maps of the world festooned with big arrows all over the world map. Written by experts in genetics, archaeology, and palaeontology, their maps differ sufficiently from one another for human genetic history to be an open field.

Flippancy aside, the trend toward multidisciplinary syntheses is essential, since no single discipline has the full story. In some parts of the reconstruction, especially with the dating, the synthesis relies on mutually supporting evidence from different disciplines joining together to give a logical whole that is not apparent from the parts.

Clearly, there is a danger of incest and circularity since several stories can show coincidental but false congruence.

As an alternative to defending my speculations (it is too late for that, after all) I should like to say something about the quality of the evidence – about where there is genetic consensus, where there is no consensus but I think the evidence is good, and where I know the evidence is shaky and expect to see raised eyebrows. Otherwise there is a strong chance that the good evidence I have presented will be tarred with the same brush as the indifferent.

Out-of-Africa is secure. There are few geneticists now working in this field who doubt that recent expansions of modern humans from Africa replaced pre-existing archaic *Homo sapiens* and older human species throughout the rest of the world. The possibility of a few genetic traces of the previous non-African lines lingering on among today's humans remains that – a theoretical possibility. The genetic logic of the *single* out-of-Africa replacement hypothesis is almost inescapable, though, surprisingly, it has yet to be generally accepted by all geneticists and archaeologists. The *southern route* out of Africa across the Red Sea has long been recognized by zoologists as a dry route for migrating mammals during the Pliocene, but it is only recently that it has been put forward as a possible parallel route among several for modern humans. The northern route for Europeans is still clung to.

In this book I have offered a synthesis of genetic and other evidence. Everything points to a *single southern exodus* from Eritrea to the Yemen, and to *all* the non-African male and female gene lines having arisen from their respective single out-of-Africa founder lines in South Asia (or at least near the southern exit). I regard the genetic logic for this synthesis as a solid foundation, and I have based the rest of my reconstruction of the human diaspora upon it. Obviously, the 'choice' of starting point (mine or theirs) determined all the subsequent routes our ancestors and cousins took. Tracing the onward trails is only possible as a result of marked specificity in regional distribution of the genetic branches today. The geographic clarity of both male and female gene trees is a big departure from the fuzzy inter-regional picture shown by older genetic studies. The degree of segregation of lines into different countries and continents is in itself good evidence that once they got to their chosen new homes, the pioneers generally stayed put, at least until the Last Glacial maximum forced some of them to move. This conservative aspect of our genetic prehistory also provides a partial explanation for the fact that when we look at a person, we can usually tell, to the continent, where their immediate ancestors came from, and underlies differences that some of us still call 'race'.

Farther along the trail, north and east from India, the genetic reconstruction of the routes becomes progressively more speculative, with some routes clearer than others. The early route to Australia is easy. The early date of Australian colonization, if confirmed, also makes a coastal beachcombing adventure round the Indian Ocean via Southeast Asia virtually the only possibility. The deep genetic differences between New Guinea and Australia tend to indicate that there were at least two separate early colonizations of these outposts.

The late colonization of Europe and the Levant from the Gulf, rather than through North Africa, is my idea and is based upon the structure of the genetic tree. It neatly explains why West Asia and Europe, alone among non-African regions, lack the Asian M superclan. The late date of Levantine colonization is explained by a dry climate before 50,000 years ago preventing access between the Gulf and the Levant. A marked improvement in climate from 50,000 years ago opened the Fertile Crescent corridor finally allowing migration north-west to the Levant, the Caucasus and Europe.

The rest of the peopling of Eurasia becomes increasingly speculative. The colonization of East Asia via the coastal beachcombing route, and of Central and North Asia by a pincer movement either side of the Himalayas, are simply the best geographical explanations of the available genetic data. The concept of the expanding East

Asian coastal flatlands being swamped by refugees from the Asian high steppe at the time of the LGM is also my idea and is bound to raise eyebrows. But there are no clear alternative explanations of the present distributions of gene lines and physical types in East Asia, and the abrupt archaeological changes in Japan and Korea at the peak of the LGM are very suggestive of an intrusion of Central Asian Upper Palaeolithic cultures.

As far as the peopling of the Americas is concerned, I choose to follow the convincing genetic consensus of an entry of all lines around or before the LGM, while putting some human behavioural perspective on the reasons for the archaeological hang-up on Clovis.

A word on prehistoric dates

Dates vary in their precision, with the method used to obtain them. Even carbon-dating has systematic errors. In certain circumstances dates calculated using the molecular clock from genetic lines provide very useful confirmation of archaeologically derived dates. The mitochondrial molecular clock is still in the process of being fine-tuned, however, and Y-chromosome dates are still very contentious. Furthermore, because the molecular clock depends on infrequent random mutations, it requires many measurements (i.e. human samples with different genetic types) to get anywhere near reliability. This means that many of the more recent archaeological dates using the radiocarbon method are much more precise or certain. However, there are consistent errors in radiocarbon dates of archaeological sites from the Last Glacial Maximum, and the method becomes seriously unreliable over 40,000 years ago. This 40,000-year ceiling does not affect the genetic clock.

The only truly reliable ancient dates are those that can be lined up unambiguously against climate records, such as those more recent ones indicated by tree rings and the analogous layers found in cores from the Greenland ice cap spanning the whole of the past

100,000 years and beyond. These cores give accurate and detailed climate records. For example, we can now see the dates of the frequent warm-ups or interstadials that affected vegetation and the movement of human populations. In our story the most accurately dated, dramatic, and unambiguous event before the last ice age was the eruption of Toba in Sumatra 74,000 years ago; and Toba ash is also found in the Greenland ice-record and submarine cores in the Indian Ocean, allowing a precise date marker.

I have stuck my neck out to place modern humans in Malaysia by this date on the basis of the Kota Tampan site where tools were found under a thick layer of volcanic ash from Toba. The key tools were indisputably artefacts, and the ash did come straight from the sky 74,000 years ago. But in spite of majority view that the Kota Tampan tools were the handiwork of modern humans, they could still theoretically have been made by other humans, since no bones have been found on-site which would confirm the identity of their makers. The only modern human remains of that antiquity found in the region are the now re-dated Liujiang skull and partial skeleton from southern China. The dating of the earliest Flores (Eastern Indonesia) occupation by modern humans remains to be published.

I have several corroborating reasons for relying on such a shaky lithic connection. First of all, the logic of the low-water colonization of Australia 65,000 years ago fits; and second, increasing numbers of genetic dates outside Africa easily reach back to this time. The next available low-water slot for the colonization of Australia would have been around 50,000 years ago, but that does not fit the other evidence so well.

The trouble is that it is difficult enough persuading a majority of Australian archaeologists that Australia was colonized by 60,000 years ago, let alone 65,000 years. The problem with suggesting any dates for modern humans outside Africa much beyond 45,000 years ago is again the radiocarbon ceiling. If one were to rely solely on radiocarbon dating, the whole human world would seem to have started just over 40,000 years ago. Only a few Australian dates of greater antiquity (e.g. in the region of 60,000 years) have been obtained by other methods, and they have so many problems it is easy to rubbish them. We could take the view that the colonization date for Australia just happens to coincide with the radiocarbon ceiling, but that is likely to be wrong. The safest thing, of course, is to say the date of first colonization is unknown. In this speculative synthesis, however, I would rather go with an earlier date which fits Kota Tampan and low sea levels than one which is more precise and recent, but eventually turns out to be wrong.

Toba is also regarded by some as having caused worldwide population extinctions as a result of the 'nuclear winter' that followed. I have taken this into account in my reconstruction. India bore the brunt of the massive ash fall, and may have suffered mass extinction, since the Toba plume spread north-west across the Indian Ocean from Sumatra. This may explain why most Indian M sub-groups are not shared elsewhere in Asia and the dates of the M clan's re-expansion are paradoxically younger in India than elsewhere in Asia and Australasia.

What of the future?

In my view it is not quite as rosy as some would hope. We are like all other species in that our evolution and survival are both subject to the controlling and moulding influence of the changing environment, whether the changes result from the ice-age cycles or from our own prodigal exploitation of the planet's resources. One of the lessons of the past is presented by the longest timescale, that of recurring glacial maxima. Eventually, it is certain, there will be another freeze-up, at which point our species will be stressed and may well hit another bottleneck. It is hard to overstate the bearing that ice-age cycles have had on our fate on the planet. Taking the long view, the effects of global warming could be little more than a blip on the way to the next glacial maximum.

However, in the short term there are more telling pressures. A key consideration throughout our story has been genetic diversity; it is, after all, the slowly evolving diversification of mitochondrial DNA and Y-chromosome lines that has been helping us to trace our past. What has not been emphasized so far is the fact that, while we are still recovering from the last ice-age cycle and previous bottlenecks, our *total* genetic diversity remains relatively low. Our lack of diversity as a species lays us open to new pandemics of infection in crowded, interacting communities.

Diversity, diversity, diversity

Here's an anecdote. When I was working in Hong Kong, one of my senior lecturers was a charming and sincere Taiwanese paediatric cardiologist. She asked me once what the difference was between killing a tiger for its body parts and slaughtering cattle. This was not an insensitive question. She did not personally take any tiger-bone medicine and felt sorry for tigers and their loss, because they were such beautiful animals. In short, she disagreed with the trade; but she was not convinced by the Western-imposed philosophical argument that the act of killing was immoral for one large animal and not for another. Nor could she see from a logical, detached point of view why it is necessarily more important to preserve a large, and to us beautiful, mammalian species than, say, a rodent.

I scratched my head for an appropriate philosophical answer to the question as posed, an answer which would avoid the issue of whether we had the right to take animal life at all, and would also avoid invoking the aesthetic appeal of big cats. Eventually, I think, I persuaded her that the objective difference between killing members of the two large species, one wild and one domestic, from the perspective of conservation was in preserving biological diversity or variety.

Domestic cattle, as a whole, have very little of their ancestral (aurochs) genetic diversity left, but they have millions of copies of that remaining diversity. Domesticating a species always reduces its overall diversity, though it may introduce variation in specific qualities such as size. By contrast, each of the few thousand remaining wild tigers still holds a significant proportion of the original diversity of their various races, so any one tiger is a unique genetic treasure house for the species and therefore much more valuable than one cow. So, apart from the fact that tigers are at greater immediate risk of extinction than cows, killing one tiger also affects a much greater proportion of species diversity than killing one cow.

Another big cat, the cheetah, is at even more at risk of extinction than the tiger. This is not just because of low numbers, but because there is virtually no diversity left in wild cheetahs – they are nearly all related to possibly a single pair that survived the last ice age. Surprisingly, non-Africans are closer to cheetahs and cattle than they are to tigers in respect of their genetic diversity, since they can all trace their lines back to a few mothers and fathers who left Africa only 85,000 years ago.

So what is so important about diversity, apart from the aesthetic aspect of variety? The answer is survival. Random diversity is nature's and evolution's fuel depot. Without randomly generated genetic diversity, species lack the flexibility to survive and adapt to the various stresses imposed upon them. Random diversity takes many generations to develop from a single breeding pair, so species which have gone through a tight genetic bottleneck have a lot of catching up to do.

Killer disease

It may come as a surprise to hear that we are still under constant evolutionary stress. The best and most important example of an ever-present and ever-changing evolutionary stress is infectious disease. Bacteria and viruses evolve much faster than we do. To combat new varieties of disease which bugs evolve to 'invade' us with, we each have built-in diversity in our immune system to enable us to identify new varieties of bugs and set up a specific defence. The capacity of the body to recognize and combat a variety of different infectious diseases is genetically determined. The diversity of immune response held in each of us has limits, however, and depends partly on the particular bugs that our own community has met in the past.

Most of such genetic variation in resistance to disease operates through the adaptive immune system. Some populations appear to have a sounder immune response to certain diseases which may have afflicted their ancestors in the past. I came across an example when I was working in Hong Kong, where ethnic Chinese children almost never fall sick with meningococcal disease (meningitis and/or septi-caemia). They usually develop detectable specific immunity to meningococci in the blood but, unlike Europeans and other non-Chinese groups, they completely avoid the disease and also do not act as carriers for the bug. In contrast, the commonest organism to find in Hong Kong Chinese with meningitis is the tuberculosis bacillus, which is extremely rare as a cause of meningitis in other developed populations. This implies that there are differences in the quality of aquired immunity to specific diseases between different modern populations.

Against other infections such as malaria, our innate defences are not solely immunological. Certain genetic disorders common in the tropics, as a result of evolutionary selection, directly impair the successful multiplication of the malarial parasite. This mechanism of genetic protection against disease in the case of malaria, one of the greatest killers, lies in inherited disorders of red blood cells, where the parasite seeks to make its home. These genetic disorders, a large proportion of which go under the general name the 'thalassaemias', are common in regions that suffer or have suffered malaria in the recent past. The name derives from Greek 'θαλασσα' for the sea, since some Mediterranean islands such as Cyprus have high rates of these diseases. These disorders however occur throughout tropical and sub-tropical regions.

As the host evolves more appropriate defences for the bugs, however, the bugs are themselves busy evolving to get round the new defences. The trouble is their evolution is faster than ours. The smartest are those that do not kill their host. Unfortunately not all bugs realize this. The evolutionary leapfrog race between infectious disease and animal hosts often takes a bad turn for the host when the bugs jump from one species to the next. Some of our most virulent viral and bacterial diseases, including bubonic plague, emerge from animals living in the wildernesses we invade. Another such hitch-hiker is the human immunodeficiency virus (HIV), which is now overtaking tuberculosis and malaria as the modern captain of death.

There is a self-comforting myth that Aids is a one-off 'bad luck' plague, uniquely super-lethal because it attacks the immune system, and its like will not appear again. Not so: it is a warning of the complex opportunism of infectious disease, which we will meet more and more as we expand into the corners of our shrinking world. In any case, the two varieties of the virus, HIV1 and HIV2, may derive independently from two different African primate species. In turn, our increasing fondness for intercontinental travel and fraternization helps spread diseases which, in the past, might have remained localized. As I write, a new infectious disease going by the acronym SARS has arisen in South China and simply adds to the list of exotic and serious infections that may have arisen in animals; it has then subsequently spread internationally from human to human aided by the jet plane.

Genetic intervention

One answer to the increasing threat of pandemic disease may seem to be genetic intervention. Every few weeks, documentaries and newspaper stories tell us of advances in genetic prediction and intervention which are going to change our lives and those of future generations. Genetic disease will be eradicated, we are told, and the more well-heeled in our societies will be able to specify designer babies or pick a clone off the shelf.

Prenatal diagnosis and genetic counselling services for lethal and serious genetically determined blood disorders have been around for some time and make an enormous difference to the lives of individuals. They have had a major influence in countries such as Cyprus, which suffers high rates of beta thalassaemia mutations as a result of previous malarial selection. Such ethically motivated interventions will continue to prevent individual misery.

However, what genetic intervention cannot do is increase our collective genetic diversity. Putting aside the ethical and technical problems, the fact is that genetic intervention can only reduce diversity. This applies equally to the abhorrent concept of culling the more subjective 'undesirable' genetic elements, as practiced by the Nazis on a variety of patients with mental and other disease as well as on Jews and gypsies, and to the *Brave New World* concept of designer humans. Even if a new breed of geneticists were able to design an especially 'good model' that found a large market among potential parents, the exercise would be self-defeating. A clone of such superhumans expanding in our midst would reduce our herd diversity, thus increasing our herd susceptibility to new infectious diseases.

Interestingly, the two characteristics of our species which interest us most, our brain size and our longevity, are potentially amenable to simple genetic interference. The former more than the latter. It seems likely that if scientists were allowed to, they could 'make' a human with an even larger cerebral cortex within decades, based on present knowledge. This could be either by manipulating single homeotic genes (genes that control the organization of the embryo and body organs) or more crudely by injecting the product of that gene at an appropriate time in embryonic development. Whether a genetically engineered 'big-brain' would be wiser or more intelligent, I do not know. I hope not to survive long enough to see it.

As far as longevity for the rich is concerned, there may be some business opportunities . . . – but there are also warnings. Ira Gershwin had a nice, though politically incorrect, take on Methusaleh's longevity in the lyrics of the song 'It Ain't Necessarily So' (from George Gershwin's Porgy and Bess): 'But who calls dat livin' / When no gal'll give in / To no man what's nine hundred years?' And there is the risk of overcrowding. According to a Vietnamese origin story, humans originally gained immortality by burying their dead under the tree of life. One day the lizard, who was fed up with having his tail trodden on by the crowd, suggested burying the dead under the tree of death. Life became easier after that.

Has evolution stopped?

Some geneticists argue that natural human evolution has stopped now that medicine allows the less fit to survive thanks to extraordinary advances in disease control and genetic interventions such as counselling and prenatal diagnosis. This seems absurd. Most of the world has limited access to such luxuries, and their influence on diversity of the world's population as a whole is relatively small. Prenatal diagnosis is in any case intended mainly for single-gene disorders, causing life-threatening disease when inherited from both parents, sufferers from which would usually have had a major reproductive disadvantage if they had survived.

As long as we continue to die, during our fertile period, from diseases that can be affected in any way by our genes, evolutionary selection will continue to operate. Apart from infection, other killer diseases, which carry a genetic predisposition, such as cancers are unaccountably on the increase. Male sperm count is also falling. While these pressures may result from chemical pollution of our environment and food, our susceptibility to them varies and is again *genetically* determined. As far as human biological evolution is concerned, it has not stopped, merely slowed down.

In the end, humans are the products of the same evolutionary forces as all other animals and will continue to be so. Hopefully, we will come to appreciate this before it is too late. We might even lose our species' arrogance and accept that we share a thin smear on the surface of a small planet and depend more on our non-human colleagues than many of them depend on us for survival. Only then can we allow our world to recover from the damage caused by our success.

My son once asked me whether a new species of human will evolve – or be artificially evolved. Well, the standard parental answer was that 'it depends'. I guess it will depend immediately on what our various cultures drive us to do to ourselves and to our environment. Our aggressive behaviour, aided by the demands our growing populations make on our environment, give us the unwanted capacity to impose stress or even to extinguish our species. Our white-hot modern technology would not be able to burn an escape hole from the impoverished prison our small planet might become for the majority of its inhabitants. How we adapt to our fouled nest, and avoid fouling it further, again depends on our immediate capacity to evolve our culture. If we do survive another near-extinction, self-imposed or otherwise, our successors may be biologically different, but there is no doubt that they will be culturally different.

APPENDIX 1:
THE REAL DAUGHTERS OF EVE

The two following pages: Names used for mtDNA lines. This table is intended as a quick reference to naming conventions of the commoner mtDNA lines outside Africa used in the text.

Pages 368 and 369: The full world mtDNA tree. Mitochondrial Eve ultimately has many daughters. The oldest branch is around 190,000 years. All non-African branches derive from two daughters, Manju and Nasreen, of L3 (Out-of-Africa Eve) who dates from 83,000 years ago. From 70,000 years ago there was a worldwide dramatic increase in daughter branches, occurring after the great Toba volcanic eruption. Specific regional distribution is shown at the foot of branches. (Branch dating by the author, where possible using complete sequence data; see Chapter 1[22]).

Eve's Line outside Africa (mtDNA)

MtDNA nomenclature*	(includes subgroups)	Distribution in non-African regions	Name in main text
L3		all non-African	OUT-OF-AFRICA EVE
2 daughters of OUT-OF-AFRICA EVE:			
N	(all non-M/non-L)	all non-African	NASREEN
M	(all non-N/non-L)	all except W. Eurasia	MANJU
many daughters of NASREEN:			
N1	—	W. Eurasia	NS**
N2	—	W. Eurasia	NS
I	—	W. Eurasia	NS
W	—	W. Eurasia	NS
R	(B, F, U, HV, JT)	Pan-Eurasia & America	ROHANI
X	—	W. Eurasia & America	X
A	—	E. Eurasia & America	A
N9	(N9a, Y)	E. Eurasia	NS
Y	—	E. Eurasia	Y
more N's in Australia	under study	Australia	NS
many daughters of MANJU:			
M1	—	E. Africa	M1
M2	—	India	M2
M3	—	India	NS
M4	—	India	NS
M5	—	India	NS
M6	—	India	NS

M8	(C, Z, M8a)	N & E. Asia	NS
M9	—	E. Asia	NS
M10	—	E. Asia	NS
M11/Q		Melanesia	NS
D	(D4, D5)	N & E. Asia	D
E	—	E. Asia	E
G	—	E. Asia	G
more M's of S.E. Asia	under study	S.E. Asia	NS
more M's of Melanesia	under study	Melanesia	NS
more M's of Australia	under study	Australia	NS
many daughters of ROHANI:			
U	(U1–7)	W. Eurasia	EUROPA
HV	(H, pre-V & V)	W. Eurasia	HV, H, Pre-V & V
JT	(J,T)	W. Eurasia	JT
B	(B1, B2 or B4, B5)	E. & S.E. Asia, Oceania, America	B & B1, B2
F	(F1, F2)	E. & S.E. Asia, Oceania, America	F
R9	—	E. Asia	R9
R10	—	Melanesia/Oceania	NS
many daughters of EUROPA: U1–7	U1, U2, U3, U4, U5, U6, U7	West Eurasia	U2, U5, U6, U7 & NS

* Richards, M. and Macaulay, V. (2000) 'Genetic Data and Colonization of Europe: Genealogies and Founders', in Colin Renfrew and Katie Boyle (eds) *Archaeogenetics: DNA and the population prehistory of Europe*, MacDonald Institute Monograph, pp. 139–141. An updated version is used in this book and is available online: (http://www.stats.ox.ac.uk/~macaulay/index.html).

** NS = non-specific reference in text; this means, for instance, that the line is identified by its immediate parent in the text and by its specific genetic marker in the endnotes.

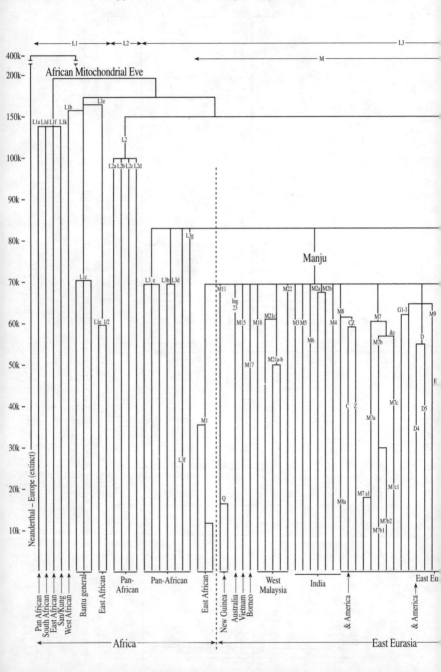

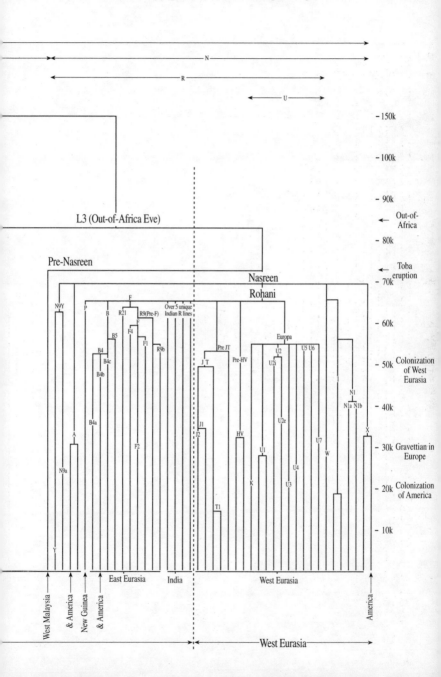

APPENDIX 2:
THE SONS OF ADAM

The two following pages: Names used for Y-chromosome lines. This table is intended as a quick reference to naming conventions of the commoner Y-chromosome lines outside Africa used in the text.

Pages 374 and 375: The world Y-chromosome tree. African Adam ultimately had at least as many sons as African Eve had daughters. All non-African branches derive from M168, the Out-of-Africa Adam and his three sons Cain, Abel and Seth. Specific regional distribution and nomenclature are shown at the foot of branches. Branch dating is not shown since there is no consensus on method or calibration. The Y-tree shown here is a fusion of Underhill et al. 2000 [Chapter 1[3]] and the Y Chromosome Consortium [Prologue[37]].

Adam's Line outside Africa (Y-chromosome)

Y-nomenclature*	(includes subgroups)	Genetic markers* (region)	Name in main text
no label	(C–R)	M168 (all non-Africans)	OUT-OF-AFRICA ADAM
3 sons of OUT-OF-AFRICA ADAM:			
C	–	RPS4Y/M216 (Beachcomber)	CAIN (Biblical)
no label	(D & E)	YAP/M145 (Middle & Far East)	ABEL/YAP (Biblical)
F	(G–R)	M89 (Worldwide – most non-Africans)	SETH (Biblical)
2 sons of ABEL/YAP:			
D	–	M174 (Asian YAP – Far East)	SONS OF ABEL/YAP
E	–	M96 (West Eurasia)	SONS OF ABEL/YAP
5 sons of SETH:			
G	–	M201 (Pan-Eurasia esp. Middle East)	NS**
H	–	M52/69 (India & Far East)	NS
I	–	M170 (Europe)	INOS (Biblical Enos)
J	–	12fa (Pan-Eurasia)	JAHANGIR (Moghul)
K	(L–R)	M9 (Pan-Eurasia & America)	KRIS-INA (Hindu deity)

3 sons of CAIN: 3 unlabelled C branches:	(L–R) (L–R)	M217 (Pan-Asian) M38 (Oceania) M8 (Australia)	SONS OF CAIN or NS SONS OF CAIN or NS SONS OF CAIN or NS
5 sons of KRISHNA: L M N O P	— — — — (Q & R)	M20/M11/M22 (mainly India) M4/M5 (Melanesia only) LLY22g/TAT (C. Asia/N. Eurasia) M175/M214 (China & S.E. Asia) M45 (Europe/C. Asia/America)	NS/SONS OF KRISHNA NS TAT HO (Ho Chi Minh) POLO (Marco)
2 sons of vPOLO: Q R	— —	P36/MEH2/M3 (C. Asia & America) M207/M173 (Europe/C. & S. Asia)	QUETZALCOATL RUSLAN
A son of RUSLAN: unlabelled	—	M17 (Europe/C. & S. Asia)	M17

* Lettering and genetic markers from: The Y Chromosome Consortium (2002) 'A Nomenclature System for the Tree of Human Y-Chromosomal Binary Haplogroups', *Genome Research* 12: 339–348. Note, not all markers shown.

** NS + non-specific reference in text; this means, for instance, that the line is identified by its immediate parent in the text and by its specific genetic marker in the endnotes.

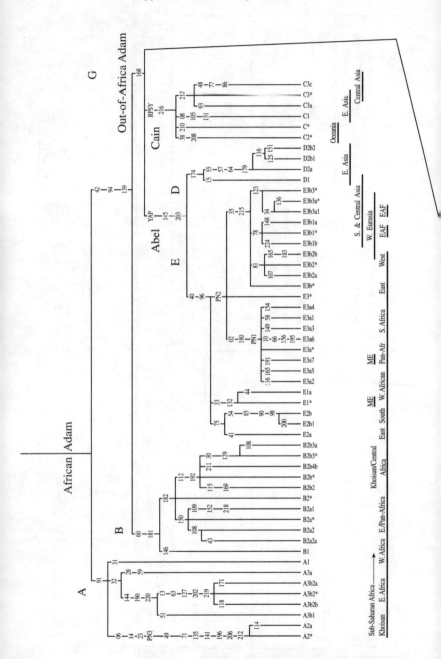

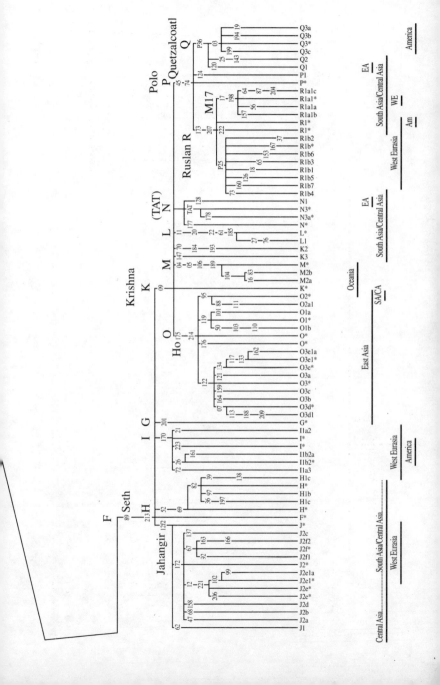

NOTES

These notes are intended as a facility to readers, academic or otherwise, seeking technical clarification and sources of evidence. They contain technical terms and detail which, in the space available, cannot be explained to the same level as in the main text. Multiple citations are merged at the end of a paragraph in many cases, to reduce total numbers of notes. In these cases each citation is keyed by a relevant text string (in bold).

Preface

1. Cann, R.L. et al. (1987) 'Mitochondrial DNA and human evolution' *Nature* **325**: 31–36; Vigilant, L. et al. (1991) 'African populations and the evolution of human mitochondrial DNA' *Science* **253**: 1503–7; Watson, E. et al. (1997) 'Mitochondrial footprints of human expansions in Africa' *American Journal of Human Genetics* **61**: 691–704.

2. Richards, M. et al. (2000) 'Tracing European founder lineages in the Near Eastern mitochondrial gene pool' *American Journal of Human Genetics* **67**: 1251–76.

3. That story was told in S. Oppenheimer (1998) *Eden in the East* (Weidenfeld & Nicolson, London); see also: Oppenheimer, S.J. and Richards, M. (2001) 'Fast trains, slow boats, and the ancestry of the Polynesian islanders' *Science Progress* **84**(3): 157–81.

Prologue

1. **Some have suggested**: Senuta, B. et al. (2001) 'First hominid from the Miocene (Lukeino Formation, Kenya)' *Earth and Planetary Sciences* **332**: 137–44. This paper controversially argues that a newly discovered hominid, *Orrorin tugenensis*, is at 6 million years ancestral to the *Homo* genus, displacing the current contender *Ardipithecus/Australopithecus ramidus* (at 4–5 million years: White, T.D. et al. '*Australopithecus ramidus*, a new species of early hominid from Aramis, Ethiopia' *Nature* (1994) **371**: 306–12) onto the *Pan* (chimpanzee) branch. The

implication is that the *Pan/*pre-*Homo* split is put back to 8 million years. **first clear evidence for bipedalism**: see the fine pictures of a hominid knee joint on pp. 44–5 in Leakey, M. (1995) 'The farthest horizon' *National Geographic* **188**(Sept.): 38–51.

2. Wheeler, P.E. (1993) 'Human ancestors walked tall, stayed cool' *Natural History* **102**(2): 65–7.

3. Elton, S. et al. (2001) 'Comparative context of Plio Pleistocene hominid brain evolution' *Journal of Human Evolution* **41**: 1–27; see p. 19 for *Paranthropus* and stone tools and p. 21 for *Paranthropus* and meat. For additional original data for hominid brain size comparisons used in this chapter, see Ruff, C.B. et al. (1997) 'Body mass and encephalization in Pleistocene *Homo*' *Nature* **387**: 173–6.

4. Elton et al., op. cit.

5. **even into the modern size range**: Saldanha 1 and Kabwe (Broken Hill 1) had brain volumes of 1,225 and 1,280 cm^3 respectively, and were both *Homo rhodesiense*. Their dates have recently been re-assessed stratigraphically to 1.07–1.3 million years – see McBrearty, S. and Brooks, A.S. (2000) 'The revolution that wasn't: A new interpretation of the origin of modern human behavior' *Journal of Human Evolution* **39**: 453–563 pp. 461, 468, 482.

6. Aiello, L.C. and Wheeler, P. (1995) 'The expensive tissue hypothesis: The brain and the digestive system in human and primate evolution' *Current Anthropology* **36**: 199–221.

7. Elton et al., op. cit. p. 23.

8. Elton et al., op. cit.

9. **1.07–1.3 million years ago**: McBrearty and Brooks op. cit. p. 482.

10. Elton et al., op. cit. pp. 19, 21.

11. Foley, R. and Lahr, M.M. (1997) 'Mode 3 technologies and the evolution of modern humans' *Cambridge Archaeological Journal* **7**(1): 3–36; see also Lahr, M.M. and Foley, R. (1998) 'Towards a theory of modern human origins: Geography, demography, and diversity in recent human evolution'*Yearbook of Physical Anthropology* **41**: 137–76.

12. **another terrible series of ice ages**: This was during Oxygen Isotope Stages (OISs) 35–32, see Rossignol-Strick, M. et al. (1998) 'An unusual mid-Pleistocene monsoon period over Africa and Asia' *Nature* **392**: 269–72, Fig. 1b. *Homo rhodesiensis*: very similar to European *Homo heidelbergensis*; the terms are sometimes used synonymously (for more clarification, see McBrearty and Brooks op. cit. p. 480). **a brain volume of as much as 1,250 cm^3**: Ruff, C.B. et al. (1997) 'Body mass and encephalization in Pleistocene *Homo*' *Nature* **387**: 173–76. op. cit. **about half a million years ago, and carried the Acheulian technology with them**: Foley, R. and Lahr, M.M. (1997) op. cit., Fig. 5.

13. **another severe ice age struck**: OIS 10, see Lahr and Foley (1998) op. cit. **archaic *Homo sapiens***: on strict cladistic grounds, *Homo sapiens sensu lato*. **To avoid confusion**: This is a contentious area; my summary is an oversimplification of the discussions in McBrearty and Brooks op. cit. p. 458; and Foley and Lahr (1997) op. cit. **the Middle Palaeolithic**: ibid.

14. **given rise to *Homo neanderthalensis***: Opinion is divided as to whether *Homo neanderthalensis* evolved in Europe and the Middle East out of this quite recent dispersal, or from an earlier out-of-Africa *Homo heidelbergensis* movement: see the discussion in Lahr and Foley (1998) op. cit. (but see also discussion in McBrearty and Brooks op. cit. pp. 480–81). Sequencing of Neanderthal mtDNA has suggested a molecular coalescent with modern humans of about 500,000 years ago. (Krings, M. et al. (1999) 'DNA sequences of the

mitochondrial hypervariable region II from the Neanderthal type specimen' *Proceedings of the National Academy of Sciences USA* **96**: 5581–5.) The coalescent for a particular molecular locus is not necessarily the same as the species (or population) split. The coalescents for other loci, e.g. some of the nuclear polymorphisms within modern humans, go back much further. Even if *Homo neanderthalensis* and *Homo sapiens* are regarded as drifted races of Archaic *Homo sapiens* (*sensu lato*) (or *Homo helmei*), their mtDNA coalescent may well go back half a million years (i.e. much earlier than the type specimen for Archaic *Homo sapiens*) irrespective of precisely when the ancestor of Neanderthals left Africa. **and had several possible relatives in India and China**: Stringer regards *Homo heidelbergensis* as the ancestor of modern humans and Neanderthals and tends to place Asian specimens such as Dali, Maba, Narmada, and Zuttiyeh in this group. See Stringer, C. (1996) 'Current issues in modern human origins' in W.E. Meikle et al. (eds) *Contemporary Issues in Human Evolution* (California Academy of Sciences, San Francisco) pp. 115–34.

15. OIS 6; note that '*Homo sapiens*' with no other qualifier means anatomically modern *Homo sapiens* (*sensu stricto*). For the population fall to 10,000, see Takahata, N. et al. (1995) 'Divergence time and population size in the lineage leading to modern humans' *Theoretical Population Biology* **48**: 198–221.

16. Ruff et al. op. cit.

17. For a discussion of Baldwinian coevolution, see Deacon, T. (1997) *The Symbolic Species* (Penguin, London) pp. 322–34.

18. For evolution of cultural traits, or 'memes', see Blackmore, S. (1999) *The Meme Machine* (Oxford University Press). See also; F. John Odling-Smee et al. (2003) *Niche Construction: The Neglected Process in Evolution* (Princeton University Press).

19. Deacon op. cit. pp. 214–16.

20. Ibid. Chapters 8 and 9.

21. Ibid. pp. 248–50.

22. **the greatest theoretical 'social capacity'**: Cetaceans have similar brain volumes to humans but have much larger bodies. As an aside, I gather that dogs, with much smaller brains, have a pretty good memory for personal smells. **a group size of over 300**: See Table 2.10 in Gamble, C. (1999) *The Palaeolithic Societies of Europe*, Cambridge World Archaeology (Cambridge University Press) p. 54. **exchanging material goods**: ibid. Chapter 2.

23. See discussion in ibid. p. 53–55.

24. See the discussion and interpretation of Köhler's work in Englefield, R. (1977) *Language: Its Origin and Relation to Thought*, eds G.S. Wells and D.R. Oppenheimer (Elek Pemberton, London) Chapter 1; and also an update in Wells, G. (1999) *The Origin of Language* (Rationalist Press Association, London).

25. **The greatest star of this story is Kanzi**: Savage-Rumbaugh, E.S. and Lewin, R. (1994) *Kanzi: The Ape at the Brink of the Human Mind* (John Wiley, New York). **Chimps have also been shown to demonstrate**: Deacon op. cit., esp. pp. 413–14.

26. **The Condillac view**: Englefield op. cit.; Wells op. cit. **The full theory sees gesture language**: For a lucid, referenced, non-technical, historical review of the evolutionary versus 'big bang' theories of language, see ibid.

27. **genetically hard-wired into our brains**: Chomsky, N. (1968) *Language and Mind* (Harcourt, Brace & World, New York). **concept originated with Plato**: see the discussion in

Englefield op. cit. p. 131. Jakob Grimm: Grimm J. (1851) *Über den Urschprung der Sprache* in L. Spiedel (ed.) (1911) *Aus den kleineren Schriften von Jacob Grimm* (Berlin) p. 268. **Max Müller, 'Language is our Rubicon . . .'**: Müller, F.M. (1891) *The Science of Language* Vol. I (Longmans, London) p. 490; **'without speech, no reason . . .'**: ibid. Vol. II p. 79.

28. Clottes, J. et al. (1995) 'Radiocarbon dates for the Chauvet-Pont-d'Arc cave' *International Newsletter on Rock Art (INORA)* **11**: 1–2.

29. **a lopsided brain**: Steele, J. (1998) 'Cerebral asymmetry, cognitive laterality, and human evolution' *Current Psychology of Cognition* **17**: 1202–14. For a less 'biologically determinist' view of cranial asymmetry, see Deacon op. cit. pp. 309–15. **Homo habilis is thought by some**: The argument for Broca's area in *Homo habilis* is less convincing since it relies too much on the concept of Broca's area as a speech organ.

30. **two important speciation events**; **mutations might be associated with cerebral asymmetry**: Crow, T.J. (2000a) 'Did *Homo Sapiens* speciate on the Y chromosome?' *Psycoloquy* **11**(001) (also at http://www.cogsci.soton.ac.uk/cgi/psyc/newpsy?11.001); Crow, T.J. (2000b) 'Schizophrenia as the price that *Homo sapiens* pays for language: A resolution of the central paradox in the origin of the species' *Brain Research Reviews* **31**: 118–29. Crow, T.J. (2002) 'Sexual Selection, Timing and an X-Y Homologous gene: did *Homo sapiens* Speciate on the Y Chromosome' *Proceedings of the British Academy* **106**: 197–216.

31. **imprinted at an early stage**: Human language ability, which includes lexical, syntax, symbolic, and syntactic inference and phoneme analysis (as opposed to learning new languages), can be acquired only during a critical period in early childhood when detailed rote learning skills are still rather poor. After this window period, normal acquisition of a first language is severely impaired. **a particular part or parts of the brain**: In any case, Broca's and Wernicke's classical speech centres evolve their critical nature during human development, i.e. they are plastic at first and their function can be taken over to a certain extent by other areas if they are damaged at a very early stage; see Deacon op. cit. pp. 282–8, 307.

32. Crow (2000a) op. cit.; Klein, R.G. (1995) 'Anatomy, behavior, and modern human origins' *Journal of World Prehistory* **9**: 167–98.

33. **humans and chimps were even more closely related**: see Table 3 of Sarich, V. (1971) 'A molecular approach to the question of human origins' in P. Dolhinow and V. Sarich (eds) *Background for Man* (Little Brown, Boston) p. 73. **split not much more than 5 million years ago**: Now estimated as 6.5 million years – see Goodman, M. et al. (1998) 'Toward a phylogenetic classification of primates based on DNA evidence complemented by fossil evidence' *Molecular Phylogenetics and Evolution* **9**: 585–98. 6.5 million years is also the age of the chimp–human split obtained by the author (see Figure 0.3) by extrapolating from another calibration approach and using complete mtDNA sequence data (unpublished analysis SJO).

34. For a personal account see Watson, J.D. (1968) *The Double Helix* (New York, Atheneum).

35. This mutation rate applies if one takes the HVS 2 segment of the mtDNA control region normally studied – see methods in Forster, P. et al. (1996) 'Origin and evolution of Native American mtDNA variation: A reappraisal' *American Journal of Human Genetics* **59**: 935–45.

36. Methods in Forster et al., op. cit.; Saillard, J. et al. (2000) 'mtDNA variation among Greenland Eskimos: The edge of the Beringian expansion' *American Journal of Human Genetics* **67**: 718–26.

37. For the consensus nomenclature, see The Y Chromosome Consortium (2002) 'A nomenclature system for the tree of human Y-chromosomal binary haplogroups' *Genome Research* **12**: 339–48.

Chapter 1

1. **reporting a major advance**: *Newsweek* 11 January 1988. *Rebecca Cann and colleagues*: Cann, R.L. et al. (1987) 'Mitochondrial DNA and human evolution' *Nature* **325**: 31–6. **clearly of African origin**: The Cann tree was better resolved in Vigilant, L. et al. (1991) 'African populations and the evolution of human mitochondrial DNA' *Science* **253**: 1503–7; and then again with further improvements on the African phylogeny, suggesting the single Out-of-Africa line, in Watson, E. et al. (1997) 'Mitochondrial footprints of human expansions in Africa' *American Journal of Human Genetics* **61**: 691–704.

2. Watson et al., op. cit.; Richards, M. and Macaulay, V. (2001) 'The mitochondrial gene tree comes of age' *American Journal of Human Genetics* **68**: 1315–20.

3. A number of trees for such sites including autosomal nuclear loci, each with their single branch coming out of Africa, have already been described: see e.g. Tishkoff, S.A. et al. (1996) 'Global patterns of linkage disequilibrium at the CD4 locus and modern human origins' *Science* **271**: 1380–97; Alonso, S. and Armour, J.A.L. (2001) 'A highly variable segment of human subterminal 16p reveals a history of population growth for modern humans outside Africa' *Proceedings of the National Academy of Sciences USA* **98**: 864–9. See also Wainscoat, J.S. et al. (1986) 'Evolutionary relationships of human populations from an analysis of nuclear DNA polymorphisms' *Nature* **319**: 491–3.

   For the Y chromosome, one single mutation on the African tree (M168) defines all non-African lines. See Underhill, P.A. et al. (2000) 'Y chromosome sequence variation and the history of human populations', *Nature Genetics* **26**: 358–61. This means that all non-African males inherit their Y chromosome from only one of the three extant African clans. The problem is that one of the three first-generation male clans descending from M168, haplogroup 'III' defined by YAP, is found both within and outside Africa, while the two others are both non-African. Peter Underhill regards YAP as having arisen in Africa, while Mike Hammer regards YAP as a re-entrant from Asia to Africa (rather like mtDNA subgroup M1 re-entering Ethiopia). I agree with Hammer – see the discussion in Chapters 3 and 4.

4. Thomas, M.G. et al. (2000). 'Y chromosomes travelling south: The Cohen modal haplotype and the origins of the Lemba – the "Black Jews of Southern Africa" ' *American Journal of Human Genetics* **66**: 674–86.

5. **geographic distributions of the branches and twigs**: Underhill et al., op. cit.; Richards, M. and Macaulay, V. (2000) 'Genetic data and colonization of Europe: Genealogies and founders' in C. Renfrew and K. Boyle (eds) *Archaeogenetics: DNA and the Population Prehistory of Europe* (MacDonald Institute for Archaeological Research, Cambridge) pp. 139–41. **A child's skeleton in Portugal**: Duarte, C. et al. (1999) 'The early Upper Paleolithic human skeleton from the Abrigo do Lagar Velho (Portugal) and modern human emergence in Iberia' *Proceedings of the National Academy of Sciences USA* **96**: 7604–9.

6. For a theoretical discussion see Wall, J.D. (2000) 'Detecting ancient admixture in humans using sequence polymorphism data' *Genetics* **154**: 1271–9. For a practical test with negative

results see Labuda, D. et al. (2000) 'Archaic lineages in the history of modern humans' *Genetics* **156**: 799–808.

7. **published in *Nature* in 1986**: Wainscoat et al., op. cit. **The technical objections**: Richards and Macaulay (2001) op. cit.

8. **Y chromosome**: Underhill et al., op. cit. **other genetic markers**: See note 3.

9. Some of the geographic, climatic and mammalian perspectives in this paragraph are loosely drawn from Turner, A. (1999) 'Assessing earliest human settlement of Eurasia: Late Pliocene dispersions from Africa' *Antiquity* **73**: 363–70. **depended on the glacial cycle**: Geoclimatic changes are from Jonathan Adams' website, http://www.esd.ornl.gov/projects/qen/

10. Dates reviewed in: McBrearty, S. and Brooks, A.S. (2000) 'The revolution that wasn't: A new interpretation of the origin of modern human behavior' *Journal of Human Evolution* **39**: 453–563, e.g. p. 455.

11. These dates depend on which approach to dating the first arrival of modern humans in Europe is used – fossil evidence or stone tools; see Chapters 2 and 3. On the former basis, some would put the first Cro-Magnons more recently.

12. While present evidence points to a dead-end failure of this first exodus, there is another interpretation: while the date of the earliest colonization of Australia keeps moving back, there is always the remote theoretical possibility that the Israel colonization was contemporary with the movement to Australia, but still failed locally.

13. Vermeersch, P.M. et al. (1998) 'Middle Palaeolithic burial of a modern human at Taramsa Hill, Egypt' *Antiquity* **72**: 475–84.

14. **Chicago anthropologist Richard G. Klein**: Klein, R.G. (1989) *The Human Career: Human Biological and Cultural Origins* (Chicago University Press); see the discussion of this and the 1999 edition in Chapter 2. **Jonathan Kingdon** and **first 'failed' northern exodus**: Kingdon, J. (1993) *Self-made Man – and His Undoing* (Simon & Schuster, London). **Stringer has taken the simplest approach**: Stringer, C. (2000) 'Coasting out of Africa' *Nature* **405**: 24–7; Stringer, C. and McKie, R. (1996) *The African Exodus* (Jonathan Cape, London), illustration (map) 48, p. 169; Vermeersch et al., op. cit.

15. **splitting the African continent into isolated human colonies**: Lahr, M.M. and Foley, R. (1998) 'Towards a theory of modern human origins: Geography, demography, and diversity in recent human evolution' *Yearbook of Physical Anthropology* **41**: 137–76. **this north-and-south viewpoint**: The multiple migration view reappears in a more recent article that Lahr and Foley co-authored with geneticists: Underhill, P.A. et al. (2001) 'The phylogeography of Y chromosome binary haplotypes and the origins of modern human populations', *Annals of Human Genetics* **65**: 43–62.

16. Kingdon op. cit.

17. Turner op. cit.

18. Richards, M. et al. (2000) 'Tracing European founder lineages in the Near Eastern mtDNA pool', *American Journal of Human Genetics* **67**: 1251–76; Richards, M, and Macaulay, V. (2000) op. cit.; Kivisild, T. et al. (1999) 'Deep common ancestry of Indian and western-Eurasian mitochondrial DNA lineages', *Current Biology* **9**: 1331–4. Most of the discussion below refers to these references (see also Chapter 3 and notes 4–6 in this chapter).

19. **50,000 years old**: Richards et al. (2000) op. cit. **the 'Out-of-Africa Eve' twig, L3**: Richards and Macaulay (2000) op. cit.

20. **U6 . . . North African lines . . . About one-eighth of maternal gene lines . . . This makes it extremely unlikely**: Rando, J.C. et al. (1998) 'Mitochondrial DNA analysis of Northwest African populations reveals genetic exchanges with European, near-Eastern, and sub-Saharan populations' *Annals of Human Genetics* **62**: 531–50. **Asian 'M' super-group . . . absent . . . from Europe, the Middle East and North Africa**: see e.g. Richards and Macaulay (2000) op. cit.

21. **If we look at the Y chromosome**: Underhill et al. (2000, 2001) op. cit. **Using markers passed down through both parents**: i.e. using nuclear autosomal markers, Tishkoff et al. op. cit.; Alonso and Armour op. cit.; see also Chapters 3 and 4. Note that the first geneticists to argue explicitly for an early southern route were Quintana-Murci, L. et al. (1999) 'Genetic evidence for an early exit of *Homo sapiens sapiens* from Africa through eastern Africa' *Nature Genetics* **23**: 437–41. Their analysis does not directly confront the European issue (which, by default, was regarded as a later northern dispersal) and mainly relates to Asian super-haplogroup M, which they regarded as originating in Ethiopia – as opposed to the Indian origin for M that I argue for.

22. The age of the L3 cluster in Africa was originally estimated at 77,000 ± 2,400 years: Watson, E. et al. (1997) 'Mitochondrial footprints of human expansions in Africa' *American Journal of Human Genetics* **61**: 691–704. This estimate increases with improved resolution of the tree round the L3 node; I have calculated a more up-to-date estimate by using complete sequence data from Ingman et al. (2000) 'Mitochondrial genome variation and the origin of modern humans' *Nature* **408**: 708–13 as 83,000 years (unpublished work by the author SJO) which uses in principle, the same dating method with calculation of 'rho' by averaging new mutations in daughter types – for methods see Forster, P. et al. (1996) 'Origin and evolution of Native American mtDNA variation: A reappraisal' *American Journal of Human Genetics* **59**: 935–45; Saillard, J. et al. (2000) 'mtDNA variation among Greenland Eskimos: The edge of the Beringian expansion' *American Journal of Human Genetics* **67**: 718–26). This estimate also shows that both M and N and the African branches of L3 and L1c re-expanded around 70,000 years ago, presumably after the worldwide effects of the great Toba explosion. See also Chapters 2 and 4. The L3 age of 83,000 years has also been independently confirmed in Hill, C. (2003) et al. 'Mitochondrial DNA variation in the Orang Asli of the Malay Peninsula' (in press).

23. Gabunia, L. et al. (2002) 'Earliest Pleistocene hominid cranial remains from Dmanisi, Republic of Georgia: Taxonomy, geological setting, and age' *Science* **288**: 1019–25.

24. Rohling, E.J. et al. (1998) 'Magnitudes of sea-level lowstands of the past 500,000 years' *Nature* **394**: 162–5; Fenton, M. et al. (2000) 'Aplanktonic zones in the Red Sea' *Marine Micropalaeontology* **40**: 277–94.

25. Stringer places late, large-brained, South and East Asian *Homo erectus* specimens such as Dali, Maba, Narmada, and Zuttiyeh in a group with *Homo helmei*, which would imply at least one additional exit by the southern route between those of *Homo erectus* and modern humans: see Stringer, C. B. (1996) 'Current issues in modern human origins' in W.E. Meikle et al. (eds) *Contemporary Issues in Human Evolution* (California Academy of Sciences, San Francisco) pp. 115–34. See also Foley, R and Lahr, M.M. (1997) 'Mode 3 technologies and the evolution of modern humans', *Cambridge Archaeological Journal* **7**: (1)3–36, Fig 5. The appearance of both

Acheulian and Middle Palaeolithic technology in India successively over the same period would effectively have increased the number of exits to four.

26. **Homo georgicus**: Gabunia et al., op. cit.

27. Foley and Lahr op. cit. Following my practice in the Prologue, I use the term *Homo helmei* loosely to distinguish Archaic *Homo sapiens* from modern humans. The term does not have general acceptance. See also next note.

28. Stringer op. cit. The summary I have given here is oversimplified. The exact details of the cladistic relationships, names, and ages of these later large-brained humans living between 130,000 and 500,000 years ago are still argued over. For our discussion the important issue is that although they looked different from and were more robust than modern humans, they had similar-sized brains and resembled us more than they did previous humans. The subject is discussed further in McBrearty and Brooks op. cit., Foley and Lahr op. cit., and Lahr and Foley op. cit.

29. Mishra, S. (1995) 'The chronology of the Indian stone age: Impact of recent absolute and relative dating attempts' *Man and Environment* **20**(2): 11–17; Acharya, S.K. and Basu, P.K. (1993) 'Toba ash on the Indian subcontinent and its implications for correlation of Late Pleistocene alluvium' *Quaternary Research* **40**: 10–19.

30. Acharya and Basu op. cit. The date of such a changeover may not be exactly 74,000 years ago: it depends on exact stratigraphic analysis of the deposits. Acharya and Basu broadly bracket this whole stratigraphic unit as 'Late Pleistocene', from 40,000 to 100,000 years ago.

31. McKie. R. (2000) *Ape-man* (BBC Worldwide, London).

32. **dated to around 130,000 years ago**: See the discussion of dating estimates in McBrearty and Brooks op. cit. **modern humans as the only survivor**: The deepest branch in the mtDNA tree (190,000 years ago, see panel diagram) is between L1a, found in the San of southern Africa, and the rest. This is consistent with isolation and separation of groups during OIS 6 and survival of only two branches from that time, possibly in southern and East Africa.

33. Oppenheimer, S. (1998) *Eden in the East: The Drowned Continent of Southeast Asia* (Weidenfeld & Nicolson, London).

34. Caton-Thompson, G. (1944) *The Tombs and Moon Temple of Hureidha (Hadhramaut)* (Oxford University Press/The Society of Antiquaries).

35. Walter, R.C. et al. (2000) 'Early human occupation of the Red Sea coast of Eritrea during the last interglacial' *Nature* **405**: 65–9. The actual dating was to between 118,000 and 132,000 years ago.

36. Watson et al., op. cit., originally estimated 60,000–80,000 years ago for the out-of-Africa expansion, but see note 22, where the mean age, $\pm$ SE) of L3 would be 83,000 ($\pm$ 6,000) years. For confirmation of the age of L3 at 83,000 years by another dating method, see Hill, C. et al. (2003) 'Mitochondrial DNA variation in the Orang Asli of the Malay Peninsula' (in preparation) (L3 age 83,500 $\pm$ SE 8,400 years).

37. **oceanographic evidence denies**: Rohling et al., op. cit.; Fenton et al., op. cit. **Such an event**: Red Sea aplanktonic episodes occurring at OIS 12, 6, and 2, ibid.

38. OIS 4; see Dansgaard, W. et al. (1993) 'Evidence for general instability of past climate from a 250-kyr ice-core record' *Nature* **364**: 218–20.

39. Rohling et al., op. cit.; Fenton et al., op. cit.; Siddall, M. et al. (2003) 'Sea-level fluctuations during the last glacial cycle' *Nature* **423**: 853–8.

40. Rohling et al., op. cit.; Fenton et al., op. cit.; Siddall et al., op. cit.

41. *Globigerinoides sacculifer*, see ibid.

42. Schultz, H. et al. (1998) 'Correlation between Arabian Sea and Greenland climate oscillations of the past 110,000 years' *Nature* **393**: 54–7.

43. Majid, Z. (1998) 'Radiocarbon dates and culture sequence in the Lenggong Valley and beyond' *Malaysia Museums Journal* **34**: 241–9.

44. Kivisild, T. et al. (2000) 'A likely post-LGM impact of Western Asian maternal lineages to Eastern Africans' Cold Spring Harbour Symposium on Human Origins & Disease. New York.

45. **74,000 years**: Kivisild, T. et al. (1999) 'The place of the Indian mitochondrial DNA variants in the global network of maternal lineages and the peopling of the Old World' in S.S. Papiha et al. (eds) *Genomic Diversity: Applications in Human Population Genetics* (Kluwer Academic/Plenum, New York) pp. 135–52. **75,000 years**: Redd, A.J. and Stoneking, M. (1999) 'Peopling of Sahul: mtDNA variation in aboriginal Australian and Papua New Guinean populations' *American Journal of Human Genetics* **65**: 808–28. **73,000 years**: Kivisild, T. et al. (2003) 'The genetic heritage of the earliest settlers persists both in Indian tribal and caste populations' *American Journal of Human Genetics* **72**: 313–33. Equal and more ancient figures have been estimated in China for two primary derivatives of the N clan: B, 74,600 ± 18,700 years ago, and R9, 81,400 ± 24,600 years ago; see Yong-Gang Yao et al. (2002) 'Phylogeographic differentiation of mitochondrial DNA in Han Chinese' *American Journal of Human Genetics* **70**: 635–51.

46. For Asian descendants, see Kivisild et al. (2003) op. cit.; Yong-Gang Yao et al. op. cit. For Australian descendants, see Redd and Stoneking op. cit.

47. Schultz et al., op. cit.

48. **no more than 47,000 years old**: or 50,000 years, depending on whether radiocarbon dates are corrected – see Chapter 3. **The Belgian archaeologist Marcel Otte**: Otte, M. (2003) *The Aurignacian in Asia* (in press), citing inter alia Olszewski, D.I. and Dibble, H.L. (1994) 'The Zagros Aurignacian' *Current Anthropology* **35**(1): 68–75; and Otte, M. (2000) 'The history of European populations as seen by archaeology' in C. Renfrew and K. Boyle (eds) *Archaeogenetics: DNA and the Population Prehistory of Europe* (MacDonald Institute for Archaeological Research, Cambridge) pp. 139–41.

49. **a date of 28,000 years ago**: Joshi, R.V. (1994) 'South Asia in the period of *Homo sapiens sapiens* up to the beginnings of food production (Upper Palaeolithic and Mesolithic)' in S.J. De Laet (ed.) *The History of Humanity* Vol. 1 (Routledge, London) pp. 256–8. **between 64,000 and 74,000 years ago**: Deraniyagala, S.U. (2001) *Prehistory of Sri Lanka* (Department of Archaeological Survey, Government of Sri Lanka) pp. 685–702.

Chapter 2

1. Gamble, C. (1994) *Timewalkers* (Harvard University Press, Cambridge, MA) p. 160, Table 8.2, p. 160.

2. Klein, R. G. (1989) *The Human Career: Human Biological and Cultural Origins* (Chicago University Press).

3. Diamond, J. (1998) *Guns, Germs, and Steel* (Jonathan Cape, London).

4. Lawrence, P. (1964) *Road Belong Cargo: A Study of the Cargo Movement in the Southern Madang District New Guinea* (Melbourne University Press/Manchester University Press).

5. **Middle Palaeolithic technology**: See the discussion, and especially Table 1 and Figures 2 and 13, in McBrearty, S. and Brooks, A.S. (2000) 'The revolution that wasn't: A new interpretation of the origin of modern human behavior' *Journal of Human Evolution* **39**: 453–563. See also the discussion in Foley, R. and Lahr, M. (1997) 'Mode 3 technologies and the evolution of modern humans' *Cambridge Archaeological Journal* **7**(1): 3–36. **Confusingly, Middle Palaeolithic stone tools**: See the simplified discussion, ibid.

6. McBrearty and Brooks op. cit.; Foley and Lahr op. cit.

7. **appeared in India about 150,000 years ago**: Mishra, S. (1995) 'The chronology of the Indian Stone Age: Impact of recent absolute and relative dating attempts' *Man and Environment* **20**(2): 11–17. **the Narmada skull**: Stringer, C. (1996) 'Current issues in modern human origins' in W.E. Meikle et al. (eds) *Contemporary Issues in Human Evolution* (California Academy of Sciences, San Francisco) pp. 115–34.

8. Harrison, T. (1959) 'New archaeological and ethnological results from Niah caves, Sarawak' *Man* **59**: 1–8.

9. I am grateful to Andrew Sherratt of the Ashmolean Museum, Oxford, who patiently took me through the Lower, Middle, and Upper Palaeolithic sequence again.

10. Foley and Lahr op. cit. This argument falls down for the Far East (see Chapters 4–6). In any case, as we shall see, blades were probably invented several times earlier during the Middle Palaeolithic, although not used for the same variety of purposes.

11. **computer analysis of sites and dates**: Bocquet-Appel, J.-P. and Demars, P.Y. (2000) 'Neanderthal contraction and modern human colonization of Europe' *Antiquity* **74**: 544–52; see also Davies W. (2001) 'A very model of a modern human industry: New perspectives on the origins and spread of the Aurignacian in Europe' *Proceedings of the Prehistoric Society* **67**: 195–217. **picked up quite a few 'modern' habits**: An example of this 'acquired technology' is the 'Chatelperronian' industry in southern France, which was a later Upper Palaeolithic tradition associated with Neanderthals. Other so-called transitional stone industries have been attributed to the Neanderthals' attempts to adapt to the pace of change. These include the Uluzzian in Italy and, much earlier in eastern Europe at the time of first appearance of moderns there around 40,000 years ago, the Szeletian, the Bohunician, and the Micoquian (named after the locations where characteristic tools were found). Unfortunately for this argument, there have always been fewer bones than stones in the record, so that it has not been absolutely confirmed who was responsible for these last four – Neanderthals or moderns. See Bocquet-Appel and Demars op. cit.

12. **being used even by Neanderthals** and **whether a particular set of bones was deliberately buried**: Solecki, R. (1972) *Shanidar: The Humanity of Neanderthal Man* (Allen Lane, London). See also the critical discussion of such evidence of early burials in Klein, R.G. (1999) *The Human Career: Human Biological and Cultural Origins*, 2 edn (Chicago University Press) pp. 395, 469–70, 550–53.

13. Klein (1999) op. cit. pp. 469–70.

14. Gamble op. cit. p. 161.

15. Both quotes from Klein (1989) op. cit. pp. 358–60.

16. **second edition of his book**: Klein, R.G. (1999) op. cit. **'to me it suggests that . . .'**: ibid. pp. 593–4.

17. Takahata, N. and Satta, Y. (1998). 'Footprints of intragenic recombination at HLA locus' *Immunogenetics* **47**: 430–41.

18. For instance, a comparison of mtDNA types between Europe and Australia found no overlap between the well delineated Caucasian N haplogroups (Table 2 of Richards, M. et al. (2000) 'Tracing European founder lineages in the Near Eastern mtDNA pool' *American Journal of Human Genetics* **67**: 1251–76; Richards, M. and Macaulay, V. (2000) 'Genetic data and the colonization of Europe: Genealogies and founders' in C. Renfrew and K. Boyle (eds) *Archaeogenetics: DNA and the Population Prehistory of Europe* (MacDonald Institute for Archaeological Research, Cambridge) pp. 139–41), and Australian or New Guinean haplotypes (Figure 2 of Redd, A.J. and Stoneking, M. (1999) 'Peopling of Sahul: mtDNA variation in Aboriginal Australian and Papua New Guinean populations' *American Journal of Human Genetics* **65**: 808–28). See also for Y chromosome: Karafet, T.M. et al. (1999) 'Ancestral Asian source(s) of New World Y-chromosome founder haplotypes' *American Journal of Human Genetics* **64**: 817–31. Crucially, none of the unique European Y or mtDNA clades can be found in full-blooded Aboriginal Australians.

19. Foley and Lahr op. cit. But see also the discussion in McBrearty and Collins op. cit. pp. 480–85.

20. Foley, R. and Lahr, M. op. cit.

21. McBrearty and Brooks op. cit.

22. Ibid.

23. **Tanzania, around 70,000 years ago**: ibid. **Sri Lanka, around 30,000 years ago**: Joshi, R.V. (1994) 'South Asia in the period of *Homo sapiens sapiens* up to the beginnings of food production (Upper Palaeolithic and Mesolithic)' in S.J. De Laet (ed.) *The History of Humanity* Vol. 1 (Routledge, Paris London UNESCO) pp. 256–8.

24. McBrearty and Brooks op. cit. p. 524.

25. Ibid p. 524.

26. Ibid. p. 526.

27. Clottes, J. et al. (1995) 'Radiocarbon dates for the Chauvet-Pont-d'Arc cave' *International Newsletter on Rock Art (INORA)* **11**: 1–2.

28. McBrearty and Brookes op. cit.

29. Bednarik, R. (1993) 'Palaeolithic art in India' *Man and Environment* **18**(2): 33–40.

30. **evidence for it from 40,000 years ago**: Table 8.2 in Gamble op. cit. **Here, 24,000 years ago**: Pettitt, P.B. and Bader, N.O. (2000) 'Direct AMS radiocarbon dates for the Sungir mid-Upper Palaeolithic burials' *Antiquity* **74**: 269–70.

31. McBrearty and Brookes op. cit.

32. **Adapting to new and varied foods**: ibid. **Neanderthals also practised beach-combing**: ibid.; Stringer, C. (2000) 'Coasting out of Africa' *Nature* **405**: 24–7.

33. McBrearty and Brookes op. cit.

34. **Here, around 125,000 years ago**: Walter, R.C. et al. (2000) 'Early human occupation of the Red Sea coast of Eritrea during the last interglacial' *Nature* **405**: 65–9. **occurred in Africa by 110,000 years ago**: McBrearty and Brookes op. cit. p. 530.

35. **Microliths start appearing**: McBrearty and Brooks op. cit. **the earliest microliths outside Africa**: Joshi op. cit.; see also a report of non-geometric microliths in a beach layer dated to 64,000–75,000 years ago in Sri Lanka: Deraniyagala, S.U. (2001) *Prehistory of Sri Lanka* (Department of Archaeological Survey, Government of Sri Lanka) pp. 685–702.

36. McBrearty and Brooks op. cit.

Chapter 3

1. **The first of these waves**: 'Earliest Upper Palaeolithic/Earliest Aurignacian' in Table 6.5 in Gamble, C. (1999) *The Palaeolithic Societies of Europe* (Cambridge University Press); see also Davies, W. (2001) 'A very model of a modern human industry: New perspectives on the origins and spread of the Aurignacian in Europe' *Proceedings of the Prehistoric Society* **67**: 195–217.

2. **after 50,000 years ago**: Uncorrected radiocarbon date, 46,000 ± 8,000 years. The earliest Aurignacian artefacts were found at Temnata, south of the Danube, west of the Black Sea in Bulgaria. There are no earlier Aurignacian tools outside Europe. See Table 6.1 in Gamble op. cit. **Fairly soon after this**: 44,300 ± 1,900 years, ibid. **to Willendorf, in Austria**: 41,700 ± 3,700 years ago, ibid. **at Geissenklösterle, Germany**: By 36,500 ± 1,500 years ago, ibid. **from Austria into northern Italy**: at Riparo Fumane 40,000 ± 400 years ago, ibid. **through El Castillo in northern Spain**: 40,000 ± 2,100 years ago, ibid. 38,000 years ago: at Gato Preto, 38,000 ± 2,100 years ago, ibid.; see also Davies op. cit.

3. **until much later**: Later Aurignacian, 25,000–33,000 years ago, Gamble op. cit. p. 287. **core homeland for the Aurignacian culture**: described as 'core typological region' in Otte, M. (2003) *The Aurignacian in Asia* (in press), citing inter alia Olszewski, D.I. and Dibble, H.L. (1994) 'The Zagros Aurignacian' *Current Anthropology* **35**(1): 68–75. The so-called 'transitional' Upper Palaeolithic industries are also found 500–5,000 years earlier than the Temnata site (i.e. 47,200 ± 9,000 years ago, see Gamble op. cit.) in the Near East at a site called Boker Tatchit in the Negev Desert.

4. Some population geneticists still regard the use of the molecular clock and the phylogeographic method as anathema.

5. Richards, M. et al. (2000) 'Tracing European founder lineages in the Near Eastern mtDNA pool' *American Journal of Human Genetics* **67**: 1251–76.

6. **J, T, U5, and I in the figure**: and in Richards et al., op. cit. **the earliest Upper Palaeolithic dates**: e.g. from the Negev Desert of 47,100 years ago – see above.

7. **over 50,000 years in the Near East**: 54,400 years ago (95% credible region (CR) 50,400–58,300 years ago), Richards et al., op. cit. **Europa, U5, also dates back 50,000 years**: 95% CR 45,100–52,800 years ago, Richards et al., op. cit. (A 95% 'credible region' is analogous to a 95% 'confidence interval', but has a different mathematical basis.) **under-recording of radiocarbon dates**: It would be easy to dismiss such a discrepancy of 4,000–7,000 years by blaming the notoriously wide error margins of the molecular clock. Another more definite reason has to do with the archaeological dating. Archaeological dates for Upper Palaeolithic sites have almost all been obtained by radiocarbon dating, the precision and accuracy of which drops off markedly for objects older than 40,000 years. In objects that old there is very little radiocarbon left to decay, and by the time we get back to 40,000 years

ago, the radiocarbon dates are systematically underestimating the true age. Using other methods of dating the same sites, archaeologists have shown the radiocarbon underestimates to be 2,000–3,500 years for dates between 20,000–40,000 years ago, and as much as 5,600 years for dates between 38,000 and 40,000 years. After 40,000 years the systematic error rises even more. With such underestimates of archaeological dates, the genetic dates (which do not have this age ceiling problem) for modern human colonization of the Levant and Europe start to look quite reasonable. See also Gamble op. cit. p. 273.

8. **Europa was genetic daughter of Rohani . . . Nasreen . . . L3**: Richards, M. and Macaulay, V. (2000) 'Genetic data and the colonization of Europe: Genealogies and founders' in C. Renfrew and K. Boyle (eds) *Archaeogenetics: DNA and the Population Prehistory of Europe* (McDonald Institute for Archaeological Research, Cambridge) pp. 139–41. Note that 'generation' is not used in a literal sense here. Each 'generation' of the gene line represents one or more new mutations and may cover a period of well over 10,000 years. **This was around 55,000 years ago**: Kivisild, T. et al. (1999) 'The place of the Indian mitochondrial DNA variants in the global network of maternal lineages and the peopling of the Old World' in S.S. Papiha et al. (eds) *Genomic Diversity: Applications in Human Population Genetics* (Kluwer Academic/Plenum, New York) pp. 135–52. The estimate in this publication is based on a poorly resolved R tree in India, and an older age of R is possible, perhaps nearer to 70,000 years. One estimate was even as much as 73,000 years in a more recent paper by Kivisild et al.: see the discussion on p. 322 of Kivisild, T. et al. (2003a) 'The genetic heritage of the earliest settlers persists both in Indian tribal and caste populations' *American Journal of Human Genetics* **72**: 313–33. **the ages of two Asian subgroups of Rohani**: e.g. R9 (81,400 years ago) and B (74,600 years ago) –Yong-Gang Yao et al. (2002) 'Phylogeographic differentiation of mitochondrial DNA in Han Chinese' *American Journal of Human Genetics* **70**: 635–51.

9. **U6 moved west round the southern shore of the Mediterranean**: Rando, J.C. et al. (1998) 'Mitochondrial DNA analysis of northwest African populations reveals genetic exchanges with European, near-Eastern, and sub-Saharan populations' *Annals of Human Genetics* **62**: 531–50. Note that U6 is present in Bedouin and Syrian Arabs at low rates of 4–7%, which is consistent with a route for U6 into North Africa via the Levant: data from Richards, M. et al. (2000), further reported in: Richards, M. et al. (2003) 'Extensive female-mediated gene flow from sub-Saharan Africa into Near Eastern Arab populations' *American Journal of Human Genetics* **72**: 1058–64. **Early Upper Palaeolithic tools**: blades and burins – Close, A.E. and Wendorf, F. (1989) 'North Africa at 18,000 BP' in C. Gamble and O. Soffer (eds) *The World at 18,000 BP* (Unwin Hyman, London) p. 47. Other evidence for early modern human presence in North Africa includes the Taramsa Hill child on the Nile, dated by Optically Stimulated Luminescence to 50,000–80,000 years ago but associated, in this case, with Middle Palaeolithic technology: Vermeersch, P.M. et al. (1998) 'Middle Palaeolithic burial of a modern human at Taramsa Hill, Egypt' *Antiquity* **72**: 475–84.

10. **U2i is clearly home grown . . .**: Bamshad, M. et al. (2001) 'Genetic evidence on the origins of Indian caste populations' *Genome Research* **11**: 994–1004.

11. Apart from R, U2, and U7, other N groups and subgroups may have a claim of ancient origin in South Asia, in particular W. Groups H, Ö, X, I, J, and T are also found in India. Kivisild et al. (1999) op. cit. pp. 137–50.

12. **Between 55,000 and 65,000 years ago the world went through a period of almost unremitting cold and dryness. During this time the Fertile Crescent corridor was shut**: For a graphic colour map description of the effect of glacial cycles on the Fertile Crescent corridor see Jonathan Adams' webpage, http://www.esd.ornl.gov/projects/qen/nercEURASIA.html **four warm and wet periods**: Interstadials (IS – not *OIS*) numbered 17–14 and dated as in Dansgaard, W. et al. (1993) 'Evidence for general instability of past climate from a 250-kyr ice-core record' *Nature* **364**: 218–20; see also Schultz, H. et al. (1998) 'Correlation between Arabian Sea and Greenland climate oscillations of the past 110,000 years' *Nature* **393**: 54–7. The last of these, 51,000 years ago: IS numbered 14 (= Glinde according to Dansgaard et al., op. cit); see also Schultz et al., op. cit. **the Indian monsoon was even wetter**: See Schultz et al., op. cit. esp. Fig. 2, p. 55. **The climatic and archaeological clock timings converge**: With correction of the radiocarbon dates – see note 7 above. **the earliest daughter lines of Nasreen**: I, and the U/Europa derivatives of R/Rohani: U/Europa root and U5, U7 (Richards et al. (2000) op. cit.).

13. The African branch that encompasses all non-Africans is defined by one bi-allelic marker, M168. Underhill, P.A. et al. (2000) 'Y chromosome sequence variation and the history of human populations' *Nature Genetics* **26**: 358–61. So far the root type for this 'Adam' marker has not been found either within or outside Africa. The three primary branches C, D/E (or YAP), and F, which account for all non-Africans, I have chosen, for simplicity, to call Cain, Abel, and Seth respectively. The letters C–F refer to the new *consensus nomenclature*. For the consensus nomenclature, see The Y Chromosome Consortium (2002) 'A nomenclature system for the tree of human Y-chromosomal binary haplogroups' *Genome Research* **12**: 339–48.

14. **J, but I shall call him Jahangir** and **north-east coast of the Mediterranean**: The *consensus nomenclature* haplogroup J (Jahangir) line is defined by M89, p12f2, and M172 (haplotypes 54–64 in Underhill et al., op. cit.) and is equivalent to Eur9 in Semino, O. et al. (2000) 'The genetic legacy of Paleolithic *Homo sapiens sapiens* in extant Europeans: A Y-chromosome perspective' *Science* **290**: 1155–9, and equivalent to haplogroup 9 according to the nomenclature of Tyler-Smith and Jobling (see Rosser, H.Z. et al. (2000) 'Y-chromosomal diversity in Europe is clinal and influenced primarily by geography, rather than by language' *American Journal of Human Genetics* **67**: 1526–43). **high frequencies in the Near East**: 57% in Syria, 51% in Palestinians, 28–45% in Jews, and 46% among Lebanese ('Med' type in Hammer, M. et al. (2000) 'Jewish and Middle Eastern non-Jewish populations share a common pool of Y-chromosome biallelic haplotypes' *Proceedings of the National Academy of Sciences USA* **97**: 6769–74) and 33% among Georgians (Semino et al., op. cit.). **highest European frequency is in Turkey**: ibid. **followed by the Balkans and Italy**: ibid.; Rosser et al., op. cit. **high frequencies in North African countries**: ibid.

15. M172 (J/Jahangir) less than 20%, Quintana-Murci, L. et al. (2001) 'Y-chromosome lineages trace diffusion of people and languages in Southwestern Asia' *American Journal of Human Genetics* **68**: 537–42; see also Underhill et al., op. cit.; Kivisild, T. (2003b) 'Genetics of the language and farming spread in India' in P. Bellwood and C. Renfrew (eds) *Examining the Farming/Language Dispersal Hypothesis* (McDonald Institute for Archaeology, Cambridge) pp. 215–222.

16. **Diversity of Jahangir**: Quintana-Murci et al., op. cit. The biggest problem comes in dating the M172 (J/Jahangir) clan. Hammer and colleagues put a date of 15,000–20,000 years on

the European expansion, although the original mutation may have been much earlier (Hammer et al., op. cit.). Hammer dated M172's immediate ancestor (DYS188$_{792}$) to 60,000 years. However, there are serious problems still with Y-chromosome dating. Kivisild (2003b) op. cit. compares different methods of dating, showing age estimates for the M172 coalescent as much as 54,700 years in Iran and 49,000 years in India, similar to the older Hammer figure. Quintana-Murci in contrast, using 'pedigree rate' to estimate time, suggests a Neolithic agricultural expansion, but the origins of this clan clearly go much further back in time and space. The people who have the highest rate of M172, the Kurds, are long-time residents of the hilly part of the Fertile Crescent who until fairly recently were nomadic herders of sheep and goats with only marginal agriculture. Descendants of M172 spread to the East as well, into Central Asia (see Chapters 4 and 5).

17. **half of all western and northern European maternal lines**: Table 2 in Kivisild et al. (1999) op. cit. **The expansion of HV has been dated to 33,500 years ago**: Richards et al. (2000) op. cit.

18. Metspalu, E. et al. (1999) 'The Trans-Caucasus and the expansion of the Caucasoid-specific mitochondrial DNA' in S.S. Papiha et al. (eds) *Genomic Diversity: Applications in Human Population Genetics* (Kluwer Academic/Plenum Publishers, New York 1999) pp. 121–134.

19. **Inos, after Seth's son Enos**: This consensus haplogroup I (Inos) clan is uniquely identified by bi-allelic marker M170 (haplotypes 49–53) in Underhill et al., op. cit., is synonymous with groups Eur7 and 8 in Semino et al., op. cit., and is largely overlapping with Tyler-Smith's Haplogroup 2 (Rosser et al., op. cit.). For an explanation of the nomenclature of I (Inos), see The Y Chromosome Consortium op. cit. **According to the Leicester-based geneticist Zoë Rosser**: Rosser et al., op. cit. **Ornella Semino and her colleagues**: Semino et al., op. cit.

20. **earliest changes from Mousterian**: 46,000–47,000 years ago – Bar-Yosef, O. (1994) 'The contributions of Southwest Asia to the study of the origins of modern humans' in M.H. Nitecki and D.V. Nitecki (eds) *Origins of Modern Humans* (Plenum Press, New York, 1994), Chapter 2. These are radiocarbon dates, and – as stated by Bar-Yosef – if correction were possible, could be much older (e.g. as much as 51,000 years ago – see comments on radiocarbon ceiling, note 7 above.) The rock shelter of Ksar 'Aqil in southern Lebanon has also been suggested as a site of the earliest transition from Mousterian technology to Levantine Aurignacian, possibly (unfortunately the date of the transition of culture could only be inferred stratigraphically) between 50,000 and 52,000 years ago; see Mellars, P. and Tixier, J. (1989) 'Radiocarbon-accelerator dating of Ksar 'Aqil (Lebanon) and the chronology of the Upper Palaeolithic sequence in the Middle East' *Antiquity* **63**: 761–8. **hiatus coincided with a climatic worsening**: The period spans two warm, wet interstadials, IS 12 and 11, with cold dry snaps preceding each of these. (IS numbering and dates according to Dansgaard op. cit) The first cold event coincided with Heinrich event No. 5. (See also Schultz et al., op. cit.)

21. The progressively worsening cold spell spanned the whole period between (IS) 12 (43,500 years) and IS 8 (34,000 years), the latter IS signalling the onset of re-warming. (Interstadial numbering and dates according to Dansgaard op. cit.) The first cold event coincided with Heinrich event No. 5. See also Schultz et al., op. cit.

22. For details of the Shanidar burial and the Baradostian culture, see Solecki, R. (1972) *Shanidar: The Humanity of Neanderthal Man* (Allen Lane, London).

23. Table 6.1 in Gamble op. cit.

24. **Earliest Upper Palaeolithic, 33,000–45,000 years ago**: Table 6.5 in Gamble op. cit. Occupation peaks for this phase occur between 40,000 and 44,000 years ago (calibrated ^{14}C dates, ibid. p. 285). **Cultures taking off from around 30,000 years ago**: Table 6.5 ibid. **third phase of high occupation**: These (the Gravettian technocomplex) correspond with a third occupation peak (or Middle Upper Palaeolithic) between 25,000 and 29,000 years ago (uncalibrated dates, Fig. 6.5 ibid.). **33,000 years ago, for example at Kostenki**: ibid. pp. 287–92.

25. **cultural additions innovations of the Gravettian**: Gamble op. cit. pp. 287–92, esp. p. 290; Soffer, O. (1993) 'Upper Paleolithic adaptations in Central and Eastern Europe and man-mammoth interactions' in O. Soffer and N. Praslov (eds) *From Kostenki to Clovis: Upper Paleolithic-Paleo-Indian Adaptations* (Plenum, New York) pp. 31–49. **may also have represented an intrusion of peoples carrying the seeds of such cultural practices from eastern Europe**: Otte, M. (2000) 'The history of European populations as seen by archaeology' in C. Renfrew and K. Boyle (eds) *Archaeogenetics: DNA and the Population Prehistory of Europe* (MacDonald Institute for Archaeological Research, Cambridge) pp. 139–41.

26. Torroni, A. et al. (2001) 'A signal, from human mtDNA, of postglacial recolonization in Europe' *American Journal of Human Genetics* **69**: 844–52.

27. **perfectly preserved Caucasoid mummies**: The point about the 3,000-year-old Caucasoid mummies on the Silk Road is merely to emphasise that there is no *a priori* reason to assume that the first populations of this part of Central Asia were Mongoloid: Barber, E.W. (2000) *The Mummies of Urumchi* (Pan, London); Mallory, J.P. and Mair, V. (2000) *The Tarim Mummies. Ancient China and the Mystery of the Earliest Peoples from the West* (Thames & Hudson, London). **two sites in the Russian Altai**: Otte, M. and Derevianko, A. (2001) 'The Aurignacian in Altai' **Antiquity 75**: 44–8; Goebel, T. et al. (1993) 'Dating the Middle-to-Upper-Palaeolithic transition at Kara Bom' *Current Anthropology* **34**: 452–8; Goebel, T. and Aksenov, M. (1995) 'Accelerator radiocarbon dating of the intial Upper Palaeolithic in Southeast Siberia' *Antiquity* **69**: 349–57.

28. **Half of these consist of HV stock**: Metspalu et al., op. cit.; Kivisild et al. (1999) op. cit. **recent eastward European emigration**: Comas, D. et al. (1998) 'Trading genes along the Silk Road; mitochondrial DNA sequences and the origin of Central Asian populations' *Molecular Biology and Evolution* **13**: 1067–77. **absent from Central Asia**: although there are matches for most European H founders. **most of the other 'west Eurasian Nasreen lines'**: U, J, and T haplogroups – U2i, U7, U5a, 1a, U4, U1, and K; see Fig. 2 in Metspalu et al., op. cit.; Kivisild et al. (1999) op. cit. **HV could have originally come from South Asia**: and J1, U1, and T.

29. **Dates of branches vary enormously**: e.g. Kivisild (2003b) op. cit.; Forster, P. et al. (2000) 'A short tandem repeat-based phylogeny for the human Y chromosome' *American Journal of Human Genetics* **67**: 182–96. **careful analysis of founder lines and mtDNA dating**: Richards et al. (2000) op. cit.; Metspalu et al., op. cit.; Kivisild et al. (1999) op. cit.

30. Underhill et al., op. cit.; Semino et al., op. cit.

31. The root haplotype 87 defined by M9 in Underhill et al., op. cit. This clade has been reclassified as K/Krishna (while M89 is F/Seth): see The Y Chromosome Consortium op. cit.

32. **the Oxford-based geneticist**: Zergal, T. et al. (1997) 'Genetic relationships of Asians and Northern Europeans, revealed by Y-chromosomal DNA analysis' *American Journal of Human Genetics* **60**: 1174–83. **his genetic father and grandfather**: haplotypes 87 and 71 respectively, defined by M9 and M89 in Underhill et al., op. cit. **a migration from Central Asia**: possibly only since the last glaciation – see Rosser et al., op. cit.; Semino et al., op. cit.

33. **Hungarians achieve the highest frequency**: followed closely by Poland, the Ukraine, and Russia at 56, 54, and 47%, respectively: Semino et al., op. cit.; Rosser et al., op. cit. **especially the Altai**: 52%, Quintana-Murci et al., op. cit.; Underhill et al., op. cit.

34. **the ultimate origin of M17**: Kivisild et al. (2003a,b) op. cit. **highest rates and diversity of the M17 line in Pakistan, India, and eastern Iran, and low rates in the Caucasus**: respectively 32, 20, 31, and 2% – Quintana-Murci et al., op. cit.; Rosser et al., op. cit. For a tabulation of the relative diversity of M17 (R1a) showing the highest diversity in South Asia, particularly Iran, see Table 5 in Kivisild et al. (2003a) op. cit. **36,000 years**: measured at 35,700 years – Kivisild (2003b) op. cit.; other methods of calculation yield much lower estimates.

35. **movement from the east to the west 30,000 years ago**: Semino et al., op. cit. Phylogenetic analysis produces a realistic age, for M17 in Europe, of 27,000 years, see: Kivisild (2003b) op. cit. In contrast, Quintana-Murci et al. (op. cit.) tentatively suggests that the expansion into Europe started only around 5,000 years ago with the advent of farming. **Ruslan**: M173 root type, i.e. Haplotype 104, in Underhill et al., op. cit. Reclassified as 'R' in: The Y Chromosome Consortium (2002) op. cit.

36. **according to one study**: M173/ht 104, in Underhill et al., op. cit. **Ruslan's genetic father, P**: Haplotype 111 in ibid.; reclassified as P in The Y Chromosome Consortium op. cit.

37. Semino et al., op. cit. It should be noted that the coalescent estimate for M17, M173, and M172 at M89 (Underhill haplotype 71) in India may be as old as 88,300 years – estimated by phylogenetic analysis, see Kivisild (2003b) op. cit.

Chapter 4

1. For a full discussion of the phylogeographic approach and founder analysis see Richards, M. et al. (1998) 'Phylogeography of mitochondrial DNA in western Europe' *American Journal of Human Genetics* **67**: 241–60; Richards, M. et al. (2000) 'Tracing European founder lineages in the Near Eastern mtDNA pool' *American Journal of Human Genetics* **67**: 1251–76.

2. **much more recent African admixture**: Richards, M. et al. (2003) 'Extensive female-mediated gene flow from sub-Saharan Africa into Near Eastern Arab populations' *American Journal of Human Genetics* **72**: 1058–64. **a number of other South Asian aboriginal groups**: India also has so-called proto-Asian groups, such as Maria Gond, Khonda Dora, and Kattuniaken. Some of these are probably, like the Munda/Mundari groups, more recent east-west re-entrants from Indo-China: see Figs 14 and 21 in Oppenheimer, S.J. (1998) *Eden in the East* (Weidenfeld & Nicolson, London). For an anthropological/genetic description of the Indian aboriginal groups see also Watkins, W.S. et al. (1999) 'Multiple origins of the mtDNA

9-bp deletion in populations of South India' *American Journal of Physical Anthropology* **109**: 147–58; Watkins, W.S. et al. (2001) 'Patterns of ancestral human diversity: An analysis of Alu-insertion and restriction-site polymorphisms' *American Journal of Human Genetics* **68**: 738–52. **beach-settling ancestors from Africa**: Kivisild. T. et al. (2003) 'The genetic heritage of the earliest settlers persists both in Indian tribal and caste populations' *American Journal of Human Genetics* **72**: 313–32.

3. **two ancient and unique Indian Manju clans, M2 and M4**: for these groups in Andamanese, see Endicott, P. et al. (2003) 'The genetic origins of the Andaman Islanders' *American Journal of Human Genetics* **72**: 178–84; Thangaraj, K. et al. (2003) 'Genetic affinities of the Andaman Islanders, a vanishing human population' *Current Biology* published online, 26 November 2002. **commonest mtDNA component among the Indian aboriginal groups**: Kivisild et al., op. cit. **On the paternal side**: for Y types in Andamanese, see Thangaraj et al., op. cit.

4. Pre-F1: Hill, C. et al. (2003) 'Mitochondrial DNA variation in the Orang Asli of the Malay Peninsula' (in preparation). For similar Pre-F1 haplotypes in Andamanese and Nicobars, see Andaman haplotypes 9 and 10 and Nicobar haplotype 1 in: Thangaraj et al., op.cit.; Prasad, B.V. et al. (2001). 'Mitochondrial DNA variation in Nicobarese Islanders' *Human Biology* **73**: 715–25.

5. Nasreen and Manju mtDNA lines in New Guinea and Australia (see also Fig. 8.2 in Appendix 1): New Guinea has three main mtDNA clades, labelled PNG 1–3 in Redd, A.J. and Stoneking, M. (1999) 'Peopling of Sahul: mtDNA variation in Aboriginal Australian and Papua New Guinean populations' *American Journal of Human Genetics* **65**: 808–28. The name labels of these three clades in the above paper corresponding to the nomenclature used in this book (Table 8.1 in Appendix 1) are as follows. PNG1 = Haplogroup B (of R haplogroup); PNG2 = local subgroup (of R haplogroup, also Group P in Forster, P. et al. (2003) 'Asian and Papuan mtDNA evolution' in P. Bellwood and C. Renfrew (eds) *Examining the Farming/ Language Dispersal Hypothesis* (McDonald Institute for Archaeological Research, Cambridge) pp. 89–98); PNG3 = Q in Forster et al. (2003) op. cit., and M11 in Richards, M. and Macaulay, V. (2000) 'Genetic data and colonization of Europe: Genealogies and founders' in C. Renfrew and K. Boyle (eds) *Archaeogenetics: DNA and the Population Prehistory of Europe* (McDonald Institute for Archaeological Research, Cambridge) pp. 139–41, Fig. 14.1. These three clades can also be confirmed unambiguously using typing data from several other publications, e.g. PNG2 = Haplotypes 6–8 and PNG3 = Haplotype 22, in Ingman, M. et al. (2000) 'Mitochondrial genome variation and the origin of modern humans' *Nature* **408**: 708–13; PNG1 = Haplogroup 1 and PNG3 = Haplogroup 2, in Sykes, B. et al. (1995) 'The origins of the Polynesians: An intepretation from mitochondrial lineage analysis' *American Journal of Human Genetics* **57**: 1463–75. For further Papuan details, see also Forster et al. (2003) op. cit.

Australian lineages have been rather less well characterized, but Redd and Stoneking (op. cit.) group them with Asians (specifically Indians – with rather less justification), rather than with Africans (see e.g. their Fig. 4). See also Ingman et al. (op. cit.), who show that Haplogroups 2 and 3 form a unique N subgroup and that Haplogroup 23 is a unique M type. No non-M/non-N Australian lineages have been demonstrated so far.

6. A recent article co-authored by Alan Thorne, a leading multiregionalist, suggested, on the

basis of mtDNA results from ancient Australian bones, that some Australians may have left Africa in an earlier migration: Adcock, G.J. et al. (2001) 'Mitochondrial DNA sequences in ancient Australians: Implications for modern human origins' *Proceedings of the National Academy of Sciences USA* **98**(2): 537–42. An immediate response from scientists working in the same field roundly condemned the study on the basis of methods, data presented, and underlying argument: Cooper, A. et al. (2001) 'Human origins and ancient DNA' *Science* **292**: 1655–6. The discussion is rather technical and involved, *and* I mostly agree with the counterarguments given in the response by Cooper, A. et al. Mainly at issue was mtDNA extracted from one of the oldest sets of skeletal remains (possibly 62,000 years old – a date challenged again recently) found at Lake Mungo in the Willandra Lakes region of south-west Australia (LM3). Adcock and co-authors (op. cit.) argued that this mtDNA came from an earlier human branch. Cooper et al. (op. cit.) convincingly undermined their claim.

A significant aspect not disputed by either side was that the skull of the LM3 individual (and all others of the same vintage) was anatomically modern and gracile (light-boned), like those of most modern non-Africans. So there still seems little doubt that the *first* immigrants to Australia were descendants of the single out-of-Africa movement. So far, there is no convincing genetic evidence among living Aboriginal Australians to challenge this view (but see my qualifications below).

To do justice to the multiregionalists, however, there remains a significant problem with later prehistoric Australian skulls, which had much more robust (heavy-boned) features. These skulls, found in Kow Swamp and the Willandra Lakes region of south-west Australia and dated to approximately the last glacial maximum (LGM) onwards, are best represented by the WLH50 skullcap. These could possibly represent a secondary migration into Australia at the very low sea level of the LGM. This scenario is implicit (if not explicitly noted) in the discussion by the leading multiregionalist Milford Wolpoff (Wolpoff, M. (1999) *Paleoanthropology* (McGraw-Hill, Boston) pp. 738–40). Multiregionalist Alan Thorne had argued that these robust skulls may represent another species, Java *Homo erectus*, who hybridized with the gracile type (Thorne, A.G. (1980) 'The longest link: Human evolution in Southeast Asia and the settlement of Australia' in J. Fox et al. (eds) *Indonesia: Australian Perspectives* (Australian National University, Canberra) pp. 35–43).

Physical anthropologist and archaeologist David Bulbeck has recently reviewed available information on this topic and, while favouring local evolution rather than di-hybrid theory, in the concluding passages he confesses that the evidence does not allow one to rule out the circa-LGM secondary colonization of Australia by robust people, themselves partly descended from Java *Homo erectus* (Bulbeck, D. (2001) 'Robust and gracile Australian Pleistocene crania: Tale of the Willandra Lakes' in T. Simanjuntak et al. (eds) *Sangiran: Man, Culture and Environment in Pleistocene Times* (Yayasan Obor Indonesia, Jakarta) pp. 60–106).

This remaining doubt has echoes in the controversial Adcock mtDNA data; mtDNA from KS8 (one of the six robust specimens described in Adcock et al. (op. cit.) and over 8,000 years old) then becomes much more interesting than LM3. On their tree, KS8 segregates from all other Australians, both modern and prehistoric. If one accepts KS8 as a valid DNA result, on the basis that the DNA is much younger and presumably more viable than others described in the paper, it can be found an approximate place early on the modern African human mtDNA tree. The Most Recent common Ancestor for all modern humans (African Eve) should have mutational differences from the European Control Region Sequence at sites 16223, 16278, 16187, (16189, 16311, 16230, 16148, and 16320. I have written these mutation sites progressively backwards on the tree towards the African Eve (MRCA). KS8 differs from the CRS at 16223, 16278, 16311, 16230, and 16284. This tends to put her way back in the African L1 branch towards the modern African Eve, whose age approaches 200,000 years (note that the genetic coalescent date estimate can be older or younger than the apparent anatomical split). This could be consistent with the mtDNA ancestor of KS8 having left Africa separately as a robust but probably modern *Homo sapiens* type either long before, at the same time as or even after the main exodus of moderns 60,000–80,000 years ago. Therefore having an L1 haplotype would not suggest that KS8 had a *Homo erectus* hybrid maternal source, merely an earlier modern one.

Similar mtDNA haplotypes sharing the 16223 and 16278 mutations appear in an Australian and Melanesian data set including Eastern Indonesians (Haplotypes 162–165 in Redd and Stoneking op. cit.). Similarly, four other non-African haplotypes belonging to African L1 and L1b haplogroups were reported by Vigilant and colleagues (Vigilant, L. et al. (1991) 'African populations and the evolution of human mitochondrial DNA' *Science* **253**: 1503–7). Two of these were described as Asian (Haplotypes V23 and V28), one as Australian (Haplotype V49), and one as being from the Pacific island of New Britain (Haplotype V50). Three of these four came from the data set of Rebecca Cann's famous *Nature* paper (Cann, R. et al. (1987) 'Mitochondrial DNA and human evolution' *Nature* **325**: 31–6). Such arguments for older African intrusions to the Antipodes have to remain speculative until (and if) ancient mtDNA from more robust fossil specimens as well as modern Australians is analysed in more detail. If such a model of a separate modern exodus carrying pre-L3 mtDNA haplotypes, which occupied Eastern Indonesia and subsequently migrated to Australia at the LGM 20,000 years ago, were substantiated, it might well pose a challenge to the hypothesis of a single out-of-Africa movement.

7. **Until the 1990s, there was no clear evidence for humans in Australia**: Roberts, R.G. and Jones, R. (2001) 'Chronologies of carbon and of silica: Evidence concerning the dating of the earliest human presence in Northern Australia' in P.V. Tobias et al. (eds) *Humanity from African Naissance to Coming Millennia* (Florence University Press, Firenze; Witwatersrand University Press, Johannesburg) pp. 239–48. **limitations of the radio-carbon method of dating**: ibid; see also note 7, Chapter 3. **between 50,000 and 60,000 years ago**: this was for the Malakunanja II shelter; Roberts and Jones later obtained similar dates for the nearby Nauwalabila I shelter: Roberts, R.G. et al. (1990) 'Thermoluminescence dating of a 50,000 year-old human occupation site in northern Australia' *Nature* **345**: 153–6; Roberts, R.G. et al. (1994) 'The human colonisation of Australia: Optical dates of 53,000 and 60,000 years bracket human arrival at Deaf Adder Gorge, *Northern Territory' Quaternary Science Reviews (Quaternary Geochronology)* **13**: 575–83.

8. **the rock art site of Jinmium**: Fullagar, R.L.K. et al. (1996) 'Early human occupation of northern Australia: Archaeology and thermoluminescence dating of Jinmium rock-shelter, Northern Territory' *Antiquity* **70**: 751–73. **two to three times as old as the Arnhem Land shelters**: Roberts et al. (1990, 1994) op cit. **the problem appeared to be solved**: Roberts, R.G. et al. (1999) 'Optical dating of single and multiple grains of quartz from Jinmium rock shelter, northern Australia: Part II, results and implications' *Archaeometry*

41: 365–95. **oldest dates of human occupation in Australia**: Since completing the Jinmium study, Roberts and Jones have redated two key samples from the Malakunanja II deposit using the same single-grain optical dating methods. These optical ages confirmed the previous ages for initial human occupation of Malakunanja II but increased somewhat the oldest age in the lowest level containing artefacts, to 61,000 years: Roberts, R. et al. (1998) 'Single-aliquot and single-grain optical dating confirm thermoluminescence age estimates at Malakunanja II rock shelter in northern Australia' *Ancient Thermoluminescence* **16**: 19–24.

9. **human occupation dates as old as 62,000 years ago**: Simpson, J.J. and Grün, R. (1998) 'Non-destructive gamma spectrometric U-series dating' *Quaternary Science Reviews (Quaternary Geochronology)* **17**: 1009–22; Thorne, A. et al. (1999) 'Australia's oldest human remains: Age of the Lake Mungo 3 skeleton' *Journal of Human Evolution* **36**: 591–612. **another 80,000 years before**: 150,000 years ago at OIS 6, Chappell, J. (1983) 'A revised sea-level record for the last 300,000 years from Papua New Guinea' *Search* **14**(3/4): 99–101.

10. **a very deep lowstand**: Siddall, M. et al. (2003) 'Sea-level fluctuations during the last glacial cycle' *Nature* **423**: 853–8 **around 100 metres vertically below today's levels**: ibid.

11. **colonization of Manus Island**: Anderson, A.J. (2000) 'Slow boats from China: Issues in the prehistory of Indo-Pacific seafaring' in P.M. Veth and S. O'Connor (eds) *East of Wallace's Line: Studies of Past and Present Maritime Cultures of the Indo-Pacific Region, Modern Quaternary Research in Southeast Asia*, Vol. 16 (Balkema, Rotterdam) pp. 13–50, here p. 17. **random accidental drifts is an unlikely scenario**: Stoneking, M. et al. (1990) 'Geographic variation in human mitochondrial DNA from Papua New Guinea' *Genetics* **124**: 717–33. **68,000-year-old date**: 68,099 years, 95% CI = 55,663–97,350 years, Redd and Stoneking op. cit.

12. **some of the earliest Australian sites**: e.g. Mungo Lake – Chapter 3 in Flood, J. (1995) *Archaeology of the Dreamtime* (Collins, Australia). **the beach nearer to its present location**: Siddall op. cit. **the next available lowstand 55,000 years ago**: ibid.

13. **Sea routes to Australia and New Guinea and inter-island visibility**: Irwin, G. (1994) *The Prehistoric Exploration and Colonisation of the Pacific* (Cambridge University Press) pp. 18–30.

14. **around 77,000 years**: 76,507 years for the PNG highlanders (PNG 2 and 3); 95% CI = 55,663–97,350 years: see Redd and Stoneking op. cit. **New Guinea may have been colonized before Australia**: This argument is highly speculative since the accuracy of genetic dating is not the best, and the earliest confirmed date of colonization of New Guinea is still only 40,000 years ago. See Groube, L. et al. (1986) 'A 40,000-year-old human occupation site at Huon Peninsula, Papua New Guinea' *Nature* **324**: 453–5.

15. Morwood, M. et al. (2002) 'The archaeology of land use: Evidence from Liang Bua, Flores, East Indonesia' paper presentated at the 17th Congress of the Indo-Pacific Prehistory Association, 9–15 September 2002, Taipei, Taiwan.

16. **as long ago as 160,000 years**: Mishra, S. (1995) 'The chronology of the Indian Stone Age: Impact of recent absolute and relative dating attempts' *Man and Environment* **20**(2): 11–17; see also the discussion in Chapters 1 and 2 (pp. 87, 118) on Sri Lankan microliths. **Middle Palaeolithic tools also abound**: Amirkhanov, H. (1994) 'Research on the Palaeolithic and

Neolithic of Hadramaut and Mahra' *Arabian Archaeology and Epigraphy* **5**: 217–28. **stone tools similar to those of the African late Middle Stone Age**: The tools are undated as yet. See McClure, H.A. (1994) 'A new Arabian stone tool assemblage and note on the Aterian industry of North Africa' *Arabian Archaeology and Epigraphy* **5**: 1–16. The North African industry referred to is the Aterian, which spread as far as the western desert of Egypt and is roughly dated from 90,000 years ago onward – McBrearty, S. and Brooks, A.S. (2000) 'The revolution that wasn't: A new interpretation of the origin of modern human behavior' *Journal of Human Evolution* **39**: 453–563).

17. **curious, rather crude, large pebble tools**: Similar large quartzite unifacial and bifacial pebble tools classified as Mode 1/2 chopper tools have been found in the southern Yemen. Since they were surface finds and undated, the same attribution to an earlier human species was made. See Whalen, N.M. and Schatte, K.E. (1997) 'Pleistocene sites in southern Yemen' *Arabian Archaeology and Epigraphy* **8**: 1–10. **tried to relate the tools to the great eruption**. Harrison, T. (1975) 'Tampan: Malaysia's Palaeolithic reconsidered' in G.-J. Bartstra and W.A. Casparie (eds) *Modern Quaternary Research in Southeast Asia* Vol. 1 (Balkema, Rotterdam) pp. 53–70. On Harrison himself, see Heimann. J.M. (1999) *The Most Offending Soul Alive: Tom Harrison and His Remarkable Life* (University of Hawaii Press, Honolulu).

18. Majid, Z. and Tjia, H.D. (1988) 'Kota Tampan, Perak: The geological and archaeological evidence for a late Pleistocene site' *Journal of the Malaysian Branch of the Royal Asiatic Society* **61**: 123–34; Majid, Z. (1998) 'Radiocarbon dates and culture sequence in the Lenggong Valley and beyond' *Malaysia Museums Journal* **34**: 241–9. The end of the Lenggong Valley culture could have been as recent as 4,000 years ago (i.e. into the Iron Age of the region), if the 'old carbon effect' of freshwater shell in karstic formations is taken into account (David Bulbeck (2002) personal communication).

19. **Two of the highest authorities**: 'Whatever the final decision on age, the tools appear to be the handiwork of anatomically modern humans' – Bellwood, P. (1997) *Prehistory of the Indo-Malaysian Archipelago* revised edn (University of Hawaii Press, Honolulu) p. 68; Bowdler, S. (1992) 'The earliest Australian stone tools and implications for Southeast Asia' *Indo-Pacific Prehistory Association Bulletin* **12**: 10–22. The description of Southeast Asian and Australian Palaeolithic tools as 'crude' or unsophisticated is more commonly used by archaeologists working in Europe or Africa. Such an appellation is often regarded by archaeologists in Australasia as a biologically determinist and Eurocentric value judgement. **tools found in the Lenggong Valley are too recent**: Majid (1998) op. cit. **finding by her team of the 'Perak Man'**: Majid, Z. (ed.) (1994) *The Excavation of Gua Gunung Runtuh and the Discovery of the Perak Man in Malaysia* (Department of Museums and Antiquity, Malaysia). **He was about 10,000 years old**: or as recent as 7,000–8,000 years old if, again, the 'old carbon effect' of freshwater shell in karstic formations is taken into account, so Perak Man is probably slightly less than 10,000 years old (David Bulbeck (2002) personal communication).

20. **these kinds of tools** (i.e. Mode 1/Chopper-chopping tool complex): see Shutler, R. Jr (1995) 'Hominid cultural evolution as seen from the archaeological evidence in Southeast Asia', Conference papers on Archaeology in Southeast Asia, Publ. Hong Kong University Museum, Hong Kong, 1995. In this paper Shutler discounts the very early dates of the Pacitanian stone tool culture in Java. In Bowdler's reviews (e.g. op. cit.) she also seems to argue that the appearance of any tools in Southeast Asia and the Antipodes coincides with the

appearance of modern humans in the region. It has been claimed that Cabengian and Pacitanian artefacts from, respectively, Sulawesi and Java may indicate modern human migrations in Island Southeast Asia by at least 74,000 years ago: Keates, S. and Bartstra, G.-J. (2001) 'Observations on Cabengian and Pacitanian artefacts from Island Southeast Asia', *Quärtar*, Band **51/52**: 9–32.

21. Bellwood op. cit. pp. 68, 160, 168, 316.

22. Geochemical analysis shows that the Kota Tampan ash belongs to the great 74,000-year-old eruption that also covered India – Shane, P. et al. (1995) 'New geochemical evidence for the youngest Toba tuff in India' *Quaternary Research* **44**: 200–204; Westgate, J.A. et al. (1998) 'All Toba tephra occurrences across peninsular India belong to the 75,000 year bp eruption' *Quaternary Research* **50**: 107–12; Acharya, S.K. and Basu, P.K. (1993) 'Toba ash on the Indian subcontinent and its implications for correlation of Late Pleistocene alluvium' *Quaternary Research* **40**: 10–19. Acharya and Basu note that both Middle and Upper Palaeolithic tools occur in Toba ash-bearing deposits.

23. **Some argue**: see e.g. the discussion in Bulbeck, D. (1996) 'Holocene biological evolution of the Malay Peninsula aborigines (Orang Asli)' *Perspectives in Human Biology* **2**: 37–61. **In the next chapter**: see also Bulbeck, D. (1999) 'Current biological research on Southeast Asia's Negritos' *SPAFA Journal* **9**(2): 14–22; Rayner, D. and Bulbeck, D. (2001) 'Dental morphology of the "Orang Asli" aborigines of the Malay Peninsula' in M. Henneberg (ed.) *Causes and Effects of Human Variation* (Australasian Society for Human Biology, University of Adelaide) pp. 19–41.

24. Hill et al. (2003) 'Mitochondrial DNA variation in the Orang Asli of the Malay Peninsula' (in press)

25. **A uranium date of 67,000 years**: +6000 −5000, Wu, X. (1992) 'The origin and dispersal of anatomically modern humans in East and Southeast Asia' in T. Akazawa et al. (eds) *The Evolution and Dispersal of Modern Humans in Asia* (Hokusen-sha, Tokyo) pp. 373–8. **but has been questioned**: Brown, P. (1999) 'The first modern East Asians? Another look at Upper Cave 101, Liujiang and Minatogawa 1' in K. Omoto (ed.) *Interdisciplinary Perspectives on the Origins of the Japanese* (International Research Center for Japanese Studies, Kyoto) pp. 105–30. **In December 2002, a Chinese group**: Shen Guanjun et al. (2002) 'U-series dating of Liujiang hominid site in Guanxi, Southern China' *Journal of Human Evolution* **43**: 817–29; see also the comment in *Science News Online* 21 December 2002. **Their preferred dating of 111,000–139,000 years ago**: Shen and colleagues (ibid.) go even further, suggesting that, if correct, the older dates could raise the possibility that the abortive exodus to the Levant 120,000 years ago may not have been quite so fruitless. The precise answer will have to wait for direct dating of the skull itself or of its calcite accretions.

26. **Several studies of Australian maternal clans**: See the discussion and references in note 4. **large studies of Y chromosomes**: Hammer, M.F. et al. (2001) 'Hierarchical patterns of global human Y-chromosome diversity' *Molecular Biology and Evolution* **18**(7): 1189–203; Underhill, P.A. et al. (2000) 'Y-chromosome sequence variation and the history of human populations' *Nature Genetics* **26**: 358–61; Kayser, M. et al. (2001) 'Independent histories of human Y chromosomes from Melanesia and Australia' *American Journal of Human Genetics* **68**: 173–90. But see the discussion on prehistoric mtDNA from robust human KS8 discussed in note 6. **same pattern is seen with genetic markers**: i.e. nuclear markers. The best

example of this is seen in a worldwide study of Alu inserts, where a neighbour-joining tree has one branch from Africa giving rise to the rest of the world, showing the Pakistanis, New Guineans, and Australians near the origin of this branch. If the Antipodes were populated by separate migrations, these would form a separate branch from the African root. See Fig. 2 in Stoneking, M. et al. (1997) 'Alu insertion polymorphisms and human evolution: Evidence for a larger population size in Africa' *Genome Research* **7**: 1061–71. For individual nuclear gene trees, see also Tishkoff, S.A. et al. (1996) 'Global patterns of linkage disequilibrium at the CD4 locus and modern human origins' *Science* **271**: 1380–97; Alonso, S. and Armour, J.A.L. (2001) 'A highly variable segment of human subterminal 16p reveals a history of population growth for modern humans outside Africa' *Proceedings of the National Academy of Sciences USA* **98**: 864–9. **dates estimated for the African L3 cluster expansion**: 77,000 ± 2,400 years, Watson, E. et al. (1997) 'Mitochondrial footprints of human expansions in Africa' *American Journal of Human Genetics* **61**: 691–704. This estimate can now be revised with improved resolution of the tree round the L3 node. A more up-to-date estimate of 83,000 years (Oppenheimer, S.J. unpublished, but again using calculation of 'rho') can be calculated by using complete sequence data from Ingman et al., op. cit. (The 'rho' methods average mutations in daughter branches and multiply by a calibrated constant – Forster, P. et al. (1996) 'Origin and evolution of Native American mtDNA variation: A reappraisal' *American Journal of Human Genetics* **59**: 935–45. and Saillard, J. et al. (2000) 'mtDNA variation among Greenland Eskimos: The edge of the Beringian expansion' *American Journal of Human Genetics* **67**: 718–26.) This method of estimation also shows that both M and N and the African branches of L3 and L1c re-expanded around 70,000 years ago, presumably after the world-wide effects of the Toba explosion (shown in Figure 8.2). See also the re-estimate of L3 at 83,500 years by an independent method based on maximum likelihood in Hill C. et al. (in preparation) op. cit.

27. **different frequencies outside Africa** (of DNA variants of functioning nuclear genes): For instance beta globin RFLP haplotypes see Wainscoat et al. (1986) 'Evolutionary relationships of human populations from an analysis of nuclear DNA polymophisms' *Nature* **319**: 491–3. For beta globin genes see Harding, R.M. et al. (1997) 'Archaic African *and* Asian lineages in the genetic ancestry of modern humans' *American Journal of Human Genetics* **60**: 772–89. For GM system see Walter, H. (1998) *Populationsgenetik der Blutgruppensystems des Menschen* (E. Schweizer'bartsche Verlagsbuchhandlung, Stuttgart). For X chromosome see Harris, E.E. and Hey, J. (1999) 'X chromosome evidence for ancient human histories' *Proceedings of the National Academy of Sciences USA* **96**: 3320–24. For dystrophin gene see Labuda, D. et al. (2000) 'Archaic lineages in the history of modern humans' *Genetics* **156**: 799–808. **The absence of specific extra packets**: e.g. Alu insertions, Stoneking et al. (1997) op. cit.

28. See especially Stoneking et al. (1997) op. cit.; Mountain, J.L. and Cavalli-Sforza, L.L. (1994) 'Inference of human evolution through cladistic analysis of nuclear DNA restriction polymorphisms' *Proceedings of the National Academy of Sciences USA* **91**: 6515–19. But also: (a) African beta globin RFLP haplotypes '– + – +' and '– – +' are found only in Oceania, Wainscoat et al., op. cit.; (b) African beta globin haplotypes C3 and A2 are found only in Papua New Guinea and Vanuatu, Harding et al. (1997) op. cit.; (c) Gm alleles 7 (and 6) are closest to African 8 and commonest in Sahul, while allele 7 is specific to Sahul – Table 5.2 of

Propert, D. (1989) 'Immunoglobin allotypes', in A.V.S. Hill and S.W. Serjeantson (eds) *The Colonization of the Pacific: A Genetic Trail* (Clarendon Press, Oxford) pp. 194–214; (d) X chromosome: A, B, O, and D are haplogroups shared between Africa and the rest of the world, Sahul has all haplogroups except B – Kaessmann, H. et al. (1999) 'DNA sequence variation in a non-coding region of low recombination on the human chromosome' *Nature Genetics* **22**: 78–81; (e) Chromosome 21: Oceania shares more haplotypes with Africa than does any other region – Li Jin et al., op. cit.

29. This paragraph, see: Fig. 2 in Stoneking et al. (1997) op. cit., southern Arabia being represented in this study by the United Arab Emirates. See also Fig. 2 in Watkins et al. (2001) op. cit.

30. **although some of these markers**: i.e. non-African 'L3*', Richards M. et al. (2003) 'Extensive female-mediated gene flow from sub-Saharan Africa into Near Eastern Arab populations' *American Journal of Human Genetics* **72**: 1058–64. **arrived from Africa more recently**: ancient Exodus types would be non-African and derived from L3, e.g. non-African L3*, M*, and N* super-clans; recent intrusions would include the 'older' specific African branches L1, L2, and African-specific L3 subgroups (for definitions/nomenclature see ibid. and Richards and Macaulay (2000) op. cit.; see also the mtDNA tree at end of this book Fig 8.2). What is clear is that, unlike North Africans and Levantines, the Hadramaut also carry roots and most of the primary branches of the Eurasian super-clans M and N (namely M*, M1, M2, M7, D, N1b, R1, R2, X, F, Pre-HV, HV1, H, U*,U2, U5, U7, J*, J1, J1b, J2, T*, T1, and K; data from Richards et al. (2003) op. cit. **a higher rate of the African ancestral types**: See Table 1 and Fig. 2 in Watkins et al. (2001) op. cit.

31. **shares some ancient mtDNA links**: i.e. both U/HV haplogroups as well as M haplogroup, e.g. U2i, U7, and Pre-HV, as well as M types: M*, M1, M2b, M4, and M-C. See Kivisild, T. et al. (1999a) 'The place of the Indian mitochondrial DNA variants in the global network of maternal lineages and the peopling of the Old World' in S.S. Papiha et al. (eds) *Genomic Diversity: Applications in Human Population Genetics* (Kluwer Academic/Plenum, New York) pp. 135–52. **They have an African Y-chromosome marker**: Hammer YAP+ Haplotype 5a defined by PN1, Mehdi, S.Q. et al. (1999) 'The origins of Pakistani populations: Evidence from Y chromosome markers' in S.S. Papiha et al. (eds) *Genome Diversity: Applications in Human Populations* (Kluwer Academic/Plenum, New York) pp. 83–91. Hammer argues that the presence of this haplotype (and its ancestral type) in Saudi Arabia, the United Arab Emirates, and Iran (and its virtual absence from Ethiopia) supports his view that the YAP+ mutation originally occurred outside Africa – Altheide, T.K. and Hammer, M.F. (1997) 'Evidence for a possible Asian Origin of YAP+ Y chromosomes' *American Journal of Human Genetics* **61**: 462–6. I agree, although the conventional opposite view – that this represents a more recent introduction by the slave trade from sub-Saharan Africa – is still possible. **Another unique Y-chromosome marker appears outside Africa only in this region**: Underhill Haplotype 12, Underhill et al., op. cit. **an early branch off the Out-of-Africa Adam**: Underhill Haplotypes 90–91, ibid.; consensus haplogroup L in Kivisild et al (2003) op. cit. and Wells R.S. et al. (2001) 'The Eurasian heartland: a continental perspective on Y-chromosome diversity' *Proceedings of the National Academy of Sciences USA* **98**: 10244–9.

32. **greatest genetic diversity of Rohani's western daughters**: Rohani types in an Iraqi
sample: H* (10), H(1–51) (17), HV* (8), HV1 (2), HV1a, HV1b, J* (6), J1 (3), J1b (5), J2,
K* (2), K2 (2), Pre-HV (5), R* (3), R1, R2, T* (3), T1 (5), T2, U* (5), U1a, U2 (2), U3 (5),
U3a, U4 (2), U5a1a, U6a*, U7 (3), U7a ($n = 116$). **unclassified root genetic types**: in
the foregoing list, an asterisk '*' indicates an unclassified paraphyletic haplotype. Data from
Richards, M. et al. (2000) 'Tracing European founder lineages in the Near Eastern mtDNA
pool' *American Journal of Human Genetics* **67**: 1251–76.

33. **for Rohani's Indian granddaughter U2i to be of a similar age**: For a comparison of
the diversity and age of Indian U types see Kivisild et al. (1999a) op. cit.; Kivisild, T. et al.
(1999b) 'Deep common ancestry of Indian and Western-Eurasian mitochondrial DNA lineages' *Current Biology* **9**: 1331–4. **several early non-African Y-chromosome genetic
groups**: in particular haplogroups 3 and 9, in: Quintana-Murci, L. et al. (2001) 'Y-
chromosome lineages trace diffusion of people and languages in Southwestern Asia' *American
Journal of Human Genetics* **68**: 537–42.

34. **Hadramaut . . . ratio . . . 5:1 Nasreen to Manju**: (Hadramaut see above, and note 30 – N
diversity also higher than M) – data from Richards et al. (2003) op. cit. **consistent with the
view that Nasreen originated farther west than Manju, in the Gulf region**: the
node type for N has not been found in India, Europe, or the Levant, although N* types have
been found in the Yemen and Tashkent – data from Thomas, M.G. et al. (2002) 'Founding
mothers of Jewish communities: Geographically separated Jewish groups were independently
founded by very few female ancestors' *American Journal of Human Genetics* **70**: 1411–20.
decreases to 2:1 in the far-western states: in the north-central/north-eastern regions
of the Punjab and Uttar Pradesh the ratio is 1:1, while in Andhra Pradesh on the east coast M
outnumbers N by 2:1, data from Kivisild et al. (1999a,b) op. cit. **Manju dominates at 5:1**:
data from ibid.

35. In Tibet, East Asian N subgroups A, B, and F constitute 31.5%, and East Asian M subgroups:
C, D, E, and G 36%, Torroni, A. et al. (1994) 'Mitochondrial DNA analysis in Tibet:
Implications for the origins of the Tibetan population and its adaptaton to high altitude'
American Journal of Physical Anthropology **93**: 189–99.

36. Bulbeck (1999) op. cit.

37. Much of this paragraph draws on Kivisild et al. (1999a, 2003) op. cit. **Manju achieves her
greatest diversity and antiquity in India**: Kivisild et al. (1999a,b, 2003) op. cit. **M2,
even dates to 73,000 years ago**: Kivisild et al (2003) op. cit. **M2 is strongly represented in the Chenchu**: ibid. **strong reasons for placing Manju's birth in India**: It
has been argued that M might have been born farther west, in Ethiopia, on the basis of a single
sub-branch, 'M1', found there with high diversity – Quintana-Murci, L. et al. (1999)
'Genetic evidence for an early exit of *Homo sapiens sapiens* from Africa through eastern Africa'
Nature Genetics **23**: 437–41. Closer inspection of Ethiopia shows no non-M1 branches or M
root (underived), nor her sister N's roots. Further, when M1 is dated in Ethiopia on the basis
of local diversity, it turns out that her age is only about 12,500 years – Kivisild, T. et al. 'A
likely post-LGM impact of Western Asian maternal lineages to Eastern Africans' abstract,
Cold Spring Harbor Symposium on 'Human Origins and Disease' October 2000. This means
that the M1's age in Ethiopia is younger than the last glaciation, and she is therefore more
likely to be a single re-entrant from South Asia.

38. **a scattering of other Europa clans**: U1, U3 – U6; see: Kivisild et al. (2003) op. cit. **a scattering of her first-generation daughters**: X, I, and, in particular, W – Kivisild et al. (1999a,b, 2003) op. cit.

39. **mother to most Westerners**: including the HV and JT clans, Kivisild, T. et al. (1999a,b) op. cit., Kivisild et al. (2002) 'The emerging limbs and twigs of the East Asian mtDNA tree' *Molecular Biology and Evolution* **19**(10): 1737–51, Kivisild et al. (2003) op. cit. **two Far Eastern daughters**: Haplogroups F and B, see the full gene network in Richards and Macaulay (2000) op. cit. **73,000 years ago**: Kivisild et al. (2003) op. cit.

40. Kivisild et al. (2003) op. cit.

41. **[Out-of-Africa] Adam's root line [absent] outside Africa**: would be defined as 'M168*' in Underhill et al., op. cit., but *all* members of the M168 clade belong to one of the three branches. **Cain, Abel, and Seth**: respectively M130 (C or RPS4Y), M1 (D'E or YAP), and M89 (or F), ibid. These three lines and their descendants are labelled by at least six different numbering systems by different scientists, so we need to give them some recognizable and consistent names. I have chosen to use the marker system (except when referring to individual haplotypes defined in cited papers in the endnotes) and haplotypes identified in The Y Chromosome Consortium (2002) 'A nomenclature system for the tree of human Y-chromosomal binary haplogroups' *Genome Research* **12**: 339–48. In the main text, as shown, I name the main branches, generally using the consensus lettering as a cue for the first letter – except in the case of Abel and Seth.

42. **One of these three root branches, C (or RPS4Y)**: M130. For the label 'Consensus type C/Cain', see the explanation above. **Cain is present at an even rate**: Kivisild et al. (2003) op. cit. **F nearly exclusively non-African with the exception of several root types**: Haplotypes 50, 58, and 71 (Underhill et al., op. cit.); Haplotype 71 is the root M89/Seth type (Consensus type F) and also appears infrequently in Sudan and Ethiopia (Haplotypes 58 and 71 are also found in India). All three haplotypes are found in Morocco (Underhill et al., op. cit.), which has a large European genetic admixture of recent origin that explains this exception. Admixture: See Rando, J.C. et al. (1998) 'Mitochondrial DNA analysis of North-west African populations reveals genetic exchanges with European, near-Eastern, and sub-Saharan populations' *Annals of Human Genetics* **62**: 531–50. For the label 'F/Seth' in place of M89, see the explanation in note 41. **high rates in Australia and New Guinea**: Kayser, M. et al. (2001) 'Independent histories of human Y chromosomes from Melanesia and Australia' *American Journal of Human Genetics* **68**: 173–90. **He accounts for 95–98 per cent of Indian male lines**: Fig. 3 in Kivisild et al. (2003) op. cit.

43. **Two of these are offspring of group K, or Krishna**: 2 Krishna sons Consensus classified respectively as L1 (which is commonest in Tamil Nadu in South India – Wells et al., op. cit. – and is also found in the Greater Andaman Islands – Chapter 5 note 44) and R2 (which is commonest farther to the east, in West Bengal) see Kivisild et al. (2003) op. cit. **third is a first-degree branch from Seth**: defined by M69 and including mainly Consensus sub-group H1, but also H* and H2, Kivisild et al. (2003) op. cit. **three types feature strongly**: Kivisild et al. (2003) op. cit.; Wells et al., op. cit. **a root Seth type in a quarter of their population, restricted to the Indian subcontinent**: F* in Kivisild et al. (2003) op. cit.

44. **another view of out-of-Africa**: Underhill, P.A. et al. (2001a) 'The phylogeography of Y-chromosome binary haplotypes and the origins of modern human populations' *Annals of Human Genetics* **65**: 43–62. **This type is M17**: data from Kivisild et al. (2003) op. cit.; Quintana-Murci, L. et al.; Wells et al., op. cit.

45. **a small, deep, early Asian branch**: 'Asian YAP': Consensus type D, Haplotypes 40–43, nodal haplotype 40, Underhill haplogroup IV (Underhill et al. (2000) op. cit) but see also Underhill et al. (2001a) op. cit. **The other, western YAP branch**: Consensus type E, Underhill haplotypes 19–39. See also above, note 31 - (Mehdi, S.Q. et al., op. cit.) **commonest back in Africa**: Underhill haplotypes 19–30; but see also Underhill et al. (2001a) op. cit., where they are also defined by PN2 and PN1 (Haplotypes 20–27). **characteristic of the Middle East**: Underhill haplotypes 31–39; but see also Underhill et al. (2001a) op. cit., where they are further defined by PN2 M35 (Underhill (2001) Haplotypes 29–38); YAP+ types in general are notably lacking in the Khoisan, except for a small number of the two commonest haplotypes with the PN2 marker. This could be consistent with an ancient YAP intrusion to Africa from the Middle East (as per Hammer's back-to-Africa YAP hypothesis) with subsequent expansion during the Neolithic and only minimal intrusion to hunter-gatherer populations.

46. e.g. Underhill et al. (2001a) op. cit.

47. i.e. mtDNA types: M1, and pre-HV; Y chromosome types: YAP+ Underhill haplotypes, especially 19–30.

48. Trask, R.L. (1996) *Historical Linguistics* (Arnold, London) p. 377.

49. Kivisild et al. (2000) op. cit.

50. **his complete absence from India**: Kivisild et al. (2003) op. cit.; Wells et al., op. cit. **[Central] Asian YAP at rates of 3–6 per cent**: Wells et al., op. cit. **much lower rates there [India] than in Central Asia**: Kivisild et al. (2003), op. cit.; Wells et al., op. cit.

51. **in Australia he is the dominant line**: Kayser, M. et al. (2001) op. cit. **Eastern Indonesia . . . the least changed or root Cain type**: Underhill, P.A. et al. (2001b) 'Maori origins, Y chromosome haplotypes and implications for human history in the Pacific' *Human Mutation* **17**: 271–80. **From which the unique Australian type is derived**: Haplotypes 2 (M210) in Underhill et al. (2001b) op. cit. **other place . . . root Cain type is found is India . . . Australoid tribal groups**: C* in Fig. 3 in Kivisild et al. (2003) op. cit. **On the neighbouring island of New Guinea**: Capelli, C. et al. (2001) 'A predominantly indigenous paternal heritage for the Austronesian-speaking peoples of insular Southeast Asia and Oceania' *American Journal of Human Genetics* **68**: 432–3; Kayser, M. et al. (2000) 'Melanesian origin of Polynesian Y chromosomes' *Current Biology* **10**: 1237–46; Haplotype 3 (M38) in Underhill et al. (2001b) op. cit. **A breakdown of Cain frequency**: Kayser, M. et al. (2000, 2001) op. cit.; Karafet, T.M. et al. (1999) 'Ancestral Asian source(s) of New World Y-chromosome founder haplotypes' *American Journal of Human Genetics* **64**: 817–31. **Asian types mainly belong to one derived clan**: M217 (Consensus group C3), Underhill et al. (2001b) op. cit.

52. **one of the two remaining founding male types**: Consensus type F/Seth = M89 base in Kayser et al. (2001) op. cit. **Seth in his ancestral or root form in all these areas**: the black shaded areas in Fig. 1 of ibid. **Krishna [at 30%] throughout Southeast Asia and Australia**: the gray shaded areas in Fig. 1 of ibid. **The third root Y line, the Asian YAP**:

Karafet et al. (1999) op. cit.; Bing Su et al. (1999) 'Y-chromosome evidence for a northward migration of modern humans into Eastern Asia during the last ice age' *American Journal of Human Genetics* **65**: 1718–24.

53. **Root and branch for Cain, Seth, and Seth's genetic sons and grandsons [in Pakistan and/or India]**: Consensus type C/Cain (RPS4Y): Haplotype 46; Consensus type F/Seth (M89): Haplotype 71; F/Seth's derivatives: M89/M172 Haplotypes 56–58, 60, 61, and 64; M89/M52 Haplotypes 65, 67, and 68; M89/M9 Haplotype 87; M89/M9/M175/ M122 Haplotypes 78 and 79; M89/M9/M70 Haplotype 88; M89/M9/M147 Haplotype 89; M89/M9/M11 Haplotypes 90 and 91; M89/M9/M45 Haplotypes 111 and 113; M89/M9/ M45/M173 Haplotype 104; M89/M9/M45/M173/M17 Haplotypes 108 and 106 – all in Underhill et al. (2000) op. cit. **several unique [western] YAP types**: Haplotypes 31 and 34, Underhill et al. (2000) op. cit. In addition to these unique YAP haplotypes which may support the Hammer hypothesis of YAP outside Africa, there are representatives from an African clan, Haplotype 12, found in India and Pakistan.

54. Fig. 2 in Metspalu, E. et al. (1999) 'The Trans-Caucasus and the expansion of the Caucasoid-specific mitochondrial DNA' in S.S. Papiha, et al. (eds), *Genomic Diversity: Applications in Human Population Genetics* (Kluwer Academic/Plenum, New York) pp. 121–34.

Chapter 5

1. Dunbar, R.I.M. (1992) 'Neocortex size as a constraint on group size in primates' *Journal of Human Evolution* **20**: 469–93.

2. Jablonski, N. and Chaplin, G. (2000) 'The evolution of human skin coloration' *Journal of Human Evolution* **39**: 57–106.

3. **selective pressure to remain dark-skinned**: e.g. seen as differential selection at the MC1R locus, which explains a substantial phenotypic component of melanin production – Harding, R. et al. (2000) 'Evidence for variable selective pressures at MC1R' *American Journal of Human Genetics* **66**: 1351–61. **tuned to local relative levels of ultraviolet light**: Jablonski and Chaplin op. cit.

4. For an in-depth study of modern human cranial variation, see Lahr, M. (1996) *The Evolution of Modern Human Diversity: A Study of Cranial Variation* (Cambridge University Press); for Mongoloid superficial features and a discussion of northern and southern Mongoloids, see ibid. pp. 316–20.

5. **physically somewhat nearer to the first out-of-Africa people**: Bulbeck, D. (1999) 'Current biological anthropological research on Southeast Asia's Negritos' *SPAFA Journal* **9**(2): 15–22. **skulls of 100,000 years ago**: Brown, P. (1999) 'The first modern East Asians? Another look at Upper Cave 101, Liujiang and Minatogawa 1' in K. Omoto (ed.) *Interdisciplinary Perspectives on the Origins of the Japanese* (International Research Center for Japanese Studies, Kyoto) pp. 105–30; see also Bulbeck op. cit.

6. Bulbeck op. cit.

7. For a comparative discussion see Lahr op. cit.

8. Ulijaszek, S. (2001) 'Ethnic differences in patterns of human growth in stature' in R. Martorell and F. Haschke (eds) *Nutrition and Growth*, Nestlé Nutrition Workshop Series, Pediatric Program, Vol. 47 (Lippincott Williams & Wilkins, Philadelphia) pp. 1–15; Ulijaszek,

S. (1994) 'Between-population variation in pre-adolescent growth' *European Journal of Clinical Nutrition* **48**(suppl.1): S5–S14.

9. **Australian skull reduction**: Lahr op. cit. **fossil skulls from Australia were actually gracile, Australians as somewhat 'changed'**: for other reasons for recent Australian Aboriginals not to look like the first colonizers see the discussion in endnote 6, in Chapter 4.

10. **Tierra del Fuegans**: Lahr op. cit. **the Ainu**: ibid. p. 319.

11. **marked shortening of the skull**: ibid. **This is most pronounced in Neolithic populations**: Ishida, H. and Dodo, Y. (1996) 'Cranial morphology of the Siberians and East Asians' in A. Takeru and E. Szathmary (eds) *Prehistoric Mongoloid Dispersal* (Oxford University Press) pp. 113–24; see also Hanihara, T. (2000) 'Frontal and facial flatness of major human populations' *American Journal of Physical Anthropology* **111**: 105–34.

12. **first modern human arrival in China**: see the discussion of the new minimum 68,000 year age of the Liujiang skull in Chapter 4; but see also the discussion of Liujiang and Upper Cave 101 skulls in Brown op. cit. Upper Palaeolithic technology and modern human remains appear at the northern Chinese site of Salawusu between 35,000 and 50,000 years ago – Chen, C. and Olsen, J.W. (1990) 'China at the Last Glacial Maximum' in C. Gamble and O. Soffer (eds) *The World at 18,000 bp* Vol. 1 (Unwin Hyman, London) pp. 276–95. **earliest undisputed Mongoloid remains**: Brown op. cit. **an isolated find of disputed significance**: described as 'a portion of frontal bone identified as having affinities to East Asians because of its flat upper nasal regions' in Wolpoff, M.H. (1999) *Paleoanthropology* (McGraw-Hill, New York) p. 740; and discussed by Alekseev, V. (1998) 'The physical specificities of Paleolithic hominids in Siberia' in A.P. Derev'anko (ed.) *The Paleolithic of Siberia: New Discoveries and Interpretations* (University of Illinois Press, Urbana) pp. 329–35. It should be noted that several other old East Asian skulls have been claimed to have 'pre-Mongoloid' status. The Okinawan Minatogawa skull (16,600–18,250 years old) has a remarkably flat nasal saddle too. These skulls differ from modern Mongoloid populations in many other respects (see the discussion in Brown op. cit.). So, although the flat nasal saddle trait may be a feature, it is not clear how discriminating it is for Mongoloids.

13. **retention of several ancestral skeletal traits in modern Europeans: Lahr op. cit. [Europeans . . . southern Indians . . . Semang . . . New Guineans] retained more African ancestral dental [features]**: Rayner, D. and Bulbeck, D. (2001) 'Dental morphology of the "Orang Asli" aborigines of the Malay Peninsula' in M. Henneberg (ed.) *Causes and Effects of Human Variation* (Australasian Society for Human Biology, The University of Adelaide) pp. 19–41. **and cranial features**: A recent craniometric study identified a cluster consisting of Andamanese, Semang, South Indian Tamils, and coastal New Guineans which hints at the retention of certain ancestral skull features as well as dental features – Bulbeck op. cit.

14. **Aboriginal Malay peoples**: also known as Proto-Malay, based on an old theory that two waves of Malays entered the region, see Carey, I. (1976) *Orang Asli: the aboriginal tribes of peninsular Malaysia* (Oxford University Press, Kuala Lumpur). **various remnant Pacific Rim populations such as the aboriginal Ainu in Japan**: Hanihara, T. et al. (1998) 'Place of the Hokkaido Ainu (Northern Japan) among peoples of the world' *International Journal of Circumpolar Health* **57**: 257–75, here pp. 273–4.

15. See Hanihara (1992) op. cit. on claims for Sundadonty in Australia. Australians' robusticity

and their dental and hair changes could all potentially be explained on the basis of (contentious) secondary, robust colonizations of Australia from Southeast Asia within the last 20,000 years (Wolpoff (1999) op. cit. p. 740). Birdsell suggested as many as three successive colonizations into Australia: a first of 'Oceanic Negritos' or Barrineans, last represented by the now extinct Tasmanians, a second of Ainu-like Murrayians, and a third of Veddoid-like Carpentarians – Birdsell, J.B. (1977) 'The recalibration of a paradigm for the first peopling of Greater Australia' in J. Allen et al. (eds) *Sunda and Sahul* (Academic Press, London), pp. 113–67. There is some archaeological and genetic support for a much more recent such intrusion during the Holocene, but the cultural impact would have been greater than the genetic one, which was relatively minor –Oppenheimer, S.J. (1998) *Eden in the East* (Weidenfeld & Nicolson, London), pp. 203–4. While secondary colonizations of Australia are out of fashion at present, and Birdsell's and Wolpoff's views are in the minority, I suspect the issue will not go away and that genetic evidence may yet provide support for several colonizations by different routes.

16. Sundadonty/Sinodonty may be an artificial categorization of a continuum. See on the one hand discussion in: Hanihara, T. (1992) 'Negritos, Australian Aborigines, and the "Proto-Sundadont" dental pattern: The basic populations in East Asia, V' *American Journal of Physical Anthropology* **88**: 183–96; see also: Scott, G.R. and Turner II, C.G. (1997) *The Anthropology of Modern Human Teeth* (Cambridge University Press). Rayner and Bulbeck (op. cit.), on the other hand, clearly regard the discrete distinction between Sundadonty and Sinodonty as artificial. They suggest more of a clinal continuum, with Sundadonty being intermediate between the undifferentiated circum-Indian Ocean type and Sinodonty. The south–north Asian cline is still preserved in this view. They also argue for a more complex variation between these Pacific Rim peoples. Although I agree with Rayner and Bulbeck on this, I continue to use the terms Sinodont and Sundadont for simplicity.

17. **genetic evidence Northern and Southern Mongoloid populations can indeed be separated**: Yong-Gang Yao et al. (2002) 'Phylogeographic differentiation of mitochondrial DNA in Han Chinese' *American Journal of Human Genetics* **70**: 635–51. **children in the south, although well nourished, are smaller than those from Beijing in the north**: Leung, S. (1990) 'Auxological and nutritional status of Hong Kong Chinese infants: Birth to two years' MD Thesis, Chinese University of Hong Kong. It may be thought that smallness and gracility are Mongoloid features. However, if Northern Mongoloids represent an exaggeration of Southern Mongoloid features, we should expect them to be smaller and more gracile rather than larger and more robust, but it should be borne in mind that Northern Mongoloid populations are admixed with Central Asian groups related to West Eurasians, as discussed later in this chapter.

18. **The other theory [adaptation to cold]**: Ishida and Dodo op. cit.; see also Coon, C.S. (1962) *The Origin of Races* (Alfred A. Knopf, New York); Akazawa, T. (1996) 'Introduction: Human evolution, dispersal, and adaptive strategies' in T. Akazawa and E. Szathmary (eds) *Prehistoric Mongoloid Dispersal* (Oxford University Press); and Guthrie, D. (1996) 'The Mammoth Steppe and the origin of Mongoloids and their dispersal' in Akazawa and Szathmary op. cit. **Guthrie has persuasively described**: Guthrie op. cit.

19. Hanihara (2000) op. cit. p. 117.

20. Ishida and Dodo op. cit. An alternative view (see Fig. 8 in Hanihara (2000) op. cit.) is that these groups have retained an ancestral *Homo sapiens* condition with regard to facial flatness, even while upper facial breadths have dramatically decreased and jaw size has just as dramatically decreased.

21. e.g. Montagu, A. (1989) *Growing Young* (McGraw-Hill, New York) p. 40; see also Gould, S.J. (1977) *Ontegeny and Phylogeny* (Belknap Press, Cambridge, MA). For those who are interested in more recent serious literature on the interactions, positive and negative, of neoteny and human evolution, see: Bemporad, J.R. (1991) 'Dementia Praecox as a failure of Neoteny' *Theoretical Medicine* **12**: 45-51; Crow, T.J. (2002) 'Sexual Selection, Timing and an X-Y Homologous gene: did *Homo sapiens* Speciate on the Y Chromosome' *Proceedings of the British Academy,* **106**: 197-216. Several rather heuristic 'reviews' on this theory may be found at www.neoteny.org/a/stephenjgould.html and www.humanevolution.net/a/asianoriental.html

22. Chou, A. (2001) 'Migration of early hominids during the Pleistocene', paper presented at the Paleoanthropology Society Annual Meeting, 27–28 March 2001, Kansas City, Missouri.

23. **arrived there by 43,000 years ago . . .**: Goebel, T. et al. (1993) 'Dating the Middle-to-Upper-Palaeolithic transition at Kara Bom' *Current Anthropology* **34**: 452–8 **Upper Palaeolithic transition across southern Siberia**: Goebel, T. and Aksenov, M. (1995) 'Accelerator radiocarbon dating of the initial Upper Palaeolithic in southeast Siberia' *Antiquity* **69**: 349–57.

24. Otte, M. and Derevianko, A. (2001) 'The Aurignacian in Altai' *Antiquity* **75**: 44–8; Kozlowski, J.K. and Otte, M. (2000) 'The formation of the Aurignacian in Europe' *Journal of Archaeological Research* **56**: 513–33; Otte, M. (2000) 'The history of European populations as seen by archaeology' in C. Renfrew and K. Boyle (eds) *Archaeogenetics: DNA and the Population Prehistory of Europe* (MacDonald Institute for Archaeological Research, Cambridge) pp. 139–41; and Otte, M. (2003) 'The Aurignacian in Asia' (in press) citing inter alia to Olszewski, D.I. and Dibble, H.L. (1994) 'The Zagros Aurignacian' *Current Anthropology* **35**(1): 68–75.

25. Goebel et al., op. cit.; Otte and Derevianko op. cit.

26. **The caves in the Russian Altai show . . . Middle Palaeolithic tradition underlying**: Otte, M. and Derevianko, A. (1996) 'Transformations techniques au Paléolithique de l'Altai (Sibérie)' *Anthropologie et Préhistoire* **107**: 131–43. **continuous indigenous graded change towards the later technology or . . . intrusive[?]**: Otte and Derevianko (1996) op. cit. **earlier modern human occupation of the Altai[?]**: Goebel and Aksenov op. cit. p. 356; Goebel et al., op. cit.; see also Derevianko, A.P. et al. (2000) *Archaeological Studies Carried out by the Joint Russian–Mongolian–American Expedition in Mongolia in 1997–98* (Institute of Archaeology and Ethnography, Novosibirsk) pp. 161, 168.

27. **Middle Palaeolithic tradition**: Blackwell, B.A.B. et al. (1998) 'ESR (Electron Spin Resonance) dating the Palaeolithic site at Tsagaan Agui, Mongolia', Proceedings of the 31st International Symposium on Archaeometry, 27 April–1 May 1998, Budapest. **Upper Palaeolithic (microlithic) traditions**: Tang Hui Sheng (1995) 'Lithic industries of the Qinghai-Tibetan Plateau' *The Artefact* **18**: 3–11.

28. Soffer, O. (1993) 'Upper Paleolithic adaptations in Central and Eastern Europe and man–mammoth interactions' in O. Soffer and N.D. Praslov (eds) *From Kostenki to Clovis: Upper Paleolithic-Paleo-Indian Adaptations* (Plenum Press, New York) pp. 33–49.

29. Cavalli-Sforza, L. et al. (1994) *The History and Geography of Human Genes* (Princetown University Press, Princetown) pp. 223–38.

30. Chan Wing-hoi (1995) 'Ordination names in Hakka genealogies: A religious practice and its decline' in D. Faure and H. Siu (eds) *Down to Earth: The Territorial Bond in South China* (Stanford University Press, Stanford) pp. 65–82. The myth of a homogenous mix throughout China is still promoted for whatever reason (see e.g. Yuan-Chun Ding et al. (2000) 'Population structure and history in East Asia' *Proceedings of the National Academy of Sciences USA* **97**: 14003–6) and then demolished, sometimes by the same authors (see e.g. Yong-Gang Yao et al., op. cit.

31. Su, B. et al. (1999) 'Y-chromosome evidence for a northward migration of modern humans into East Asia during the last ice age' *American Journal of Human Genetics* **65**: 1718–24.

32. **palaeoclimatological studies**: see the maps at http://www.esd.ornl.gov/projects/qen/NEW_MAPS/eurasia1.gif and http://www.esd.ornl.gov/projects/qen/euras(2.gif **deep genetic diversity of south-west Central Asia**: see Fig. 2 in Metspalu, E. et al. (1999) 'The Trans-Caucasus and the expansion of the Caucasoid-specific mitochondrial DNA' in S.S. Papiha et al. (eds) *Genomic Diversity: Applications in Human Population Genetics* (Kluwer Academic/Plenum, New York) pp. 121–34. See specific maps on Jonathan Adams' ESD ORNL reference website: www.esd.ornl.gov/projects/qen/euras18k.gif and www.esd.ornl.gov/projects/qen/euras(2.gif. See also the archaeological evidence presented in the next chapter.

33. Groups A and X are first-generation from N/Nasreen, while B and F derive from Nasreen through Rohani. Groups C, D, E, G, and Z all derive directly from M/Manju (see Figures 5.9 and 5.10). The first full description of Groups A to G all shown on one tree was by Torroni, A. et al. (1994) 'Mitochondrial DNA analysis in Tibet: Implications for the origins of the Tibetan population and its adaptaton to high altitude' *American Journal of Physical Anthropology* **93**: 189–99. For the first naming of Group X, see Forster, P. et al. (1996) 'Origin and evolution of Native American mtDNA variation: A reappraisal' *American Journal of Human Genetics* **59**: 935–45. A further group, Y, appears almost exclusively among the Nivkhs of Sakhalin Island in the north; it is a very young group, and therefore peripheral to this discussion (see below). For Groups Y and Z and the most recent published updates of the Asian mtDNA tree, see Kivisild, T. et al. (2002) 'The emerging limbs and twigs of the East Asian mtDNA tree' *Molecular Biology and Evolution* **19**(10): 1737–51; Yong-Gang Yao et al., op. cit.; and Fig. 2 in Forster, P. et al. (2003) 'Asian and Papuan mtDNA evolution' in P. Bellwood and C. Renfrew (eds) *Examining the Farming/Language Dispersal Hypothesis* (McDonald Institute for Archaeological Research, Cambridge) pp. 89–98.

The first task is to identify distinct northern and southern genetic lines among Mongoloid populations. C and Z are both related M types (on newly identified parent group M8, Yong-Gang Yao et al., op. cit.), and are found almost entirely in North Asia (and C also in the Americas), and not in Southern Mongoloids. A, although common in north-east China, north-east Siberia, and North America (Kolman, C.J. et al. (1996) 'Mitochondrial DNA analysis of Mongolian populations and implications for the origin of New World founders' *Genetics* **142**: 1321–34) is also found at appreciable frequencies and diversity in south and south-west China, Tibet, and Xinjiang (Yong-Gang Yao et al., op. cit.), but is absent from India and West Eurasia (Kivisild, T. et al. (1999) 'The place of the Indian mitochondrial DNA variants in the global network of maternal lineages and the peopling of the Old World' in S.S. Papiha et al. (eds) *Genomic Diversity: Applications in Human Population Genetics* (Kluwer Academic/Plenum, New York), pp. 135–52). So, a south-west China source, with movement up the Yangtzi to Tibet and thence to Central and North Asia, seems more likely for the A group origins than either an Indian or North Asian source. Y, a daughter of N, is found only in Northeast Asia (Stariovskaya, Y.B. et al. (1998) 'mtDNA diversity in Chukchi and Siberian Eskimos: Implications for the genetic history of Ancient Beringia and the peopling of the New World' *American Journal of Human Genetics* **63**: 1473–91; Torroni, A. et al. (1993) 'mtDNA variation of aboriginal Siberians reveals distinct genetic affinities with Native Americans' *American Journal of Human Genetics* **53**: 591–608). But Y has an age of only around 5,000 years, and is ultimately derived from a Southeast Asian N branch, N9. X, another daughter of N, is limited to Europeans and Americans (Brown, M. et al. (1998) 'mtDNA Haplogroup X: An ancient link between Europe/Western Asia and North America?' *American Journal of Human Genetics* **63**: 1852–61), and there is one reported instance in Siberians (see below). Although any of these three northern lines (C, X, and Z) could theoretically be characteristic Mongol-oid genetic lines, they are absent from Southern Mongoloids, and also are found in other populations, thus making this less likely. Several more Asian clades found throughout China have recently been added: three are from M (M7, M9 and M10) and a fourth is from N (N9, estimated age 64,300 ± 20,000 years and ancestral to Group Y): see Yong-Gang Yao et al., op. cit.

The two Asian granddaughters of N (B and F) are the only known East Asian offspring of R/Rohani (except for a newly described but ancient clade, R9, estimated age 81,000 years ± 24,600 years: see Yong-Gang Yao et al., op. cit., which has been shown to be ancestral to F in the south and thus has already been relabelled F4 in: Hill, C. et al. (2003) 'Mitochondrial DNA variation in the Orang Asli of the Malay Peninsula' (in preparation); See also Fig. 5.6). B and F have their greatest diversity and frequency in Southern Mongoloids of Southeast Asia (Torroni et al. (1994) op. cit.; Yong-Gang Yao et al., op. cit.). They are also both found north of the Himalayan barrier in Central Asia (Fig. 2 in Metspalu et al., op. cit), Mongolia (Kolman et al., op. cit.), and Tibet, Korea, and Japan (Torroni et al. (1994) op. cit.; Horai, S. et al. (1996) 'mtDNA polymorphism in East Asian populations' *American Journal of Human Genetics* **59**: 579–90). They are not, however, found farther north in Siberia in the Subarctic region. Of these southern lines, B is also found in America, although again below the Subarctic region (see Chapter 7). Since B and F are present on both sides of the Himalayas, they are potential candidate original Mongoloid lines, but there is still a question mark over whether they define all Mongoloids (F is absent from America).

We have looked at three Asian lines from the north and three Southeast Asian probables, so that leaves D, E and G. These daughters of M/Manju are potentially related at their origin (since they are all M's and share a mutation at the fast (unstable) site of 16362 – see Kivisild et al. (1999, 2002) op. cit.). D and G are widely distributed throughout the Mongoloid dispersal right down as far as Indo-China. Unique local versions of D are found at high rates throughout China, Japan, Mongolia, Tibet, Korea, Central and Northeast Asia, and the Americas (Torroni et al. (1994) op. cit.; Torroni, A. et al. (1993) 'Asian affinities and continental radiation of the four founding Native American mtDNAs' *American Journal of Human Genetics* **53**: 563–90; Kolman et al., op. cit.; Kivisild et al. (1999, 2002) op. cit.). Although found in southern

China, D is not a feature of Southeast Asia (Torroni et al. (1994) op. cit.). Unique versions of G are found in Central Asia (see Fig. 2 in Metspalu et al., op. cit.), Tibet (Torroni et al. (1994) op. cit.), the Ainu (Horai et al., op. cit.) and Northeast Asia (Torroni et al. (1994) op. cit). Group E has its own unique subgroup in Island Southeast Asia, and is also found in Tibet (Torroni's types 83, 89, 94, 104, 106, 109, and 119 – misidentified due to the presence of RFLP site at base 16517, Torroni et al. (1994) op. cit.; Fig. 2 in Metspalu et al., op. cit.). A newly described clade, M7 (age 61,000 ± 20,000 years) has a broad East Asian coastal distribution, like D but, like E, extends down into Southeast Asia: see Kivisild et al. (2002) op. cit.; Yong-Gang Yao et al., op. cit.

34. Data for Central Asia from Fig. 2 in Metspalu et al., op. cit.; for Tibet, Torroni et al. (1994) op. cit.; for Mongolia, Kolman et al., op. cit.; for China and Korea, Torroni et al. (1994) op. cit.

35. **age of four of these lines in Mongolia**: Kivisild et al. (1999) op. cit. (note that there is the possibility of carried-over diversity affecting local age estimates in Mongolia). **ages of the same lines farther south in China**: Table 3 in Yong-Gang Yao et al., op. cit. Note that in Yong-Gang Yao et al. individual branches of D and G age at 51,000–60,000 years, and these two haplogroups coalesce with M9/E even earlier (Kivisild et al. (2002) op. cit.).

36. Group B, with an estimated Asian age of about 75,000 years (74,600 ± 18,700 years, Yong-Gang Yao et al., op. cit.), achieves its highest frequencies in peoples of Southeast Asia, Oceania (excluding New Guinean highlanders and Australians), and the west Pacific coast.

37. For B and F diversity and antiquity in the south, see Ballinger, S.W. et al. (1992) 'Southeast Asian mitochondrial DNA analysis reveals genetic continuity of ancient Mongolid migrations' *Genetics* **130**: 139–52. Data also from Fucharoen, G. et al. (2001) 'Mitochondrial DNA polymorphisms in Thailand' *Journal of Human Genetics* **46**: 115–25; and Oota, H. et al. 'Extreme mtDNA homogeneity in continental Asian populations' *American Journal of Physical Anthropology* **118**: 146–53; see also Kivisild et al. (2002) op. cit.; Yong-Gang Yao et al., op. cit.: Groups B (estimated age 74,600 ± 18,700 years) and R9(F4) (estimated age 81,000 ± 24,600 years) which is ancestral to F in the south (see above in note 33). For the **newly identified pre-F haplogroup** now, by agreement re-classified as R9, see Hill, C. et al. op. cit. See Fig 5.5. The newly described M7 haplogroup mirrors B and F. M7 dates to 61,000 years, and its oldest branch, M7b, is a feature of Vietnamese populations – Kivisild et al. (2002) op. cit.

38. **two common subgroups of B**: The oldest in Mongolia (40,500 years), B1, is the dominant type throughout Southeast Asia, the Pacific, and the Americas. B1 is also the type found in Tibet – Kivisild et al. (1999) op. cit.; Torroni et al. (1994) op. cit. B1 and B2 are differentiated respectively by 16217 (now generally classified as B4) and 16243/16140 (now reclassified by Kivisild et al. (2002) op. cit. as B5b) in Kolman et al., op. cit. The younger of the two, B2 (33,500 years in Mongolia), features rather more than B1 on the west Pacific coast (Eastern China, Korea, Japan) – Horai, S. and Hayasaka, K. (1990) 'Intraspecific nucleotide sequence differences in the major non-coding region of human mitochondrial DNA' *American Journal of Human Genetics* **46**: 828–42; Nishimaki, Y. et al. (1999) 'Sequence polymorphism in the mtDNA HV1 region in Japanese and Chinese' *Legal Medicine* **1**: 238–49; Horai et al. (1996), op. cit; Seo, Y.B. et al. (1998) 'Sequence polymorphism of mitochondrial DNA

Notes (pp. 234–8)

control region in Japanese' *Forensic Science International* **97**: 155–64. **both B types during the Palaeolithic**: Fig. 2 in Metspalu et al., op. cit.

39. **three partly related Manju lines D, E, and G**: the most dominant of these, D at 44,500 years (Kivisild et al. (1999) op. cit.), is commonest in Siberia, and is present in South China and the whole of the Americas but not Southeast Asia, i.e. Sundaland (Torroni et al. (1994) op. cit.). D is also present at low rates in India (Kivisild et al. (1999) op. cit.). D and E are also common in western Central Asia (Fig. 2 in Metspalu et al., op. cit.; for E see Ballinger et al., op. cit). A variant of E known to occur in Korea is found commonly in Southeast Asia, raising the possibility that the ancestor of this group also ultimately came from the south. There is also a link between G and unique Semang M group M21c, again suggesting a possible ultimate southern source for this group (non-coding site 5108 in Hill et al., op. cit.). **sister branches C and Z reach their highest rates**: Kolman et al., op. cit.; Bamshad, M. et al. (1999) 'Genetic evidence on the origins of Indian caste populations' *Genome Research* **11**: 994–1004; Yong-Gang Yao et al., op. cit.; Kivisild et al. (2002) op. cit. **Groups C and Z in India, Turkey, Central Asia, and Mongolia**: Kivisild et al. (1999) op. cit. (C only in India), Bamshad et al., op. cit. **age of C in Mongolia**: Kivisild et al. (1999) op. cit. .

40. X: **a single report from southern Siberia**: Derenko, M.V. et al. (2001) 'The presence of mitochondrial Haplogroup X in Altaians from South Siberia' *American Journal of Human Genetics* **69**: 237–41. **up to 30,000 years old**: Brown et al., op. cit.

41. D/E, C, and F are the new consensus names respectively for YAP+, RPS4Y/M216, and M89 – see The Y Chromosome Consortium (2002) 'A nomenclature system for the tree of human Y-chromosomal binary haplogroups' *Genome Research* **12**: 339–48.

42. **Eastern Indonesia, Australia, and New Guinea**: Haplotype 48 to eastern Indonesia and New Guinea, and Haplotype 49 to Australia; **around the Indo-Pacific coast to Japan**: Haplotype 50; **a unique progenitor Asian son**: M217 or Haplotype 52, giving rise to Haplotypes 51 and 53 – all haplotypes in Underhill, P.A. et al. (2001) 'The phylogeography of Y-chromosome binary haplotypes and the origins of modern human populations' *Annals of Human Genetics* **65**: 43–62. **into Mongolia and Central Asia**: Haplogroups 21–26 and 31–34, respectively, Karafet, T.M. et al. (1999) 'Ancestral Asian source(s) of New World Y-chromosome founder haplotypes' *American Journal of Human Genetics* **64**: 817–31. **into the Americas**: ibid.; Underhill et al., op. cit.; Underhill, P.A. et al. (2000) 'Y-chromosome sequence variation and the history of human populations' *Nature Genetics* **26**: 358–61.

43. **no further north than Korea**: Karafet et al., op. cit. **Mongolia and the Russian Altai**: Data in ibid.; see also data in Bing Su et al. (1999) 'Y-chromosome evidence for a northward migration of modern humans into Eastern Asia during the last ice age' *American Journal of Human Genetics* **65**: 1718–24.

44. **12,127 Asians and Pacific islanders**: M89 (defines Consensus group F/Seth) in Ke, Y. et al. (2001) 'African origin of modern humans in East Asia: A tale of 12,000 Y chromosomes' *Science* **292**: 1151–2. This paper incidentally also shows that all these 12,127 Asians share the M168 Out-of-Africa Adam mutation as do 99.9% of other non-Africans. **as several geneticists have suggested**: The view that Seth came as a later exodus from Africa is elaborated in Underhill et al. (2001) op. cit. For **Seth types, in relict beachcomber populations**: See (a) M89 (consensus Group F) 23% and M95 (consensus Group O) 65% respectively in Orang Asli aboriginals of the Malay Peninsula – see data in Bing Su et al. (2000) 'Polynesian

origins: Insights from the Y chromosome' *Proceedings of the National Academy of Sciences USA* **97**: 8225–8; (b) M9 (consensus Group K including Subgroups O, L, and P) 100% in Greater Andamans, while Asian YAP+ (Cain or consensus Group D) 100% in other Andaman Islanders – see data in Thangaraj, K. et al. (2002) 'Genetic affinities of the Andaman Islanders, a vanishing human population' *Current Biology* (published online 26 November); (c) M9, 98% in Australoid tribal groups in India: Chenchus and Koyas – see data in Kivisild et al. (2002) op. cit.; (d) M9, 35% in Australians and 94% in New Guinea Highlanders – see data in Kayser, M. et al. (2001) 'Independent histories of human Y chromosomes from Melanesia and Australia' *American Journal of Human Genetics* **68**: 173–90.

45. **Seth represents a quarter of all Indian Y chromosomes and his sons most of the rest**: For Seth see Fig. 1 and Table 1 in Hammer, M.F. et al. (2001) 'Hierarchical patterns of global human Y-chromosome diversity' *Molecular Biology and Evolution* **18**(7): 1189–1203; for representatives of Seth's sons, Haplotypes 19–24, see Fig. 1, ibid.

46. Hammer et al. (2001), op. cit., Haplotypes 20–23, see also Fig. 1, ibid. See also Chapters 3 and 4. Consensus group F/Seth accounts for G–R in The Y Chromosome Consortium (2002) op. cit.

47. **40 per cent of Y-chromosome types**: Underhill et al. (2001) op. cit.; Hammer et al., (2001) op. cit. **suggests that he was born in India very soon after the initial out-of-Africa dispersal**: One estimate (using the 'Phylogenetic method') of the age of Krishna's immediate ancestor line M89 (Seth) is 88,000 years; the age of a sub-branch (M17) of Polo in India is estimated at 51,200 years using this method. M17 later moved to Central Asia and Europe – see Table 3 in Kivisild, T. (2003) 'Genetics of the language and farming spread in India' in P. Bellwood and C. Renfrew (eds) *Examining the Farming/Language Dispersal Hypothesis* (McDonald Institute for Archaeological Research, Cambridge) pp. 215–22. **Several [sons] are local to Pakistan and India**: Haplotypes 90 and 91 in haplogroup defined by M11, in Underhill et al. (2000) op. cit.; Haplotypes 90 and 91 defined by M147 and M70, inibid. **another is found only in Melanesia**: Haplotypes 94–97 in haplogroup defined by M4G/M5T/M9G, in Kayser et al., op. cit. and in Capelli, C. et al. (2001) 'A predominantly indigenous paternal heritage for the Austronesian-speaking peoples of insular Southeast Asia and Oceania' *American Journal of Human Genetics* **68**: 432–43. **another (TAT) is exclusive to Central Asia**: TAT, Haplotype 92, Underhill et al. (2000) op. cit.

48. **M175 or Consensus type O . . . Ho**: M175 branch in Underhill et al. (2000, 2001) op. cit. O/Ho corresponds to Haplogroup O in The Y Chromosome Consortium (2002) op. cit. **Ho splits easily into three branches . . .; One remained in southern China, Indo-China and Southeast Asia**: M95; **southern China . . . concentrating on Taiwan**: M119; **Japan, Korea, and Northeast Asia**: M122 – see data in Bing Su et al. (1999, 2000) op. cit.; Karafet et al., op. cit.; Underhill et al. (2000) op. cit.

49. **the other major Asian son of Krishna – Polo**: the M45 branch in Underhill et al. (2000) op. cit. **P/Polo corresponds to Haplogroup P in**: The Y Chromosome Consortium (2002) op. cit. **Kets and Selkups**: Karafet et al., op. cit.

50. Soffer, O. and Praslov, N.D. (eds) (1993) *From Kostenki to Clovis: Upper Paleolithic – Paleo-Indian Adaptations* (Plenum Press, New York).

Chapter 6

1. **from the Russian Altai . . . through Lake Baikal in southern Siberia to the Aldan River in the east**: Klein, R.G. (1999) *The Human Career: Human Biological and Cultural Origins* (Chicago University Press) – there is an excellent map of Upper Palaeolithic sites on p. 536. For the Ikhine II, Ust' Mil' (eastern Siberia) and Malaia Syia (Altai) sites, see Velichko, A.A. and Kurenkova, E.I. (1990) 'Environmental conditions and human occupation of northern Eurasia during the Late Valdai'; in C. Gamble and O. Soffer (eds) *The World at 18,000 bp*, Vol. 1 (Unwin Hyman, London) pp. 254–65; Goebel, T. et al. (1993) 'Dating the Middle-to-Upper-Palaeolithic transition at Kara Bom' *Current Anthropology* **34**: 452–8. For the Lake Baikal area, see Goebel, T. and Aksenov, M. (1995) 'Accelerator radiocarbon dating of the initial Upper Palaeolithic in southeast Siberia' *Antiquity* **69**: 349–57. **the Arctic Circle was penetrated**: Pavlov, P. et al. (2001) 'Human presence in the European Arctic nearly 40,000 years ago', *Nature* **413**: 64–7; see also Velichko and Kurenkova op. cit. **on a northern bend of the Yellow River**: at Salawasu/Shuidonggou, Chen, C. and Olsen, J.W. (1990) 'China at the Last Glacial Maximum' in C. Gamble and O. Soffer (eds) *The World at 18,000 bp*, Vol. 1 (Unwin Hyman, London) pp. 276–95.

2. **first flowering of the mammoth culture**: Soffer, O. (1993) 'Upper Paleolithic adaptations in Central and Eastern Europe and man–mammoth interactions' in O. Soffer and N.D. Praslov (eds) *From Kostenki to Clovis: Upper Paleolithic Adaptations* (Plenum, New York) pp. 31–49. **first possible evidence of Mongoloid features**: Alekseev, V. (1998) 'The physical specificities of Paleolithic hominids in Siberia' in A.P. Derev'anko (ed.) *The Paleolithic of Siberia: New Discoveries and Interpretations* (University of Illinois Press, Urbana) pp. 329–35.

3. See e.g. the description in Oppenheimer, S.J. (1998) *Eden in the East: The Drowned Continent of Southeast Asia* (Weidenfeld & Nicolson, London) pp. 23–7.

4. Zhang, D.D. and Li, S.H. (2002) 'Optical dating of Tibetan human hand- and footprints: An implication for the palaeoenvironment of the last glaciation of the Tibetan Plateau' *Geophysical Research Letters* **29** (published online DOI: 10.1029/2001GL013749).

5. **The first [refuge] . . . characterized by . . . the Solutrean culture**: Otte, M. (1990) 'The northwestern European Plain around 18,000 bp'; Chapter 3, Gamble, C. and Soffer, O. (eds) (1990) *The World at 18,000 bp*, Vol. 1 (Unwin Hyman, London), pp. 61–5; for more details of Solutrean in SW Europe see also Chapters 2, 4–6. pp. 40–169. **other southern refuges . . . described more generally as Epi-Gravettian**: Otte, M. (1990) in Gamble and Soffer op. cit. **second refuge area was Italy**: ibid.; Mussi, M. (1990) 'Continuity and change in Italy at the Last Glacial Maximum' in Gamble and Soffer op. cit. pp. 126–43. **third was the Ukraine**: Gamble and Soffer op. cit, and Chapters 3, 7, 10–12; Soffer (1993) op. cit. **Two other regions of Central Europe**: Kozlowski, J.K. (1990) 'Northern Central Europe *c.*18,000 bp' in Gamble and Soffer op. cit. pp. 204–27.

6. Soffer (1993) op. cit.

7. Torroni, A. et al. (1998) 'mtDNA analysis reveals a major late Paleolithic population expansion from Southwestern to Northeastern Europe' *American Journal of Human Genetics* **62**: 1137–52; Torroni, A. et al. (2001) 'A signal, from human mtDNA, of postglacial recolonization in Europe' *American Journal of Human Genetics* **69**: 844–52.

8. **the post-glacial dates of expansion of V**: Torroni et al. (1998) op. cit. The high

frequency of V in the Saami is thought to be a founder effect. See also Richards, M. et al. (2000) 'Tracing European founder lineages in the Near Eastern mtDNA pool' *American Journal of Human Genetics* **67**: 1251–76. **Pre-V found further east (and Trans-Caucasus) . . . and older**: Torroni et al. (2001) op. cit. **Exactly the same [geographic] pattern . . . for Ruslan**: Semino, O. et al. (2000) 'The genetic legacy of Paleolithic *Homo sapiens sapiens* in extant Europeans: A Y-chromosome perspective' *Science* **290**: 1155–9. Note in this context, Ruslan in Semino is 'Eu 18' – i.e. M45/M173 without the further M17 (or R without R1a1 in consensus nomenclature)

9. **persisting preglacial mtDNA lines**: Table 5 in Richards et al., op. cit. Note the LGM partition comes between lines 4 (Middle Upper Palaeolithic) and 3 (Late Upper Palaeolithic) of the table. **a feature of the Ukraine refuge**: ibid.

10. Table 4 in Richards et al. (2000) op. cit.

11. **they still mark a clear genetic boundary**: Stefan, M. et al. (2001) 'Y-chromosome analysis reveals a sharp genetic boundary in the Carpathian region' *European Journal of Human Genetics* **9**: 27–33. **M17 is still found at high frequencies**: Later post-glacial expansions into that region could have had the same effect – Semino et al., op. cit. (M17 is Eu 19 in Semino et al.) In the consensus nomenclature, M17 would now be called R1a1 – see The Y Chromosome Consortium (2002) 'A nomenclature system for the tree of human Y-chromosomal binary haplogroups' *Genome Research* **12**: 339–48.

12. **population of southern Central Asia . . . severely reduced**: Davis, R.S. (1990) 'Central Asian hunter-gatherers at the Last Glacial Maximum' in Gamble and Soffer op. cit. pp. 267–75; but see also signs of life in Tibet at the LGM in Zhang and Li op. cit. **human activity north even of the permafrost line . . . Afontova Gora . . . scattered archaeological sites**: Velichko and Kurenkova op. cit.

13. Table 2 in Forster, P. et al. (2003) 'Asian and Papuan mtDNA evolution' in P. Bellwood and C. Renfrew (eds) *Examining the Farming/Language Dispersal Hypothesis* (McDonald Institute for Archaeological Research, Cambridge) pp. 89–98.

14. **[?] no Mongoloid types . . . in East Asia until around 7,000–10,000 years ago**: Brown, P. (1999) 'The first modern East Asians? Another look at Upper Cave 101, Liujiang and Minatogawa 1' in K. Omoto (ed.) *Interdisciplinary Perspectives on the Origins of the Japanese* (International Research Center for Japanese Studies, Kyoto) pp. 105–30. **[?]none in Southeast Asia until well after that**: Bellwood, P. (1997) *Prehistory of the Indo-Malaysian Archipelago* revised edn (University of Hawaii Press, Honolulu pp. 70-95).

15. **B and F . . . great local antiquity in the south**: See discussion in Chapter 5. For pre-glacial age of B in Southern Mongoloids, see: Taiwan (B4a: 30,500 years) in Table 1, Richards, M. et al. (1998) 'MtDNA suggests Polynesian origins in Eastern Indonesia' *American Journal of Human Genetics* **63**: 1234–6. See also discussion and summary re Southern origin of B and R9, and estimated ages of B (and sub-groups) and R9 (F4) in Table 3 Yong-Gang Yao et al. (2002) 'Phylogeographic differentiation of mitochondrial DNA in Han Chinese' *American Journal of Human Genetics* **70**: 635–51.

16. Oppenheimer op. cit.

17. Ibid.; see also note 22 below and Bellwood op. cit.

18. **Largest population expansion in ISEA . . . arrival of the Metal Age**: The metal age arrived much later in Island Southeast Asia than on the mainland – see Higham, C. (1996) *The*

Bronze Age of Southeast Asia (Cambridge University Press) pp. 301–4. **When rice agriculture greatly expanded**: Paz, V. (2003) 'Island Southeast Asia: Spread or friction zone?' in P. Bellwood and C. Renfrew (eds) *Examining the Farming/Language Dispersal Hypothesis* (McDonald Institute for Archaeological Research, Cambridge) pp. 275–86. And Bulbeck F.D. (2002) 'Recent Insights on the Chronology and Ceramics of the Kalumpang Site Complex, South Sulawesi, Indonesia' *Indo-Pacific Prehistory Association Bulletin* **22 (Vol 6)**: 83–99.

19. Nasreen types originating in the south: B and F (B* found among Aboriginal Malays), R9 (found in Yunnan (South China) and Xinjiang from a branch ancestral to F), pre-F (common among Aboriginal Malays and ancestral to both R9 and to F), pre-N, N*, and N9, all found in Aboriginal Malays (N9, found throughout Southeast Asia and in South China, is ancestral to Y;) – see Chapter 5; R21 (found only among the Semang and Senoi from a Rohani branch, but may be ancestral to pre-F, F4, and F – shares HVS1 site 16304, but not certain key non-coding sites –thus providing a possible deep anchor between the Aboriginal Malays and other aboriginal groups of the Malay Peninsula) – see Chapter 4. Manju types originating in the South: M7 – see Chapter 5. Y-chromosome types originating in the South: Ho (Consensus type 'O') – see Chapter 5.

20. Rayner, D. and Bulbeck, D. (2001) 'Dental morphology of the "Orang Asli" aborigines of the Malay Peninsula' in M. Henneberg (ed.) *Causes and Effects of Human Variation* (Australasian Society for Human Biology, University of Adelaide) pp. 19–41.

21. Oppenheimer op. cit.

22. Richards, M. et al. (1998) 'MtDNA suggests Polynesian origins in Eastern Indonesia' *American Journal of Human Genetics* **63**: 1234–6; Oppenheimer, S.J. and Richards, M. (2001a) 'Polynesian origins: Slow boat to Melanesia?' *Nature* **410**: 166–7; Oppenheimer, S.J. and Richards, M. (2001b) 'Fast trains, slow boats, and the ancestry of the Polynesian islanders' *Science Progress* **84**(3): 157–81.

23. **Cambridge geneticist, Peter Forster**: Table 2 Forster et al., op. cit. **Similar postglacial dates for intrusive Y**: M119 in Table 5 in Kayser, M. et al. (2001) 'Independent histories of human Y chromosomes from Melanesia and Australia' *American Journal of Human Genetics* **68**: 173–90; M122 in Table 2 in Kayser, M. et al. (2000) 'Melanesian origin of Polynesian Y chromosomes' *Current Biology* **10**: 1237–46.

24. Data from Torroni, A. et al. (1994) 'Mitochondrial DNA analysis in Tibet: Implications for the origins of the Tibetan population and its adaptaton to high altitude' *American Journal of Physical Anthropology* **93**: 189–99 (note, the new clade M7 is identified in this older dataset by RFLP site 9820g). The presence of southern paternal line (M95) and the two dominant southern maternal clans B and F in Indo-China and Island Southeast Asia may simply indicate that they had been there all along among Sundadont populations (see Chapter 5), but their presence in Melanesia clearly indicates migration. The finding of maternal group C in the south (by e.g. Yong-Gang Yao et al., op. cit.), however, implies migration from the north.

25. Hill, C. et al. (2003) 'Mitochondrial DNA variation in the Orang Asli of the Malay Peninsula' (in preparation).

26. Consensus line O/Ho = M175: spread of this genetic line in Southeast Asia and intrusion across the Wallace Line reviewed in Oppenheimer and Richards (2001b) op. cit.; data from Kayser et al. (2001) op. cit.; Capelli, C. et al. (2001) 'A predominantly indigenous paternal heritage for the Austronesian-speaking peoples of insular Southeast Asia and Oceania' *American*

Journal of Human Genetics **68**: 432–43; Bing Su et al. (1999) 'Y-chromosome evidence for a northward migration of modern humans into Eastern Asia during the last Ice Age' *American Journal of Human Genetics* **65**: 1718–24. See also The Y Chromosome Consortium (2002) op. cit.

27. **Mongoloid remains . . . in Java . . . dated to 7,000 years**: Widianto, H. and Detroit, F. (2001) 'The prehistoric burial customs in Indonesia during early Holocene: Nature and age' abstract, Symposium 16.1, 16th Congress of the Union Internationale des Sciences Préhistoriques et Protohistoriques, 2–8 September, Liège. **From the LGM up until about 10,000 years ago**: Oppenheimer op. cit. pp. 78–83. **People of New Guinea . . . morphologically similar to the Negritos**: Bulbeck, D. (1999) 'Current biological research on Southeast Asia's Negritos' *SPAFA Journal* **9**(2): 14–22; Rayner, D. and Bulbeck, D. (2001) 'Dental morphology of the "Orang Asli" aborigines of the Malay Peninsula' in M. Henneberg (ed.) *Causes and Effects of Human Variation* (Australasian Society for Human Biology, University of Adelaide) pp. 19–41; see also Chapter 5.

28. **[Niah 'deep skull'] Carbon–dated to around 42,000 years ago**: Barker, G. et al. (2001) 'The Niah Cave Project: The second (2001) season of fieldwork' *Sarawak Museum Journal* **56**: 37–119, here pp. 56–8. **like the now extinct Tasmanians**: See note 15 in Chapter 5. **a partial skull from Tabon Cave**: Bulbeck, F.D. (1981) 'Continuities in Southeast Asian evolution since the Late Pleistocene', MA thesis, Department of Prehistory and Anthropology, Australian National University, Canberra.

29. **For more than a century arguments . . . Proto–Australian**: Dubois, E. (1922) 'The proto-Australian fossil man of Wadjak, Java' *Koninklijke Akademie van Wetenschappen te Amsterdam* B **23**: 1013–51; Weidenreich, F. (1945) 'The Keilor skull: A Wadjak type from south-east Australia' *American Journal of Physical Anthropology* **3**: 225–36; Wolpoff, M.H. et al. (1984) 'Modern *Homo sapiens* origins: A general theory of hominid evolution involving the fossil evidence from east Asia' in F.H. Smith and F. Spencer (eds) *The Origins of Modern Humans* (Alan R. Liss, New York) pp. 411–84. **The skulls have been claimed to be early Mongoloid**: Coon, C.S. (1962) *The Origin of Races* (Alfred A. Knopf, New York); Jacob, J.T. (1967) *Some Problems Pertaining to the Racial History of the Indonesian Region* (Drukkerij Neerlandia, Utrecht) pp. i–xiv, 1–162; Bulbeck, D. (1981) op. cit. **modern (Mongoloid) Javanese**: Storm, P. (1995) 'The evolutionary significance of the Wajak skulls' *Scripta Geologica* **110**: 1–247. **like the Ainu**: Bulbeck, D. (2002) 'South Sulawesi in the corridor of island populations along East Asia's Pacific Rim' in S. Keates and J. Pasveer (eds) *Quaternary Research in Indonesia, Modern Quaternary Research in Southeast Asia*, Vol. 17 (Balkema, Rotterdam). **either 10,560 or 6,560 years old**: Storm op. cit.; Shutler, R. et al. (2002) 'AMS bone apatite C14 dates from Wajak, Indonesia' in Keates and Pasveer op. cit. Bulbeck also makes a similar Jomon connection for the cranial and dental morphology of pre-ceramic (before they made pots) Toaleans in Sulawesi.

30. **There may not be a single date at all . . . gradual local evolutionary process**: Storm op. cit. **their original name, 'Proto–Malays'**: Glinka, J. (1981) 'Racial history of Indonesia' in I. Schwidetsky (ed.) *Rassengeschichte der Menschheit*, Vol. 8, *Asien I: Japan, Indonesien, Ozeanien* (Oldenbourg, Munich) pp. 79–113.

31. Forster et al., op. cit.

32. **the ice-age Japanese Minatogawa 1 skull**: Brown op. cit. **the modern Ainu**:
    Hanihara, T. et al. (1998) 'Place of the Hokkaido Ainu (Northern Japan) among peoples of the
    world' *International Journal of Circumpolar Health* **57**: 257–75.

33. **In Okinawa, . . . the rare Asian YAP+ marker achieves frequencies of 55%**:
    Hammer, M.F. and Horai, S. (1995) 'Y chromosomal DNA variation and the peopling of
    Japan' *American Journal of Human Genetics* **56**: 951–62. **The other beachcombing Y
    marker [Cain]**: Consensus group C/Cain = RPS4Y, Karafet, T.M. et al. (1999) 'Ancestral
    Asian source(s) of New World Y-chromosome founder haplotypes' *American Journal of Human
    Genetics* **64**: 817–31; Bing Su et al., op. cit. C corresponds to the consensus nomenclature for
    this haplogroup, The Y Chromosome Consortium op. cit.

34. Brown op. cit. See also Cunningham, D.L. and Wescott, D.J. (2002) 'Within-group human
    variation in the Asian Pleistocene: The three Upper Cave crania' *Journal of Human Evolution* **42**:
    627–38; Wu, X. and Poirier, F.E. (1995) *Human Evolution in China* (Oxford University Press,
    New York) pp. 158–70.

35. Karafet et al., op. cit.; Ke, Y. et al. (2001) 'African origin of modern humans in East Asia: A
    tale of 12,000 Y chromosomes' *Science* **292**: 1151–2.

36. The 'backward' epithet is probably a Eurocentric slur, since the available stone was poor and
    the most pliant materials used by Southeast Asians for their tools were of perishable wood,
    fibre, and bamboo. See the discussion in Chapter 4 and in Shutler, R. Jr (1995) 'Hominid
    cultural evolution as seen from the archaeological evidence in Southeast Asia', Conference
    papers on Archaeology in Southeast Asia, Publ. Hong Kong University Museum, Hong Kong,
    1995.; Pope, G.G. (1989) 'Bamboo and human evolution' *Natural History* (October) pp. 49–
    56.

37. **What became known as the Movius Line**: Movius, H.L. (1948) 'The Lower Palaeolithic
    cultures of southern and eastern Asia' *Transactions of the American Philosophical Society* (new
    series) **38**: 329–420. **at least a million years ago**: Pope, G.G. and Keates, S.G. (1994)
    'The evolution of human cognition and cultural capacity: A view from the Far East' in R.
    Corrucin and R.L. Ciochon (eds) *Integrative Paths to the Past: Paleoanthropological Advances*
    (Prentice Hall, Englewood Cliffs, NJ) pp. 531–67. **around 70,000 years ago**: Shutler
    op. cit.; see also Bowdler, S. (1992) 'The earliest Australian stone tools and implications for
    Southeast Asia' *Indo-Pacific Prehistory Association Bulletin* **12**: 10–22; Keates, S.G. and Bartstra,
    G.-J. (2001) 'Observations on Cabengian and Pacitanian artefacts from Island Southeast Asia'
    Quärtar, Band **51/52**: 9–32; Pope and Keates op. cit.

38. **It has been surmised**: Shutler op. cit.; Pope op. cit. **bamboo**: ibid.

39. Chen and Olsen op. cit.

40. Ibid.

41. Ibid.

42. Kuzmin, Y.V. et al. (1998) '14C chronology of Stone Age cultures in the Russian Far East'
    Radiocarbon **40**(1/2): 675–86.

43. This paragraph draws on Reynolds, T.E.G. and Kaner, S.C. (1990) 'Japan and Korea at 18,000
    bp' in C. Gamble and O. Soffer (eds) *The World at 18,000 bp*, Vol. 1 (Unwin Hyman, London)
    pp. 276–95.

44. **The regions around the Yangtzi Kiang**: at Tonglian – Chen and Olsen op. cit. **the
    coastal regions of southern China**: The preglacial southern Thai sites of Moh Khiew and

Lang Rongrien, however, are reported to show a high percentage of utilized flake tools – F.D. Bulbeck (2003) 'Hunter-gatherer occupation of the Malay Peninsula from the Ice Age to the Iron Age' in J. Mercader (ed.) *The Archaeology of Tropical Rain Forests* (Rutgers University Press, New Brunswick) pp. 119–60, here p. 129.

45. **gap in occupation** (of SE Asia and the Malay Peninsula at LGM): ibid. **the former continent of Sundaland**: Oppenheimer op. cit. **They thus simply followed the sea**: Bulbeck op. cit., but see also Bellwood op. cit. pp. 159–61.

46. **inland caves were reoccupied**: for re-occupations in: Malaysia, lowland Gua Sagu from 14,400 years ago; Lenggong Valley from 13,600 years ago (Gua Runtuh) – Fig. 1 in Majid, Z. (1998) 'Radiocarbon dates and culture sequence in the Lenggong Valley and beyond' *Malaysia Museums Journal* **34**: 241–9. In Indo-China, Son Vi from 9,000 to 12,000 years ago, Hoabinhian from 7,000 to 11,000 years ago, Bacsonian from 7,000 to 10,000 years ago – Fig. 2.3 in Higham, C. (1991) *The Archaeology of Mainland Southeast Asia* (Cambridge University Press). **the old lithic traditions continued**: Majid op. cit. **moved back from lower altitudes**: Bulbeck op. cit.

47. **ancestors of the nomadic Negrito forest hunter-gatherers**: e.g. Bellwood (op. cit. p. 85) argues that the Semang are descended from the earliest inhabitants of Gua Cha Cave, in the centre of the Malay Peninsula. But dentally the Gua Cha inhabitants both pre- and post-Neolithic look more similar to Pacific Rim peoples or Aboriginal Malays than Semang: see table 5 in Bulbeck D. (2000) 'Dental Morphology at Gua Cha, West Malaysia, and the Implications for Sundadonty' *Indo-Pacific Prehistory Association Bulletin* **19 (Vol 3)**: 17–41. **Zuraina Majid argues further**: Majid op. cit.

48. **colonization of the Philippines**: but excluding the island of Palawan, which was connected to the Sunda Shelf and was colonized much earlier – Thiel, B. (1987) 'Early settlement of the Philippines, Eastern Indonesia and Australia-New Guinea: A new hypothesis' *Current Anthropology* **28**: 236–41. Solheim: **a late Pleistocene intrusion**: Solheim, W.G. II (1994) 'Southeast Asia and Korea from the beginnings of food production to the first states' in S.J. De Laet (ed.) *The History of Humanity* (Routledge, London) pp. 468–81, here p. 476.

49. **the shores of the extinct Lake Tingkayu**: Bellwood op. cit. pp. 175–9. **'unique in the whole of Southeast Asia . . .'**: ibid. p. 179. **the two other preglacial sites**: ibid. p. 160. For each site there is ambiguity over the dates, but they are late Upper Pleistocene.

50. Ibid. p. 179.

Chapter 7

1. **Thomas Jefferson**: Jefferson, T. (1955) 'Query XI: A description of the Indians established in that State?' in *Notes on the State of Virginia* (ed. William Peden) (University of North Carolina Press, Chapel Hill, NC). **Jesuit scientist and traveller**: José de Acosta (1590) *Historia Natural y Moral de las Indias* (Seville).

2. Thomas, D.H. (1999) 'One archaeologist's perspective on the Monte Verde controversy' in 'Monte Verde under fire' *Archaeology* Online Features, 18 October 1999 (www.archaeology. org).

3. **the so-called Clovis orthodoxy**: Rose, M. (1999) 'The importance of Monte Verde' in 'Monte Verde under fire' *Archaeology* Online Features, 18 October 1999 (www.archaeology.

org). **mantle of authority for this gatekeeper role**: ibid. **Hrdlicka was singled out**: Deloria, V. Jr (1995) *Red Earth, White Lies: Native Americans and the Myth of Scientific Fact* (Scribner's, New York).

4. For a longer review of the discoveries mentioned in this paragraph, see Rose, op. cit.

5. **American geochronologist C. Vance Haynes**: Haynes, C.V. (1964) 'Fluted projectile points: Their age and dispersion' *Science* **145**: 1404–13; see also Haynes, C.V. (1969) 'The earliest Americans' *Science* **166**: 709–15. **dates of various Clovis-point sites**: these are uncalibrated radiocarbon dates; the calibrated or corrected date bracket would be around 2,000 years older i.e. 13,000 years ago. **age was significant for geologists**: Marshall, E. (2001) 'Pre-Clovis sites fight for acceptance' *Science* **291**: 1730–32; Rutter. N.W. (1980) 'Late Pleistocene history of the Western Canadian ice-free corridor' *Canadian Journal of Anthropology* **1**: 1–8.

6. **eighteen contender sites**: Frison, G.C. and Walker, D.N. (1990) 'New World palaeo-ecology at the Last Glacial Maximum and the implications for New World prehistory' in C. Gamble and O. Soffer (eds) *The World at 18,000 bp*, Vol. 1 (Unwin Hyman, London) pp. 312–30, here pp. 313–15. **Only a few have survived**: the still-embattled sites include Pedra Furada in north-east Brazil, which has a claimed antiquity of 35,000 years, and Taima Taima in Venezuela, at 15,350 years.

7. Dillehay, T. (1997) *Monte Verde, A Late Pleistocene Settlement in Chile*. Vol. 2, *The Archaeological Context and Interpretation* (Smithsonian Institution Press, Washington, DC).

8. Marshall op. cit.

9. **The group's consensus report**: Meltzer, D. et al. (1997) 'On the Pleistocene antiquity of Monte Verde, southern Chile' *American Antiquity* **62**: 659–63. **A further article**: Taylor, R.E. et al. (1999) 'Radiocarbon analyses of modern organics at Monte Verde, Chile: No evidence for a local reservoir effect' *American Antiquity* **64**: 455–60. Note that contamination can occur as a result of coal (fossil carbon) or older peat leaching into younger sources of carbon.

10. Fiedel, S. (1999) 'Monte Verde revisited: Artifact provenence at Monte Verde: Confusion and contradictions' in Special Report 'Monte Verde revisited' *Scientific American Discovering Archaeology* **6**(November/December): 1–12.

11. Adovasio, J.M. (1999) 'Paradigm-death and gunfights' in Special Report 'Monte Verde revisited' *Scientific American Discovering Archaeology* **6**(November/December): 20.

12. Meltzer, D.J. (1999) 'On Monte Verde' in Special Report 'Monte Verde revisited' *Scientific American Discovering Archaeology* **6**(November/December): 16–17.

13. Collins, M.B. (1999) 'The site of Monte Verde' in 'Monte Verde under fire' *Archaeology* Online Features 18 October (www.archaeology.org).

14. Thomas, D.H. (1999) 'One archaeologist's perspective on the Monte Verde controversy' in 'Monte Verde under fire' *Archaeology* Online Features 18 October (www.archaeology.org).

15. 16,175 years bp corrected ± 975; deepest layer with (disputed) Paleoindian association 21,070 years BP corrected ± 475: Adovasio, J.M. et al. (1990) 'The Meadowcroft Rock-shelter radiocarbon chronology 1975–1990' *American Antiquity* **55**: 348–54. Reviewed in Marshall op. cit.

16. **Adovasio is reported, 'I will never run another date . . .'**: reported in Marshall op. cit.

17. McAvoy, J.M. and McAvoy, L.D. (1997) 'Archaeological investigations of Site 44SX202, Cactus Hill, Sussex County, Virginia' Virginia Department of Historic Resources, Richmond, Research Report Series No. 8. See also Rose, M. (2000). 'Cactus Hill update' *Archaeology* (April 10), available at http://www.archaeology.org/online/news/cactus.html

18. Reviewed in Marshall op. cit.

19. Goodyear, A.C. (2001) 'The stratigraphy story at the Topper site' *Mammoth Trumpet* (Center for the Study of the First Americans, Department of Anthropology, Texas A&M University) **16(4)**; also reviewed in Marshall op. cit.

20. Marshall op. cit.; see also D.K. (1999) 'Breaking the "Clovis barrier": Were the first Americans in South Carolina?' *Scientific American Discovering Archaeology* September/October.

21. Rose, M. (1999) 'Monte Verde fallout: Beyond Monte Verde' in 'Monte Verde under fire' *Archaeology* Online Features 18 October (www. archaeology.org).

22. Rose, M. (1999) 'Beyond Clovis: How and When the First Americans Arrived' *Archaeology* **52**(November/December): (book review of Dixon, E.J. (1999) *Bones, Boats, and Bison: Archeology and First Colonization of Western North America* (University of New Mexico Press, Albuquerque), which argues for a west-coast route).

23. Wallace, A.F.C. (1999) *Jefferson and the Indians: The Tragic Fate of the First Americans* (Belknap Press, Cambridge, MA).

24. **Polynesians' spread through the empty islands**: Oppenheimer, S.J. and Richards, M. (2001) 'Fast trains, slow boats, and the ancestry of the Polynesian islanders' *Science Progress* **84**(3): 157–81. **genetic picture fits the linguistic trail very well**: ibid., but this does not work farther west from Polynesia, where the migration history is more complex – see ibid.

25. Trask, R.L. (1996) *Historical Linguistics* (Arnold, London) p. 377.

26. **between about 12,000 and 20,000 years ago**: Dixon, R.M.W. (1997) *The Rise and Fall of Languages* (Cambridge University Press) p. 94. **explain the present diversity of American language families**: Nichols uses a particular definition of families defined as 'stocks' – see e.g. pp. 24–5 and 233 in Nichols, J. (1992) *Linguistic Diversity in Space and Time* (University of Chicago Press). **English linguist Daniel Nettle**: see the discussion on stocks, phylogenetic diversity, and the Americas in Chapter 6 of Nettle, D. (1999) *Linguistic Diversity* (Oxford University Press).

27. **167 American language 'stocks'**: Nichols op. cit. These stocks do not exclude the probability of higher-order nodes or groups based on looser rules. Such higher-order groups can be found in other common secondary classifications; clearly, fewer nodes means fewer stocks, and that can more than halve the estimates. **a simple function of time**: simple = linear, but see also the comment by Nettle op. cit. p. 120.

28. **difficulties with all these analyses**: Nettle op. cit. (in his Chapter 6) has criticized Nichols' methods and suggested an alternative model, again using 'stocks'. **languages per stock varies**: Nettle op. cit.

29. **The exception is Australia**: It has even been suggested that the present dominant language family in Australia, Pama-Nyungan, was introduced with the dingos – Flood, J. (1995) *Archaeology of the Dreamtime* (Collins, Australia) pp. 206–8; but see also Dixon op. cit. pp. 89–93. **interesting, almost a caricature**: These figures are from my own unpublished analysis.

30. Greenberg, J.H. et al. (1986) 'The settlement of the Americas: A comparison of the linguistic, dental, and genetic evidence' *Current Anthropology* **27**: 477–97.

31. Although I accept that Greenberg's synthesis of a single Amerind group is difficult to sustain, I shall, for convenience in the genetic discussion below, use the term 'Amerind' for Native American languages that are neither Na-Dene nor Inuit-Aleut.

32. Ward, R.H. et al. (1991) 'Extensive mitochondrial diversity within a single Amerindian tribe' *Proceedings of the National Academy of Sciences USA* **88**: 8720–24.

33. Horai, S. et al. (1993) 'Peopling of the Americas founded by four major lineages of mitochondrial DNA' *Molecular Biology and Evolution* **10**: 23–47.

34. **Their early mtDNA results**: Wallace, D.C. and Torroni, A. (1992) 'American Indian prehistory as written in the mitochondrial DNA: A review' *Human Biology* **64**: 403–16 **further clarified the mtDNA types**: Torroni, A. et al. (1993a) 'Asian affinities and continental radiation of the four founding Native American mtDNAs' *American Journal of Human Genetics* **53**: 563–90; Torroni, A. et al. (1993b) 'mtDNA variation of aboriginal Siberians reveals distinct genetic affinities with Native Americans' *American Journal of Human Genetics* **53**: 591–608.

35. **Just one of these clusters, A**: Torroni et al. (1993a) op. cit.; **the identifying mutations**: Torroni et al. (1993b) op. cit.

36. **There were surprising results**: In America, A came out at 22,750–45,500 years, B at 6,000–12,000 years, C at 24,000–48,000 years, and D at 13,250–26,500 years – Table 8 in Torroni (1993a) op. cit., p. 584. **They suggested a distinct origin for the Na-Dene and Inuit-Aleut**: although this could not be definitely inferred from the data.

37. See also Stariovskaya, Y.B. et al. (1998) 'mtDNA diversity in Chukchi and Siberian Eskimos: Implications for the genetic history of Ancient Beringia and the peopling of the New World' *American Journal of Human Genetics* **63**: 1473–91.

38. Dates vary from 22,000 to 29,000 years ago (e.g. Torroni, A. et al. (1994) 'A mitochondrial DNA "clock" for the Amerinds and its implications for timing their entry into North America' *Proceedings of the National Academy of Sciences USA* **91**: 1158–62) to 30,000–40,000 years ago (e.g. Bonatto, S.L. and Salzano, F.M. (1997a) 'A single and early migration for the peopling of the Americas supported by mitochondrial DNA sequence data' *Proceedings of the National Academy of Sciences USA* **94**: 1866–971; Bonatto, S.L. and Salzano, F.M. (1997b) 'Diversity and age of the four major mtDNA haplogroups, and their implications for the peopling of the New World' *American Journal of Human Genetics* **61**: 1413–23); to expand the horizon to 23–37,000 years ago, see Stone, C.A. and Stoneking, M. (1998) 'mtDNA analysis of a prehistoric Oneota population: Implications for the peopling of the New World' *American Journal of Human Genetics* **62**: 1153–70. Although I prefer Forster's genetic date of entry at 22,000 years, just before the LGM (Forster, P. et al. (1996) 'Origin and evolution of Native American mtDNA variation: A reappraisal' *American Journal of Human Genetics* **59**: 935–45), it is clear from these date brackets that Dillehay's (op. cit.) most controversial earliest dates of Monte Verde occupation 35,000 years ago are not completely ruled out by the genetics.

39. **Initially they had thought**: Torroni et al. (1993a,b) op. cit.; **It was also soon realized**: Forster et al., op. cit.

40. **the three Greenberg groups as a 'family'**: albeit a distant family, since the split was rather deep – Forster et al. op. cit. **Neither A1 nor A2 are found in Asia**: ibid.

41. **Inuit populations in both North America and Greenland**: Saillard, J. et al. (2000) 'mtDNA variation among Greenland Eskimos: The edge of the Beringian expansion' *American Journal of Human Genetics* **67**: 718–26. **D2 was a feature of Inuit-Aleuts**: Forster et al., op. cit. This blossoming D relationship was, however, broken more recently with the discovery that D2 was a more recent introduction from the Siberian side – Stariovskaya et al., op. cit.

42. Shields, G.F. et al. (1993) 'mtDNA sequences suggest a recent evolutionary divergence for Beringian and northern North American populations' *American Journal of Human Genetics* **53**: 549–62.

43. Forster et al., op. cit. In passing I should mention that geneticists were not the first to point to the importance of Beringia in American ice-age prehistory. Archaeologists such as Knut Fladmark (see below) had been beating this drum for some time.

44. **the Bering Strait was then a land bridge**: For a comprehensive chronological map of Beringia, see http://www.ngdc.noaa.gov/paleo/parcs/atlas/beringia/index.html For maps based on bathymetry and the sea-level curve, see Bard, E. et al. (1996) 'Deglacial sea-level record from Tahiti corals and the timing of global meltwater discharge' *Nature* **382**: 241–4. **The summers were for sure cooler**: Schweger, C.E. (1997) 'Late Quaternary palaeo-ecology of the Yukon: A review' in H.V. Danks and J.A. Downes (eds) *Insects of the Yukon* (Biological Survey of Canada (Terrestrial Arthropods), Ottawa) pp. 59–72. **being an Arctic desert at this time**: see maps on Jonathan Adams' ESD ORNL reference website, at http://www.esd.ornl.gov/projects/qen/euras18k.gif and http://www.esd.ornl.gov/projects/qen/euras(2.gif **linked to America through their A1/A2 group gene tree**: An important piece of support for this scenario was that the deepest A2 founder type was a feature of the Na-Dene and rare-to-absent in the Inuit-Aleut, while the derived A2 types were found throughout Eskimo populations. This meant that A2 most probably originated in the Na-Dene and later diversified in the Inuit-Aleut, including the Siberian Inuit, and spread to their neighbours the Chukchi. In other words, the source of the Beringian A2 founder was from the original American genetic stock on the Alaskan side and not a latecomer from Asia. Saillard et al., op. cit.

45. **Central Americans at 16,000 years**: This is likely to be a gross underestimate of human occupation of that region, since 81% of the Central American sample were from the Chibcha culture, known from archaeological evidence to have a time depth of approximately 10,000 years – Torroni et al. (1994) op. cit. **a case for the founding lineages . . . arriving before 21,000–22,000 years ago**: There is an interesting anomaly in the various ages of B, which was 25,000 years in South America but rather younger, at 19,000 years, in North America. The latter seems to disprove Stariovskaya's theory (see note 37 above) that B came in after the ice age by a coastal route, but might be still consistent with a re-expansion of B in North America associated with Clovis. **the expansion age came out at 11,300 years**: Since this date specifically estimated a post-glacial expansion, it hides the real age of the A2 founder type in the ancestors of the Na-Dene and Inuit-Aleut. That age comes out at 25,000 years, which is similar to, in fact rather older than, A2 in Amerinds. In other words, this older date supports the view that the original A1 and A2 ancestors of all three American language groups arose in North America before the last ice age. Saillard et al. (op. cit.) recently reanalysed A2 gene trees and expansion ages among Na-Dene and Inuit-Aleut. Their results

give a fascinating account of the continuing cyclical fight against extreme cold climates right down to historical times. They noted first that the Haida Na-Dene inhabiting Queen Charlotte Island off the west coast of Canada must have split from the ancestors of the Inuit-Aleut and the mainland Na-Dene rather early. This was because they share no types with the latter except for the founder A2 root type. For instance, one sub-branch of A2 (16192) originates after this, in Beringia or on the mainland, around 22,000 years ago, subsequently expanding among both Na-Dene and Inuit in the peri-Arctic zone from 6,300 years ago. Another sub-branch of A2 (16265G) is much more recent, being found only in Inuit-Aleut and expanding from 3,000 years ago. Saillard et al. trace repeated genetic re-expansions of this Inuit branch to archaeologically proven recolonizations of Greenland over the past few thousand years as mini ice ages waxed and waned. **they still owe much of their genetic heritage**: Just how much they owe to America is another interesting question explored by Saillard et al. (op. cit.). Stariovskaya et al. (op. cit.) demonstrated that the other Inuit founding lineage, D2 was derived not from the American D1 but from Beringian contact with Siberia. This is the only clear evidence for a late separate entry into the Americas. Clearly this implies that Inuit and Aleuts are to a small extent an admixed American/Siberian population, not simply a new migration. Saillard and colleagues point out that the Siberian D2 input may only be very recent, within the past thousand years or so.

46. Bonatto and Salzano (1997a, op. cit.) say essentially the same thing about the Beringian refuge and re-expansion, while Stone and Stoneking (op. cit.) and Stariovskaya et al. (op. cit.) have variations on the theme. What differs in all these other reports is that their dates of first entry into the Americas are even earlier than Forster's, generally in excess of 30,000 years. It is inappropriate to go into the virtues of different methods of genetic dating in this book. As an observer, my own preference is for the method used by Forster and colleagues, i.e. calculation of rho (Forster et al., op. cit.) That is the method I have used for most of the estimates in this book, and is based on calculating the average number of mutations in a gene tree. It has the advantage that it is relatively independent of unknown past variations in population size (which produces more conservative estimates in this case). Whichever method is used, however, the result easily breaks the Clovis-first mould and means that the Americas were most likely colonized before the last ice age.

47. **Argentinian geneticist Graciela Bailliet**: Bailliet, G. et al. (1994) 'Founder mitochondrial haplotypes in Amerindian populations' *American Journal of Human Genetics* **55**: 27–33. **his new method of genetic tree-building**: Fig. 7 in Bandelt, H.-J. et al. (1995) 'Mitochondrial portraits of human populations using median networks' *Genetics* **141**: 743–53. **a European X group**: Torroni, A. et al. (1996) 'Classification of European mtDNAs from an analysis of three European populations' *Genetics* **144**: 1835–50.

48. **rates of 5 and 11–13 per cent . . .**: Brown, M.D. et al. (1998) 'mtDNA Haplogroup X: An ancient link between Europe/Western Asia and North America?' *American Journal of Human Genetics* **63**: 1852–61; see also Ward et al., op. cit. **rates of 25 per cent**: Brown et al., op. cit.

49. DNA was extracted from remains in the Norris Farms ancient cemetery – Stone and Stoneking op. cit.; also reported and discussed in Brown et al., op. cit.

50. Chatters, J. (2002) http://www.mnh.si.edu/arctic/html/kennewick_man.html Originally published in *Newsletter of the American Anthropological Association*, 1996. Also Chatters, J.C.

(2000) 'The recovery and first analysis of an early Holocene human skeleton from Kennewick, Washington', American Antiquity 65: 291-316.

51. Letter from Secretary of the Interior Bruce Babbitt to Secretary of the Army Louis Caldera, 21 September 2000, regarding disposition of the Kennewick Human remains; Report on the Non-Destructive Examination, Description, and Analysis of the Human Remains from Columbia Park, Kennewick, Washington, October 1999; Powell, J.F. and Rose, J.C. (1999) Report on the Osteological Assessment of the 'Kennewick Man' Skeleton (CENWW.97. Kennewick) Chapter 2 in F.P. McManamon (ed.) Report on the Non-Destructive Examination Description, and Analysis of the Human Remains from Columbia Park, Kennewick, Washington. Washington, D.C.: National Park Service, Department of the Interior. (CENWW.97.Kennewick).

52. Chatters op. cit.

53. Chandler, J.M. and Stanford, D. (2001) 'Immigrants from the other side?' *Mammoth Trumpet* (Center for the Study of the First Americans, Department of Anthropology, Texas A&M University) 17(1): 11–16.

54. Stanford, D. and Bradley, B. (2000) 'The Solutrean solution: Did some ancient Americans come from Europe?' *Discovering Archaeology* (Feb. 2000). See review of this old theory: Holden, C. (1999) 'Were Spaniards among the First Americans?' *Science* 286: 1467–8.

55. Brown et al., op. cit.

56. Stone and Stoneking op. cit. p. 1168.

57. Karafet, T.M. et al. (1999) 'Ancestral Asian source(s) of New World Y-chromosome founder haplotypes' *American Journal of Human Genetics* 64: 817–31; Merriwether, D.A. et al. (1996) 'mtDNA variation indicates Mongolia may have been the source for the founding population for the New World' *American Journal of Human Genetics* 59: 204–12.

58. **Spirit Cave Man, at around 9,400 years**: uncorrected radiocarbon date, Barker, P. et al. (2000) 'Determination of cultural affiliation of ancient human remains from Spirit Cave, Nevada' Report, Bureau of Land Management, Nevada State Office; Jantz, R. and Owsley, D. (1997) 'Pathology, taphonomy, and cranial morphometrics of the Spirit Cave mummy' *Nevada Historical Society Quarterly* 40: 62–84. **Three other atypical Palaeo-Indians**: An excellent map showing Palaeo-Indian finds and their dates may be found at: http://www.csasi.org/July2000/Earliest%20Americans.htm (author David Heath).

59. http://www.antropologiabiologica.mn.ufrj.br/english/luzia/estrela1.htm

60. **rather robust East Asian skulls**: e.g. Niah, Wajak, Liujiang, Minatogawa, and Upper Cave (see Chapters 5 and 6, and specifically Brown, P. (1999) 'The first modern East Asians? Another look at Upper Cave 101, Liujiang and Minatogawa 1', in K. Omoto (ed.) *Interdisciplinary Perspectives on the Origins of the Japanese* (International Research Center for Japanese Studies, Kyoto) pp. 105–30. **Neves did actually find links**: e.g. with Upper Cave 101: Neves, W.A. and Pucciarelli, H.M. (1998) 'The Zhoukoudien Upper Cave skull 101 as seen from the Americas' *Journal of Human Evolution* 34: 219–22; Neves, W.A. et al. (1999) 'Modern human origins as seen from the peripheries' *Journal of Human Evolution* 37: 129–33. See also Fig. 8 in Hanihara, T. (2000) 'Frontal and facial flatness of major human populations' *American Journal of Physical Anthropology* 111: 105–34.

61. Lahr, M. (1996) *The Evolution of Modern Human Diversity: A Study of Cranial Variation* (Cambridge University Press).

62. Powell, J.F. and Neves, W.A. (1999) 'Craniofacial morphology of the first Americans: Pattern and process in the peopling of the New World' *Yearbook of Physical Anthropology* **42**: 153–88.

63. Powell and Neves (ibid.) point out, however, that several other scenarios could lead to the same result.

64. Underhill, P.A. et al. (2000) 'Y-chromosome sequence variation and the history of human populations' *Nature Genetics* **26**: 358–61; see also Fig. 1 and Table 1 in Hammer, M.F. et al. (2001) 'Hierarchical patterns of global human Y-chromosome diversity' *Molecular Biology and Evolution* **18**(7): 1189–203. The M45 clade has been reclassified as P (Polo) – The Y Chromosome Consortium (2002) 'A nomenclature system for the tree of human Y-chromosomal binary haplogroups' *Genome Research* **12**: 339–48.

65. **still common in North Asia**: Hammer haplotype 36, 103/495 = 21%, Hammer et al., op. cit. **the main American founder**: 69/439 = 15.7% of Native American Y chromosomes – ibid., data combined with those in Underhill et al., op. cit. **found in Europe**: Eu 20 at 1%, Semino, O. et al. (2000) 'The genetic legacy of Paleolithic *Homo sapiens sapiens* in extant Europeans: A Y-chromosome perspective' *Science* **290**: 1155–9. **Lake Baikal region is the homeland**: Karafet et al., op. cit. **dominant European subgroup . . . is also . . .**: Hammer haplotype 37 (Semino haplotype Eu18/ Consensus type R1b). Comparison of the observed rate in Native Americans with the rate expected from gene flow from North Asia yields an odds ratio of 4.51, based on Hammer et al., op. cit.; R/Ruslan is the reclassified label of M45/M173 – The Y Chromosome Consortium (2002) op. cit.

66. **a direct branch derivative of the Polo root, Q**: Q/Quetzalcoatl refers to a haplogroup defined by M45/M3 – The Y Chromosome Consortium (2002) op. cit. **all share the special American Y-chromosome type**: Karafet et al., op. cit.; Karafet, T.M. et al. (2001) 'Paternal population history of East Asia: Sources, patterns, and microevolutionary processes' *American Journal of Human Genetics* **69**: 615–28. **which comes out at 22,000 years ago**: Bianchi, N.O. et al. (1998) 'Characterization of ancestral and derived Y-chromosome haplotypes of New World native populations' *American Journal of Human Genetics* **63**: 1862–71.

67. Based on odds-ratio comparisons using data from Hammer et al., op. cit.

68. **an extra mutation, M217**: For the marker M217 and its East Asian and American distribution, see Underhill P. A. et al. (2001) 'Maori origins, Y-chromosome haplotypes and implications for human history in the Pacific' *Human Mutation* **17**: 271–80. **highest frequencies are found nearer the Pacific coast**: Karafet et al. (1999) op. cit.

69. Afontova Gora II on the Yenisei River in southern Siberia (see Chapter 5).

70. **The X line has recently been unambiguously identified**: Derenko, M.V. et al. (2001) 'The presence of mitochondrial Haplogroup X in Altaians from South Siberia' *American Journal of Human Genetics* **69**: 237–41. But note that a single reported instance like this could still be due to recent European intrusion, since the Siberian haplotypes are not unique root types, but lie on a sub-branch shared with some European haplotypes. **The 30,000-year-old link**: Brown et al., op. cit.

71. **In Asia, B is represented by two main branches**: B4 and B5 correspond to B1 and B2 as defined in Kolman, C.J. et al. (1996) 'Mitochondrial DNA analysis of Mongolian populations and implications for the origin of New World founders' *Genetics* **142**: 1321–34. For their exact correspondence, see note 38, Chapter 5. **Piman Indian Group B4**: Haplotype 4 in

Ingman, M. et al. (2000) 'Mitochondrial genome variation and the origin of modern humans' *Nature* **408**: 708–13. **Japanese Group B4**: Haplotype analysed in Japan and reported in Maca-Meyer, N. et al. (2001) 'Major genomic mitochondrial lineages delineate early human expansions' *BMC Genetics* **2**: 13. Additional matched sites (apart from those defining B4 itself) between the two haplotypes: HVS 16189; non-HVS 499, 827, 13590, 15535. **The matches are strong**: The Ingman Piman haplotype 4 has a close match in another Piman Indian, Haplotype 21, in Torroni et al. (1993a) op. cit.

72. **particular individual mtDNA types**: so-called 'private' or 'tribal polymorphisms'. **This has been interpreted to mean . . . quickly split**: Torroni et al. (1993a) op. cit.

73. **three unique types not found anywhere else**: the Ojibwa also have A1, which is rare in North America anyway and has been found only in Ojibwa, defined by 16126 in Torroni et al. (1993a) op. cit. (Great Lakes and Canada). Other similar A1s have been found in DNA tests on ancient bones from a pre-Columbian cemetery (Norris Farms) in Minnesota, near the Great Lakes (Stone and Stoneking op. cit.). **the highest rates of the rare X type**: Brown et al., op. cit. **having only the dominant Y founder**: Scozzari, R. et al. (1997) 'mtDNA and Y chromosome: Specific polymorphisms in modern Ojibwa: Implications about the origin of their gene pool' *American Journal of Human Genetics* **60**: 241–4. **Ojibwa share . . . even some northern cultural features with the Na-Dene**: Algonquin tribes share the earth-diver myths of recovery from the Flood with Na-Dene speakers and with peoples living either side of the Bering Strait: Oppenheimer, S.J. (1998) *Eden in the East: The Drowned Continent of Southeast Asia* (Weidenfeld & Nicolson, London) pp. 236–37.

74. By a further coincidence, one of the other participants, an American of Greek ancestry, also belonged to the X clan, thus demonstrating in this very small sample the power of mtDNA to trace ancient relationships.

75. **The picture of A in the rest of North America**: Stone and Stoneking op. cit.; Kolman et al., op. cit. **the Fremont cultures of Great Salt Lake**: Parr, R.L. et al. (1996) 'Ancient DNA analysis of Fremont Amerindians of the Great Salt Lake wetlands' *American Journal of Physical Anthropology* **99**: 507–18. **the extinct Fuegan tribes**: Fox, C.L. (1996) 'Mitochondrial DNA haplogroups in four tribes from Tierra del Fuego–Patagonia: Inferences about the peopling of the Americas' *Human Biology* **68**: 855–71. The Fuegans contrast strongly with the Central American Chibcha tribes, who all have A and B but lack C and D (Stone and Stoneking op. cit.).

76. **B remained younger in Central America**: Torroni et al. (1993a) op. cit.; Forster et al., op. cit. **She is old in South America**: Table 2 in Stone and Stoneking op. cit.; Forster et al. op. cit.

77. **Russian geneticist Yelena Stariovskaya**: Stariovskaya et al., op. cit. **at least one close B4 match**: see note 71.

78. **First raised thirty years ago**: Fladmark, K.R. (1979) 'Routes: Alternate migration corridors for early man in North America' *American Antiquity* **44**(1): 55–69; see also Fladmark, K.R. (1990) 'Possible early human occupation of the Queen Charlotte Islands, British Columbia' *Canadian Journal of Archaeology* **14**: 183–97. **Two sites on the southern Peruvian coast**: Sandweiss, D.H. et al. (1998) 'Quebrada Tacahuay: Early South American maritime adaptations' *Science* **281**: 1830–32; Keefer, D.K. et al. (1998) 'Early maritime economy and El Niño events at Quebrada Tacahuay, Peru' *Science* **281**: 1833–5.

ɔnard, J. et al. (2000) 'Population genetics of Ice Age brown bears' *Proceedings of the National Academy of Sciences USA* **97**: 1651–64.

80. **remains and artefacts on Prince of Wales Island**: Dixon, E.J. (1999) *Bones, Boats, and Bison: Archaeology and the First Colonization of Western North America* (University of New Mexico Press, Albuquerque) **evidence of beachcombing dating to 11,600 years ago**: Erlandson, J.M. (1996) 'An archaeological and palaeontological chronology for Daisy Cave (CA-SMI-261), San Miguel Island, California', *Radiocarbon* **38**(2): 355–73. The date of first human presence of 10,500 years ago given in this publication has now been pushed back to perhaps 11,600 years ago. **Radiocarbon tests from a woman's bones**: This redating was first reported by the Santa Barbara Museum of Natural History in the *San Francisco Chronicle*, Monday 12 April 1999.

81. Fedje, D.W. and Josenhans, H. (2000) 'Drowned forests and archaeology on the continental shelf of British Columbia, Canada' *Geology* **28**: 99–102.

INDEX